THE
SINK

Books by Jeffrey Robinson

Fiction

A True and Perfect Knight
The Monk's Disciples
The Margin of the Bulls
The Ginger Jar
Pietrov and Other Games

Non-Fiction

Prescription Games
The Merger
The Manipulators
The Hotel
The Laundrymen
Bardot – Two Lives
The End of the American Century
The Risk Takers – Five Years On
Rainier and Grace
Yamani – The Inside Story
Minus Millionaires
The Risk Takers
Teamwork
Bette Davis

JEFFREY ROBINSON

THE
SINK

TERROR, CRIME AND DIRTY MONEY
IN THE OFFSHORE WORLD

CONSTABLE • LONDON

Constable & Robinson Ltd
3 The Lanchesters
162 Fulham Palace Road
London W6 9ER
www.constablerobinson.com

First published in the UK by Constable
an imprint of Constable & Robinson Ltd 2003

A copy of the British Library Cataloguing in
Publication Data is available from the British Library

ISBN 1-84119-682-7

Printed and bound in the EU

for my old pal
Mort Shuman
1936–1991
tu nous manques

Contents

The Sink

When the government of Antigua granted an offshore licence to Hanover Bank Ltd, the deal was typical and straightforward. The company could operate as a bank anywhere in the world, except Antigua.

After all, that government had long ago predetermined, if any offshore bank licensed on the island was going to scam someone, it was not going to be an Antiguan. Which was fine with the owner of Hanover, an Irishman with absolutely no banking experience, because he never had any intention of scamming anyone in Antigua. A former public relations adviser to Irish Prime Minister Charles Haughey, he didn't even plan on opening an office in Antigua. The reason he chartered his bank on the island was because no one there particularly cared about how he ran his business, that is, as long as he didn't do it in Antigua.

Not that Hanover had a physical presence anywhere else. There was no building, there were no tellers, there were no drive-thru cash machines. The bank was nothing more than a plaque on a wall in the office of a company formation agent in the Caribbean and some files in a sitting room in Ireland. Its two clients were an international fraudster and a US-based convicted money launderer. No one in Antigua audited Hanover's books. For that matter, neither did anyone in Ireland, where the Central Bank didn't have a clue that Hanover was in business.

Still, Hanover had a correspondent relationship with a bank in the Channel Islands which, in turn, had a relationship with the New York branch of a Chicago bank. Such is the nature of the offshore world that a bank that didn't exist could do business in the United States.

Five thousand miles to the north-east of Antigua, in Moscow, the Soviet Union was little more than a bad memory. During the heyday of the Communist Party, there was only one bank in town – the State. When the Iron Curtain disintegrated, however, banks rose from the ashes. By the end of the 1990s, there were around 2,000 banks in

Moscow alone, 85–90 per cent of them owned by, run by or otherwise managed by organized criminal groups.

One of those new banks was controlled by speculators who were systematically raping the Russian economy by stealing funds from former Soviet industries. The money was funnelled out of the country to shell companies with bank accounts in the Channel Islands. From there, it was moved to New York. In the course of six months, no fewer than 10,000 transactions were lodged in a single account, amounting to $4.2 billion. Eventually $7 billion was moved out of Russia this way, laundered through those accounts and dropped into the Bank of New York.

The paramount lesson of Russian capitalism is clear. In the global business environment where there is such easy access to the offshore world, bad guys don't need to rob banks; they can buy them.

Twenty-eight hundred miles south of Moscow, a financial institution in Sudan was doing business according to the strict teachings of Islam. The Al-Shamal Bank had its headquarters in the centre of Khartoum. At least until 1998, the bank had correspondent relationships with American Express, Citibank, the Arab American Bank, ING Bank in Indonesia, Commerz Bank in Germany, Credit Lyonnais in Switzerland and Standard Bank in South Africa. Although some of those agreements were inactive by 9/11, each bank maintained correspondent accounts in the United States, Britain, Canada, Australia, New Zealand and throughout the West.

Correspondent banking is an acknowledged necessity of global finance. Nevertheless, it allows institutions in dubious offshore jurisdictions to conduct business in countries where they are not licensed. Al-Shamal opened in 1982 backed by Saudi money. The US State Department maintains that Osama bin Laden invested $50 million in the bank. Al-Shamal refutes that. In a written statement, the bank acknowledges that bin Laden held three accounts there from 1992 to 1997, but asserts that he was never a founder or a shareholder. Whether he was or he wasn't, it remains that Al-Shamal's correspondent relationships gave bin Laden open access to Western banking.

According to a US Senate report, virtually every major bank in the world – especially the biggest in North America and Europe – holds accounts for offshore banks and/or banks in suspect jurisdictions. Even though recently passed laws make it more difficult for US banks to hold accounts for 'shell-banks' such as Hanover, loopholes in the laws are gaping. The banking lobby in Washington made sure of that, fighting the various bills that would have restricted such relationships. In their eyes, it was vital to guarantee that the offshore world would survive and flourish. After all, business is business. And the business of moving money into and out of shady jurisdictions is so colossal, so hugely profitable for the banking industry, that most people outside the industry never saw it as anything but a money spinner, at least not until 9/11.

The cornerstone of twenty-first century globalization was laid during the final decade of the twentieth century, which brought about the greatest quantum leap in technology since man invented the wheel. Satellites, faxes, mobile phones, the Internet and e-mail reduced the planet to the size of a Palm Pilot.

Although national sovereignty was not yet dead, the concept that we've lived with since the seventeenth century, has been administered last rites. Radical changes in transport and communication seriously impede governments' ability to exercise controls over the movement of goods, services, people and ideas. Not just in the West, where change is often welcome, but in the closed societies of Asia and the Middle East, where change threatens the power base of dictatorial rule. The momentum is such that, inevitably, it is unstoppable. The rivers, mountain ranges, oceans and imaginary lines which originally defined borders would always be there, but the national supremacy that those borders imply is swiftly evaporating. Real power no longer lies in London or Washington or Frankfurt or Paris. Military might does. But real power is exercised in boardrooms. Real power is pharmaceutical companies and telecoms and insurance companies and banks, which are no longer British or American or German, Japanese or French. They are not even, any longer, multinationals. They are 'beyond-nationals'. They are command and control. And in the globalized world of the twenty-first century, corporate command and control is *real politik*.

As corporations replaced nation-states – serving markets which fused like single-cell amoebae to form larger, more powerful, more intelligent creatures – globalization of the legal economy simultaneously globalized the underworld. As newly globalized exchanges found emancipation beyond territorial control, so did terrorism and organized crime. Money drives all of them, and while money has always been a political force, never before has it been so easy for people intent on committing crimes to harness that energy. Burrowing inside the confusion created by the global flood of goods, services, people, ideas and 'megabyte bucks' – blips on computer screens that are not tethered to central banks or geography – transnational organized criminals and terrorist mobs like Al-Qaeda emerged with the capacity to impose themselves way beyond their station.

In the globalized world of the twenty-first century, there is, at any given time, an estimated $600–$700 billion in dirty money circling the planet looking to get clean. The lion's share is drug money. But, as crime and terrorism are twins, it is increasingly difficult to separate drug money from terrorist money. At times they look alike. At times they are the same. All too often, the link that binds them is weapons – handguns for assassinations, automatic rifles for insurrections, weapons of mass destruction to promote political ideals.

In the globalized world of twenty-first century, drugs, arms and dirty money are the Holy Trinity. They move like a malignant virus through the system, driving crime and terror, breeding unabated offshore in the murky heart of the legitimate, global financial world. Organized criminals and global terrorists work the same neighbourhoods, deal in the same 'currencies' – be it drugs, diamonds, or fissile materials – and bank with the same people.

Until 9/11, many European and North American politicians considered foreign sponsored terrorism something that happened only in other countries, and believed that organized crime needed to be defined locally. The reasons are obvious: they couldn't do much about global terrorism anyway, except sit on committees, issue reports and point fingers; and, by insisting that crime was a local issue, they could convince themselves that they were solving the problem. But law enforcement is a declaration of sovereignty. The state dictates: you may not comport yourself in a certain manner while inside this imaginary line. So, while the politicians passed laws and funded law enforcement to stop and punish those who did not comply, like old generals, they were sending their armies out to fight the last war. In this globalized world of twenty-first century crime and terror, those who do not comply have created wealth and safety by purposely functioning beyond reach.

More bobbies on the beat may mean fewer little old ladies having their purses stolen, but it has no effect whatsoever on real crime and real terror. It simply gives politicians the right to boast that the crime rate is coming down – making them worthy of re-election – because diminishing crime rates is what's supposed to happen when politicians promise to do something about crime. Except that when the bottom line of the business of crime and terror jumps from where it was at the beginning of the 1990s – around $100–$300 billion – to $600–$700 billion by the end of that decade, there is reason to suggest that politicians don't know what they're talking about.

Which, until 9/11, most of them clearly didn't.

Just look at the way inattention, incompetence and narrow 'local issue' thinking has allowed money launderers, criminals, bankers, accountants, brokers, company formation agents, financial advisers and lawyers to get rich off the back of dirty money. That $600–$700 billion represents a mere 10 per cent of the wealth that is today hidden offshore. In other words, there is $6–$7 TRILLION – that's twelve zeros – moving through the offshore world, beyond the reach of Western laws and out of sight of Western law enforcement. What's more, that money is protected from oversight by those same bankers, accountants, brokers, company formation agents, financial advisers and lawyers – and with the conscious support of dozens of governments – by the system itself, which has been deliberately designed to short-circuit oversight.

Out of 190 or so jurisdictions in the United Nations, at least 65 offer secret banking that, in some cases, is absolutely airtight. It has been estimated that 4,000 banks operate in the offshore world, most of them with no physical presence anywhere. The Swiss, once famous for their numbered accounts, are no longer at the top of the league. Dozens of jurisdictions do it better than Switzerland, more efficiently and with much lower risks of detection. The reason why comes down to a simple commercial fact: secrecy sells like hotcakes.

It's no wonder, then, that no jurisdiction selling secrecy will even entertain a debate about the elimination of it without first drawing comparisons to suicide by starvation. And in every case, starvation is where the debate on hotcakes ends.

Most offshore centres have two things in common: unsustainable population growth and limited natural resources. Banking and company fees add up quickly to become an important source of income. They're derived from a non-polluting, employment hungry industry. As long as banks and companies are restricted from doing business in the home jurisdiction, the population is safe from the frauds and felonies that might be associated with shell banks and international business corporations (IBCs).

Surrounding this are legitimate financial institutions, which charge handsome fees to provide special services, euphemistically called 'Private Banking'. Under the banner of tax-efficient investment, tax avoidance and ultimate discretion, the world's major banks offer these services to clients willing to pay those handsome fees. That banking secrecy does not legally exist in Britain or Australia or New Zealand does not hinder British and Australian and New Zealand banks from offering the service to their wealthiest clients. In some cases, those wealthiest clients are legitimate businesses which use the offshore world for both legitimate and illicit reasons. In that respect, there is no inherent difference between the Mafia's money, Al-Qaeda's money and Enron's money.

During the first few months of the Bush administration – a Texas-oil-connected White House – official US policy was to turn a blind eye to money laundering as a tax evasion tool in the Caribbean. It is perhaps no coincidence that this happened at the same time that the Texas-based energy company, Enron – with no fewer than 3,000 shell companies offshore – was fighting to stay alive. Enron called their shell companies 'corporate subsidiaries' and 'partnerships'. They were set up for only two reasons: to avoid taxes, which the company success-fully did in four of its final five years; and so that the regulators, analysts and shareholders couldn't find out what Enron's management was doing with the company's money, which was stealing it.

That the offshore world is the financial equivalent of a black hole can come as no surprise to anyone who looks at the basic economics of jurisdictions offering secret banking, totally opaque corporate duck-blinds and economic citizenship. But this colossal force, sucking money into offshore banking and corporate secrecy, has reached the point where it poses a serious risk to Western stability.

Within days of the World Trade Center and Pentagon atrocities, as the financial war on terrorism slowly gathered momentum, atten-tion rightly turned to the offshore world. In response, foreign bankers in jurisdictions that had customarily been shut tight to outside scrutiny, voluntarily announced that they would take the initiative to root out any terrorist money hidden there. Some accounts were, in fact, frozen. At the same time, certain jurisdictions simply gave them-selves a clean bill of health – *terrorists have not been, nor will they ever be welcome here* – in the obvious hope that such proclamations would allow them to return to business as usual.

In other words, the offshore world was saying, no one here will do business with terrorists as long as no one anywhere else worries about the way we do business with criminals of other persuasions, be it some organized Russians or Enron.

This remains the anthem of the sink that is the offshore world.

As so much of that world is enveloped by the British Commonwealth, a fair question is: why doesn't Parliament do something about it? The answer is simple – and this holds true for the Netherlands and France, two other nations with heavy investments in the offshore world – there are no votes in it. Sure, everyone looks for terrorist money. But, direct intervention in the offshore world is too hard a sell for politicians at home. Shutting down an island somewhere offers no immediate political capital. Anyway, the cost is too high. There are no substitute crop programmes for out-of-business offshore banks. There are no alternate jobs for out-of-work company formation agents. Throughout the eastern Caribbean, offshore money has become the mainstay of the local economy. In other areas, it has become the mainstay of political corruption. A draconian crackdown would not feed the poor or pave the roads. Instead, it would ruin the local economy, threaten the financial infrastructure, possibly destroy the tourist industry and put natives on the breadline.

More menacingly, dirty money is now estimated to be as much as 2 per cent of the world's GDP, making it so vital to the global economic system that a thorough purging would have severe economic ramifications throughout the First World.

And yet:

From the Channel Islands, funds disguised as Islamic charities were laundered on their way to America to support Al-Qaeda.

In Cyprus, Russian criminal organizations control a huge percentage of the 48,000 shell companies registered there, 47,000 of which have no physical presence whatsoever – no roof, no phone number, not even a post box.

From Dubai, the offshore banking capital of the Gulf States, five times as much money moves back and forth to the Indian sub-continent through the *hawallah,* or underground, banking system than through legitimate banking channels. *Hawallah* bankers in Dubai – and in Afghanistan and in Pakistan, and in ethnic neighbourhoods across North America and Europe – assert their cultural right to do business in this traditional way. Which means, no paperwork or money trail.

In four US cities, a Somalian-based wire remitter was shut down in dawn raids in November 2001 by US Customs officers who suspected that the Al-Barakaat network was funding terrorist cells. Among the evidence uncovered was a connection with an Islamic charity whose money was in the Channel Islands. The jury remains out on just how much money moved through these offices, but it took 9/11 for someone to act, even though Al-Barakaat had been suspected of moving money illegally for at least two years prior to 9/11.

From Toronto, telephone-marketing fraudsters have managed to hold onto a large share of the $40 billion global industry they helped to create by defrauding foreigners, and then moving their money through the offshore world, depriving Canadian law enforcement of access to the victims and to the proceeds of crime.

In the totally phoney offshore jurisdiction of Niue, some 2,000 people living on a rock in the middle of the Pacific earn an estimated $2 million a year in fees from licensing phoney banks and dubious shell companies, representing 7–10 per cent of the national economy. Relatively nearby, in the equally phoney offshore jurisdiction of Nauru, 10,000 natives licensed 400 offshore banks, which, at one point, accounted for more than 5 per cent of government revenue.

The offshore world is a place where money trails evaporate into thin air, where dirty money mingles with the financial traffic of the world's legitimate businesses, where connections smudge and are then erased, and where anyone looking for the truth is confronted by so many man-made barriers – many of them frequently cloaked in the guise of legality – that inquiries are, in the end, mostly futile. With so much at stake, the people best positioned to put a stop to this are the very same people making money from it – bankers, accountants, brokers, company formation agents, financial advisers and lawyers. It's hardly surprising that they don't have much incentive to do so.

Again, the Caribbean is the best example. The banks are there. The shell companies are there. The Colombians are nearby. The Italians are willing to meet there. And these days the Russians are there too, having turned the Caribbean into organized crime's version of the warm water port the Soviet navy could never establish.

That bank secrecy is a service many people are willing to pay for, goes without saying. But to claim, as many of these jurisdictions do, that selling such a service is their sovereign right as long as no laws are being violated in that sovereignty – with total disregard to laws being violated elsewhere – is more than just disingenuous. Most people who hide money are doing so for reasons which, at best, might be questionable, and at worst, are blatantly illegal somewhere.

By taking the moral high ground in their defence of secrecy, these jurisdictions ignore the fact that, as long as stealth is the product, no matter how it's disguised – whether as an International Business Corporation, a numbered bank account, or an insurance trust, two questions must be asked: who is buying that product? and, why are they paying for it? Unless those questions are then satisfactorily answered, the offshore world will continue, intolerably, to be the sink that washes dirty money in direct support of crime and terror.

Money laundering facilities evolved because there was enough money that needed to be laundered to create laundromats. At the same time, those laundromats generated enough cashflow and reinvestment for criminals and terrorists, that greater sums needed to be laundered. Accordingly, by reducing the amount of money looking to get clean, you effect the laundromats. By abolishing the laundromats, you severely disrupt the cash flow and reinvestment of the business of crime and the business of terror. As long as drug traffickers, terrorists, fraudsters, tax evaders and other criminals – both private and corporate – are permitted to use legitimate means to achieve illegitimate ends, then any attempt by any jurisdiction to corral money laundering and somehow interrupt the financial activities of these drug traffickers, terrorists, fraudsters, tax evaders and other criminals, is tantamount to pissing in the wind.

Despite constant protestations from countries who sell secret banking and shell companies and their own sovereignty – despite the gripes about sovereign rights to protect one's own interests and to determine one's own future – there is this indisputable fact: the world offshore is a smoke-and-mirrors fiction, purposely constructed so that money can be in one place, the management of it can be halfway around the world, and the beneficial owner of it can remain well hidden, somewhere else again.

Until the wars on crime and terror are fought on the beaches of the offshore world, organized criminals and global terrorists will remain what they have worked so hard to become – the most powerful special interest group on the planet.

CHAPTER ONE

Like a Thief with a Blueprint

*Show me an attaché case that can hold $2 million
and you can have the $2 million.*

— Frank Sinatra

It's more than a century later but there really aren't many differ-ences in the way it's made. Sure, the 'kitchens' are modern today, and the lighting is much better and, of course, there's air conditioning. Otherwise, everything is pretty much the way it was then. The glass flasks and the ceramic containers are the same. So is the necessary plumbing. It still takes three people — a master chef and two appren-tices — to cook it. And the six-step recipe is identical, too.

1. Bind ten kilos of pure morphine base in a container with ten kilos of acetic anhydride and simmer the mixture at 185 degrees Fahrenheit for six hours.
2. Treat this mixture — which is impure diacetylmorphine — with water and chloroform, to eliminate some of the impurities.
3. Drain this into a second container and add sodium carbonate until solid particles form and drop to the bottom of the gooey liquid.
4. Purify the solid particles in a solution of alcohol and activated charcoal, then burn off the alcohol.
5. The result is a pile of granules which you dissolve in alcohol and mix in a solvent of ether and hydrochloric acid, transforming the granules into tiny white flakes.
6. Now filter out the tiny white flakes — you should have ten kilos' worth — and allow them to dry into a white powder.

The first time anyone cooked up a batch was in 1898. Interestingly enough, it was in the same laboratory in Leverkusen, Germany, where aspirin was conceived. That's when the Bayer Chemical Company invented heroin. But the recipe was formulated by an English chemist named C.R. Wright in 1874. And that's the date that matters.

The moment Wright committed this recipe to paper, that was the 'Big Bang' that created the modern offshore world.

On a blustery Friday morning, 13 March 1931, a panel of 23 random citizens who'd never met before sat down on hard wooden chairs in a dingy, windowless room of the ancient federal courthouse in downtown Chicago and, with the door guarded by armed US marshals, listened to US Attorney George E.Q. Johnson – a tall, thin, stern man wearing gold rimmed glasses – as he asked them to formally inculpate the most notorious gangster in the country for failing to pay $32,488.81 in income tax seven years earlier.

After several days of hearing evidence, the men and women of this Grand Jury returned an indictment which, the judge ordered, would be kept secret until further investigations were completed concerning Alphonse Capone's subsequent tax years 1925–9. The same group met again on 5 June to return a second indictment, charging Capone with 22 counts of tax evasion totalling over $200,000. The following week, they indicted him again, along with 68 members of his gang, this time on 5,000 violations of the Volstead Act – the law that created Prohibition by banning the manufacture, transportation and sale of beverages containing more than 0.5% alcohol.

Facing a possible 34 years behind bars – for running a £75 million a year industry that was built on illegal booze, gambling, prostitution and 500 murders – Capone agreed to plea guilty in exchange for a short sentence. Johnson was willing to discuss it for several reasons: he was concerned with potential jury tampering; recognized the real possibility that witnesses might wind up dead; and feared that defence lawyers might successfully argue that the statute of limitations had run out on some of the charges. So after lengthy negotiations with Capone's attorneys, Johnson recommended a custodial sentence of two to five years. Believing it was a done deal, Capone started bragging that he'd be out in under 30 months. That incensed the judge who accepted Capone's guilty plea but then handed down 11 years. Furious, Capone reneged on his plea and decided to take his chances with a jury. The trial didn't last long and on Saturday, 17 October, he was found guilty on some, but not all, of the tax evasion charges. The judge accepted the jury's decision and gave Capone 11 years anyway.

Watching this from the sidelines, a 29-year-old New York

bootlegger named Meyer Lansky couldn't believe that, where G-Men with guns had failed, accountants with pencils had succeeded.

Capone's dim-witted brother Ralph – a.k.a. 'Bottles' Capone – suffered a similar fate. The way Lansky viewed life, that should have been warning enough. Capone's lieutenants, Frank Nitti and Jake Guzik, were also charged with tax evasion. Ironically, four decades later, Lansky himself would have to face those charges. But now, in 1931 – the same year that gambling was re-legalized in the State of Nevada – Lansky was shocked that Capone had fallen for 'the rum runner's myth'.

Throughout Prohibition, bootleggers had convinced themselves that because booze was illegal, the money they made on it was not taxable. The same false impression was shared by gamblers taking illegal bets on horse racing. 'The income tax law is a lot of bunk', Capone had insisted. 'The government can't collect legal taxes from illegal money'.

Lansky, aghast at how easily Capone's world had crumbled, was determined not to fall into that same wide trap. At first glance, he was staring at a no-win situation. Pay taxes and you admit your guilt. Don't pay taxes and you get done like Capone. Eventually, though, he realized there was a third possibility. The Internal Revenue Service (IRS) could only make a tax evasion case if they could find the money. If the Feds couldn't find the money, he reasoned, then the money was, by default, not taxable. With this as his premise, he turned to the one place where secrecy was already a business – Switzerland.

Long before Holocaust money needed a place to hide, or James Bond gave secret Swiss banking a patina of cinema glitz, the gnomes of Zurich were selling stealth. Several banks offered anonymous banking to clients during the French Revolution. By the end of the nineteenth century, all of them were offering numbered accounts. But it took New Jersey, Delaware and Great Britain to help the Swiss find their niche.

Facing a budgetary crises in the mid-1880s, the governor of New Jersey passed a law which permitted businesses located across the Hudson River in New York to incorporate in his state. For a small fee, New York businesses could pretend to be New Jersey businesses, which would save them from paying New York's higher taxes. Based on New Jersey's success, Delaware went one step further. Towards the end of the 1890s that state offered incorporation to anyone looking to avoid taxes anywhere. Today, Delaware is America's foremost offshore centre.

The tax advantages of becoming a registered company somewhere else were further defined by British case law. Judges ruled that a company was resident for tax purposes in the jurisdiction where it was controlled. If the management was in Britain and the factory was in Germany, then the company was British. By that same principle, a company doing business in the UK was not subject to British tax as long as the business was entirely 'controlled from outside' the UK. To define that term, judges asked several questions: Where do the directors permanently reside? Where is the seal of the company? Where are the minutes of the meetings kept? Where are the books of accounts and transfer kept? And, where are transfers approved?

As long as the answers to all those questions was 'some place besides Britain', the company was deemed to be non-resident in the UK for tax purposes. The significance of the ruling is that it applied to the entire British Empire, which opened the door for Bermuda and the Bahamas to sell companies resident in their jurisdiction but controlled from elsewhere and therefore not subject to tax in Bermuda or the Bahamas.

The Swiss got into the game when they realized they could use dummy companies to create a second barrier of secrecy. Lawyers formed shell companies for clients whose names never appeared on the incorporation documents. A numbered account would be opened by the lawyer in the name of the shell, and those few bankers who knew about the account would never know who the beneficial owner was. Only the lawyer knew, and he could not be forced to reveal his client's name because attorney-client privilege was written in stone. The Swiss also allowed the shares of one dummy corporation to be held by second shell.

In 1934, the Swiss added another ingredient, making it a criminal offence for anyone working in a bank to reveal any details whatsoever of any account, creating a system that was, in those days, impregnable.

Because there was money to be made in this, Liechtenstein decided to compete with Switzerland by inventing trusts which were even more secret than anything the Swiss had for sale. Luxembourg went the Swiss one better, as well. Where Swiss banking rules dictated that two senior executives in each bank needed to know a client's identity, the Luxembourgois limited that to one. Not to be left out, the Austrians entered the fray, declaring that no one in any bank needed to know anyone.

As new markets for corporate, financial and individual protection grew — and competed with each other for business — some very wealthy men figured out how to use companies formed in the Bahamas to mask business transactions. Notable among them were the heirs of J. P. Morgan and the American financier Andrew Mellon, a man who served Presidents Harding, Coolidge and Hoover as secretary of the treasury. In this scenario, Bahamian companies purchased goods from all over the world destined for import into the United States, marked-up on them, then sold the goods to their own companies in the States. The US companies showed little or no profit for tax purposes, sheltering those, instead, in the no-tax Bahamas.

From such humble beginnings, this highly profitable practice of 'transfer pricing' came to effect as much as 60 per cent of the world's trade. That's how much is estimated to take place inside the confines of multinational enterprises. Although Britain's Inland Revenue cannot come up with figures which would quantify tax avoidance through transfer pricing in the UK, a report in the United States suggests that the US Treasury lost $53 billion (£34 billion) in revenues to transfer pricing in 2001.

But that was still a fledgling industry in 1936, a time when bankers in the Bahamas were also working out the advantages of moving money through offshore trusts. Originally made available to wealthy Brits, then to wealthy Canadians, one of those first trusts, Bahamas General, was taken over by National Westminster Bank. Of course, as soon as one big bank got involved, others followed, and offshore trusts were soon widely offered in the UK and Canada. Essentially, this was the birth of 'private banking'. British and Canadian banks opened throughout the British overseas territories, including Anguilla, the British Virgin Islands (BVI) and, eventually, the Cayman Islands.

Yet, Switzerland was still the best bet for hiding cash. This being an era when no one cared where cash came from, Lansky had no trouble hiding his in Switzerland. However, stashing money in the faraway Alps, out of the taxman's reach, also put it beyond his reach. And therein lies the difference between capital flight (hiding assets to protect them) and money laundering (hiding assets to protect them, then repatriating those protected assets in a different guise, in order to enjoy them).

The 'Lansky Syllogism' became: if the Feds can't follow the money, they won't be able to find it; if the Feds can't find it, it's not taxable; consequently, if you can camouflage this untaxable money to make it look like taxable money, then the Feds won't recognize it when you show it to them, which means you can bring it home and use it.

That prompted the question: how do you bring your hidden money safely home from wherever it's been hidden?

And a few winters after Al Capone took up long-term residence on a rock in the middle of San Francisco Bay, Meyer Lansky, wintering in Florida, looked south and could almost see the answer.

Opium has played a role in the politics of the world for the past 4,000 years. Its influence spread from the Mediterranean where it was first used as a folk medicine, through Asia and back to the Indian sub-continent where it was first used recreationally. The commercialization of opium opened the trade routes and, along with coffee and tobacco, sustained European mercantilism for 200 years. By the middle of the nineteenth century, opium was already one of the world's major commodities. In 1805, pharmacologists turned raw opium into the pain killer morphine and in 1858 doctors decided that the speediest way to deliver it into the bloodstream was with a hypodermic needle. By then, the drug had already been misused for nearly 40 years. For a while, the opium derivative heroin was an ingredient in commercial cough medicines. Thanks largely to opium, the European chemical industry became the European pharmaceutical industry.

But the downside effects of opium were so dangerous and abuse became so widespread, that by World War I most western governments began to outlaw it. The League of Nations imposed codes on opiates, the 1925 Geneva Convention restricted the manufacture and export of heroin, and the 1931 Limitation Convention attempted to confine heroin to medical use. To fill gaps in the market, Chinese criminal syndicates in Shanghai and Tientsin supplied European and North American criminal syndicates with product. Within a few years, organized criminal enterprises in the West were producing it in sufficient quantities to compete with the Asian suppliers. They met the demands of the market and assured huge profits for everyone along the supply chain.

World War II saw controls imposed on shipping that cut into the easy transport of opiates, creating a new market in North America for Mexican heroin. After the war, it was business as usual and addiction rates began to climb. Governments responded by escalating the drug wars, the sale and distribution of heroin became increasingly more dangerous and, as a result, increasingly more profitable. Poppy fields expanded, refineries sprouted up, and Lucky Luciano rewrote his epitaph by inventing the 'French Connection'.

While this was going on, the rise of Italian and French communism brought the newly formed US Central Intelligence Agency (CIA) into the game. By recruiting local mobsters to take on the local communists, the CIA heavy-handedly tipped the balance in favour of the mobsters who then used their new found powers in the pursuit of illegal activities, notably drug trafficking. It is a scenario that would be repeated many more times over the next 50 years: from the Golden Triangle of Burma, Thailand, and Laos to the Golden Crescent of Iran, Afghanistan and Pakistan; throughout Latin America stretching from Mexico all the way down through Panama, then across Venezuela, Colombia, Ecuador and Peru; from unofficial support of the Nicaraguan Contras to official support of corrupt governments in Bogota fighting the FARC; from Luciano's labs in Marseilles to the establishment of a Corsican Mob presence in Afghanistan and the subsequent colonization of the poppy fields there by the Taliban. Wherever there was heroin, there was the CIA and every time the Agency got involved, it was with predictably detrimental long-term results.

Heroin was king, and for organized crime the Eighteenth Amendment to the Constitution merely ushered in a sideshow. Prohibition created an era when everybody wanted booze and only some people wanted heroin, so the Mob concentrated on booze. But in 1933, when the Twenty-First Amendment put an end to bathtub gin, allowing the government to tax all that whiskey coming down from Canada, drugs were once again the best game in town.

There is really only one reason why criminals work at the business of crime.

Putting psychopaths and people who commit crimes of passion to the side, most people commit crimes for money. That's why they rob banks. That's why they work extortion. That's why they hijack lorries. That's why they run numbers. That's why they invent frauds. That's why they traffick heroin. Criminals are criminals because they think crime pays.

And for the really smart ones – like Maier Suchowljansky – it often does.

Born in Grodno, then Russia, now Poland in 1902, he arrived in Brooklyn with his parents in 1911 and, after Americanizing his name to Meyer Lansky, dropped out of school at the age of 14. For a time, he worked as an apprentice toolmaker. But there was never going to be a lot of money in that, and this was a boy who wanted to have a lot of money. So he looked for it on the streets and took it when he saw it. Even though the diminutive Lansky needed thick-heeled shoes to hit 5 ft - 4 inches, he turned out to be tough enough that he never walked away from trouble.

One of the street kids who tried to give him trouble was Salvatore Lucania. But the tiny Jew stared back at the lanky Italian and a life-long friendship was born.

The Lucania family had emigrated to the States in 1907 when Salvatore was just 10. Within a few years, he was a reluctant resident of a home for juvenile delinquents. He followed that, in 1916, with a spell in prison for possession of heroin. As soon as he got out, having Americanized his name to Charlie Luciano, he set about working his way up the ladder of the organized crime and before long, was a prime suspect in a series of gangland murders. By then, his pals Frank Costello, Albert Anastasia and Vito Genevese were calling him 'Lucky'. He'd survived a brutal knife fight and legend had it that's where the nickname came from. The truth is less romantic. They dubbed him Lucky because he was extraordinarily successful at picking horses.

Lansky's other boyhood friend was a Jew named Benjamin Siegel. Born in Brooklyn in 1906, Siegel had a volatile temper and was said, by some of the other kids, to be 'as crazy as a bedbug'. The handle stuck, he came to be known as Bugsy, and got as crazy as a bedbug whenever anyone called him that. Lansky and Siegel started as small time extortionists and street level hoodlums, moving whatever heroin the 'Bug and Meyer Gang' could handle. Like everyone else, they changed tack with Prohibition. They got good at what they did – which was street-level whiskey sales – and it didn't take long before Lansky's smarts and Siegel's sheer nastiness got them noticed by a real player.

Arnold Rothstein was perhaps the most important criminal of the era. Today, he is best remembered as the gambler who fixed the 1919 World Series – baseball's famous 'Black Sox Scandal' – which earned him a walk-on role in F. Scott Fitzgerald's *The Great Gatsby*. He is also, supposedly, the model for Nathan Detroit in the musical *Guys and Dolls*.

One of the brightest men in the business history of crime, Rothstein realized early on that life as a criminal exposes you to personal risk. So, to minimize personal risk, he established himself as backer. He started in the heroin business, expanded into stolen diamonds and various black markets and, eventually, became America's premier bootlegger. He also wrote the textbook on the care and feeding of politicians and judges, turning graft and corruption into an art form. He met Lansky somewhere around the start of Prohibition, liked him and brought him under his wing. Siegel came along as part of the deal. Rothstein backed their early ventures and, by example, taught Lansky a lesson that served him his entire life: stay in the background, don't trample on egos, and become indispensable to everyone else's business by carving out your own niche in their supply chain. Rothstein's niche was the finance of smuggling. Lansky's was the finance of dirty money.

Yet Rothstein's real contribution to twentieth-century crime must be the word 'organized'. He wasn't like so many of his contemporaries, a thug who committed crimes. He was a criminal who comported himself like a businessman. At a time when almost everything was divided along ethnic lines, he crossed those lines to put diverse people together.

Sound business, it was also a mean trick because neighbourhoods had definable boundaries and most people stayed within them. It was that way with schools, clubs and at work, especially in New York where melting pot immigrants spent a generation or two denying the melting pot process. The Mob was no different. The Italians stuck with Italians, the Jews stuck with Jews. Rothstein's legacy is of a Jew who was accepted by them all. He was close to the Italians, notably Al Capone. He could hobnob with Irish gangsters like Owney Madden who ran Manhattan's Hell's Kitchen, and with Irish millionaires in plush Back Bay Boston estates like John F. Kennedy's bootlegging father, Joe. He accepted Luciano as Lansky's friend and brought him into the clique. He saw to it that Luciano's friend Frank Costello — whose real name was Francesco Castiglia and who would come to be known as the Mafia's Prime Minister — accepted Lansky and Siegel as his friends. He showed them all how to forge bonds across tribal lines and how to establish 'syndicates', which turned into 'organized crime', which made Luciano and Lansky and the others men to be reckoned with.

Rothstein would be murdered by gamblers to whom he owed money in November 1928. But by then, his 'syndicate' business model was firmly in place. Lansky and Siegel were operating several distilleries, supplying whiskey to Italian, Irish and Jewish distributors and speakeasies. While Luciano, who had a piece of the action with them, was now a made-member of Joe Masseria's crime family.

None of these guys were businessmen in the Rothstein mould. That would come with time. At this point, they were still thugs playing at business. But Rothstein left a huge void and these guys were smart enough to fill it. In April 1931, Luciano reshuffled the deck by conspiring with Masseria's sworn enemy, Salvatore Maranzano, to kill his boss. If Lansky and Siegel weren't actually in on the hit – and there is reason to believe they might have been – they certainly knew about it and helped Luciano arrange it. Maranzano then divided New York into five families and rewarded Luciano by naming him head of one of them. In turn, Luciano appointed Costello as his underboss and promoted Vito Genovese into a position of responsibility. Four months later, Luciano – and very likely Lansky and Siegel – struck again, this time eliminating Maranzano.

Luciano, Lansky and Siegel were now the biggest players in the East. They ran businesses, jointly and separately, that employed tens of thousands of people and generated tens of millions of dollars. But it didn't last long because so much of it was based on whiskey. When Congress made booze legal again, that was the end of that. Some of the Mob stayed in the whiskey business. But the commodity was nothing special, competition was everywhere and profits were a shadow of what they'd been. For men like Luciano, Lansky and Siegel – and their cohorts Costello, Genovese, Joe Bonanno, Carlo Gambino, Johnny Torrio, Longy Zwillman, the Fischetti brothers, Santos Trafficante, Tony Accardo, Sam Giancana, Joe Adonis, Carlos Marcello and all the others who whose names would become legendary in the history of twentieth-century crime – the fallback position was heroin.

Prostitution was still a thriving investment, but risks were too high for profits which seemed too low, as Luciano would find out. Extortion, fraud and numbers rackets were much less risky, but the profits reflected that. Booze had been special because it had defied the ratio – it was a low-risk, high-profit commodity. The lament became, 'If only they'd make whiskey illegal again!'

Slowly, however, it began to dawn on some of these men that whiskey might not have been quite so unique after all. It was illegal and therefore fruitful, but illegal only proved fruitful in this case because a wide section of the population wanted it enough that they would openly flout the law to have it. That's what increased profits and reduced the risks. It wasn't the whiskey, it was the demand for whiskey. The greater the public appeal, they realized, the easier it was to entice local politicians and cops to look the other way, which in turn reduced risk. That's when some of them – and Meyer Lansky was clearly at the forefront – wondered, what else does the public want enough to break law for?

The answer was gambling.

It was illegal everywhere, except Nevada. Yet, anyone who wanted to shoot craps or play roulette could always find a roadhouse somewhere with tables. And anyone who wanted to place a bet on a horserace or a ballgame could go to their barber shop because barber shops across the country were tied into a bookies' wire. By 1932, the national bookies' wire was controlled by Moe Annenberg. He's the father of Walter, who owned Triangle Publications, published *TV Guide*, the *Philadelphia Inquirer*, and *Seventeen Magazine*. He also owned radio and TV stations, was patron of the University of Pennsylvania's school of communications and Temple University's main library – both of which bear his name – and, during Nixon's reign in the White House, served as US Ambassador to the Court of St James.

Annenberg Senior fought with, and eventually made peace with, the Mob to control the national wire. He already owned the daily racing form which, with gangster money and muscle, gave him a virtual monopoly on information coming out of the nation's racetracks. To suggest that either Moe or Walter Annenberg ever allowed that information to be misused, is pure speculation. To suggest that criminals with access to that information wouldn't use it to their advantage, flies in the face of reason.

As everything was already in place, all the Mob had to do was upgrade the product. Speakeasies traded booze for craps tables and roulette wheels. Roadhouses became 'carpet joints' – sawdust was no longer the floor covering of choice – and the business prospered for the next 20 years. From the end of Prohibition through the 1940s, the public wanted to gamble and the Mob did what the Mob does best – supply illegal demand.

Typically kitted out with a dozen roulette wheels, half a dozen craps tables and half a dozen card tables, there was the Piping Rock and the Arrowhead Inn, next to the racetrack in Saratoga, New York; the

Agua Caliente in Tijuana, Mexico, an afternoon's drive from Los Angeles; the Beverly Club in Louisiana; the Riviera across the bridge from Manhattan in New Jersey. There were gambling barges in southern California taking punters beyond the three-mile limit where laws against gambling didn't apply; and wall-to-wall carpet joints in Hot Springs, Arkansas, and Galveston, Texas, and Cleveland, Ohio, too. Entire cities were transformed by illicit gaming, much the way Branson, Missouri, today is a city of supper clubs and show palaces. As competition increased, the product improved. Carpet joints started offering food and dancing and big name entertainers like Jimmy Durante, Sophie Tucker, Joe E. Lewis and an up-and-coming kid from Hoboken, New Jersey named Sinatra. There were carpet joints wherever there was room for one. But it was in Hallandale, Florida where Lansky made his mark on this era.

It began with a small-time Chicago operator named Julian 'Potatoes' Kaufman, who'd been on the run and fallen under the paid protection of a Genovese Family lieutenant named Vincent 'Jimmy Blue Eyes' Alo. In those days, Hallandale was nothing more than a way-station for itinerant fruit pickers. Kaufman opened a bookies' shop in a fruit-packing shed on a small parcel of land and, because the itinerant workers had cash on pay-day to spend, he added a roulette wheel and a craps table. He called it The Plantation.

Luciano had introduced Alo to Lansky some years before and those two had become mates. Alo was only a year older than Lansky, equally short and equally shy. Where Lansky had the brains to devise a scheme, Alo had the back-up muscle to guarantee that it worked. Eventually Alo would be the watchdog positioned between Lansky and the Mob. He would keep one eye on Lansky, to make sure that Lansky played straight with the boys, and the other eye on the boys, to make sure that none of them ever muscled in on Lansky. In turn, both Lansky and the boys took care of Alo.

So now, when Alo told Lansky that some locals had shut down The Plantation, Lansky concocted a plan to reopen it next door. Potatoes unexpectedly found himself with more partners than he'd ever imagined, including Lansky, Alo, Luciano, Costello and Siegel. Lansky dubbed the place The Farm, and put his brother Jake in charge of doling out bribes to local politicians to keep it open. On the back of The Farm, this group – minus Potatoes – opened the much grander Colonial Inn right next door to Gulfstream racetrack. From Hallendale, their carpet joints spread south into Dade County and Miami, and north to Palm Beach. The public wanted to play, the locals grew rich on the gamblers, and the cops were paid to worry more about traffic than the mobsters who were bringing economic prosperity to south Florida.

By design, carpet joints, like all casinos, were profitable because the odds are always with the house. What made them extremely lucrative – and the reason why the Mob has always revered casinos – was 'the skim'. A basic 'fingers in the till' game, it's about helping yourself to a share of the winnings after the money moves from the tables and before it gets to the accountant's office. If there's a 100-grand at the roulette wheel and you only hand 80-grand to the accountant – which is what the tax man and your partners get to see – the 20-grand difference is yours, free and clear. All you have to do is make it disappear. But Lansky came to see the carpet joints as more than mere cash cows. They were a near-perfect washing machine. By adding heroin money to the daily take, street cash could be disguised as house profits.

Gambling money was pouring in, and the skim was making a lot of people very rich. But there was also so much heroin money coming in that the Mob in Hallandale needed to do something with it. The carpet joints couldn't absorb it fast enough. That's why Siegel headed west to build the biggest, most spectacular carpet joint ever. Financed by his friends, he would invent the Las Vegas Strip, construct The Flamingo hotel and casino, sustain huge cost overruns, open it disastrously, infuriate his partners by stealing from them and, eventually, suffer the ultimate fate for betrayal.

Lansky, in the meantime, was still haunted by Capone's mistake. With more cash than he'd ever seen as a bootlegger, he was more anxious than ever to keep the IRS from finding it. He theorized that if he could put a casino outside the jurisdiction of the IRS, sitting between his cash businesses – especially heroin trafficking – in the States and his secret bank accounts in Switzerland, he'd have the perfect cogwheel to turn his two money engines in tandem.

And the place to do that, he decided, was Cuba.

Only 90 miles away, and easily accessible by boat and plane from Florida, the island was a popular, albeit under-developed, vacation spot. In 1933, a 31-year-old army sergeant named Fulgencio Batista y Zaldívar had rallied the military to overthrow the government of Gerardo Machado. He'd installed himself as chief of the armed forces, had seized control of the country and had inaugurated a reign of massive political corruption. He'd also put out the welcome mat for organized crime.

It's not entirely clear when Lansky first visited Cuba, but by 1937 he'd acquired a franchise on some gaming tables in the casino at Havana's Hotel Nacional. A chaotic place, with different people owning different table rights in the same room, the casino provided Lansky with the opportunity to move money from Florida to the safety of Havana and also move money hidden in Switzerland through Havana and back to Florida. The taxman wouldn't know about the money leaving the country, but he'd be welcome to count whatever was coming in, as that was a 'legal' return on an overseas' investment.

Two years after Lansky set up in Cuba, Batista decided to do something about the disarray in the gambling industry. He hired a New England racetrack owner to modernize Oriental Park racetrack and asked Lansky to reorganize Havana's casinos. Accordingly, one of the first things Lansky did was to take over the racetrack casino so that he could launder money through there, too.

The operative verb being, 'to launder'.

It's called what it is, not because Al Capone had a string of launderettes that he used to hide his income — that's a bedtime fable — but because it aptly describes the process. Dirty money, being the proceeds of illegal activity, is fed into legitimate businesses and through them into the legitimate financial system, washed through a deliberate strategy to obscure the money trail — moved in and out of shell companies, secret bank accounts and multiple jurisdictions so that law enforcement can't follow it — and then, brought out the other end scrubbed and shiny, looking exactly like legitimately earned income.

What's more, Lansky never used the term money laundering. That didn't come into the English language until the Watergate scandal in 1973. In Lansky's mind, he was merely taking capital flight to the next level. But there's no doubt that he laid the groundwork for what would come, and that first giant step for mankind left its footprint in Cuba.

Seven years after seizing power, Batista decided to validate his dictatorship by running for president. He won the 1940 election, but somehow mismanaged the rigged election four years later and got voted out. He retired to a well feathered nest in Florida. By then, Lansky and his chums had taken over a substantial part of the action at the Nacional and were settling into casinos all over town. By then, too, Lansky was fast becoming the single most powerful foreign investor in Havana.

Along the way, Lucky's luck ran out. Manhattan District Attorney Thomas Dewey busted Luciano in June 1936 on 62 counts of compulsory prostitution and shipped him off to serve two 15-year terms at Dannemora Prison in Clinton, New York. Referred to by fellow inmates as 'Siberia' because of it's remote and harsh conditions, Luciano spent six years there before his lawyers and Lansky worked out a way to get him moved.

With the war in Europe and the Pacific in full swing, Lansky sent out feelers through lawyers suggesting that Luciano could be of real assistance to the Pentagon. There's no doubt that the government seriously considered enlisting his help. Luciano claimed that he could – and later, swore that he did – exert his influence with the longshoremen to keep Italian stevedores working in the ports of New York when the US declared war on Italy. He also maintained that, during the planning stages for the invasion of Sicily, he personally supplied American intelligence with underground contacts on the island.

Records do indeed show that the US Navy was concerned about sabotage at the docks in Brooklyn, and that the Office of Naval Intelligence (ONI) in Manhattan looked to the Mafia for help. Sometime around 1942, officers contacted Joseph Lanza, a mobster with ties to the longshoremen. There is serious doubt, however, about Luciano's role.

When he applied for a suspension of his sentence on 8 February 1943, Luciano cited some vague assistance he'd rendered to the Navy. The New York State Parole Board's recommendation that Luciano's sentence be reduced – based largely on testimony from an ONI officer who claimed to have visited Luciano in Dannemora and secured his co-operation – was sent to Thomas Dewey, now governor of New York. But there's no hard evidence to show that Luciano's collaboration with the government ever transpired. There was a project called 'Operation Underworld' – which today sounds like a silly and unlikely name – but that refers to Lanza's help. The likelihood is that Luciano's support in the war effort was nothing more than a put-up job by Lansky.

But that didn't stop Luciano from insisting that he had lived up to his end of the deal and, on the basis of the Parole Board's now-suspect endorsement, Dewey acquiesced. On 3 January 1946, he granted Luciano a reprieve on the condition that Luciano agree to deportation and promise never to return. On 10 February 1946, Luciano sailed out of New York Harbour on the SS *Laura Keene*, bound for Italy. Knowing that the press would be at the pier reporting on mobsters waving goodbye, Lansky deliberately stayed away.

Luciano settled in a villa on the Via Lucillo in Montemario, a quiet residential neighbourhood just to the north of Vatican City in Rome. He was there eight months before taking the first step in reneging on his pledge not to come back.

On 29 October 1946, this time without any press coverage, Meyer Lansky was waiting on the tarmac at Camaguey Airport to welcome Lucky to Cuba.

Lansky installed his old pal in the Presidential Suite at the Nacional. A few weeks later, Luciano took up more permanent residence at No. 29, Calle 30, in the fashionable Miramar district of Havana. He spent the days at Oriental Park playing the horses with Lansky and, later in the evenings, they gambled together at the Nacional. Like the celebrity he'd become, Luciano held court with American tourists and wealthy Cubans who'd previously known him only by reputation, and met often with old friends and associates who arrived from the States to pay homage. Shadowed by the FBI, Luciano was overheard telling people that while he had no present business connections in Cuba, he planned to remain there for a long time and was, 'Hoping to establish himself in some legitimate business in the near future'.

In January 1947, around the same time that Al Capone died in Florida, Luciano put out the word that he wanted 'the boys' to come to Cuba for a summit. He didn't say as much, but he intended to enthrone himself as *capo di tutti capi,* the boss of bosses of the American Mafia. Attendance was mandatory, as was 'a little something' to welcome Lucky back. That translated to cash. The legitimate business in which he was hoping to establish himself was the Nacional's casino. The $150,000 that he expected to collect was to pay for his share of it.

On 11 February, two Chicago gangsters – Joe and Rocco Fischetti – flew to Havana from Florida for the meeting that was to begin the following day. They brought along with them their friend, Frank Sinatra. Years later, Sinatra's FBI file would suggest that he had an obscure family tie to the Capones. The three Fischetti brothers – Charlie was the third one – operated carpet joints in Chicago and Miami and were also related to Capone. Not that this explains Sinatra's lifelong fascination for wiseguys, simply that the Sinatra–Fischetti friendship might somehow be part of the confused Mafia concept of family. Certainly the friendship lasted a long time. Perhaps more importantly, through that friendship, Sinatra forged what has to be his most significant Mob association – one he often denied but one that would have very serious repercussions – with the Fischettis' boss in Chicago, Sam Giancana.

Many years later, Sinatra's presence at the so-called 'Havana Conference' would assume mythical proportions as tales of the meeting grew with each telling. In one version, Sinatra had been invited along as a bag man for the Fischettis who worried that if they carried money to Luciano they might be stopped, but reckoned that if Sinatra carried the cash it would be safe because no one would bother to check him. In 1963, when the Nevada Gaming Commission held licensing hearings on Sinatra's Cal-Neva Lodge hotel and casino – where Giancana was, illegally, his secret partner – they asked him about that meeting. Sinatra confirmed that he'd gone to Cuba in early 1947, but insisted that he was there on vacation and swore under oath that he did not have anything to do with gangsters.

One of the Commissioners fired point blank, 'Did you fly to Havana with $2 million in an attaché case?'

That's when Sinatra retorted, 'Show me an attaché case that can hold $2 million and you can have the $2 million.' He wasn't asked if he was carrying any money for the Fischettis, so he never had to answer that one. Nor did he ever bother to explain how or why, when the Italian police raided Luciano's home, they found a gold cigarette case inscribed, 'To my dear pal Lucky, from his friend, Frank Sinatra.'

The oft-repeated version of this story has it that Luciano was discovered living in Cuba only when the Havana Conference ended with a Christmas party in Sinatra's honour. But FBI records reveal that isn't so. The US Embassy in Rome had been informed in October 1946 that Luciano – travelling on an Italian passport in the name of Salvatore Lucania – had left Italy, and the US Embassy in Havana had been informed a few days later by the Cuban intelligence service that he'd arrived. FBI records also indicate that Luciano was kept under constant surveillance by both the Cubans and the Americans. There was no Mafia Christmas bash and his discovery there had nothing to do with Sinatra. The Cuban press had already stumbled across Luciano at the racetrack several days before Sinatra arrived with the Fischettis. An

article appeared in *Tiempa En Cuba* on 9 February 1947, noting
Luciano's presence on the island. That article tipped US press to the
story. When Sinatra's name got thrown into the mix, coupled with
Luciano's, the story stayed in front of the public for weeks.

Both governments were suddenly faced with the dilemma of what
to do with Luciano. An official American report labelled Luciano's
presence in Cuba 'sufficiently dangerous', and on 21 February
Washington issued an ultimatum. Either Cuba deport Luciano or shipments of much needed American pharmaceuticals would be halted.
The Cubans arrested Luciano the following day and declared him an
undesirable. They held him at the Tiscornia Immigration Camp until
20 March when, despite last-ditch legal wrangling by Luciano's friends
in high places, the Cubans stuck him on a Turkish freighter bound
for the Canary Islands and Genoa, Italy.

While that event changed Luciano's life, it didn't alter much, if
anything, for Lansky. He continued commuting between Florida and
Cuba, representing his own interests, and also the interests of his partners, especially Luciano. Although that same year, when some locals
in Hallandale moved to shut down the Colonial Inn, Lansky began
selling out. It was just in time because, what did change things, materially, for Lansky, were the lofty ambitions of a Democrat from
Chattanooga, Tennessee and an out-of-work Cuban president in
Daytona Beach, Florida.

In May 1950, Senator Estes Kefauver launched a 15-month-long,
15-city pilgrimage to challenge the Mob. His 'Special Committee to
Investigate Organized Crime in Interstate Commerce' was uniquely
armed with an executive order from President Harry Truman which
gave Kefauver the right to examine the tax returns of anyone the
committee chose to subpoena as a witness. Television was becoming
America's most powerful medium, and Kefauver understood that, by
putting every known crook in the country in front of the cameras and
forcing them to testify about gambling and racketeering, even if they
evaded answering his questions – which most of them did – the glare
of publicity would take its toll. In all, he and his four committee
members called 600 witnesses, compiled 12,000 pages of testimony
and delivered hundreds of hours of public hearings into more than 25
million living rooms.

Although Kefauver never actually proved the existence a formal
mobster alliance, he concluded, 'There is a nationwide crime syndicate known as the Mafia, whose tentacles are found in most large

cities.' He even described it as, 'The cement that helps to bind the Costello-Adonis-Lansky syndicate of New York and the Accardo-Guzik-Fischetti syndicate of Chicago.'

Gambling, he decided, was the root of this evil. 'Gambling profits are the principal support of big-time racketeering and gangsterism. These profits provide the financial resources whereby ordinary criminals are converted into big-time racketeers, political bosses, pseudo-businessmen and alleged philanthropists. Thus the $2 horse player and the 5-cent numbers player are not only suckers because they are gambling against hopeless odds, but they also provide the moneys which enable underworld characters to undermine our institutions.'

The 'Kefauver Hearings' popularized the word 'Mafia', demonstrated clearly the power of organized criminals – especially their ability to corrupt the political system – launched a national assault on the Mob, and set the tone for Congressional hearings for the next 20 years which probed further into the business of organized crime in America. Among the people subpoenaed to testify were Tampa Mob boss Santos Trafficante Sr, who would be ruined by these hearings; 'Murder Incorporated' boss Albert Anastasia, who would be killed before the decade was out; 'Prime Minister' Frank Costello, who became famous overnight for shielding his face from the cameras which then focused on his trembling hands; and the naturally shy Meyer Lansky, whose demeanour made him look as dangerous as your average bank teller. The hearings also helped to popularize the Fifth Amendment of the Constitution, as over and over again, questions were answered with, 'I plead the Fifth' and 'I refuse to answer the question on the grounds that it may tend to incriminate me.'

Kefauver set his sights on Florida. Although he never actually went to Hallandale, he described it as, 'The sin city capital of the South.' That didn't please Lansky who, following one of his three appearances before Kefauver, got into a now-much-quoted conversation with him. Knowing that Kefauver was a gambler, Lansky asked, 'What's wrong with gambling? You like it yourself. I know you've gambled a lot.'

The Senator acknowledged that was true. 'But I don't want you people to control it.'

Lansky assumed that by 'you people' Kefauver was referring to Jews. He snapped, 'I will not allow you to persecute me because I am a Jew.'

Kefauver's response was to get a federal grand jury to return a 21-count indictment against Lansky. The charges were mostly for 'corrupting racetrack gambling'. Lansky pleaded guilty to five counts, was fined $2,500 and given a three-month suspended sentence. Even though his conviction would be overturned 20 years later, this slap on the wrist reminded Lansky that his carpet joint innings were over.

What Kefauver never counted on when he began his hearings were two very specific after-effects. First, the Mob's ardour for Las Vegas intensified which, consequently, touched off a building boom there. Second, by shutting down cities like Hallandale, he greatly enhanced the attraction of Cuba.

As for the out-of-work president in Daytona Beach, Batista's ego ultimately got the best of him. He headed home to Cuba, snatched back power two months before the 1952 elections and, having learned his lesson in 1944, shamelessly rigged the ballot so that this time he could not be defeated. By now, the gambling Mecca he'd helped to create was being run by crooks who were acting like crooks – everyone was stealing from everyone else. Batista believed that if the punters were being robbed they'd go somewhere else, so he decided to replace those crooks with his own crooks.

The crook he trusted the most was his old chum Meyer Lansky.

Having recently taken over Havana's Montmartre Club, Lansky also understood that high-stakes gambling was most profitable when it was run honestly. He accepted Batista's invitation to become Cuba's unofficial 'minister of gambling', which came with a $25,000 yearly salary. For Lansky, it was a licence to print money.

In turn, at Lansky's behest, Batista's police ran the worst of the crooks off the island, meaning Lansky's major competitors. Lansky then convinced Batista to subsidize his clean up of the gambling industry with government grants, and to enact 'Hotel Law 2074'. That awarded tax exemptions plus a casino licence to foreigners investing more than $1 million. Taking full advantage of both, Lansky wound up controlling the Nacional for less than 50-cents on the dollar. He installed his brother Jake as manager of the Nacional and the Montmartre Club then acquired a stake in the Tropicana. Lansky's sometimes-associate, Santos Trafficante Jr – who'd lived on the island for more than 20 years and was *de facto* head of the Tampa Mob – was allowed to take over operations at the Sans Souci, the Sevilla-Biltmore, the Commodoro and the Deauville. The two were part owners of the Capri, where another Lansky friend, actor George Raft, had a share. The only hotel and casino that even came close to a Mob-free zone was the Havana Hilton, because the chain's founder, Conrad Hilton, promised to keep it honest. But Batista sold the casino licence to a consortium of Lansky's friends for a $1 million cash kickback and that effectively neutered Mr Hilton.

It goes without saying that everyone had to kick-back Batista and his entourage at every turn. That included a nightly share of the gambling tables, in addition to what he was taking for the rights to control prostitution and, in Trafficante's case, to tranship heroin. It meant that, for all intents and purposes, the Mob was running its own country.

Now, Lansky decided to furnish it better. In partnership with Luciano and Costello, Lansky arranged for the Batista government to fund the jewel in Havana's crown – The Riviera Hotel. A 440-room, 21-storey extravaganza, it would be the largest, most luxurious purpose-built casino-hotel outside of Las Vegas.

Bizarrely, as this was Lansky's monument to himself, he would not allow his name to appear on any of the official documents. Not even the casino licence. That was held by Eddie Levinson, a Lansky crony from New York. Nor would Lansky put his name on the books of the corporation that would own the hotel. That was fronted by Ben and Harry Smith, out of Toronto. The only place where Lansky's name appeared was as director of the kitchens.

For the man who supposedly once said 'Crime is bigger than US Steel,' the pieces had fallen neatly into place. Even if Lansky didn't actually say it, and there is some doubt that he did, comparing crime to US Steel wouldn't have been too far from the truth. Each casino maintained bank accounts in Miami. Checks and cash were couriered from Cuba to those banks daily and from Florida, the funds were wired elsewhere. Some money went to legitimate businesses in the States. Some just disappeared into the night. Money also moved from Cuba to Switzerland, then came back to Mob accounts in the States as legitimate earnings from businesses in Cuba. By the time the Riviera opened for business, just before Christmas 1956, so much heroin money was pouring into Cuba that Lansky's laundromat – an anti-Disneyland – had become the most decadent spot on the planet.

Havana was 'America's whorehouse'.

By now, too, the Batista regime had grown so wildly corrupt that unrest was spilling onto the streets and, more importantly, about to come down from the Sierra Maestra mountains. A former baseball player, law student and political prisoner named Fidel, together with his brother Raul, their comrade Che and 128 other malcontents, were making ready to take the island.

Batista had secured promises from Washington that, should he have to leave Cuba in the dead of night, he'd be permitted to enjoy unhindered asylum in Daytona Beach. But there's not a lot of evidence that Lansky had an exit strategy. For a man as bright as him, it's unthinkable that Lansky didn't see the writing on the wall. Perhaps he figured that the kickbacks to Batista – which had climbed to a high of 30% of the Riviera's gaming table receipts – were some sort of insurance policy to guarantee safe harbour no matter what happened.

Perhaps he was, as some historians have recently asserted, hedging his bets by getting money to Castro.

Or, perhaps, he was simply blinded by his own success.

After all, like a thief with a blueprint, he'd just invented the world's first offshore financial centre.

CHAPTER TWO

The Next Cuba

Winning isn't the most important thing, it's second to breathing.
— New York Yankees owner, George Steinbrenner

Meyer Lansky's dream of a world beyond the reach of the IRS suffered a rude awakening when the rebels came down from the mountains and with the help of guns provided by American gangsters — notably Lansky's own associate, Santos Trafficante Jr — seized control of the island. Che Guevara took Havana on New Year's Day, 1959. Batista had escaped on New Year's eve, carrying $40 million. Castro marched in on 8 January. Lansky had fled the night before, leaving $17 million behind. A few days later, as if to say thank you for coming to my insurrection, Castro shoved Trafficante into jail and left him there for a year.

For a while, Washington played the anxious suitor and, for a while, it appeared as if Castro was available for the courting. But fleeting romance succumbed to protracted acrimony. Castro tossed out the Americans, claimed control of the casinos and saved his goodnight kisses for the Russians. Lansky put a $1 million bounty on Castro's head, payable to anyone upon his return to Havana, although deep down, he must have known it was a lost cause. Some of his cohorts blamed Lansky for staying with the wrong horse so late in the race, but there was no way he could have predicated that a ragtag band of merry men would pull off an entire revolution. Besides, Cuba had served the Mob well.

Nursing his wounds back in Miami, Lansky had lived to play again another day. He'd also learned some valuable lessons about 'the next Cuba'. It would have to be small and close enough to the US mainland to get tourists and gamblers in and out easily. In that respect, it would look a lot like the last Cuba. It, too, would have to come furnished with a thoroughly corrupt political regime, held together by a despot greedy enough to welcome the Mob with open arms. But unlike Batista, that tyrant would have to be so firmly in place that the political environment would remain stable no matter what. And the Mob's money would have to be spread so thick and so wide that, if some other tyrant seized power, he'd need them to maintain his own stability.

At first glance, the Dominican Republic seemed to fit the bill. The man in charge was General Rafael Leonides Trujillo, one of the bloodiest autocrats in Latin American history. With Trujillo's blessings, mobster Joe Bonanno was already moving heroin through the Dominican Republic to the United States. So clearly, Trujillo was someone the Mob could deal with. But because Lansky and his friends did not necessarily trust Bonanno, they looked for a different way to get to Trujillo. The key became his ex-son-in-law, Porfirio Rubirosa.

Forever described as a 'playboy' – as if that was his job description – when Rubirosa wasn't chasing women around Palm Beach and New York, or marrying Trujillo's daughter, or marrying French actress Danielle Darrieux, or marrying tobacco heiress Doris Duke, or marrying Woolworth heiress Barbara Hutton, or just sleeping with actress Zsa Zsa Gabor, he was working as the General's bagman. It was Rubirosa who collected the various fees and commissions that Trujillo claimed from deals his government arranged with American businesses. Along the way, he got to know Frank Sinatra, who introduced him to John Kennedy – birds of a feather – who in turn took an interest in the Dominican Republic.

Kennedy feared that the Russians might try to move in on yet another Caribbean island. That worry, together with his distaste for Trujillo, was shared with Allen Dulles, the CIA chief he'd inherited from President Eisenhower. What Kennedy didn't know until Dulles told him was that Bonanno and Trujillo were trading drugs for weapons. Eisenhower had been furious and, consequently, the CIA had approved a plot by seven Trujillo colleagues to kill the Dominican ruler. At the end of May 1961, barely four months into the Kennedy presidency, JFK refused to pull the plug on Trujillo's assassination.

Unknowingly, Kennedy was now on a collision course with the Mafia boss of Chicago's 'Outfit', Sam Giancana.

The Outfit and the Kennedys had history. Like many of America's major gangsters in the early 1960s, Giancana and his pals had run booze with Kennedy's father Joe during Prohibition. Some of the money Kennedy Senior made as a whiskey smuggler was reinvested in Chicago when, in 1945, Joe bought the Merchandise Mart. Supposedly the largest commercial establishment in the world, it remained the bedrock of the Kennedy family fortune for 50 years. Needless to say, no business that size could function in Chicago in those days without certain people being taken care of. Workers were supplied by the city's Democratic machine. Where 'jobs for the boys' went, so went the Teamsters Union. Along with the Teamsters came the Outfit.

In 1960, Giancana played his part in JFK's presidential campaign. He not only delivered cash to the Kennedys – using Sinatra as his intermediary – but sat back and watched as one of his girlfriends, Judith Campbell, was introduced to Kennedy by Sinatra, and quickly became a Kennedy girlfriend, too. Giancana used Campbell as a conduit for more campaign cash.

For the November election, Giancana and the Outfit were in the shadows of the Cook County 'cemetery vote', helping to stuff Chicago's ballot boxes with votes from dead people. Some historians contend that those were the votes that carried Illinois for Kennedy, which swung the election away from the Republican candidate, Richard Nixon. The Democratic Party political machine of Mayor Richard Daley, with the Outfit in the background, are the indisputable chief suspects. And while other historians argue that the votes stolen for Kennedy in Illinois were nullified by votes stolen for Nixon in other states and, therefore, did not play such a momentous a role, it doesn't belie the fact that Giancana felt Kennedy owed him.

The assassination of Trujillo upset Giancana's plans. He'd staked a hefty share of his Outfit's financial future on Las Vegas and was now looking to move offshore. As a corporate entity in Vegas, the Outfit controlled the Sands, the Sahara and the Riviera. But Nevada, like Cuba, had been declared an 'open' city, in effect, a free trade zone where any Mob family could work gambling or hookers or drugs or extortion for as long as they could hold onto the business. And everybody was there. Lansky had part of the Thunderbird; the Cleveland Mob ran the Desert Inn and the Stardust; New England's Patriarca family had the Dunes; and a Lansky-Costello partnership was behind the Tropicana. The Teamsters were mixed into this as well, at Caesar's Palace, the Dunes and the Fremont. Although there was plenty of money to be skimmed, there were a lot of fingers dipping into the pot. Giancana wanted some place that would belong to Chicago and he'd set his sites on the Dominican Republic

His scheme revolved around Bobby Baker, a very powerful man whom Giancana had slipped into his own pocket. In the days when Lyndon Johnson was the omnipotent Democrat in the Senate, Baker

– Johnson's closest and most trusted confidant – was referred to as
'the 101st Senator' and 'Little Lyndon'. Now, with Johnson as Vice
President, Baker's corrupt influence was such that he was being paid
by Trujillo to be his lobbyist on Capitol Hill, and was being paid by
Giancana to seduce legitimate hotel chains (mainly Intercontinental)
and airlines (mainly Pan Am which owned Intercontinental) into a
Dominican investment.

While Giancana was manoeuvring the Outfit's takeover of Santo
Domingo, Allen Dulles and the CIA were busy cooking up 'Operation
Mongoose'. A series of conspiracies to overthrow Castro, one of the
plots included hiring the Mafia to kill him. When word reached
Giancana that he might be called on to show his patriotism, he made
certain that Kennedy knew he'd signed on. But the Attorney General,
John's brother Bobby, had other ideas about Giancana. Bobby had
already annoyed Giancana by labelling him a dangerous gangster in
his 1960 book, *The Enemy Within*. Now, learning that Giancana was
eyeing the Dominican Republic, Bobby moved against the Outfit and,
at the same time, extracted John from his friendship with Giancana's
pal, Frank Sinatra.

A financial scandal took Bobby Baker out of circulation, killing
Giancana's offshore plans. For good measure, Bobby ordered the FBI
to get in Giancana's face. Agents hounded the Chicago mobster at
every turn, harassing him when he could least afford to find himself
targeted by law enforcement and severely hampering his ability to
earn a living. Bobby also set off in hot pursuit of the Teamsters Union.

FBI records reveal that Giancana took this as a personal affront.
They leave no doubt that he was fed up with Bobby's Justice
Department and their bellicose harassment of him. He was aggravated
when the Kennedys abandoned Sinatra. And he was exasperated by
Bobby's relentless targeting of the Teamsters. In Giancana's eyes, the
brothers were disloyal and infidelity was not something he could accept
gracefully. Which is why, if you believe in conspiracy theories – especially the one that goes, the Mafia murdered John F. Kennedy – it's
easy to give credence to claims that the Kennedy's 'betrayal' of
Giancana lies somewhere at the heart of it.

The Dominican Republic would have suited the Mob, at least in
the short term. But that was gone. So Lansky, still in search of the
next Cuba, needed to find somewhere else. By this time, casinos were
happening all over the Caribbean, notably in the Netherlands Antilles
– Aruba, Bonaire, Curacao and Sint Maarten – and in Haiti. Some

were legit, most were not, Haiti being the worst of the bunch. But after taking a good look around, none of those places seemed quite as enticing to Lansky as the 700 islands and cays that made up a British colony just 30 minutes by air from Miami. Communications were good, real estate was cheap, access was easy, the political system was stable enough and the politicians were corrupt enough that the place was ripe for plucking.

Best of all, the route into the Bahamas was already paved.

In July 1944, representatives from 44 nations gathered at Bretton Woods, New Hampshire, to put the final touches on an agreement to stabilize the world's postwar economy. They established the International Monetary Fund (IMF), fixed the price of gold at $35 an ounce, tied the US dollar to gold, then tied the exchange rate of other convertible currencies to the dollar. The theory behind Bretton Woods was that, by imposing monetary stability, the Western powers could guarantee money supply, stabilize interest rates and slow recession.

Everyone recognized the benefits of this, especially, Joseph Stalin.

The Russian rouble, in its non-convertible state, might have been a symbol of fiscal sovereignty for the Soviet dictator, but the truth of the matter was that, when it came to imported goods and services, he was dependent on the stability of Western economies in general and the strength of the US dollar in particular. And while dollar dependency might have looked like an obstacle to the Soviets on their road to world dominance, it was hardly insurmountable because Russia is an oil producer, oil is a dollar commodity and Stalin had dollar revenues. What he didn't have was some place safe to bed down his dollars until he spent them. In those days, the only banks holding dollar deposits were American, which put the Communist Party of the USSR in the odd position of being a commercial client of their avowed Capitalist enemies.

Stalin was uncomfortable about that, for two very practical, decidedly non-ideological, reasons.

The first was the Tsar's IOUs. Three decades after the October Revolution, the world was still awash with Russian bonds. For all intents and purposes, the bonds were worthless because the Communists said they were. These were the Tsars' debts and as long as Stalin had no intention of honouring them, bondholders had no way of collecting on them. But that could change if someone discovered Soviet dollars sitting in New York. Bond values would soar before the ink was dry on the first lawsuit.

The second reason was the Cold War. Stalin feared that, as friction between the two super-powers increased, Washington might be tempted to hold the Soviets to ransom by seizing Russian money in the States.

Now, it may be apocryphal, but there's a story told about the ruler of Abu Dhabi who was keeping all his money stacked in the basement of the royal palace. One day, his finance minister came to him to announce that rats were eating the bank notes and warned that, if he didn't get his money out of the basement immediately, there wouldn't be any left. When the ruler of Abu Dhabi confessed that he had no place else to put his money, the finance minister suggested he deposit it in a bank. So, the ruler ordered that his money be removed from the basement, piled into oxen carts and driven to a bank. A week later, the ruler called for his finance minister and commanded, take me to the bank, I want to see my money. Needless to say, banks don't stash money, they loan it out to people, businesses and even other banks. Now, an embarrassed finance minister had the awkward task of explaining to the ruler why his money wasn't actually at the bank, even though it was in the bank.

When a bank doesn't have enough money immediately available – if cash reserves are inadequate and someone wants to see his money – the bank has a liquidity problem. To get around it, they ask the government to print more money and lend it to them through the discount window. In Stalin's day, the Federal Reserve – America's version of a central bank – did that for American banks but was not inclined to do it for foreign banks. Theoretically, Washington allowed banks outside the States to hold dollars as long as they could jump through some very narrow hoops. Among other things, foreign banks were required to maintain liquidity levels much steeper than most of them could afford.

What Stalin couldn't foresee, and what the Americans never counted on when they signed Bretton Woods, was that by pinning the world's currencies to the dollar, Washington was creating a monster with an enormous appetite for dollars. The Marshall Plan injected a gigantic $13 billion into Europe between 1948 and 1951, and European central banks were buying substantial quantities to bolster their own depreciating currencies. Suddenly, a colossal amount of dollars was housed outside the United States. Those dollars needed some place to go, and two banks that slipped quietly into the business of housing them were the Moscow Narodny Bank in London and the Banque Commerciale Pour l'Europe du Nord in Paris. Both just happened to be Soviet-owned and both just happened to be served by British financial advisers.

In the aftermath of the 1956 Russian invasion of Hungary, the Kremlin's British financial advisers – who were in touch with the two banks' British financial advisers – agreed that it would be especially prudent to move Russia's dollars out of America's clutches and into Paris. Their timing was good because the following year, when the Moscow Narodny Bank in London faced a crisis – triggered by a British balance of payments emergency which itself had been brought on by the Suez Crisis – Banque Commerciale could loan Moscow Narodny enough dollars to assure liquidity. The cable address of Banque Commerciale was 'Eurobank' and the loan was described as 'Eurobankdollars', which was eventually shortened to 'Eurodollars'.

Seeing how liquidity could be assured through dollar loans negotiated outside the United States, several international banks piled onto the bandwagon. At the same time, responding angrily to Suez – which Washington had bluntly warned the British not to precipitate – the Americans seized dollar assets held in the States by all the participants. The freeze didn't last long but it infuriated the Arabs, and once it was over, Arab governments moved their money out of US banks and into this brand new Eurodollar market. That meant bedding down dollars in London – ironically, the enemy from Suez – which was the heart of this brand new market.

Without realizing it, the Russians had stuck a dagger into Bretton Woods and unwittingly provided nutriment at a critical moment in the gestation of the modern offshore world.

Rich Americans had wintered in the Bahamas and sports fishermen had plied the waters there for years. But in the mid-1950s, tourism in the islands was a far cry from what it is today. For tourism to develop, there had to be an infrastructure. And the story of how that infrastructure evolved – how the pieces got put into place for the Mob – is filled with a cast of screwballs and eccentrics, any one of whom could have come straight off the pages of Damon Runyan.

It begins with a swindler from Baltimore named Wallace Groves who first showed up during the Great Depression and lived in the Bahamas on and off – the notable off period being 1941–1944 when his residence was a US federal prison – for most of his adult life. A man who was forever dreaming up schemes that entailed bilking the local treasury, his partner in crime was Sir Stafford Sands, a Bahamian attorney and power broker who stroked the heart of the white minority 'Bay Street Boys' government. Conveniently, Sands was also chairman of the Development Board which, effectively, made him the minister for tourism.

More than just 'vaguely villainous', as some Bahamians remember him today, Sands was thoroughly corrupt. He was also a bigot who would leave his country when black majority rule was introduced, to die in stubborn exile in 1972 at London's Dorchester Hotel. And yet, his legacy as the architect of the island's modern economy is such that his oval, eye-glassed face stares back from the Bahamian ten dollar bill.

Sands' strategy to bring the islands into the twentieth century – while all the time insuring his own financial security – saw Groves play the front man. In 1955, Groves applied for a government grant of 50,000 acres, all sorts of tax breaks plus the promise of more land, to create the Grand Bahama Port Authority. Needless to say, the scheme was approved. But when Sands admitted that this was far too substantial a project to pull off on their own, he and Groves fast-talked the enigmatic Daniel K. Ludwig into backing them.

A postwar financier who showed up on everybody's 'richest men in captivity' list, Ludwig owned the world's largest merchant shipping fleet and therefore had the wherewithal to guarantee the project's success. He dug the harbour while Groves and Sands developed the land. The result was Freeport, the Caribbean's first significant industrial centre and purpose built parking lot for cruise ships. Groves and Sands next step was to parlay Freeport into a tourist resort. For that, Groves brought in a Canadian conman friend, Lou Chesler.

Known as 'Moose', because he weighed nearly 300 pounds and looked like one, Ontario-born Chesler made his first million in 1946, at the age of 33, flogging dodgy Canadian mining stocks. He took his money to Florida, sold swamps to the gullible, bought dry land for himself and by 1960 had multiplied his fortune fifty fold. Along the way, he went out to Hollywood, bought Associated Artists, named himself chairman and, through various share manipulations, turned one company into another to become chairman of Seven Arts. Chesler had learned the art of duplicity back in the early 1940s from a skilful fraudster named John Pullman.

Born in Russia, Pullman spent his early years in Canada, emigrated to the States and, after serving in the US Army, wound up in Chicago bootlegging whiskey. In 1931, he was convicted for violations of the Volstead Act and served six months. While in jail, Pullman met a rumrunner from Minneapolis named Yiddy Bloom. When they both got out, Bloom introduced his new friend Pullman to his old friend Meyer Lansky and, some years later, Pullman introduced his new friend Lansky to his old friend, Lou Chesler.

Chesler and Lansky hit it off and worked several scams together, most notably injecting Mob money into the 1958 redevelopment of Miami International Airport. So now, when Groves brought Chesler into the Freeport project, Chesler arrived holding hands with Lansky.

In the meantime, Pullman concluded that he didn't like being an American criminal any more, so he gave up his citizenship to become a Canadian criminal. Except, he didn't like the Canadian weather, so he moved to Switzerland where he hooked up with the intensely mysterious Tibor Rosenbaum.

A Holocaust survivor, Rosenbaum was either an agent for the Israeli intelligence service Mossad, or a businessman whom Mossad could call for favours. The extent of his service has never been made clear and probably never will be. It is known that, between the end of World War II in 1945 and mid-1948, Rosenbaum ran guns from Czechoslovakia to Palestine. He is remembered today as one of those men who helped forge Israeli statehood. It is also known that, at some point over the following ten years, Rosenbaum spent a great deal of time in – of all bizarre places – Liberia. After doing whatever it was he did there, by the time he moved to Geneva, Rosenbaum was carrying a black diplomatic passport as an Honorary Counsel of Liberia.

In 1959, almost certainly with Mossad backing, Rosenbaum created the Banque International de Credit (BIC) which was to become a legendary laundry. Liberian diplomatic passports would also, in their own way, become part of the offshore world's myth.

So Pullman joined Rosenbaum in Geneva while Chesler, in the Bahamas, formed a company called Devco which acquired land from Groves' and Sands' Port Authority in exchange for Devco shares. Chesler then folded Devco into a pair of bogus Canadian shell companies and announced plans to build the deluxe Lacayan Beach Hotel. Incongruously, included in the blueprints for a hotel where people would be spending most of their time outside on the beach in perfect weather, were several large indoor squash courts.

Despite having failed to attract enough tourists to support Chesler's resort, Sands formed a company with Chesler and Groves called Bahamas Amusement. The ink was still wet on the incorporation documents when the government granted Bahamas Amusement – part owned by the man in charge of tourism – an exclusive ten-year licence to operate casinos on the island. Seconds later, miraculously, by connecting a few dots on the Lacayan's blueprints, the squash courts metamorphosed into a casino.

Called the Monte Carlo, the casino opened in January 1964, several weeks before the hotel itself was completed. Lansky bankrolled it and put his own guy, Dino Cellini, in to supervise it. When the deceit, conflicts and corruption became too obvious even by Bahamian standards – when Sands' puppets in government 'suddenly realized' that the country was overflowing with mobsters – Premier Roland Symonette had little choice but to do something. He ordered out a handful of the most prominent goons, with Cellini heading the list. But the extradition paperwork got lost in the bureaucratic maze and everyone, except Cellini, was allowed to stay for up to four years, by which time suitable replacements had been found. Lansky dispatched Dino Cellini to England, where he joined his brother Eddie in the background of the Colony Club, one of London's most notorious casinos. Fronted by actor George Raft, Dino and Raft were eventually declared undesirables and tossed out of the UK.

No sooner was the Monte Carlo up and running when John Pullman moved from Geneva to Freeport to open the Bank of World Commerce (BWC). Years later, the New Jersey Casino Control Commission would describe BWC as a sink for 'some of the nations' top gangsters' where 'millions of dollars passed through the door and were reinvested in syndicate controlled projects in the United States.'

The casino skim from Vegas now mingled with casino skim from the Bahamas and moved through BWC on its way to BIC in Switzerland. To oil the works, Rosenbaum opened a local subsidiary of BIC in Freeport called Atlas Bank. He then turned to Africa, to help despots there bring stolen booty into the West, laundering it through BIC and Atlas and, from the Bahamas, investing it for them in North America. Not to be left out in his own backyard, Stafford

Sands opened a bank in Nassau called Intra Bahamas Trust Ltd, which was tied to Intra Bank of Beirut, headquartered in Lebanon, which is one of the world's most under-rated drug money laundering centres.

Enter here the hapless George Huntington Hartford II.

A man born with a $90 million silver spoon in his mouth, he was heir to the A&P grocery store empire that once stretched across the US. Hartford was also a man struggling to make his own dreams come true. By the time he'd graduated Harvard in 1934, he'd dropped the George and replaced the II with tags such as art collector, museum benefactor, magazine publisher, author and property developer. The problem was that, most of the time, he lost money and by the end of his life he'd gone through a sizeable amount of his fortune.

In the early 1950s, Hartford had 'discovered' a 700-acre beach ten minutes by boat from Nassau called Hog Island. Measuring four miles by two-thirds of a mile, it got its name because it was overrun with pigs. Hartford bought it the same day he spotted it, never thinking it might be a good idea if his lawyers come down first to read the small print on his $11 million purchase. Hartford intended to develop the place into one of the world's great tourist resorts. He renamed it Paradise Island and, over the next several years, dropped another $19 million trying to make it look like its new namesake.

At the heart of his plans was a hotel and casino complex. At the heart of his downfall was the fact that he chose the wrong law firm to advise him. Instead of going with Stafford Sands, he opted for honest lawyers and was, therefore, never able to acquire the necessary gaming licence. Compounding the sin, Hartford sank money into the underdog, black power Progressive Liberal Party, which was tantamount to treason in the eyes of Sands and his white United Bahamians.

That Hartford soon ran into cash flow troubles simply exposed his carcass to the circling vultures. He was forced to sell part of his interest for $750,000. Inexplicably, Hartford then turned around and lent $2 million to the man who'd bought that part interest, accepting repayment in unregistered stock, which he quickly discovered he couldn't sell to anyone. So his new partner – the same fellow who still owed him $2 million – offered to help out with a $1 million loan, which wound up being secured with another hefty chunk of Paradise Island shares. The original guarantees were quickly pulled and the loan was called in. Hartford's stake was sold and the net result was that his $30 million investment in Paradise Island produced a $28 million tax loss.

The group that moved in on Paradise Island was called Mary Carter Paint. They'd already tied up with Groves and Chesler in Freeport and would, in time, evolve into Resorts International. With Sands help, it was Mary Carter Paint that secured the casino licence and saw Paradise Island rise out of Hartford's ashes.

Lansky, in the meantime, was feeling the all-too familiar chill of political change. So he followed Hartford's lead by quietly backing the Progressive Liberals. By the time the black Bahamian opposition just barely squeaked into power in 1967, Sands was on his way into exile and the island's new leader – Lynden Pindling – was on his way into the pocket of the great survivor, Meyer Lansky.

Back in the good old days, Lucky Luciano oversaw a network that smuggled Turkish opium into Lebanon, where Italian chemists turned it into heroin, where it was handed off to Corsican smugglers who shipped it to Montreal, where the Bonanno family moved it by truck through Buffalo and Detroit and onto the streets of New York. When those Italian chemists got busted, Luciano moved the factory to Marseilles, where French chemists and Corsican smugglers expanded the connection into the single most important heroin cartel of the century.

But times were changing and younger men were coming into the business, bringing with them, younger ideas. There had always been infighting among Sicilian clans however, the mammoth influx of money that now came along with the heroin business exacerbated differences and jealousies. Luciano had not been able to maintain sufficient control and from the mid-1950s until his death in 1962, infighting jeopardized the Sicilians' ability to do business. Almost as soon as Luciano was gone, the younger generation moved against the older leaders, seriously weakening the Mafia's authority around the world. Gangland murders increased. Law enforcement took advantage of the confusion and began to break up old alliances. At the same time, the Americans coerced the Turks to crack down on opium production, which created a source of supply crisis for Luciano's 'French Connection' labs in Marseilles.

The Mafia's fallback position became Southeast Asia. The French had colonized the region and, until they got thrown out in 1954, French and Corsican gangs had smuggled vast quantities of gold, currency and heroin from there back to the Mediterranean. Now, with more than 70 per cent of the world's opium grown in the Golden Triangle countries of Thailand, Laos and Cambodia, those same French and Corsican gangs re-ignited old friendships and reopened the Saigon–Marseilles smuggling routes.

In 1965, John Pullman went to Hong Kong to check out gambling, banking and the narcotics business. The war in Vietnam was bringing tens of thousands of drug-hungry American GIs into the region, creating a brand-new customer base. That the Mob intended to exploit this, goes without saying. That the Mob showed this kind of market-vision, is testimony to their capacity for freewheeling capitalism.

Santos Trafficante had by then inherited what was left of Luciano's heroin interests. The same year that Pullman went to Hong Kong, Trafficante – looking to maintain market share – sent one of his young lieutenants to Vietnam. Frank Furci opened clubs in Saigon, and infiltrated others on military bases, using them to move black-market money and drugs. Though stiff competition soon forced the inexperienced Furci to retreat, Trafficante himself showed up in 1968 to underwrite both his concerns for and increasing investment in the region.

The following year a summit took place at the Continental Palace Hotel in Saigon. With the war in full swing, French and Corsican syndicates looked to opium producers in the Golden Triangle to assure their own supply. Within two years, Golden Triangle heroin was moving through Chinese labs in Hong Kong, onto Chile, across the border into Paraguay then north and into the Caribbean.

The Bahamas were geographically ideal for transhipping drugs into the US, and had been used for that since the 1950s. Starting with Jamaica marijuana and Paraguayan cocaine, it escalated with the arrival of Southeast Asian heroin and Colombian cocaine. Not only did all those islands and cays offer thousands of hiding places, but the traffickers were protected by Pindling. He served as premier for seven years before independence and as prime minister for 19 years after independence. In 1984, he was implicated in a corruption and drug scandal that, predictably, went nowhere. An inquiry exonerated him after hearing his explanation for spending eight times more on his personal life than his official salary. According to Pindling, legitimate business associates gave him cash presents because they liked him.

His regime ended with a plea for a laundering of his character. In Pindling's farewell speech, he asked, 'I hope that future generations will not find me sorely wanting.' Many didn't, still don't, and yet he was. His legacy is one of popular liberation and education for the masses, underpinned by corruption, cocaine and criminals.

Pindling was a manipulator who sold out to dirty money. He set a tawdry example for the rest of the offshore world, opening a door – that still isn't shut – to a multitude of crooks and conmen. Yet, few of those crooks and conmen have ever been able to equal the panache of the original eccentric who now appeared in the doorway.

Born in Turkey in 1927, Benno Cornfield was raised and educated in Brooklyn, where his family changed their last name to Cornfeld and he changed his first name to Bernard, except that everybody always called him Bernie.

Short, stocky, bearded and bald, he was extremely intelligent, incredibly funny, almost always unconditionally charming and almost always wonderful company. He had a ferocious temper, which he occasionally lost and a total lack of respect for time, which he hardly ever kept. Plans to meet for lunch at noon didn't guarantee he'd even be there for dinner. He was also, always, distracted by two overwhelming obsessions which took demonic control of his life: money and women.

Different ways of keeping the same score, one fed off the other, giving him the air of a man incredibly good at both. But when you saw him up close, when you knew him well enough to get past the paraphernalia of image, it became apparent – especially at the end of his life – that, in fact, he wasn't extraordinarily adept at either. Although he surrounded himself with the trappings of success, which more often than not included dozens of totally gorgeous women, it was as if he was wearing boutonnières because he liked the message, not because he appreciated flowers. Once he'd lost the accoutrements of serious wealth, when the planes, the yachts, the mansions, the cars, the famous hangers-on and his own model agency were all gone – toys locked away forever – it was not just the quantity of his ladies that dried up.

An incessant hustler, Bernie never stopped working a room, never stopped stalking opportunity – financial or female – and many women felt uncomfortable in his presence. If he liked you, he might not hit on your wife, but there was usually a moment when you suspected he was pondering her underwear. For the same reason, men occasionally found his company disconcerting. It wasn't easy to have a serious, lengthy conversation with him if there was a short skirt within 200 yards.

That said, he was an absolute original and, if you happen to like absolute originals, it was impossible not to like Bernie.

Throughout his life, people were always saying that he was a born salesman and therein lay his genius. Had that been true, had his talent been that simple to define, he might be remembered today as the best mutual fund salesman ever. But having known him well and having listened to him tell stories of how it used to be, it's evident that his real genius was his capacity to isolate problems and then go about solving them in a unique way. His cunning was unequalled.

After graduating from Brooklyn College, he spent a year or so as a Trotskyite intent on changing the world. Once he discovered that radical socialists don't eat as well as old fashioned capitalists, he hooked up with a young mutual fund manager just out on his own named Jack Dreyfus.

Bernie decided that American GIs in Europe had money to spend, so with Dreyfus's blessing, he moved to France to flog mutual funds to soldiers. This was the mid-1950s. His territory included bases across Europe, but his bachelor lifestyle revolved around Paris. There he concocted a one-room operation called Investors Overseas Services (IOS) and collected a staff of otherwise-out-of-work American ex-pats. Under his tutelage, this bunch of semi-misfits got extremely good at high-pressure selling and before long, they were all making a lot of money.

Before long, too, Bernie was coming to realize that IOS could be more than just a cash cow, that he'd created an infrastructure which could be put to better use than churning out clients for Dreyfus. To make real money he needed management fees, not commissions, so instead of selling Dreyfus funds, he decided to sell his own. In 1960, he created International Investors Trust, followed shortly by a mutual fund that held shares in other mutual funds, called the Fund of Funds. He pitched these investments with the brilliantly conceived question, 'Do you sincerely want to be rich?' And so many people answered yes, that he found himself inundated with their money.

Needless to say, there was considerably more to IOS than he allowed outsiders to see. Bernie was making himself seriously rich by tapping into middle class anxieties. Until he and IOS came along, only the wealthy could call on personal banking connections. The middle-classes in many countries, who were just as worried about asset protection, didn't have those connections or the necessary funding to buy fiscal refuge. That's what Bernie sold them. Together with a Harvard lawyer named Edward Cowett – who was the legal mastermind behind all this – IOS structured itself and its funds to exploit tax breaks, secret banking, legal loopholes and the paucity of offshore oversight. Which is what brought Bernie to the Bahamas. He nested his funds there, in shell companies designed to prevent scrutiny. His army of salesmen spread out around the world, smuggling trunks of cash out of Latin America, Asia and the currency controlled nations of Europe, and flew them into the Bahamas where Bernie deposited them in Tibor Rosenbaum's Atlas Bank.

While Bernie advertized IOS as an investment, and wrapped IOS in a shawl of integrity – peppering his board of directors with the former Governor of California Pat Brown, with FDR's son James Roosevelt, and with advisers to the Governor of the Bank of England – his real business was capital flight and tax evasion.

From the Bahamas, Rosenbaum moved IOS's money to Geneva where Bernie arranged to lend it back to his investors so they could purchase IOS shares. It meant that someone in, say, Brazil, who wanted to protect his assets, had access to a smuggling service to get money out of the country, and paperwork from a Swiss bank to show his taxman that the IOS shares he was holding – which he'd actually paid for – were only mortgaged.

This concept of back-to-back loans quickly became the flavour-of-the-month money laundering ploy of Colombian drug traffickers. Following Bernie's lead, they spent all of the 1970s, 1980s and most of the 1990s dumping drug cash offshore, borrowing their own money to buy real estate, and declaring the income from the real estate to the taxman in Bogota in order to justify their wealthy lifestyles.

Unquestionably, this basic laundering system served Bernie well for five or six years, permitting him to enjoy the fruits of global empire building. By the mid-1960s, he was reportedly worth $1.5 billion, enough to buy a lot of fruit. It also bought him the Overseas Development Bank (ODB). His friend Rosenbaum objected, contending that Atlas in the Bahamas and BIC in Switzerland could handle whatever it was he needed. But owning a bank was one of the ultimate toys and while IOS was riding high, Bernie bought a lot of toys. For good measure, Rosenbaum went partners with him and owned 20% of ODB.

What most people didn't realize about Bernie, until it was much too late, was that his toys lived inside a house of cards. And the house that Bernie built took a serious knock in 1966. The Brazilians cottoned onto what he was doing, arrested 13 IOS salesmen and seized records for more than 10,000 clients. Bernie hired his own SAS-like commando team to get his salesmen out of Brazil – which they did – but not before the government charged IOS with smuggling $100 million out of the country.

The following year, the Swiss decided they didn't like the way he was running his business, either. IOS was offshore in the Bahamas and, before long, in Panama too. But Bernie, now living in Switzerland, was trying to make people believe that IOS had a Swiss pedigree. The Swiss reckoned it didn't matter where he lived because the Bahamian and Panamanian incorporation documents stipulated that the companies were managed offshore. Although they couldn't yet make a criminal case against him, they put enough pressure on him that Bernie moved across the border to France. Hardly forced to slum, he owned a castle in France stocked with antique furniture, gourmet food, vintage wine and centrefold playmates. For good measure, he also had the similarly equipped, 40-room Douglas Fairbanks mansion in Beverly Hills.

Years later, Bernie would say that the Swiss hounded him, not because he pretended that IOS was Swiss, but because the bankers didn't like how he'd made offshore funds popular, in direct competition to secret Swiss banking. There might be some truth in that because by 1967, the offshore world was awash with several hundred funds – IOS imitations and wannabes – holding assets of close to $4 billion. The Bahamas was booming. As was Panama, which was so aggressively turning itself into an offshore sink that someone would later remark, 'Panama isn't a country, it's a business.' Other jurisdictions were also cottoning onto the idea that they could sell shell companies to help people hide assets, or allow foreigners to incorporate banks as long as those foreigners didn't take deposits from any locals.

As laundering facilities grew more plentiful, insuring cash flow and reinvestment for illicit activities, crime and intrigue kicked up a gear. Honduras turned itself into a cocaine bridge. Guatemala offered mobsters sanctuary by selling passports. Costa Rica and Nicaragua sold out to the CIA. Paraguay set out its stall, with anything and everything for sale in the wide open, frontier town that was then called Ciudad del Stroessner and is today called Ciudad Del Este. Argentina responded by becoming a major drug transhipment point, moving cocaine from Colombia east to Africa and Europe, and moving heroin from the Mediterranean north to the Caribbean, the US and Canada. As drug trafficking and illicit activities increased, creating more cash, laundromats multiplied. More laundromats meant more room for dirty money, which in turn brought about more laundromats.

And the parade of people with dirty money to wash seemed endless.

Allen Jones Lefferdink, a man who once said, 'I have only two kinds of days, happy and hysterically happy,' was a fraudster from Nebraska who bilked investors in Colorado, came to the islands, started Mutual Funds of America, used investors' money to buy himself an insurance company and two banks offshore, then disappeared with $15 million.

Jerome Hoffman started a Liberian company called International Investors, turned that into a pair of mutual funds in Bermuda, and disappeared with $12 million.

Lansky's pal Ed Levinson, together with another friend, Ben Siegelbaum, opened the Exchange Bank of Geneva, bringing along with them Yiddy Bloom and John Pullman, to create yet another extension of Pullman's and Rosenbaum's operations in the Bahamas.

A fraudster named Clovis McAlpin liked the loan-back scheme so much he bought his own Swiss bank to make it work. He invited one of his friends in on the deal – a stock manipulating crook from Detroit named Robert Vesco – and together, they bought Standard Commerz of Lucerne. Although that partnership didn't turn out to be as successful as McAlpin had promised, it opened Vesco's eyes to the offshore world and IOS.

All this time, Lansky himself was more active than ever, running his own bank. Purchased secretly in 1958, Miami National was not only the national collection centre for silver dollars used in Las Vegas's slot machines, it was the conduit for dirty money coming back from the Bahamas and Teamster money heading offshore. The bank financed the Mob's move into south Florida real estate and connects with other local banks of dubious pedigree, especially the highly suspect Bank of Perrine which turned out to be a sink used by the CIA in various covert operations. Investigations later revealed that Miami National was an important link between the Teamsters and Charles 'Bebe' Rebozo, the Cuban American who owned Key Biscayne Bank, was tied into the Cleveland Mob and is best remembered as Richard Nixon's bagman.

Rebozo and Miami National underwrote the purchase of Nixon's 'winter White House' in Key Biscayne. They managed it through a company called Keyes Realty, which had previously been identified in the Kefauver hearings for its links to organized crime. The property passed through the hands of a Cuban 'investment' group, the Teamsters and Miami National, before being sold by Keyes to Nixon at substantially less than market value. Furthermore, Keyes ties into the Bay of Pigs invasion – some of its Cuban exile employees were directly involved – and to some of the men who took part in the Watergate break-in. It was also used to launder money for Nixon's re-election campaign funds. Following the money trail through Keyes, you can connect Rebozo to Lansky, to casinos in the Bahamas and from there to Resorts International. For good measure, Bernie Cornfeld was a shareholder in Resorts International.

In his heyday, Bernie had IOS offices in 100 countries, a sales force of 15,000 and funds valued at $2.5 billion. But he couldn't make it work forever, and wasn't the kind of man to quit while he was ahead. Facing a two-pronged attack by the Brazilians and the Swiss, Bernie was unable to sustain his Latin American capital flight business, which seriously cut into his cash flow. He couldn't carry his monstrous overheads and was unwilling to cut back on his own lifestyle. He believed the answer was to go public. But that turned out to be too wild a ride, with IOS shares bouncing all over the place, from $5 to $19 then sinking to under $3. The Securities and Exchange Commission refused to buy into Bernie's claim that a mutual fund holding shares in a dozen other mutual funds was a dozen times better than any one of the funds it was holding, and moved against him for securities' violations. The IOS board turned against Bernie and pressure mounted on him to stand down. He held on as long as he could, which was much too long.

If Bernie was a likeable scoundrel, then the vulture who now came sweeping out of the sky was a detestable sleazebag.

When Robert Vesco's interest waned in Standard Commerz of Lucerne, he looked around and spotted IOS. The board was in the market for a bailout and he somehow conned them into letting him do just that. Once inside the company, instead of saving it, he simply stole the assets. Some $260–$300 million disappeared into offshore shells.

By then, Vesco was under indictment in New York for illegal contributions to Nixon's 1972 presidential campaign. He couldn't go back to the States, so he headed for the safety of Costa Rica, where he lived under the protection of presidents Jose 'Pepe' Figueres and Daniel Oduber. He invested $13 million in radio and television stations, a newspaper and a hotel. He also acquired tens of millions of dollars worth of Costa Rican bearer bonds, enough that he purportedly had it within his power to create an instant financial crisis. Such was Vesco's way of insuring he'd always have some place safe to sleep.

In 1976, he was indicted again in the US, this time for the theft of $224 million of IOS funds. Two years later, a new president in Costa Rica withdrew the welcome mat. Vesco settled in the Bahamas, where he opened a bank and assured his continued residency by offering various members of Mr Pindling's government a rare kind of account – one that featured perpetual withdrawals without the pain of ever having to make a deposit. His generosity was rewarded with a Bahamian diplomatic passport.

Immunity was a handy thing to have, especially now, because Vesco was embarking on a business venture that would really piss-off the Americans. Installed on his own non-extraditable Bahamian island, Cistern Cay, Vesco went into business with his neighbour, who lived on the private island of Norman's Cay. Carlos Lehder was then an associate of cocaine trafficker Pablo Escobar. Vesco helped Lehder turn the Bahamas into the primary transhipment point for cocaine going to North America. Finding a niche for himself as their *consiglieri*, Vesco's corporate skills lifted Lehder and Escobar from second-rate smugglers to entrepreneurs running the vertically integrated Medellin Cartel.

When Vesco ultimately became an embarrassment to the Bahamians – even by Pindling's standards – he fled to Nicaragua. He'd been courting some influential Panamanians, including Manuel Noriega, who might have given him shelter there, except that Noriega had his own troubles. From Nicaragua, Vesco headed for Antigua, where the government of Vere Bird sold him sanctuary and a passport with a false name. Bird resisted American pressure to hand over Vesco just long enough for Vesco to phone Pepe Figueres in Costa Rica, and beg a favour. On Vesco's behalf, Figueres personally rang Fidel Castro to negotiate safe haven. Castro agreed, not as a courtesy to Figueres but because Vesco was willing to pay Castro a gigantic premium for the privilege. Myth has it that the figure was $1 billion, but it's doubtful that Vesco had that much to play with. Then, too, even if the payment was only 10 per cent of that – which Vesco did have – it's hardly chump change.

So Castro installed Vesco in a guest villa in La Coronela, the most exclusive district of Havana, and assigned a detachment of security guards, as much to protect him as to keep him leashed in. Vesco was permitted to mingle with the diplomatic set at the country's most fashionable golf club, to send his children to the International School, to throw lavish parties, to invest in sugar and tobacco, to build a series of beachfront homes, to deal in coffee futures, and to run a huge money-laundering operation out of Cayo Largo in southern Cuba. He used his Colombian connections to turn Cuba into a cocaine transhipment point – generating 'rent' for the Castro brothers – and to call on his Panamanian connections to help Fidel beat the US Embargo on Cuban goods. To manage that, Vesco designed a system where sugar was shipped from Havana to Panama, relabelled and re-invoiced there as Panamanian sugar, then brought into the States. The same tactic worked for Cuban lobster. Conversely, Vesco arranged for US goods, which could not legally go to Cuba, to be laundered through Panama, where invoices showed them heading one way when they were actually on a ship bound for Havana. The best the Americans could do was indict Vesco yet again, this time for conspiring to smuggle cocaine into the United States.

Inevitably, the Swiss reopened their file on Bernie Cornfeld. While they scrutinized IOS, they locked him up for 11 months. Unable to summon help from the commandos who'd once freed his salesmen in Brazil, Bernie hired the finest restaurants in Geneva to cater his meals inside. He was charged with embezzling $7 million, but the Swiss couldn't make the charges stick and he was acquitted. Bernie spent much of the rest of his life living in a small mews house in London, still hustling. In 1995, on a visit to Israel, he suffered a stroke and friends had to chip in to bring him back to the UK. He died a few weeks later.

That same year, Castro charged Vesco with being an 'agent provocateur' for unnamed foreign governments. Vesco had embarked on a scheme with Richard Nixon's nephew Donald to develop a wonderdrug which would cure cancer and arthritis. It turned out to be less than wonderful. The US State Department was put on notice that Cuba might be prepared to hand him over, but that didn't happen.

Bernie had once predicted that the day would come when Vesco would simply outlive his usefulness, that Castro would unceremoniously turn his back on Vesco. Which is exactly what happened. Castro sent Robert Vesco to jail for 13 years.

Somewhere, Bernie was having a posthumous last laugh.

CHAPTER THREE

The Rules of Nowhere

Faith is believing in something you know can't be so.
                                        – Huckleberry Finn

In the early 1960s, the pool of dollars beyond the control of US authorities finally reached the point where the value of dollars held in foreign hands actually exceeded the value of America's gold reserves. For the first time in American history the risk of a 'ruler of Abu Dhabi scenario' was very real.

Not having enough gold at Fort Knox directly threatened the international monetary system, the dollar's standing as the world's primary currency and the economic might of the United States. The situation was further aggravated by America's increasing involvement in Vietnam, which added considerable sums to the amount of currency flowing overseas. The balance of trade became widely disproportionate and draconian measures seemed inevitable.

Starting with the Kennedy administration in mid-1963, and going through Lyndon Johnson's term which ended in January 1969, the Americans attempted to tighten financial regulations and institute capital controls, in the vain hope of restricting the flow of dollars overseas. But the war in Vietnam wreaked havoc on the balance of payments. Johnson made the controls voluntary until they failed, then made them mandatory, which also failed. Major international banks viewed these interventions as unnatural restraints on the natural flow of money, and invented ways around them. Johnson argued that the measures were a political necessity, but to pacify big business, he permitted companies operating overseas to keep those profits outside of the country. The question for those companies was, where do we put those profits? The obvious answer was, in our own backyard – the Bahamas.

The new Gold Rush was on. American banks headed south to open offshore branches, companies followed those banks offshore, and more banks followed those companies. Gangsters had shown big business the way, and by the time Richard Nixon replaced Lyndon Johnson in the Oval Office, the Bahamas had become one of the world's foremost money centres.

As money accumulated beyond the reach of those governments where that money was originally issued, the concept of sovereignty suffered yet another blow. Once upon a time, rule was defined by a mountain range or a river; or by a beach plus three miles of ocean, which happens to have been the distance a canon ball could travel; or in the sky, to the altitude that a hot air balloon could fly. While the three-mile limit was later extended to 12 miles to give fishing fleets a monopoly on catches which would otherwise have been in international waters; and while altitude was later extended to 50.55 miles because of jet planes; much of what sovereignty used to mean now lay in tatters because the offshore world is, by definition, beyond sovereignty.

Nation states could dictate supply, and finance ministers could tinker with interest rates, but governments were ultimately losing control over their own currency. It was being waylaid by countries with no real international influence, except their ability to sweep great sums of money away from those nation states that backed the money. The power vacuum left in between was filled by banks and corporations. As a result, all these years later, any government that thinks it controls its own financial destiny has failed to understand the political might that has been seized by businesses – both legitimate and illicit – through their offshore holdings.

History makes that abundantly clear.

In the late 1960s, mirroring Lyndon Johnson's concerns, finance ministers and Central Banks across Europe were equally worried about their currencies. Increased speculation was creating too much volatility in the markets which destabilized political agendas. Equating control of their currency to control of their destiny, several governments teamed up to bully banks with legislation aimed at limiting currency trading. The Brits, French, Swiss and Germans all said to the banks, if you trade the pound, the two francs and the deutschmark, you have to play by our rules, and if you don't play by our rules, if you create too much misery for our currency, we're going to throw you out of the country. That sounded like a good idea to the politicians, but bankers knew it was never going to work. The horse hadn't merely bolted, it was living in a beachfront condo in the Caribbean.

A trader at Citibank came up with the scheme that beat the finance ministers. Instead of booking trades in London or Paris, Zurich or

Frankfurt – where those finance ministers could monitor them – he decided to book his trades out of sight and beyond the horizon at the 'Nassau Desk'. For Citibank, it didn't matter where the trades were booked, as long as the paperwork showed they weren't booked in London or Paris, Zurich or Frankfurt. And he got away with it for quite a while, that is, until someone in Switzerland discovered that his trades were not actually being booked in the Bahamas. Instead, they were going to New York, landing on a desk in Citi's trading room where the bank flew a cardboard sign that read, 'Nassau'. Eventually, after the trades were booked there, a clerk copied them into a second set of books in the Bahamas, just in case someone ever showed up and asked to see them.

The Swiss screamed foul, the other European governments complained, and the SEC launched its own investigation. In the meantime, Citibank brought a new computer system on-stream which allowed them to book trades made anywhere in the world, instantaneously, somewhere else. So now, a trade made in London or Paris could be legitimately booked in the Bahamas, which eliminated the need for the cardboard sign in Manhattan and, effectively, rendered the case moot. Anyway, by then, almost all of the major US banks had cottoned onto the trick and were running their European trades through the Bahamas.

Seeing so much money heading south, the State of New York came up with a variation on the theme of offshore banking in the heart of Manhattan. The Bahamian government was pledging to protect assets by imposing strict secret banking laws and reinforcing a commitment to shelter money from foreign tax authorities. In response, the New Yorkers created International Banking Facilities (IBFs), which loosened fiscal restrictions, made capital markets more user-friendly and offered tax advantages to foreign banks. Some dollars flowed back onshore, but nowhere near as many as the Americans were hoping for, because New York couldn't offer the most important product of all – capital flight. To do that, the state would have had to put the two big ticket items on the menu: secret banking and shell companies to facilitate tax evasion. That was out of the question.

New York's inability to compete with the Bahamas highlighted the great divide between onshore and offshore. It all boiled down to 'regulatory risk'. Where is your money most likely to get found? In onshore New York, regulatory risk was very high. In offshore Nassau, it was very low.

Put another way, people with money to hide sent it to banks offshore, because they worked for their customers, and not to banks onshore, because they worked for the taxman.

Bernie Cornfeld pioneered the way, demonstrating how the offshore world was designer-made for capital flight and tax evasion. By using IOS to move money from Brazil through the Islands, into Switzerland and some-times back again, he established one of the most important rules of offshore commerce: create confusion through multiple jurisdictions.

The more borders you put between yourself and the authorities, the less likely it is that those authorities will get across all the borders. It was one thing for the Brazilian police – or the Argentine police or the Swiss authorities – to investigate Cornfeld locally. But the moment they stepped across the border, they faced intertwining shells in multiple jurisdictions where foreign cops had no authority. That formula remains the bedrock of the offshore philosophy of several industries, for example, shipping.

As far back as the 1950s, Aristotle Onassis and his brother-in-law, Stavros Niarchos decided they were paying too much tax to the Greek government on their merchant shipping fleets. To save money, they bought 'flags of convenience'. Registering each ship as an IBC in the Bahamas, they then listed the shell company as a vessel on Panama's shipping register. It meant that their Greek fleets, which were now Bahamian, could pretend to be Panamanian. Onassis and Niarchos not only avoided Greek taxes but, as each ship was an anonymous company, they could hide behind those shells to protect their personal wealth.

Today, Liberia and Panama are the most important maritime registries of convenience, accounting for somewhere around 75–80 per cent of the world's merchant tonnage. Not by coincidence, Liberia and Panama are also among the world's most prominent dirty money sinks. Liberian shell companies are *de facto* suspect, especially since Liberia became a leading force in Africa's illicit arms market. A recent United Nations report singled out Liberia for funnelling revenues from ship registration to weapons purchasing and smuggling, in direct viola-tion of UN embargoes. Meanwhile, Panama remains a pivotal player in drug money laundering.

The reason why flags of convenience are popular becomes obvious every time an oil tanker breaks up on rocks and destroys hundreds of miles of coastline. The Panamanian ship is owned by a Bahamian shell, which is insured through a shell in Bermuda, which has reinsured the policy with a shell in Antigua, that turns out to be nothing more than a plaque on an office door and an answering machine. Some people call it smoke and mirrors. Other's label it a fiction.

The most commonly made case for offshore banking and shell companies revolves around three areas: private investment, so that you can minimize your tax liabilities while maximising privacy; asset protection, so that you can safeguard your holdings from political, fiscal and legal attempts to confiscate them; and estate planning, so that you can leave your property to whomever you choose without having legal restraints and conditions imposed on your wishes. It is no coincidence that offshore banking, offshore insurance and offshore ship registration – which make up the three main money spinners – are all heavily regulated in the rest of the world.

Walter Wriston, former chairman and CEO of Citicorp, confirms that, 'Capital goes where it is wanted, and stays where it is well treated. It will flee onerous regulation and unstable politics, and in today's world technology assures that that movement will be at near the speed of light.'

He insists, 'No amount of rhetoric or spin control can fool capital for long.'

By the 1970s, transfer pricing and trade between companies tied together in cross-border alliances, were big enough money spinners to assure prosperity for the offshore world. Capital flight was right up there with them. Offshore banks were now holding more Latin American money than US banks were sending to Latin America to keep those countries afloat. But a new money spinner was entering the equation and, in both volume and velocity, it would quickly dwarf the others.

It was, drugs.

The explosion of demand, and the production that geared up to meet it, multiplied exponentially both the supply of and the demand for offshore banking and shell companies. It happened because the offshore world was there to help it happen, and the offshore world was there to help it happen because it was happening.

'The significance of this,' says Washington lawyer Jack Blum, a world-class expert on money laundering and the offshore world, 'was lost on the vast majority of people. In the main, they believed, it wasn't important. It hadn't reached the scale of, "If you don't pay attention to this you're going to get clobbered". We hadn't yet been through all the successive mergers that produced mega-corporations. Executives weren't yet making hundreds of millions a year. Being multinational was relatively new. Things hadn't yet got out of kilter. It wouldn't be until communications improved and transportation improved and money became totally portable, exchangeable and interchangeable that anyone would sit up and scream, "What the hell's going on here?"'

For some jurisdictions, it was a process of natural evolution – a political version of the biblical prophesy that the meek shall inherit the Earth. For others, it was good business. For many, it was both. The US State Department estimates that 40 per cent of all the cocaine and 30 per cent of all the heroin that shows up on North American streets transits through the Caribbean. As drug trafficking increases offshore, so does offshore banking. In a country as poor as Haiti, for example, in recent years as drug transhipment noticeably increased, the number of banks on the island quadrupled.

Selling stealth and deception to hide foreign assets is a clean, non-polluting industry. Protecting someone's assets from whatever civil or criminal liabilities he or she would otherwise encounter at home, doesn't require any significant capital investment. Nor does it require a skilled workforce. You become a haven by declaring yourself a haven. You legislate secrecy for the financial products on sale, hang out your shingle and just like that, you're in business.

As Blum confirms, 'You're in the United States, you're under American law. You cross the border, it's Mexican law or Canadian law. Traditionally, law has always gone hand in hand with the territory. But when you're dealing with money moving around the world, when it can move anywhere, when it can be booked anywhere, then where's the law? In this instance, the law is wherever you chose to make it.'

Sovereignty was finally dead.

Paul Helliwell understood that better than most.

So did Manuel Noriega.

Helliwell was an intelligence operative in World War II who never got out of the game. A lawyer by trade, he set up his Miami practice to work like a CIA cut-out.

Noriega was chief henchman to Panama's dictator Omar Torrijos. He was also the man who eventually unseated the men who murdered Torrijos to seize power.

As an attorney, Helliwell helped the Disney Corporation disguise a 37,000-acre interest in Orlando – which would become Disney World – by running purchases through shells in Panama and the Cayman Islands. He counted among his other clients the Grand Bahamas Port Authority. He was head of the Republican Party in Florida and a confidant of Bebe Rebozo. As a part-time spook, Helliwell set up shells throughout the offshore world to hide funding for CIA gunrunning and the Bay of Pigs invasion. He also put together a holding company called Florida Shares which owned several small financial institutions, including the CIA cut-out Perrine Bank. But his masterpiece was his 1964 creation of Castle Bank and Trust. Born out of a shell in Panama – part owned by Daniel K. Ludwig – Helliwell housed the bank in Nassau, opened a branch in the Caymans and established correspondent relationships around the world. On the surface, the bank was selling tax evasion to wealthy Americans. Below the waterline, Helliwell was laundering money to pay for the CIA's expeditions into drug trafficking.

Unaware of the CIA connection, the FBI and DEA stumbled across Castle Bank while looking at a trafficking ring. They brought the IRS in to peruse the bank's clients. But, just as the taxmen discovered some wealthy Americans hiding money, their investigation was abruptly wound down. That's because, the CIA pulled strings to get it wound down.

The moment Castle was exposed, the Agency decided it had outlived its usefulness and the bank quickly collapsed. As soon as it was gone, a tiny bank opened in Australia, mirroring Castle's operation. The Nugan Hand Bank picked up many of the pieces left on the floor by Castle, became a player in the Pacific and opened in the Caribbean, too. It's directors were mostly retired Americans, high placed spooks and former military intelligence officers. Nugan Hand suffered the same fate as Castle, and sank just as quickly. What records were left showed that fraud, extortion, money laundering and drug trafficking were what this bank was all about. The difference between the two banks, however, was starkly seen in the difference between the fate of the men fronting it. Paul Helliwell died in his own bed. Frank Nugan was found dead with a bullet hole in his head, an apparent suicide, and Michael John Hand just disappeared, never to be seen again.

Manuel Noriega fared much better in his offshore adventures by living to tell the tale, but only just. He'd been Torrijos' intermediary with the Colombian cocaine cartels and had arranged several lucrative deals with Robert Vesco's partner and neighbour in the Bahamas, Carlos Lehder. In exchange for a piece of the action, Panama provided Lehder with storage and transhipment points for his cocaine, and with banking facilities to launder his money. Panama's secret banking laws, first established in 1927 and considerably tightened over time, make Switzerland's appear almost transparent.

By the time he'd taken rule of the country in 1983, Noriega had embarked on a spectacular series of deals with both the Colombians – to help traffic their drugs and launder their money – and also with the DEA. As their guy in Panama, the DEA were paying Noriega up to $200,000 a month to tip them off to drug trafficking and money laundering. He was also earning $10 million a month from Lehder.

Playing both ends against the middle, Noriega handed Lehder's competitors to the DEA, which kept them both happy. Although, in one case, he shut down a bank belonging to the Cali Cartel, which didn't exactly endear him to the Orejuella brothers who owned the cartel. Legend has it, they put out a contract on Noriega which only got lifted through the direct intervention of Fidel Castro, who was also paying Noriega to help Cuba break US sanctions.

To hide his own money, Noriega first used Panamanian banks, then diversified around the world – both onshore and offshore – opening accounts at BCCI, Banque National de Paris, First American and the Algemene Bank Nederland. He moved money through the Caribbean, sometimes in his own name, at other times in the name of the Panamanian Defence Force, at still other times, in the names of offshore shells he'd set up to hide the true ownership of his money. When he was finally taken down – kidnapped in Panama, brought to Florida and thrown into prison for 43 years – the nation he left behind had mixed emotions about his departure. He was an ugly dictator and many democratic loving Panamanians were glad to see the back of him. But he'd also helped create a laundromat that has made many Panamanians very rich.

Thanks, in large part, to Noriega, the Panama Free Trade Zone is a home away from home for the drug cartels and other transnational organized criminal groups. It is the second largest free trade zone in the world – after Hong Kong – and the largest cash business on the planet. It is a magnate for drug trafficking, contraband and money laundering.

And thanks, almost entirely, to the Free Trade Zone, dirty money turns out to be the backbone of the Panamanian economy.

With 350,000 shell companies and 150 banks thriving in its shadow, it's not surprising why one US Customs official notes, 'The country is filled with dishonest lawyers, dishonest bankers, dishonest company formation agents and dishonest companies registered there by those dishonest lawyers so that they can deposit dirty money into their dishonest banks. The Free Trade Zone is the black hole through which Panama has become one of the filthiest money laundering sinks in the world.'

Whereas Noriega is still a hero to certain folks in Panama, someday there will be statues of Harold Wilson, James Callaghan and Denis Healey all over the Channel Islands, a sign of gratitude from a prosperous people to two British Prime Ministers and one Chancellor of the Exchequer for singularly having failed to understand the realities of economics.

In October 1973, the OPEC oil embargo quadrupled the price of a barrel in a mere few weeks, creating colossal wealth for the producing nations, especially the Gulf States.

Those 'petro-dollars' had to go somewhere and their natural home was London's Euromarket. So tens of billions of dollars gushed into Britain, followed quickly by American banks looking to grab their share of the action. It could have been boom-time for everyone, except that the Labour government, under Wilson, Callaghan and Healey, decided to screw it up by instituting currency and other monetary controls. Misguidedly, they believed that the way to guarantee Britain's financial prosperity was to limit free trade by stopping the mass exportation of the national currency. They didn't realize that money had become stateless, that it was beyond the control of any government, that the market for money was bigger than many governments put together, and that several banks were bigger than those governments, as well.

These days, no politician could afford to be so foolish. The market for money is so vast that, when central banks step into the ring, they usually get their noses bloodied. As business guru Peter Drucker puts it, 'Money has slipped the leash.'

Messrs. Wilson, Callaghan and Healey never stood a chance. The big banks and big business easily side-stepped controls. So did the wealthy. Smaller banks, the ones that couldn't afford to stay at the table, also headed offshore. The islands were cheaper, welcomed large dollar deposits and spoke English. Most of them were more or less politically stable. Most of them had reasonable communications and transportation facilities. None of them had exchange controls or imposed interest rate ceilings. Much of the Caribbean was in the same time zone as New York. The Channel Islands were in the same time zone as the City of London.

By dramatically raising the cost of doing business in the UK, the Labour Regime penalized the poor, empowered the rich and created newfound wealth offshore. Islands everywhere owe them a thank you, but none more so than Jersey, Guernsey and the Isle of Man.

Crown Dependencies, the Channel Islands are not legally part of the United Kingdom, which means that acts of Parliament do not automatically apply. As self-governed jurisdictions, they'd been minor players in the offshore world for a long time, going all the way back to Ivar Kreuger.

The Swedish financier made his original fortune in construction, before branching out to banking and film finance. As a movie mogul, he paid for Greta Garbo's first role. As a banker, he learned how to hide money. In 1915, Kreuger discovered he could buy supplies of phosphorus and potash at a time when established match manufacturers couldn't. Within two years, he'd taken full control of Sweden's match industry. From there he moved into France, Yugoslavia, Turkey, Eastern Europe, and Central and South America, multiplying one match monopoly into another. He layered his empire with off-shore holdings so that he could secretly move money to wherever he needed it. By the mid-1920s, Krueger was the 'Match King' of the planet, owning or controlling 75 per cent of the world's matches.

Roaming the globe with great panache, he put together flamboyant deals that filled the financial pages of the daily papers. But while Kreuger's companies were making money, none of them was making enough to cover the whopping dividends he was paying investors. To keep up grand appearances, he began forging financial instruments. No petty thief, he wrote himself one from the Italian government for $143 million. It was easy to fool bankers in the Channel Islands, who in those days didn't have the experience to know better. But by 1931, the stress of juggling so many frauds got to be too much and Kreuger suffered a stroke. A year later he ended his life with a pistol, even though he was still worth $200 million.

Kreuger's exploits opened the eyes of bankers in the Channel Islands to a growing market of businessmen with multinational aspirations.

Fast on their way to becoming a first class refuge for European tax evasion, it took the Nazis to lay waste to just about everything in Jersey and Guernsey. And then, it took more than a decade and a half to nurse wounds, and rebuild lives and business there. But in the 1960s, Phil Wilson picked up where Kreuger left off and gave the Channel Islands a much needed boost, plus the bad name that still – in many cases, erroneously – reverberates today.

No relation to Harold, this Wilson was a thief from St Louis who, after years of dealing in forged securities, saw the Channel Islands offering opportunities he couldn't buy elsewhere. Needing to raise money, all three governments were aggressively selling IBCs and banking licences. Wilson bought the right to be a financial institution in Guernsey for $200, and called himself the Bank of Sark. He rented a room above a hairdressers, installed a telephone and a telex machine, printed stationery, printed business cards, printed glossy brochures, forged letters of credit, found a bent accountant in the Bahamas to swear that the bank's assets were $72.5 million – as shown in audited statements which Wilson also printed – and got himself listed in a legitimate banking directory.

Suddenly, all the worthless paper he'd been selling could be backed by a bank that had its own stationery. He spent the end of the 1960s and the first few years of the 1970s convincing real banks that his assets were genuine. Enough real banks believed him that he walked away with $40 million. His mistake was to take the Bank of Sark to Miami, where he hoped to work his scam on a much larger scale. Instead, he ran up against some very tough characters connected to traditional Italian organized crime, and wound up on the short end of the deal. He also wound up convicted by the Feds for fraud and other crimes, and shipped off to jail.

Back in Britain, currency controls were proving to be what currency controls always are, an exercise in futility. The folks who got stuck were working-class holidaymakers needing to take more than £50 out of the country to fund two weeks in Mallorca. The rich, who could afford lawyers and accounts, were offered dozens of schemes to beat the controls, and many of those schemes were anchored in the Channel Islands. If wealthy Brits on the mainland were not doing what the government required them to do, that was hardly the worry of anyone in Jersey, Guernsey or Man. Paying taxes and obeying the law in England was an Englishman's responsibility. Protecting wealth was the business of the Channel Islands.

Their financial infrastructure and offshore significance grew quickly. Wilson, Callaghan and Healey had caused them to put everything in place and, inadvertently, had made certain they would succeed. Paradoxically, it wasn't until the abolition of exchange controls in 1979 that the Channel Islands joined the major leagues.

Mrs Thatcher was now in Downing Street and she ignited the British markets. For the wealthy, once bitten twice shy, the fear remained that some future Labour government could reinstate currency controls. So smart money now rushed out, legally. Today, 55–60 per cent of Jersey's and Guernsey's GDPs come from offshore finance. In Man, the figure is only about 40 per cent. But the three islands have a combined bank deposit total of around £130 billion, with almost 100,000 companies incorporated there. Adding trusts and insurance, the islands manage assets of about £300 billion.

Once it became clear that Mrs Thatcher's pro-business Tory government was going to stick around for a while, capital flight from Britain to the Channel Islands was replaced by tax evasion. As more people made more money in the City boom of the 1980s, a lot of that money was moved offshore. All anyone needed to do to keep the Inland Revenue at bay was buy an IBC registered in the Isle of Man and find a friendly banker in Guernsey or Jersey. The trick was that your name could never appear on the paperwork in Man. So, accountants there turned to folks who lived on a tiny island off the coast of Guernsey. The so-called 'Sark Lark' was a pretty sound gimmick. Manx licensed IBCs came ready-made with offshore company directors in Sark. No one in Man knew who owned the company and no one in Sark knew where the company's money was. It worked so well, that before long, companies formed in Jersey and Guernsey also came equipped with Sark-based directors. At one point, Sark's 575 residents held directorships in 15,000 companies. Some 16 residents acted as directors in, and received fees from, no fewer than 135 companies. While three Sark residents held between 1,600–3,000 directorships.

Since those days, a lot of this baloney has been stopped. In the face of criticism from groups like the Financial Action Task Force (FATF) – the money laundering watchdog established by the then G-7 Nations in 1989 – jurisdictions all over the offshore world began giving lip service to cleaning up their act. In a few cases, some even managed it.

Guernsey is a good example. The government finally said enough is enough and, in recent years, has purged a lot of the island's less-than-scrupulous customers. A conscious effort was made to weed out poor-quality business and poor-quality professionals hiding behind Guernsey corporations. The island also signed a multitude of mutual legal assistance treaties assuring that anyone hiding dirty money in Guernsey, will be seriously disappointed.

'There can be no place in a globalized economy for non co-operating jurisdictions,' explains the island's former attorney general, Geoffrey Rowland. 'Guernsey is no safe home for tax evasion, no safe haven for organized crime or insider dealing, no safe haven for money laundering, no safe haven for the proceeds of corruption and no safe haven for terrorists and those who assist and finance them.'

When Guernsey opted for legitimate-only offshore business, dirty money abandoned the island for jurisdictions with less adequate regulations. Jersey cracked down, too, and to some extent, so has the Isle of Man. Sadly, though, around much of the rest of the offshore world, pressure for change merely became a challenge to criminals to find more sophisticated ways of doing the same thing.

At the same time that the Wilson, Callaghan and Healey Troika were doing their bit for the Channel Islands, Lynden Pindling was doing his for the Bahamas, by liberating the island state from British control.

As a direct result of Bahamian independence in 1974, some bankers started having second thoughts about the financial sector there. With Britain in charge, they saw the island as safe. But the WASP banking world didn't have a particularly high opinion of native politicians, most of whom seemed to have been cut from the same cloth as Pindling. Some of those WASP bankers decided it might be time to start looking for some place else to go.

That racism played a part in the development of the offshore world is undeniable. As one person put it, 'White bankers wouldn't trust a black crook. White crooks, okay. But not black crooks.' Which is also why nearby ports of call in the Eastern Caribbean didn't land the business. Instead, money began to head westward, past Jamaica to a British crown colony – which meant it was still acceptable to the white world – called the Cayman Islands.

Some 480 miles south east of Miami, the Caymans is a British crown colony of three islands, 525 banks, 900 mutual funds, 400 insurance companies, 40,000 IBCs and about the same number of residents. As there are no direct taxes on income, profits, wealth or capital gains, the government must make its money on indirect taxes, which include sales tax, import duties, stamp duty, plus the sale of banks, mutual funds insurance companies and IBCs.

Commercial finance came slowly. In 1953, Barclays opened the island's first foreign branch. Ten years later, a second bank arrived – the Royal Bank of Canada – being the opening salvo in a campaign by Canadian money managers to colonize the Caribbean. The island's third foreign bank, a year after that, was the Canadian Imperial Bank of Commerce. As more and more money left the Bahamas, the pace in the Caymans picked up and, within 20 years, the Caymans could boast one bank for every 49 residents. Abuse brought embarrassment and several banks have since been shut. So now, there's only one bank for every 76 residents, which still isn't bad considering that by holding assets of nearly $900 billion – more than twice the amount on deposit in all the banks in New York – it works out to $22.5 million per resident.

Not that every resident has that much. For that matter, you won't find $900 billion on the island. A few years ago, a local businessman needed to raise a lowly $1 million in cash to pay for a banknotes-on-the-table deal, and it took him several weeks to manage it. Unlike financial centres in Europe where vaults are filled with the stuff, the water table in the Caymans is so high that there are no basements.

No basements, no underground vaults, no cash.

But even if they had vaults, you still wouldn't find $900 billion there because it's never been there and there's no reason for it to go there. The money is in New York, London, Paris, Frankfurt and Hong Kong, where it's always been. Whatever transactions are booked in the Caymans have nothing to do with moving money, they're just blips on a computer screen pretending to be the location of the money.

'What is all this money doing off-shore?' New York's legendary District Attorney Robert Morgenthau answers his own question. 'It is not there because of the sunshine and the beaches. To be blunt, it is there because those who put it there want a free ride, depositors, investors, banks and businessmen want to avoid or evade laws, regulations and taxes.'

Morgenthau is unrelenting in his aversion to the Cayman Islands and the way they do business. 'Tax havens which rely on bank and corporate secrecy are knowingly assisting customers of theirs to commit tax fraud. Unlawful tax shelters do not need to be kept secret.'

One of the engines that drove this long period of prosperity was drug money. It poured in from the 1970s well into the 1990s. Then the Russians arrived on the wings of capital flight. Since 1992, it is estimated that as much as $300–$400 billion has bled out of the Russian economy. Some of it stayed in Europe – London, Frankfurt and Vienna, and less obvious financial centres such as Cyprus, Latvia and Turkey. Some if it went to Dubai. A lot of it wound up being invested in the United States. But at some point, a lot of it either moved through the Caribbean or was bedded down there for a while. And in some cases it still lives there. In the Caymans, at least in the beginning, they welcomed the Russians with open arms.

Russian money was followed by money that used to be in Hong Kong. Fearing the Chinese takeover of the colony, a great deal was shipped out to be bedded down in the Caymans for safe keeping. Some of it was legitimate money. Some of it was owned by Asian organized criminals. But, by the time it got to the Caribbean, it all smelled sparkling clean. What's more, just because it now lived in the Caymans, that didn't mean the money wasn't still in, and being managed from, Hong Kong.

These days when you mention money laundering in the Caymans, you get the same answer, almost verbatim, from everyone you speak with: no one here wants money launderers, we systematically reject dirty money, we've cleaned up our act; the Caymans is no longer a sink for the world's drug cash.

When it comes to drug cash, there may be some truth in their avowals. It's a lot tougher for a Colombian cocaine trafficker to hide his money there. Although it's not beyond the realm of belief that the trafficker might have a lawyer in Switzerland, who manages a Luxembourg company, that is financing a huge land development project in Haiti, which is being financed with a back-to-back loan out of the Caymans. They also insist there is no terrorist money there, either. And, it must be said, over the past few years, the Caymanians have got better at looking for both drug cash and terror dollars. But that's not the same as saying there's no dirty money regularly coming into the Caymans. UPS and Fedex 737s arrive daily, filled to the brim with express envelopes for banks and trusts and mutual funds and IBCs registered on the island. It's hard to imagine so many flights a week, filled with that many 'documents', flying into any other jurisdiction of 40,000 people.

Throughout the history of the Caymans as a financial centre, there has been tax evasion. People tell you there, too, that tax evasion –

like drug money and capital flight – is not what the Caymans is all about. They're fast to point out that, in 2000, the government nego- tiated a treaty with the US ending, once and for all, ambiguities in tax evasion cases. The island agreed to provide American prosecutors with some banking and corporate information. And, for a while, it seemed as if one former Caymanian banker's rebuke – 'The Cayman Island government is knowingly aiding and abetting tax evasion' – was a thing of the past.

That is, until the Caymanians announced in 2002 that, maybe it wouldn't sign the treaty after all.

That there is a legitimate place for offshore banking and offshore companies, is an accepted fact of global finance. That there is legiti- mate room for confidentiality – especially where business dealings and personal finance are concerned – is also a given. But necessary confi- dentiality and ultimate secrecy are two different things, and that distinction is not often made when there is profit to be had by confusing the two.

Jean-Pierre Roth, chairman of the governing board of the Swiss National Bank, typified the offshore banker's stance in a recent speech in Basle. 'The beneficiary of banking secrecy is the client, not the bank.'

While that may sound true, without strict banking secrecy, the money goes elsewhere. Proof lies in the fact that, as some jurisdictions have 'liberalized' and begun to co-operate with foreign authorities, there's been an observable shift of funds to jurisdictions that don't co- operate. In the Caymans, for example, when the government announced that they would sign that tax treaty, money moved away. When they reneged on the deal, money came back. So despite Roth's claims, secrecy is a product for sale which does, indeed, benefit the bank.

'In Switzerland,' Roth went on, 'privacy rules are not limited to the banking sector, but they apply with equal vigour to professions such as doctors, lawyers, solicitors and the clergy.'

That's as true in Switzerland, as it is throughout much of the world. But if you live in say, Liverpool, the fact that a doctor in Geneva won't publicize your medical condition is of little consequence. Neither would a doctor in Liverpool. Anyway, you don't go to Geneva because a doctor there keeps your secrets. You go because, by law, a banker must.

Roth then insisted, 'Swiss people would not comprehend, and indeed they would not support, any initiative aimed at throwing out financial privacy principles simply because some dishonest people have taken advantage of them, any more than they would accept giving up medical secrecy because of a few cases of health insurance fraud. Nor could the Swiss understand, or accept, that the foreign clients of our banks be treated any differently, i.e. without the same amount of due trust and respect.'

Of course not. To do so would cost them too much money.

Sharing Roth's agenda, the Swiss Bankers Association (SBA) talks an equally good, equally disingenuous game. A pamphlet published in 2001 called, *'Dirty Money? No, Thanks!'* tries to buttress their morally responsible face of secret banking. 'The Swiss financial centre has many assets, but its sound reputation is surely the most important . . . every attempt at money laundering is considered a risk to its reputation.'

The pamphlet cites an FATF report crediting Switzerland with 'extremely effective measures to combat criminal activities.' Pointing to the 1998 law – which is directed at all persons active in the financial sector, not just bankers – the SBA stresses how it obliges everyone to identify clients and to establish the beneficial owners of the assets. What's more, the SBA notes, that law comes on the back of more than 20 years of codes enforcing the strictest due diligence.

That said, a fair question is: if 20 years of codes had successfully enforced due diligence, how come they needed yet another law in 1998?

The answer is obvious: because 20 years of codes didn't work. Just look at 20-years worth of Swiss embarrassment after they got caught red-handed, hiding money for crooks named Abacha, Marcos, Noriega, Bhutto, Sese Seko and Duvalier, plus the Cali Cartel, the Medellin Cartel, the traditional Sicilian Mafia, the N'Drangheta, the Camorra, the Russian Maffiya, and enough fraudsters and tax evaders to fill a small stadium. How long does the list have to be to prove the SBA wrong?

Nor does the 1998 law work all that well. Granted, it puts increased responsibilities on the private sector, through mandatory reporting where corruption or criminality is suspected, and expands reporting responsibilities from banks to 'financial intermediaries'. But, co-operation has been so minimal that, two years after the law came onto the statute books, the head of Switzerland's Money Laundering Reporting Office

(MROS) quit. So did the rest of his office, all of five of them. They left because, despite the law, the government flatly refused to put its money where it's laws were and give the office real powers to do something about money laundering. The 1998 law is filled with loopholes through which 'financial intermediaries' can claim that reporting is not required. As a result, the MROS has been receiving fewer than one report of suspected criminal activity per bank per year!

To give the dog its due, secrecy in Switzerland is not what it used to be. But that's not because the gnomes got religion, it's because pressure from European governments over transparency in tax matters, and from the US in the fight against money laundering, rudely muscled the Swiss into a corner.

When groups in North America went in search of Holocaust money, stringent denials came from Switzerland, categorically refusing the notion that this money was hidden there. Swiss bankers assumed their best air of utter indignation, furious that anyone would even insinuate they were party to such heinous behaviour. That is, until Holocaust money was, indeed, found in Switzerland and those bankers were proven to be outright liars. They responded with rage that anyone would suggest how the mere presence of Holocaust money automatically meant they were harbouring dirty money.

Having reputational risk shoved down their throats left them with no alternative but to become better global citizens. That's not to say they're good. Just better. Underneath it all, the gnomes seem less concerned with being accused of brokering dirty money, than they are with how forced changes benefit other jurisdictions.

If you can't hide it in Switzerland, you can walk it across the border to Liechtenstein.

In 2000, the tiny principality found itself included in an OECD list of 35 countries that had laws or policies which were deemed to be obstructive for foreign tax authorities. Fearing an effect on business, the good people of Vaduz – Liechtenstein's only city – redressed the windows by changing the law that otherwise guaranteed secrecy for certain classes of criminals. But they refused to kill the goose. In the end, they couldn't even fool the characteristically gullible OECD into thinking that real change was afoot. Two years after finding themselves on that list, the Liechtensteiners were still on it.

Looking for a scapegoat, they conveniently blamed the Swiss. The prime minister's office announced that Switzerland was behind attempts to change the banking regulations in Liechtenstein, in order to secure an unfair competitive commercial advantage.

Hardly a revelation of earth-shattering proportions, when the United Nations looked into Swiss banking, they found the gnomes desperately worried that erosion of client confidentiality diminished the nation's competitive advantage. One Swiss banker told the UN, 'The time has come to take a stance and defend, in a lucid and resolute manner, an asset of which the country may be proud and which it cannot do without.'

Hoping to occupy the moral ground, Niklaus Blattner, chief executive of the SBA, suggested his members would opt for doing what's right. 'In the scramble for a share of the global wealth management market, the long-term prize will go to those financial centres with the highest regulatory standards'. This flies in the face of conventional wisdom which dictates that the prize belongs to those bankers who, under the guise of self-regulation, don't self-regulate, giving themselves a competitive advantage over those who do.

The fallacy of self-regulation lies at the heart of the matter for offshore bankers. That money hidden in an account may contribute to crime, violence and corruption outside the jurisdiction where the bank is registered, is not their concern. And laws in most offshore centres reflect that. It's only a crime if it's a crime in the jurisdiction, except sometimes, when the jurisdiction simply can't avoid it, like with terrorism.

No, what really worries folks in offshore jurisdictions goes back to that SBA pamphlet and the concept of reputational risk. But, it's not reputational risk the way the SBA put it. It's the risk that comes from first having to deny you're involved, then getting caught at it, then having to retract your denials. It's the reputational risk that the Swiss suffered when they denied hiding Holocaust money, got caught with it, were exposed as liars and were then forced to admit they'd had it all along.

In other words, getting caught is bad for business.

'The offshore world was created as an answer to a simple question,' lawyer Jack Blum is fast to conclude. 'That is, how do we step out of our responsibility for our actions in the place where we live? The idea is to remove legal responsibility from our own society so that we can say, we don't have any responsibility here. So that we can say, we're governed by the rules of nowhere. And a lot of people, for a lot of different reasons, like the rules of nowhere. You don't want to pay taxes? You don't want some government to insist that an investment is truly an investment and not just a scam? You want to run a hedge fund and put other people's money in fairy dust and cotton candy? Then you need a place where there are no rules, where you can do everything, where there is no accountability. It's the rules of nowhere that built the offshore world.'

CHAPTER FOUR

Sinks R Us

You never know what you can get away with unless you try.
– Colin Powell

It took 16 years for most people even to begin to understand how the rules of nowhere connected dirty money, organized crime and global terrorism. Then, it took several bent banks and a bunch of crooks to drive the notion home.

The point of departure for what would prove to be a very steep and costly learning curve was America's 1970 'Financial Recordkeeping and Reporting of Currency and Foreign Transactions Act', otherwise known as the 'Bank Secrecy Act (BSA)'. It recognized the necessity to identify dirty money at the earliest stage of the laundering process when cash is fed into the banking system. Primarily, the BSA required banks to file Currency Transaction Reports (CTRs) for cash deposits over $10,000.

The next co-ordinate came in 1984, when Ronald Reagan's Commission on Organized Crime issued it's watershed report, *Cash Connection*. This was the first time that any government anywhere officially acknowledged the links between organized crime, financial institutions and money laundering. That report was followed by two more from the Commission: *America's Habit-Drug Abuse, Drug Trafficking and Organized Crime,* and *The Impact-Organized Crime Today*.

Those three reports successfully laid the groundwork for passage of the 1986 Money Laundering Control Act (MLCA), which established criminal penalties for washing the proceeds of 'unlawful activities'. That term widened the offence of money laundering away from drug trafficking to include all sorts of criminal conduct. In effect, it made the charge of money laundering similar to the charge of conspiracy, a kind of catch-all offence that prosecutors could use in conjunction with other charges. Simply put, as long as money was involved with the crime – which it almost always is – and as long as that money was somehow disguised to avoid detection, then laundering could be charged.

The rest of the world did nothing. There were stirrings in Australia, Canada and Britain, suggesting that money laundering was an area that they needed to deal with, but it would take several more years before they got around to it. Australia was the first nation, after the United States, to require reporting of cash transactions in excess of US $10,000. Canada and Britain opted for 'suspicious cash transaction' reporting, a popular but otherwise lame system that allows bankers to decide what's suspicious.

In the meantime – during that 16-year period, 1970 to 1986 – drugs bombarded the United States, coming at the country from every direction: cocaine from Colombia; cocaine and heroin from Mexico; marijuana and heroin from the Orient; heroin from Turkey and Nigeria via Europe; marijuana, cocaine and amphetamines from Canada. As drugs saturated America's streets, the money from those drugs was dumped into the banking system. As law enforcement geared up to go after individual bankers, traffickers diversified to wire remitters and businesses, like supermarkets, where they could feed cash into the system. As the cops got wise to that, the traffickers began bulking cash out of the country. The money headed for Canada – once described as the Maytag of North America, because so much got washed there – or was shipped south into the Caribbean. Just like the drugs which arrived by boat, plane, on the backs of mules, in steamer trunks, in refrigerators, in sacks of coffee and in car bumpers, cash left the same way the drugs had come in.

It was easy getting cash across the northern border, where Canadian banks and wire remitters operated oblivious to US laws and without much interference from Canadian laws. It wasn't any more difficult getting cash across the southern border, where Mexican banks, wire remitters and Cambios set up on the banks of the Rio Grande to handle the influx. But it was easiest of all once the cash reached the Caribbean, where nations like Antigua deliberately turned themselves into laundromats. There was even an in-transit bank at the airport to handle cash from arriving couriers, managing it so efficiently that the courier could deposit the money and get back onto the same plane for the flight home.

In Anguilla, a wooden shack at the end of the runway had the word 'Bank' painted on the front of it so that pilots could taxi up and not have to shut down their engines.

In Montserrat, hundreds of banks were chartered by a government desperate for money, with total disregard to the people chartering those banks or to the fact that absolutely none of the banks had a physical presence on the island.

Money flashed around the world, across borders, in and out of shell companies, through banks in the Channel Islands and Switzerland, through shell companies registered in Luxembourg and Liechtenstein, and somehow arrived, finally, back into the hands of Colombians and Mexicans, Turks and Nigerians, Chinese, Japanese and traffickers from all over Southeast Asia. It wasn't stopped, because the people who could stop it were getting rich: dealers on street corners in Philadelphia and Manchester; bankers in Miami, Geneva, London and the Bahamas; wire remitters in Montreal; lawyers in Panama; company formation agents in the Caymans and the Isle of Man; and, of course, the traffickers themselves. They all raked in unbelievable heaps of money. At one point, the Cali cartel had annual profits of $7 billion, three times greater than General Motors.

But during those 16 years, American law enforcement came to understand that the way to stop it was by going after the money, and little by little, that's what they learned how to do. Prior to the MLCA, four American law enforcement agencies looked at financial crimes, and their parameters were very specific: the Internal Revenue Service dealt with tax matters; the FBI with bank fraud and racketeering; Customs dealt with imports and restrictions on exports; and the SEC dealt with securities fraud and stock market manipulation. Where drugs were involved, the emphasis was mostly on smuggling and street corner busts.

The first of the big 'follow the money' cases was the famous 'Pizza Connection'. An offshoot of Lucky Luciano's French connection, morphine base from Turkey was shipped to Sicily, where it was refined, then moved through Canada and into the States. From 1979 to 1984, nearly $1.6 billion worth of heroin was distributed through a franchised network of pizzerias that stretched across the industrial Northeast and into the Midwest. The Mafia's original intention was to wash cash from the drug sales through the tills with the pizza sales. But all too soon there was far too much money for the restaurants to launder, so the traffickers turned to Wall Street. The various money trails led through major financial institutions including Merrill Lynch, Chemical Bank, E.F. Hutton, Handelsbank and Credit Suisse. The case was prosecuted by the brash young US Attorney for Manhattan, Rudy Guiliani.

While the Pizza Connection was in full swing, the DEA was

working a two-year undercover that saw agents posing as bankers to expose a $150 million money laundering operation through Panama for a Colombian trafficker named Orozco-Prada. In a similar case, the Feds targeted the financial dealings of a trafficker named Oscar Cuevas, who smuggled $123 million out of Los Angeles and into Britain and from there had it transferred into Swiss banks.

Other operations followed. In 'Greenback', federal agents posing as launderers moved money through a bank in Miami to the Cayman Islands branch of the Costa Rican bank BAC International. In 'Pisces', the DEA washed drug cash straight into Panama. In 'Expressway', the FBI moved $16 million for the Medellin Cartel through US banks and into Panama. In 'Polar Cap', the government exposed a multi-billion dollar laundering network which indicted Pablo Escobar, head of the Medellin Cartel. His money was washed through jewellery stores in Los Angeles and, with the use of offshore shells plus banks in Canada, Switzerland, Italy, Germany and Uruguay, wound up in the Panamanian subsidiary of Colombia's Banco de Occidente. A second phase of 'Polar Cap' saw $121 million seized in the UK, Switzerland, Luxembourg, Austria, Panama and in 1,035 US-based bank accounts. In 'Dinero', the DEA established the RHM Bank in Anguilla, through which agents laundered $12 million in 40 days for six Cali Cartel connected clients. 'Dinero' was important for many reasons: it exposed links between the cartel and the traditional Sicilian Mafia; uncovered a drugs-for-arms swap, demonstrating how drugs, money and arms all function together; and showed how legitimate businesses, such as supermarkets and car rental agencies, could be used to launder money.

But it was 'Operation C-Chase' in Florida – the C standing for 'cash' – that really made the case for following the money. Customs agents working an undercover sting of the Medellin bunch, collected drug cash in Los Angeles, Miami and New York, then dumped it in the Tampa branch of the Bank of Credit and Commerce International (BCCI), at the time, one of the ten largest banks in the world.

This hugely complicated and costly five-year operation – which moved $34 million through BCCI Tampa – produced more than 1,200 secretly recorded conversations and 400 hours of clandestinely recorded video tape, which exposed offshore networks running through Britain, France, Italy and Panama. In 1990, the evidence that the agents had amassed led to dozens of convictions, including BCCI bankers.

But the real significance of C-Chase was in what followed.

When they began, the undercover agents and their handlers believed that the laundromat they were targeting – the biggest they'd ever seen – was inside BCCI. By the time they finished, they realized that the laundromat wasn't inside BCCI – it was BCCI.

Created in 1972 by a 50-year-old Indian-born banker named Agha Hasan Abedi, BCCI was originally backed by the ruler of Abu Dhabi, Sheikh Zayed Bin Sultan Al-Nahayan, members of the Saudi royal family and the Bank of America. It was capitalized at $2.5 million. Five years later, Abedi was boasting 146 branches in 32 countries and claiming to control assets of $2.2 billion. Only the Bank of America sussed that something wasn't right and pulled out. The rest of the world fell for Abedi's scam, especially the British.

Abedi had registered the holding company that owned BCCI in Luxembourg, a jurisdiction with strict banking secrecy. However, what he really wanted was the credibility that being a British bank could give him, so he opened branches in Asian neighbourhoods across the UK. He registered BCCI a second time, now in the Cayman Islands, then moved his top management to London. Over the next 15 years, the Bank of England (BoE) gave Abedi and BCCI a clean bill of health. With hindsight, it's easy to see why: Abedi made certain that there wasn't much for anyone to see; the British government had it's own agenda; and the Bank of England was generally incompetent.

Oddly, the BoE did show some concern at the very beginning, because it refused to charter BCCI as a bank. Instead, it handed Abedi the less weighty title of 'licensed deposit taker'. Abedi later claimed it was because BCCI operated 'outside the club' suggesting a racist motive for refusing to accept his bank as the real thing. And there might have been a grain of truth in that, except that his bank wasn't the real thing. Not that it mattered to the public if BCCI wasn't officially a bank because they didn't know the difference between a bank and a licensed deposit taker. BCCI had 45 offices in Britain that looked like banks and operated like banks and, for all intents and purposes, were banks. Except in the minds of a few folk along Threadneedle Street.

That BCCI was chartered in Luxembourg and the Caymans, deliberately placing it beyond BoE regulation, should have set off alarm bells. Instead, the BoE turned up its highfalutin nose and left it to the Luxembourgois and the Caymanians to regulate BCCI. Except, the Luxembourgois and Caymanians were counting on the Bank of England to do it. What they all would have seen, had anyone bothered to look, was massive fraud at every level. Abedi was creating capital accounts in the Caymans by using the bank's money in Luxembourg, then creating capital accounts in Luxembourg, by using the banks money in the Caymans. Abedi hired different auditors for every jurisdiction. As long as they didn't compare notes – which there was no reason to believe they would – no one would find out that the banks were capitalized by thin air.

In 1976, Abedi tried to buy the Chelsea National Bank in New York but state regulators nixed that deal. Among other things, they objected to the B in BCCI standing for bank. As a licensed deposit taker, it was not legally allowed to call itself a bank. The BoE failed to stop it.

Thwarted in New York, Abedi went south to Atlanta, hired Jimmy Carter's pal and disgraced former budget director Bert Lance, and through him, surreptitiously acquired the National Bank of Georgia. It was one of Abedi's mates, Saudi businessman Gaith Pharaon, who officially bought that bank, and the Independence Bank of Encino California, too. He paid for them with a $500 million loan from Abedi, secured with the shares of the two banks. Abedi then sold National Bank of Georgia to Financial General, a holding company in Washington secretly owned by more of his friends. And just like that, Abedi illegally gained control of three US banks.

When the SEC figured out what was going on, it threatened to take action against Abedi and his backers. There was even talk of a criminal case. So Abedi worked out a deal to pull the wool over the SEC's eyes. Financial General was renamed First American Bankshares and, he said, would be independent of BCCI. In reality, it was always Abedi's. To give First American a pedigree, Abedi installed two prominent Americans on the board. Clark Clifford – an exalted DC attorney and elder statesman who'd served as an adviser and friend to almost every President since Harry Truman – was named chairman. His law partner Robert Altman, husband of TV's 'Wonder Woman' Lynda Carter, was named president.

By then, Abedi had opened BCCI offices in Panama, where Manuel Noriega was his largest single depositor. Middle Eastern terrorist Abu Nidal was soon channelling funds through BCCI, followed quickly by the Medellin Cartel. By 1988, Abedi's laundromat had 417 branches in 73 countries and reported assets of $20 billion. And, all this time, the Bank of England maintained that everything was just dandy.

The drug money pouring into BCCI Tampa turned out to be the tip of a gigantic iceberg. Massive amounts of cash were also coming into BCCI Miami. From there, the money would be flown by private jet to Panama and the Caymans, wired onto BCCI Luxembourg, then transferred to the traffickers' BCCI accounts anywhere in the world, but especially Colombia. BCCI opened seven branches there, five of them in Medellin.

To cover the cash deposited in Florida and confound anyone looking for a money trail, Abedi invented a ghost bank. His computers were programmed to show the Florida cash as having been deposited first in BCCI Bahamas – which didn't exist – and then bulked to Miami as part of a normal internal bank transfer. BCCI Miami even fulfilled the requirements of the Bank Secrecy Act by filing the proper forms with US Customs to account for the concocted importation of cash.

Diversifying further afield, Abedi sent some of BCCI's laundry work to Canada and expanded throughout the Caribbean, opening in marijuana-rich Jamaica, Barbados, Curacao and Trinidad. He also set up in the United Arab Emirates (UAE), to serve the heroin trade in the 'Golden Crescent' of Pakistan, Iran and Afghanistan. And he set up in Hong Kong, to serve the heroin trade in the 'Gold Triangle' of Laos, Burma and Thailand. Ultimately Abedi even opened in the Bahamas, where hundreds of shell companies were formed to disguise the movement of dirty money back and forth with BCCI Miami.

But Abedi was chasing shadows. His balance sheet was fiction. Although many of his liabilities were real, most of his assets weren't. The faster he opened banks, the faster the system sprang leaks. To plug holes, he stole $150 million from a staff pension fund. Eventually, Abedi would steal $10 billion of depositors funds. International banking supervisors in Basle had grown increasingly concerned with his management of BCCI's assets, and reported this to the BoE. But auditors there failed to see Abedi's frauds.

Fearing that the British might one day cotton onto him, Abedi moved the treasury out of the UK to Abu Dhabi. By then BCCI was the object of investigations in Switzerland, Canada, France, Luxembourg, Brazil, Singapore, Bermuda, the Caymans, Cyprus and even Nigeria.

In the States, indictments came down from C-Chase. Senator John Kerry, presiding over the Subcommittee on Narcotics Terrorism and International Operations – under the auspices of the Senate Foreign Relations Committee – opened hearings on BCCI's association with

Noriega. Under oath, two convicted drug dealers claimed they'd laundered funds through BCCI Panama and that their introduction to the bank had come from Noriega. A further Senate inquiry would reveal that Noriega had used BCCI to wash tens of millions of dollars.

Kerry's chief investigator on the subcommittee, Jack Blum, realized right away that BCCI might be the biggest laundromat of all time and tried to interest the C-Chase investigators in the wider picture. They were too busy with their own case. So Blum went to the IRS and the Justice Department to bring them in. Neither shared his enthusiasm. Finally, he went to see the New York District Attorney. And Robert Morgenthau was very interested. Able to claim jurisdiction because First American Bankshares had offices in New York, Morgenthau's tenacious assistant John Moscow led the charge.

A sturdily built native New Yorker now in his mid-50s, Moscow is deceptively friendly. Everyone who likes him – and after 30 years of chasing financial crooks there are plenty of cops and prosecutors and government officials who like him – really likes him a lot. When you mention his name to people who have been on the same side of the courtroom, you always get a broad smile and are reminded, 'John's my friend'. He is hospitable, witty and seriously bright. Very few people know the ins-and-outs of financial crime better than John Moscow. But the people who run up against him in his role as the DA's Deputy Chief of the Investigations Division – those people who find themselves on the wrong side of the courtroom – soon discover that *bonhomie* doesn't count and that tangling with him can end in tears. He is relentless when he investigates crimes, resolute when he pursues people who perpetrate them, and ruthless when he prosecutes people who need to be prosecuted.

Although it embarrasses him to hear it, John Moscow is a star.

He set his sites on BCCI, Abedi and everyone involved with BCCI's takeover of First American, including Clifford and Altman. But when Moscow turned to the BoE for help, folks there became obstructive.

In March 1990, the BoE's governors were informed by the intelligence services that Abu Nidal controlled 42 accounts at BCCI branches around London. Eight months later, they were handed two reports, one from the City of London Fraud Squad, the other from a Middle Eastern accountant, outlining massive frauds at BCCI. Two months after that, the governors learned that BCCI had amassed some $600 million in unrecorded deposits.

Refusing to let the BoE off the hook, Morgenthau and Moscow

showed their files to Deputy Governor Eddie George. In no uncertain terms, they threatened to raise public hell if the Bank of England didn't do something about BCCI. Eddie George returned from that meeting in New York to warn the Bank's governor, Robyn Leigh-Pemberton, that the New Yorkers were on the warpath. In March 1991, Leigh-Pemberton ordered an audit. When it was finished, in July of that year, the BoE was out of excuses and BCCI was shut down.

Morgenthau and Moscow indicted Clifford, Altman, Abedi and the number two man at BCCI, Swaleh Naqvi. Clifford and Altman were ordered to stand trial, although the case against them subsequently fizzled out. Naqvi was arrested in Abu Dhabi, extradited to the United States, charged with conspiracy, wire fraud and racketeering, pleaded guilty and was sentenced to 11 years. In Abu Dhabi, a court convicted 12 BCCI officials *in absentia* – including Abedi and Naqvi – and sentenced them all to lengthy prison terms. But Abedi never saw the inside of a courtroom. He became the subject of an extradition battle with the Pakistanis, which the Americans lost. By then, he was ill and bedridden. He died in Karachi in August 1995. He was 73.

It is now known that there were several parties interested in keeping BCCI's pipeline open through the offshore world. Among them: the BoE, which had been told to keep its distance by the British security services as they were using BCCI to monitor several people, including Saddam Hussein; the CIA, which was using BCCI to launder funds for the Iran-Contra affair and also washing money for Afghan rebels; the US Defense Intelligence Agency, which maintained a slush fund at BCCI; and MI-6, which had a relationship with Abedi frontman Kamal Adham – the former chief of Saudi intelligence – that provided a convenient channel to the Gulf States. Furthermore, BCCI had been involved in financing the transfer of North Korean Scud-B missiles to Syria; had helped to broker and finance the sale of Chinese Silkworm missiles to Saudi Arabia; and had acted as financial middleman when the Saudis needed Israeli guidance systems for those missiles.

When the BCCI affair ended, ruining the lives of so many, innocent depositors who'd entrusted Abedi with their savings, Leigh-Pemberton testified to a House of Commons Select Committee that he had never been 'particularly happy' with BCCI's presence in the UK. Which is as close as anyone at the Bank has ever come to admitting a mistake.

To this day, still impervious to criticism and despite a mountain

of evidence to the contrary, officials at the BoE arrogantly insist that
the bank did nothing wrong.

Astonishingly, Leigh-Pemberton actually told that Committee, 'If
we closed down a bank every time we found an incidence of fraud,
we would have rather fewer banks than we do at the moment.'

There's no reason to believe that the lessons of BCCI have been
indelibly stamped on the brains of banking regulators around the
world. However, they were definitely learned by some Russians looking
to do the same thing, but better.

In the old days under the Soviets, unless you were one of the chosen
few, bilking the system was what you did to stay alive. When the
fraud of Communism disintegrated and a fledgling, kind-of-capital-
istic Russia tried to extract itself from the quicksand, the people carried
with them into this new world their cynicism, their deep-seeded
distrust of all things official and their well-honed instincts for self-
preservation.

The government opted for privatization of the old Soviet industrial
complex, but that was strictly a Western concept. Corruption was
what the people understood. They'd learned their lesson in the rigid
world of the forced economy. Standing on line for hours to buy whatever might be at the end of that line was how they'd paid their dues.

Now, in the sudden freedom that was 1990s, it was as if the rules
had vanished with their rulers, and their right to steal was inalien-
able. Everything was for sale, and anything that couldn't be bought,
could probably be filched. Companies, over-taxed and over-burdened
by extortion, produced documents to show that they were importing
something – it hardly mattered what – and so to pay for the goods,
they transferred money out of the country. Like contrails in the sky
marking the paths of high flying jets, throughout the past decade,
tens of thousands of money trails have come out of Russia. That the
corresponding goods never arrive back in the country surprises no one.

One popular destination for this mass capital flight is Britain. In
addition to modern financial facilities provided throughout the City
of London, there are fashionable properties to live in, expensive private
schools for Russian children, art and antiques to be bought at auction,
elite shopping and until recently, money laundering laws lax enough
to be almost non-existent. For the Russians, London is a hub with

easy access to other western financial centres, especially the Channel Islands and the Caribbean. A few years ago the Moscow-based financial newspaper Kommersant noted, 'Tens of millions of dollars have left the former Soviet Union, specifically bound for Britain.' Today, the figure is into the tens of billions. And a chunk of that came from a group of Russians who set up a circuit through Britain and the Channel Islands that turned out to be the Bank of New York (BoNY) scandal.

At the heart of it were two young women.

Lyudmila Pritzker was born in Leningrad in 1958. At the age of 19 she married an American named Brad Edwards and moved with him to the States. She Americanized her name to Lucy, had a child, divorced her husband and wound up working as a teller for the Bank of New York. In 1988, BoNY bought Irving Trust, an old established Manhattan-based financial institution that had been actively pursuing business in Eastern Europe. Edwards soon found herself working in BoNY's newly acquired Eastern European Division.

Her manager there, Natasha Gurfinkel, was also Russian-born. Three years older than Edwards, Gurfinkel was married to Konstantin Kagalovsky, Russia's representative to the International Monetary Fund (IMF). Kagalovsky and his financier chum Mikhail Khodorkovsky shared business interests in a Russian bank called Menatep. That bank is believed to have had an interest in the totally crooked European Union Bank of Antigua (EUB).

Records show that EUB was owned by a Bahamian shell company called Swiss Investment Association. It was the brain child of either Khodorovsky, who appears to have been a major shareholder, or Alexandre Konanykhine who, at the time that EUB was chartered in July 1994, was in jail in the States for violating his visa conditions. According to the Washington Post, Konanykhine was also wanted in Russia for embezzling $8.1 million from another Moscow bank in 1992.

In September 1995, EUB opened its doors or, more accurately, turned on its computer. Because, the bank didn't exist in Antigua, or anywhere else for that matter, except in cyberspace. It's only presence was on the Internet. The bank's website pitch read, 'Since there are no government withholding or reporting requirements on accounts, the burdensome and expensive accounting requirements are reduced for you and the bank.'

Within nine months, EUB was claiming to have assets of $2.8 million and 144 accounts in 43 countries. Naturally, EUB was also

claiming to maintain the strictest standards of banking privacy, reinforced by the claim – somehow made with a straight face – that
Antigua was a serious financial centre with serious penalties for anyone
violating its serious banking secrecy laws. Shortly after EUB went on
line, the Bank of England warned the US Federal Reserve Bank that
while Menatep was denying any involvement in EUB, Konanykhine
had asked the Antiguans to keep Menatep's involvement in EUB a
secret.

Among many things not publicly disclosed was that EUB's
computer server – which was, effectively, the bank – was located in
Washington DC. And that the man operating the computer server,
who was effectively the banker, was in Canada. How much money was
ultimately funnelled through the bank – washed by Russians for other
Russians and, as well, for some of their Latin American drug trafficking friends – is not known. Nor will it ever be. Because one day
in mid-1997, just like that, someone unplugged the computer. That
was the last anyone ever heard of the depositors' money. Upwards of
$12 million is said to have disappeared.

There are links between EUB and Menatep and further links
between Menatep and the scandal plagued, now-defunct Moscow-based
financial institution, Inkombank. Both Menatep and Inkombank had
relationships with BoNY. In fact, Inkombank was one of several clients
brought to BoNY by Natasha Gurfinkel, who'd wrenched it away
from rival Republic Bank. A much heralded coup, by 1995 Inkombank
was BoNY's largest generator of fee income, making BoNY the most
important clearing bank in Russia for domestic transactions. Only
later did anyone learn that Republic had filed suspicious activity
reports about Inkombank with federal regulators and were glad to see
Inkombank take its business elsewhere.

About a year after going to work under Gurfinkel, Edwards remar-
ried. Peter Berlin was a molecular chemical physicist from Moscow
who'd recently arrived in the States. The couple lived in New Jersey
and Berlin worked out of their flat, which was the registered address
for his company, Benex. Before long, Berlin was brokering sales of
electronic goods to Russia. And it was while running this phase of
his business that he was asked by some of his clients to provide false
invoices on the back of which they could ship money out of Russia.
Berlin had the means of facilitating the movement of funds and his
wife had access to a bank they could use. So in 1996, Benex
International opened an account at BoNY's Wall Street headquarters.

Six months later, a company called Becs International also opened an account at the same BoNY branch. Lucy Edwards was listed as a Becs employee and had a signature authority on the account.

Unaware of Edward's involvement with Benex and Becs, BoNY promoted her to vice-president and assigned her to their London offices, specifically to seek out new Russian business. By this time, Berlin had moved into a one room office at 118–21 Queens Boulevard, in Forest Hills, New York, just across the East River from Manhattan. And that's where Peter Berlin and his wife Lucy Edwards might be today – commuting between London and New York – had it not been for a scam in Canada and a kidnapping ransom in San Francisco.

Britain's National Criminal Intelligence Service (NCIS) was investigating the YBM Magnex scandal, a fraud perpetrated on the Toronto Stock Exchange. The man behind it was, allegedly, Semion Mogilevitch, an alleged Russian Maffiya boss. One of many shell companies NCIS stumbled across in that investigation was Benex. At first glance, it looked like just another empty shell through which money flowed. That Benex was using an account at the Bank of New York didn't seem out of the ordinary either, because shell accounts pop up all the time at legitimate banks. But, when the NCIS officers took a really close look at Benex, they were dumbfounded by the amount of money moving through one Benex account in Jersey, and into BoNY. During a single six-month period, 10,000 transactions shifted $4.2 billion!

NCIS passed the intelligence along to the Americans.

Around the same time, the Russian police asked the FBI for help in a kidnapping case. A $300,000 ransom had been paid to secure the release of a man named Edouard Olevinsky. The Bureau traced the payment from the victim's bank in San Francisco through BoNY and an offshore account in the Channel Islands to the Sobin Bank in Moscow. The offshore account belonged to Benex.

The NCIS file wound up at the New York DA's office. The FBI file wound up at the US Attorney's office in Manhattan. Suddenly, two US based investigations plus the NCIS investigation in Britain were all looking at Benex and BoNY. Unbeknown to those three, the National Crime Squad in London had also stumbled across Benex and Becs in their pursuit of a separate case dealing with drug money laundered through the Channel Islands.

When the four investigations finally converged, they turned into the largest international money laundering inquiry in history. It entailed 87,000 electronic transfers to move $15 billion. Some of those transfers involved Russian companies evading taxes. Some of them linked Benex and Becs with Russian organized criminals. The New York Police Department, the Federal Reserve Board and the Comptroller of Currency also took an interest in this. Before long, investigators had widened the case to include banks and financial relationships in more than 50 jurisdictions.

Blissfully unaware of law enforcement's interest in their business, the Gurfinkel–Edwards team mined sources that other foreign banks left untapped. By summer 1999, they were dealing with Russian clients that other foreign banks had turned down. That's when the *New York Times* broke the story of the enormous sums being washed through BoNY.

For more than a month, from the middle of August until early October, this was a fast moving, front-page news story. Denials, shock and horror by BoNY officials were followed by Edwards' dismissal. Then Gurfinkel resigned. Her husband, Konstantin Kagalovsky, denied any wrong doing – everybody involved with this denied wrong doing throughout most of it – and the IMF grew concerned. Press reports suggested that some of the money funnelled through Benex and BoNY might have been IMF funds originally intended to keep the Russian economy afloat.

Edwards' and Gurfinkel's offices at BoNY were searched, documents were removed and sealed, and their homes were searched as well. When British police raided the Edwards' London flat they found business stationery imprinted with both Benex and Bank of New York logos. When Berlin's office in Forest Hills was raided, four new companies came to light. Two of them had banking relationships with BoNY. And one of them was registered at an address that tied it to a network of companies, including an offshore bank, licensed by Russians in the highly suspect offshore Pacific Island jurisdiction of Nauru.

At this point, the chief culprit appeared to be Mogilevitch. Based in Budapest during the YBM Magnex scandal, the US State Department had pressured the Hungarians into doing something about his presence there and he'd been given the bums rush back to Russia in July 1999. In April 2003, the US Justice Department unsealed an 86-page, 45-count indictment relating to the YBM Magnex case, charging Mogilevitch and three others with racketeering, wire fraud, mail fraud, securities fraud and money laundering. The FBI issued a warrant for his arrest. Money was moved through dozens of banks, including Royal Bank of Scotland, Barclays, Royal Bank of Canada, CIBC, Mellon and Chase Manhattan; and some 20 countries, including Britain, Canada, the US, the Caymans, Nevis, Cyprus, and Nauru. Mogilevitch's name also continues to pop up in connection with the BoNY matter. The FBI believes that some of the $15 billion that went through the Benex account in the Channel Islands was proceeds of the YBM Magnex scam.

But not all of that money came from YBM. Enter here a new and even more worrying connection.

While investigating a Russian mobster named Yuri Essine and his Italian-based export business, authorities in Italy took an interest in the growing Russian presence along the Adriatic coast. In particular, they wanted to know more about Russian organized crime links in the city of Rimini.

A typical beach resort with a pleasure boat port, hotels and fish restaurants, Rimini is also filled with nightclubs and travel agencies where the signs out front are written in Cyrillic. It's a city that lost its way in the tourist battle against more fashionable resorts, went in search of new markets and discovered the Russians. Planeloads of them now show up every week. But these aren't tourists who sit on the beach and eat ice cream. Instead, they step off their chartered flights and are bussed directly to a wholesale leather goods market just outside of town. Carrying wads of brand new $100 bills, they buy up whatever they can, sending their purchases back home by the plane load. Some of these Russians may be legitimately working for an import/export business. Most of them are not.

The Russians invading Rimini are believed, by the Italian police, to be part of a huge money laundering circle. It starts with drugs sold in Russia. That street cash is washed through Rimini's leather wholesalers who, it must be said, are more than happy to have this influx, which they then bank in nearby San Marino, safely out of reach of Italian tax inspectors. The goods shipped back to Russia are sold in the new markets there and the profits generated are reinvested in drugs.

The Italians only stumbled across this while looking at Yuri Essine. He led them to Rimini and while looking at Rimini, they discovered Benex. A major investigation was launched, dubbed Operation Spiderweb, which rounded up 50 people and indicted 100 others. The investigation continues in Italy, France, Switzerland and Germany, where more than 300 bank accounts have been seized. According to the Italian police, by tracing money moved through Benex, one offshoot leads to Boris Yeltsin's family. Others point to several important Russians suspected of money laundering, fraud and, in one case, arms smuggling. Most worrying of all, there are financial connections through Benex that suggest links exist between Russians in Italy and Chechen rebels in the former Soviet Union who, in turn, have financial ties to Al-Qaeda.

When the BoNY scandal shook out, Gurfinkel was not charged. She sued BoNY in Moscow for $270 million, alleging illegal suspension from her job and libel. In September 2001, the Russian court threw out most of her case. What remained was settled two months later, when BoNY paid her $5 million, including $300,000 to cover her legal fees. The Yeltsin family has immunity from prosecution, although BoNY have admitted that two accounts held by a family member at BoNY's Cayman Islands branch, contains $2.7 million. Edwards and Berlin pleaded guilty to various felonies, including conspiracy to commit money laundering. As of mid-2003, neither had been sentenced because they were actively co-operating with the authorities. The information that led to Spiderweb is said to be the first of several leads that could keep Edwards and Berlin out of jail for the foreseeable future.

That leaves BoNY.

The bank got its wrists slapped for sloppy bookkeeping, so the board put its best face forward and came up with double-talk. A press release was issued saying that the board had full confidence in the Chairman and Chief Executive Officer, Thomas Renyi, noting that Renyi had 'no direct responsibility for the events'. But then, the board obviously felt the need to add that the Chairman and Chief Executive Officer has ultimate responsibility for the bank. Consequently, they lowered Renyi's annual compensation for 1999 by around 11 per cent to $6.58 million for 1999. His total package the year before had been $7.38 million which, on the face of it, seemed to be saying that Renyi's parking ticket for the fiasco was going to cost him $800,000.

Except, the following year, Thomas Renyi made it all back in spades, pocketing a whopping increase, for a combined salary and compensation package of nearly $21 million.

CHAPTER FIVE

Potentates in the Citi

Much that we had done to keep Private Banking private becomes 'wrong' in the current environment. The business itself is very highly attractive and there is no reason why we cannot pursue it in a sound way but it will take an adjustment.

— John Reed, then CEO of Citicorp

For the chairman of a public company like Thomas Renyi to pocket a $21 million thank you from the board when his bank, during his watch, had just gone down in history as the centrepiece of the largest money laundering scandal ever, is, even by American corporate standards, bad taste.

That said, corporate America's version of bad taste pales by comparison with what goes on in the rest of the world when it comes to people in positions of trust helping themselves to money. Just look at what's been going on for decades in Latin America, the Indian sub-Continent, Asia and throughout Africa. Even then, there are few places on the planet where corruption and political criminality has reached the unimaginable heights that it has in Nigeria.

Since independence in 1960, it is estimated that as much as $120 billion has been siphoned out of the Nigerian treasury and moved into the offshore world for safekeeping by dishonest politicians. Nigeria today is a monument to the former heads of state and the gaggle of crooks surrounding them who ravished the nation and jettisoned their own people to destitution. Among the accused stands Ibrahim Bobangida, president from 1985–1993, whose entourage allegedly left the country $20 billion poorer.

If it's true that in confusion there is profit, then the sheer complexity of Nigeria is one reason for this swamp of political depravity. Nigeria became a British colony late in the colonial era only because Germany was threatening to colonize it. What the British left behind is not so much a nation as it is a confederation of tribal states with unnatural boundaries drawn up simply to suit the whims of the colonial masters.

Twice the size of California, it's assumed that around 130 million people live there, but no one can be certain because the usual state of affairs in Nigeria is utter confusion and census taking is a practical impossibility. There are 250 ethnic groups and nearly as many different dialects spoken. About 30 per cent of the population is Hausa-Fulani, living in the northern half of the country. The Yoruba make up a little over 20 per cent and populate the southwest corner which includes Lagos. The Ibo are just shy of 20 per cent and are found mainly in the southeast. The rest are minority groups like Ijaw, Kanuri, Ibibio and Tiv. Religiously, the country breaks down into Muslim, Christian and indigenous beliefs.

During the days of British rule, it was said that the Hausa-Fulani ran the army, the Ibo ran the government and the Yoruba were the entrepreneurs. But that would suggest that the Hausa-Fulani and the Ibo aren't as opportunistic as the Yoruba, which they are. Historically, Nigerians have always been the best traders in Africa. They have created a well documented transhipment hub for heroin and cocaine, moving drugs in all directions: north to Europe; south to South Africa; and, either directly across the Atlantic or through Latin America for the US and Canadian markets. Nigerians also oversee a significant money-laundering centre. At the same time Nigerians are Africa's most talented, free-wheeling fraudsters. Their reputation is well deserved, having set loose a plague on the world known as '419 Fraud'.

Named after the Nigerian law that made this particular scam illegal, millions of letters and e-mails are sent around the world from Nigerian criminal enterprises offering overly-generous cuts for helping someone get money out of one country and into another. The only thing you have to do is allow that person to deposit a large sum into your bank account. Once the funds clear, you agree to forward some of that money to your benefactor, and get to keep the rest for your troubles.

In the past, the Nigerians used the post office to deliver their 419 letters, counterfeiting stamps for bulk mailings. But postal authorities got wise to that and annually pull millions of letters out of the system instead of delivering them. Anyway, snail mail is a risky and expensive way of doing businesses. So they turned to e-mail. And while some people have been accused of over-hyping the business potential of the Net, there's no denying that it has worked wonders for fraud. Using e-mail not only diminishes the possibilities of getting caught – hiding in cyberspace is akin to being invisible – but greatly reduces operating expenses to near-negligible. It costs around $50 to buy one million e-mail addresses and almost nothing to spam letters across the globe.

A recent example, a gem filled with spelling and grammatical errors, comes from someone calling himself Mr Day:

Dear Sir: This may reach you as a surprise, I am sending you this mail due to my present urgent position.

I am Mr Deoff Day, the officer in charge of special projects to Mr John Mendelson who recently resigned as a member of the board of directors of Enron Energy Corporation, a multi billion dollar energy corporation in the United States of America.

My job description amongst others is auditing, verification and recommending for payment, funds for our overseas operations and projects for work done by our Europe and Far East countries clients.

Just before Enron filed for bankruptcy, we were in the process of paying out huge funds to some of our foreign clients, this was however suspended after the federal agents stepped in following the discovery that our accounting firm Arthur Anderson was carrying out some accounting irregularities.

Incedentaly (sic), before the company was sealed, I succeeded in securing some vital classified documents in collaboration with my boss who ordered that the documents be destroyed. These documents shows (sic) how funds meant for overseas payment are lodged abroad. These funds are safely in offshore bank accounts.

Presently, I am in the island of Haiti and need a reliable friend that can assist in standing in as a client of Enron, of which payment for work done is long overdue.

If you agree to work with me in this venture, I will provide all information and details in respect of the funds deposited, that will empower and enable you collect the funds on my behalf.

I would provide you with more details as soon as you acknowledge receipt of this mail.

Please note that this venture is completely safe as we shredded all documents concerning the whereabout (sic) of our offshore accounts before the company folded up and the funds can not be traced anywhere in the world.

I expect your prompt response. And please respond only to this my confidential mail address. Kind regards, Deoff Day.

Once you provide Mr Day with all your banking details, if there's enough in your account, he will empty it. If not, he'll slip into advance fee fraud mode and explain that, in order to get your share of the money, you'll need to pay certain bank charges. Or he'll ask you to put up some money at the last minute to bribe an official. Or you'll have to pay an unexpected legal fee. Whatever his excuse, once the money is paid, he'll come back for more and keep coming until you stop paying him. And that's the last you'll see or hear about your promised millions.

Sometimes, the author of these letters is a government official, or a senior adviser to a political leader of another country, or a family member of an important Nigerian official: the Ministry of Petroleum of Nigeria is due a payment of $23.5 million that has been held up by government currency controls and you can take a quarter of that if you'll help them launder it through your account; an aide to the late Mobutu Sese Seko of Zaire wants to get his hands on $22 million that's been stashed in a secret offshore bank account and will allow you to have 25 per cent of it if you will allow him to transfer the entire sum into your bank account; the widow of the late President, is due $45 million but the money is being blocked by corrupt tax officials who are trying to steal it and you can have a big cut of this money simply for helping her get it away from them and out of Nigeria.

To create a scenario which sounds real, current events are often used. In one letter that followed the World Trade Center and Pentagon attacks, the author claimed to be representing the families of Nigerians killed on 9/11, whose money has been blocked because bank records were also destroyed that day. In another, a Nigerian government employee named Richard Moore was listed as one of the victims of the attacks. The bank manager holding his $10 million account put the money in escrow. But miraculously, Moore survived and now wants his money. Unfortunately, the courts won't release it to him because he was proclaimed legally dead. So the bank manager is looking to run the monies through someone else's account and for that service, Mr Moore will happily allow that person to keep $3 million.

Like all frauds, 419 plays directly on greed. Many people simply can't resist the opportunity to make a fast $10 million, even when their better judgement tells them this is too good to be true. Which, of course, it is. Around 1–2 per cent of the people who receive the 419 letters fall for the scam and average loss in the $200,000 range per victim.

Making the scam additionally dangerous, some people are foolish enough to show up in Lagos and demand their money back. They risk getting killed, or beaten up and put on the first plane home, or sold yet another scam on the back of the first one, which winds up costing them even more.

In addition to spamming e-mails to anyone and everyone, the criminals behind these letters also frequently hone in on specific groups. They often pry on charities. They also like to go after bankers. One bunch of Nigerian fraudsters, including a man pretending to be Chief Paul Ogwuma, Governor of the Nigerian Central Bank, hit on a director of the Banco Noereste Brazil. They convinced him that they were brokering a massive energy deal and he duly forwarded funds to offshore shell companies with bank accounts in Switzerland, China, the UK, Nigeria and the US. It turned out to be the biggest 419 swindle to date, as the Nigerians walked away with $181.6 million.

Leading the charge against the conmen is the United States Secret Service. They maintain a mammoth database of letters and e-mails, coordinate investigations with law enforcement around the world, and recently opened an office in Lagos specifically to pursue 419 fraud. The problem is that attempting to use Western law enforcement techniques in a nation that is, for all intents and purposes, lawless can prove frustrating. To begin with, you're never sure with whom you're dealing.

Bureaucracy in Nigeria is a series of overlapping systems – tribal, feudal, regional, federal – based on nepotism, favours, bribes, plus a myriad of contradictory alliances and allegiances. There are hundreds of elected tribal chiefs with fealty to the kings of different regions. Conflicting agendas are the norm, to the point where rule in Nigeria is a room full of people all talking at the same time in different languages. It's tough to get heard. Rationally, the whole process is irrational. There's no way to run this country. There's no way to police it. And there is certainly no way to catch bandits if you've come from the outside.

A nation of massive oil wealth, the king of the hill is the man who knows how best to distribute the booty. Following a fairly standard model, the man in charge is expected to divvy the oil revenues with the people below him. Those people must then share their take with the people below them. The money flows down through the immediate circle of advisers and to the military commanders. If the king of the hill gets too greedy or allows the system to run amok, he's toppled and someone else takes over the distribution system. It goes without saying that none of this money ever trickles down to the average guy, which is why just over half of Nigeria's population are living today on less than a dollar a day.

The civilian government that the British left in place on independence fell to a military coup in 1966. Generals held onto power for the next 13 years before handing the reins back to civilians.

In 1979, the price of oil had skyrocketed and the country should
have prospered. But elected president Shehu Shagari and his mates were
so incompetent and so corrupt that they plunged the country into near-
bankruptcy. They ran up foreign debts of $18 billion, while hustling
$15 billion out of the country for themselves. They bought all sorts of
goods and services no one needed at prices four times above the market,
helping themselves to kickbacks at every stage. One of the commodities they over-bought was cement. And at one point, Lagos harbour was
so overcrowded with hundreds of cement ships waiting for months to
unload that, eventually, the cement in the holds hardened and the ships
had to be scuttled. The military finally said enough is enough and
General Muhammadu Buhari sent the president packing. Two years of
severe repression later, General Ibrahim Babangida ousted Buhari.

Under Babangida's rule, in 1989, a North American oil company
tried to put a deal together with the government. Refineries in Nigeria
were operating at 40 per cent capacity and Babangida was importing
oil to meet the country's needs. This, at a time when Nigeria was a
major OPEC oil producing nation. So the North Americans suggested
a swap. In exchange for crude oil, plus drilling concessions and royal-
ties on any oil discovered, they would repair the refineries and guarantee to get them running at 90 per cent capacity, eliminating the
need to import. Negotiations went on for months, and wound their
way all the way up to the Minister of Petroleum, which is where the
deal got killed. Unbeknown to the North Americans, key Babangida
supporters owned interests in oil refineries in the Ivory Coast and
Benin. They were making a fortune refining Nigerian oil, then selling
it back to Nigeria. There was no way the government was going to
change that.

Eventually Babangida declared that he would hand the country back
to civilian rule and organized elections for 1993. But when his former
business partner Chief Moshood Abiola won, Babangida cancelled the
results. He hung on only long enough to create an interim civilian government, which was quickly overthrown by General Zachary Sani Abacha.

By comparison, this man who now became king of the hill, made
all the others look virtuous.

The 1980s saw the world economy lose its balance.

Oil prices shot sky high and interest rates spiralled, topping 20 per cent. The industrial world toppled into recession and the Third World was swamped with mega-debts. Many developing countries that had borrowed beyond their means when rates were low, were unable even to meet interest payments. Poland defaulted in 1980, so Western banks pulled the plug on several eastern bloc countries. Two years later, Mexico defaulted. And suddenly the crisis was full-blown.

For the major western banks, ever in search of profits, throwing more money at Latin America was out of the question. But as the Third World sank in the mire, wealthy Latinos rushed to get their funds into safer places, willing to pay handsome fees to ship money by the ton from Argentina, Brazil and Venezuela. Bernie Cornfeld was only one tour leader taking them to the offshore world. The big banks couldn't fill their sightseeing buses fast enough. There was plenty to be made servicing anyone in search of asset protection. In many cases, the people who were now trying to escape the confusion and misman-agement of their governments were the same ones who'd helped create the plight by ripping off the loans that the banks originally made to keep the countries afloat. Not that this was going to stop any major bank from getting its share of this burgeoning new market. So they created banks inside their own banks – private banking – as an enclave for the a select group of wealthy clients willing to pay steep fees for the privilege of organized capital flight.

Higher returns and tax avoidance might have been the agenda when private banking was still a fledgling idea in the 1970s. But when demand for capital flight was highlighted by the debt crisis, many wealthy individuals concluded that capital flight was their best chance for survival. Responding to that, the big banks opened offices for their private banks in all those places where the wealthy were threatened. An obvious end of the road for this money was Zurich or Geneva, where non-Swiss private banking groups – especially British, Canadian and American – could effectively sell Swiss banking secrecy. But Switzerland wasn't the only destination on offer. The trick was to spread accounts over several jurisdictions because the more borders you put between the money and someone looking for it, the less chance there is that anyone will be able to go the full route and find it. So private banking was about selling Cayman Island trusts and Bahamas shell companies that could open bank accounts in Luxembourg and Liechtenstein. It was about selling Uruguayan bank secrecy to nearby Argentines, Caribbean anonymity to Canadians, Venezuela banking to Brazilians and Channel Island banking to Venezuelans.

One estimate suggests that perhaps as much as 80 per cent of the loans made by commercial banks to governments in Latin America during those crisis years of the 1980s never reached their destined countries, remaining instead in western bank accounts. In Latin America, two-thirds of total debt is thought to have been deposited in western banks.

For public consumption, the major banks have always made it appear as though private banking was just another name for personalized asset management, investment, trust and estate planning. But people with serious money always had those services available to them. In reality, private banking during the debt crisis was mainly about capital flight. And not that much has changed today. Each client is assigned a private banker whose job is, simply put, to make sure that the client doesn't take his money somewhere else. One way a private banker does that is by helping clients get better returns on their money. Another way is by keeping clients' money out of the reach of other people who might want a share of it, such as governments, ex-spouses and creditors.

In 2001, when the US Senate's Permanent Subcommittee for Investigations opened a lengthy and very thorough look at private banking and the offshore world, one banker admitted under oath that his superiors forbade him from keeping any records in the US which could link shells to their owners. At any given time, he said he dealt with 30–40 clients, some of whom maintained as many as 15 shells. To remember which was which and who owned what, he used 'cheat sheets', which he kept secret from bank officers who actually launched surprise inspections to assure themselves that if law enforcement ever raided their offices, they would never find evidence which could incriminate their clients.

Just three years previous, the US Federal Reserve had queried Bankers Trust on exactly this issue. The bank agreed to establish a database that they would consult should a subpoena order them to identify which shells belonged to which clients. And Bankers Trust did create that database. But they deliberately housed it in Jersey where US subpoenas had no standing.

Needless to say, fees for such services have never come cheap, and are usually pegged to the client's net worth. It's not uncommon to find fees exceeding $1 million a year. Which is how private banking came to be the industry's major growth area. The lure of big profits brought more banks into the arena. Heightened competition meant more services on offer. The next logical step from tax avoidance is tax evasion, and the next logical step from capital flight is money laundering. Which is how drug money and funds pilfered by people in high office got mixed into this.

From Jean-Bedel Bokassa, the flesh eating Emperor of the Central African Republic, to Romania's first family, Nicholas and Elena Ceausescu, despots everywhere rushed into private banking.

In Haiti, the Duvalier 'Docs' – Papa and Baby – helped themselves to $16 million of a $22 million grant from the IMF. Much of it was washed through Canada and hidden in private banking in the Channel Islands. An additional $400 million was stashed in offshore companies and private Swiss banks.

During their reign in the Philippines, Ferdinand and Imelda Marcos made the Duvaliers look like amateurs. Those two were so crude in their greed that even the Swiss were embarrassed by them. When Ferdinand died in exile in Hawaii in 1989 and Imelda stuck him in a refrigerated box to await burial at home, Swiss bankers refused to comment on the rumours that the family had stashed $15 billion in private banking vaults. The Marcos' horde was said to include 1241 tons of gold in storage at Zurich's Kloten Airport. Swiss officials searched the customs-free storage area at the airport – or at least they said they did – and announced that no gold was found. It turned out that the $13.2 billion worth was a hundred yards away in the UBS bank's private airport vault. However, by the time Ferdinand's fridge was turned off and he was buried in the Philippines, the gnomes had miraculously found, and agreed to return, $500 million of pilfered assets. They obviously didn't look very hard because before long, another $356 million showed up in numbered accounts at Credit Suisse and Swiss Bank Corporation. Marcos money has also since been located in four Liechtenstein foundations and one Panamanian shell company. Ten years after Marcos' death, the government of the Philippines was still trying to freeze some Swiss accounts and had only accounted for around $2 billion of the supposed $5 billion that Marcos stole.

Then there was Indonesia's President Suharto. Forced from office at the age of 77, after 32 years, his family had also bilked the country out of billions of dollars. The old man positioned himself, his family and his friends to share on a near 50–50 basis with Indonesia's economic prosperity. Foreigners invited in to mine gold or to build toll roads, were required to have local partners. Those Indonesian companies, which provided no capital, were owned by the Suhartos and their friends. For example, Suharto's oldest daughter built power plants and owned toll roads. His son, Bambang, owned a bank. Another son, Hutomo – known as Tommy – built cars under special dispensation from the government that exempted him from tariffs and taxes, raising costs for his competitors by a 60 per cent. Tommy also controlled the sugar, paper, cement and flour industries.

The World Bank believes that as much as 30 per cent of the money lent to Indonesia disappeared without a trace, most of it going into the private banking accounts of the Suharto family and their chums. Forbes magazine estimates the family is worth $16 billion. The CIA says $40 billion.

It was much the same story with Mobuto Sese Seko, the last of Africa's old-time potentates and the ruler of Zaire. He'd run the country into the ground with an iron hand for three decades and, during that time, acquired a personal fortune worth $5 billion. Said to be the only world leader who could pay off his country's national debt from his own pocket, Mobuto's style was to treat the national treasury as his own bank account. When the US sent him $1.4 million to help his troops fight a civil war, he simply pocketed the entire amount. Despite his enormous wealth and Zaire's huge natural resources, he never seemed especially troubled by the fact that his country was the fifth poorest in Africa. Nor did it seem to bother him that one out of every six children in Zaire died before the age of five from malnutrition. His money disappeared into private banking.

One of the dominant institutions in private banking throughout this period was Citibank. Under Walter Wriston's chairmanship, capital flight became the bank's single most profitable business. Citi set up outposts – they called it International Private Banking (IPB) – in various countries specifically to bring in new business. Wriston emphasized Citi's role in the Third World and his successor, John Reed, was Argentine born and innately understood Latin America. So Citi easily took the lead.

But competition for the Latin American market was rough and aggressive. Chase and Swiss Banking Corp were players there, too, as were UBS, Bank of Boston and Bankers Trust. American Express Bank got into the private banking game in Panama, then expanded to Miami – by then fast becoming the financial capital of Latin America – and also opened in London, Paris, Geneva, and Singapore. Brokers rushed in, as well. Merrill Lynch International, Shearson, Bear Stearns, E.F. Hutton, Bache, Morgan Stanley, First Boston, and Goldman Sachs all became private bankers to some degree. Not to be left out, Lloyds, Marine Midland, Natwest, Royal Bank of Canada, Bank of Montreal, Deutsch Sudamerikanische – everybody jumped on this bandwagon. By 1986, the world's top 12 banks had grabbed 40 per cent of the capital flight market. The top 50 controlled 75 per cent.

Mexico quickly became a significant battleground. In 1988, Harvard-educated Carlos Salinas de Gotari was elected President. Four years later, Mexican billionaire Carlos Hank Rhon – a Citibank IPB client – introduced his private banker to his friend Raul Salinas, the President's brother. That private banker was Cuban born, Amelia Grovas Elliott, known to everyone as Amy. A native Spanish speaker, she was IPB's lead officer in New York for the bank's business in Mexico.

Interestingly enough, a couple of years later, Elliott would be called as a witness in the Texas money laundering trial of an American Express banker who'd laundered funds for Mexican trafficker Juan Garcia Abrego. At the time, she didn't have a clue that Raul Salinas was tied into this. Nor could she guess that Abrego was the source of some the Salinas' funds that she was helping to hide in Switzerland and the Caymans. During that trial, Elliott asked her how she saw her job. She responded, 'Private banking is the area of the bank that deals with clients with more money than the general public, that does it on a more white gloved kind of environment.'

A white gloved environment was exactly what she provided for Salinas. IPB set him up with accounts in New York, London and Switzerland which, in and of itself, would not otherwise have been suspect. But the way Elliott did it and the amount of money that went through the bank – $87 million, most of it in Mexican cashier's checks – should have raised very loud alarm bells at Citi. That they didn't, made the case noteworthy.

To begin with, Elliott listed Raul Salinas as 'Confidential Client #2'. Carlos Hank Rhon was already CC-#1. IPB then opened five accounts for CC-#2 in New York. Another account, in the name of a shell company, was opened at the bank's trust company in Switzerland. The account itself was called Bonapart. Cititrust Cayman Islands then formed a shell called Trocca which was listed as the owner of all CC-#2's private bank accounts. Three additional shells were listed as Trocca's shareholders and three more shells were listed as Trocca's board of directors. A Trocca account was also opened at IPB London.

The name Salinas was deliberately omitted from all IPB files, and never appeared in connection with anything. The one piece of paper that showed Raul Salinas was the beneficial owner of Trocca, and therefore all of this money, was purposely kept in the Caymans, where bank secrecy laws forbid anyone from divulging its existence and no foreign country could subpoena it.

IPB loaned CC-#2 some $3 million which they invested for him. They also gave him credit cards for his accounts in the names of the shells so that whatever charges he made would never be associated with him directly, or ever appear in Mexico, thus allowing him to use his money without paying taxes on it. Furthermore, IPB helped obscure any money trails by moving some funds deposited by CC-#2 through 'concentration accounts'.

That's one of the tricks of private banking.

Sometimes called 'settlement accounts', they're temporary homes for money without a home, monies that are waiting to be claimed or monies that have not yet been properly designated to an account. For example, funds arrive for J. Smith with the account number 12345, and someone realizes that while there is a client named J. Smith, his account number is 54321. That money is left in a concentration account until the confusion over J. Smith's money is straightened out. By putting CC-#2's money through the concentration account, Citi allowed it to co-mingle with other funds, clouding the money trails both inbound and outbound. Since then, Citi has prohibited the use of concentration accounts for client transactions. But other private banks still regularly use them.

What no one at Citi realized when Carlos Hank Rhon brought Raul Salinas to the bank, was that the client they were taking was carrying a lot of baggage. Salinas led Elliott and her bosses to believe that the bulk of his money came from the sale of his construction company and family wealth. In truth, it came from Abrego, and also from political corruption during the Salinas presidency. IPB had accepted Raul as a client without bothering to investigate his background or his financial situation. Elliott also waived the requirement for several references, accepting the word of Carlos Hank Rhon that Raul Salinas was who he said he was. The initial $2 million deposit that opened his account did not come from him. It was transferred from one of Carlos Hank Rhon's accounts, on the grounds that Hank Rhon owed Salinas the money for a deal that hadn't gone through. So IPB violated its own rules right from the start by not knowing its customer or the source of his funds. Had IPB done the due diligence that Citi normally should have required, the bank would never have taken Salinas as a client, and never wound up being associated with a murderer.

At the time of Carlos Salinas de Gotari's election as President of Mexico, Francisco Ruiz Massieu was secretary-general of the country's ruling Institutional Revolutionary Party. But he was no fan of the Salinas family and at one point he posed a real threat to Carlos's political career. In turn, Raul understood, that threatened his own livelihood. So Raul did what any loving brother would do – he assassinated Ruiz Massieu.

He got away with it for several years, but justice finally caught up with him once his brother left office in 1994. An investigation was opened into the Ruiz murder and in February 1995, Raul was arrested for it. The next day, an officer at IPB London suggested that they should quickly move Salinas' $20 million out of the country and into Switzerland so that law enforcement couldn't find it. When it was decided that they couldn't manage it without leaving a money trail, IPB decided to cover its own butt and call in Salinas' $3 million loan.

Towards the end of that year, Raul's wife Paulina Castanon left Mexico for Switzerland to withdraw $84 million from one of Raul's accounts at Banque Pictet where it was deposited under the false name, Juan Guillermo Gomez Gutierrez. The Swiss arrested her. At one point, the officer who interrogated her said he couldn't understand why she tried to take $84 million, which attracted attention. He asked, 'why didn't you just take out a little bit every time?' She answered, 'That's what I was doing.'

The Swiss froze that account and others in six cantons that they believed were owned by Raul. The total came to $132 million, including $27 million at IPB Switzerland. The investigators also located the $20 million in London. Raul was found guilty of Ruiz's murder and is currently in prison. Carlos Salinas de Gotari left Mexico for exile in Ireland. Which is where the Salinas family saga ends. But for IPB – which, over a four-year period, earned around $2 million on the Salinas account – worse was yet to come.

This client's name was Asif Ali Zardari. A Pakistani legislator and former government official, Zardari also happened to have been married to Pakistan's Prime Minister, Benazir Bhutto.

Ignoring the fact that Bhutto had been dismissed as PM in 1990 for alleged corruption – she was re-elected in 1993 and would be dismissed a second time in 1996 – and also ignoring the fact that Zardari himself had spent more than a year in jail on charges of corruption, IPB never-theless opened three private accounts for him in Switzerland, and allowed him to maintain one in Dubai, with an initial deposit of $18 million. Just as they had for Salinas, IPB formed shells for Zardari through which he could move money, in this instance basing two of them in the British Virgin Islands. Using those shells, over the next three years, Zardari laundered $10 million in kickbacks on a gold scheme he was running.

The government of Pakistan finally shut Zardari down, indicting him and his wife. A Swiss court then froze his accounts and indicted him for money laundering. A court in Pakistan then convicted him of accepting the kickbacks.

Citicorp Chairman, John Reed, summed up the Zardari business for his board of directors, by saying, 'I do not yet understand the facts but I am inclined to think that we made a mistake.'

More mistakes were to follow.

El Hadj Omar Bongo had been Gabon's President since 1967. A former public servant who'd never earned more than a few thousand dollars, Bongo was taken on by IPB as a client in 1970, opening his first account with them in Bahrain, making an initial deposit of $52 million. IPB subsequently opened accounts for Bongo and members of his family in London, Paris, Luxembourg, Switzerland, Jersey, Bahrain and New York. And while Gabon is the richest country in sub-Sahara Africa, with a per capita GDP of $6300, Bongo's Citibank private bank accounts held as much as $130 million. Following the usual pattern, IPB established shell companies in the Bahamas and gave Bongo a coded account name. They loaned him $50 million, issued credit cards to him and his family and helped invest his money for him. His fees at IPB were running over $1 million a year. At no point did Bongo ever give IPB a clear explanation of where his funds came from. Although it was later discovered that IPB listed Bongo's wealth as coming from government funds.

In spring 1997, allegations began circulating that Bongo was being investigated by French authorities in conjunction with a corruption scandal at the French oil company, Elf Aquitaine. Certain officers at Elf were believed to have bribed certain officials in Gabon. The Swiss authorities responded to a French request to freeze bank accounts, and some of them included funds belonging to Bongo. A Swiss court reportedly described Bongo as, 'The head of an association of criminals'. The case is still ongoing.

The Office of the Comptroller of the Currency in Washington DC was also unhappy about Bongo holding accounts with Citibank and wanted to know more about the source of his funds. Explanations were slow in forthcoming but when the accounts came up for regular review, IPB decided they would close them. The official reason they came up with was that the accounts had caused too many questions to be asked, required too much paperwork and had incurred too many incremental costs.

A more believable excuse might have been that someone at IPB was suddenly afraid of getting caught. Still, closing accounts is unusual in the private banking industry, where business as usual means doing whatever you have to in order to keep clients.

It was business as usual for IPB when Nigeria's General Abacha showed up with government funds in his pocket.

A career soldier and civil servant all his life, in 1988 Abacha had dispatched his oldest sons, Ibrahim and Mohammed to begin a relationship with IPB New York. A shell was created, called Morgan Procurement, and three accounts were opened in code names. Among them were Gelsobella for the account in New York and Navarrio for the account in London.

Oddly, the IPB 'relationship manager' who handled the accounts later claimed that he didn't have any idea that Ibrahim and Mohammed were related to General Abacha – a man recognized on the world stage for his audacious brutality – and wouldn't become aware of that fact for nearly three years. It was only after the Abacha family relationship with IPB ended that documentation came to light suggesting that at least one IPB officer knew who his clients were. The bank's paperwork read: 'Father of Ibrahim and Mohammed, General Sani Abacha, is the current military ruler of Nigeria, where there is a lot of corruption.'

By then, Abacha had dissolved all political parties in Nigeria, forbidden demonstrations against the new military regime, put in place draconian media censorship and locked up a lot of people who'd opposed him. But instead of cancelling the account, the Abachas remained IPB clients for 11 years and moved more than $110 million through accounts in New York, London and Jersey.

It must be said that Citibank was not the Abachas only bank. Twenty different banks in Switzerland held more than 140 Abacha accounts. A substantial portion of the funds located there arrived after the 1998 Swiss money laundering codes were put into law. Those codes had been held up to the rest of the world by the Swiss themselves as positive proof that the bad old days of dirty money were over, that money stolen by dictators was no longer welcome in Switzerland.

Sani Abacha died in June 1998, apparently of a heart attack. He was 54. A best-estimate has it that he stole $4.3 billion, some $2.3 billion of it directly from the national treasury. The remaining two billion came in equal halves from contracts that he put through his own shell companies and bribes from foreign contractors. Shortly after his death, his widow Mariam was stopped at Lagos airport trying to leave for Saudi Arabia carrying 38 suitcases filled with foreign currency. Reports vary on the amount involved, ranging from $50 million–$100 million. She said she was going to the Hajj.

Around the same time, Mohammed Abacha contacted IPB in London and asked that $39 million held in his account there be sent to three different accounts outside the UK. But that money was on time deposit and wouldn't come due for another two weeks. Mohammed clearly sensed the urgency of the matter and begged Citibank London to find a way around the time lock. IPB responded favourably by offering Mohammed an interest free overdraft of $39 million. IPB had it secured against the money on deposit, and Mohammed Abacha got his $39 million out of the country. Unfortunately for him, when Mohammed returned home he was arrested and charged with murder in connection with the death of the wife of one of his father's political opponents. He was promptly locked up.

The man who succeeded Sani Abacha, General Abdulsalami Abubakar, now went to all of his predecessor's cronies and demanded that they return whatever money they'd got from him. He collected $770 million and confiscated some property. He made good on his promise to call elections and another former general, Olusegun Obasanjo – who'd been a political prisoner under Abacha – became president in May 1999. It was Obasanjo who intensified the international efforts to reclaim Abacha money.

By then, Credit Suisse Private Banking had discovered Abacha accounts holding $232 million. The Swiss Federal Banking Commission (SFBC) ordered a search of all banks in the country and in October put a freeze on Abacha accounts at five other banks.

In January 2000, the Swiss police announced that a total of $645 million had now been identified and frozen. Although a Swiss judge would later unblock $115 million of that. Six banks were reprimanded by the SFBC for serious omissions and individual failures in handling the Abacha accounts. Another six were castigated for discernible weaknesses in their controls. And six Swiss bank personnel were actually convicted for money laundering and other offences over the Abacha money. By sheer coincidence, the gnomes at UBS suddenly discovered they too were holding Abacha accounts funds. And another $60 million was frozen there.

Authorities in Luxembourg froze $670 million in eight separate accounts for seven offshore shell companies that the Abacha brothers held in that country. Authorities in Liechtenstein froze $109 million sitting in one shell company account and another DM100 million in another.

The Nigerians had turned to the UK for help but no banks in Britain or Jersey seemed particularly anxious to co-operate. When asked to freeze accounts, they refused on the grounds that no criminal proceedings were underway in Nigeria. However, in Spring 2001, Britain's Financial Service's Authority (FSA) announced the discovery of $300 million sitting in 42 Abacha accounts held in 23 different banks. The turnover of these accounts for the period 1996–2000 was nearly £1 billion (then about $1.3 billion). But instead of pressing for prosecution against the banks and bankers in violation of UK money laundering laws – if nothing else, they were dealing in stolen funds – the FSA suffered an enormous loss in credibility by simply slapping the wrists of 15 banks for 'significant weaknesses' in money laundering controls.

In July 2002, Nigeria's Supreme Court ruled there was insufficient evidence to prosecute Mohammed on the murder charge, leaving him still facing 111 counts of laundering and corruption. While the court decision mystified some people, President Olusegun Obasanjo ordered negotiations to begin with the Abacha family for the return of Nigeria's money.

The two sides worked out a deal, brokered by the Swiss, wherein the Abachas agreed to hand back $1.35 billion in exchange for the government agreeing to free Mohammed from the cell where he'd been for the past three years. Under the terms of the agreement, the Abacha family would be permitted to keep around $100 million, which they somehow convinced the Swiss they'd acquired prior to Sani Abacha taking over as President. That a career soldier and public servant could amass such a fortune legally belies belief. But the Swiss fell for it and Obasanjo agreed the deal, hoping to put the matter behind his government. When Mohammed agreed to the settlement, Obasanjo ordered

him released. As soon as he got out, Mohammed denied agreeing to
return the family's billion and the settlement collapsed.

There is a PS to the Citibank story.

Shoddy stewardship of IPB took its toll. Careers were ruined and
reputations suffered, notable among them, Citi's.

Senator Carl Levin publicly chastized the IPB directors for getting
involved with the Abacha family. 'They weren't just asleep at the switch,
they were in a deep sleep on this one.'

Not everyone was quite so diplomatic. 'There was a time,' one prosecutor at the New York DA's office says, 'when you heard the words
money laundering and private banking and the first bank you thought
of was Citi.'

In 1998, Sandy Weill, then chairman of Travelers Group – a brokerage
and insurance conglomerate – orchestrated a $70 billion takeover of
Citigroup, then America's third largest bank. Among the many problems he inherited was Citi's reputation. But very early on in his stewardship of the company, Weill undertook a massive cleanup of private
banking, and ordered that controls and due diligence be severely tightened. His cleanout, and the changes he instituted of what he called 'the
old bank', were so dramatic that, these days, Weill's era at Citi is known
as 'the new bank'.

Heads of state and former heads of state – referred to as 'politically
exposed persons' (PEPs) – are no longer welcome and, in fact, openly
discouraged. Every client is now thoroughly vetted. Multi-layered
controls put in place to monitor business are, Citi believes, the most
severe in the industry.

One senior executive insists that, people with dirty money to hide
belong to the 'old bank'. So much so that, even if an extremely well
disguised potentate, trafficker, fraudster or laundrymen foolishly bothered to show up, a relationship with the 'new bank' would be 'virtually impossible'.

Ironically, that executive says, the change has not only affected the
people they deal with —radically so – it's boosted profits. He contends
that Citi's private banking makes more money these days by deliberately keeping the wrong customers out, than it did when the 'old bank'
deliberately went looking for them.

CHAPTER SIX

Caribbean Wash

The big hurricane destroyed those documents.
— Lester Bird, Prime Minister of Antigua and Barbuda

For a couple of years in the mid-1980s, a fellow in Boston named John Fitzgerald worked as the principal laundryman for a well organized marijuana smuggling cartel run by the Murray family.

The head of the clan was Joseph Murray, late of Charlestown, Massachusetts, an avid IRA supporter who was totally dedicated to the British defeat in Ulster. His Irish roots gave him a natural affiliation with another IRA sympathizer, James 'Whitey' Bulger, then leader of Boston's 'Winter Hill' crime gang. In turn, Bulger was connected to New England's most important La Cosa Nostra (LCN) family, the Patriarcas.

It was only a matter of time before the groups joined forces. When they did, the result was a archetypal drugs, arms and dirty money connection. The Murrays brought marijuana in on fishing boats. Bulger financed the purchases and took a share in the distribution. Drug money was mixed with monies collected by NORAID, the IRA-backed charity. It was washed through the Bank of Boston, then used to pay for illegal arms, supplied by the Patriarcas. The guns were shipped to the IRA on the same boats that brought in the drugs.

It was down to Fitzgerald to look after the Murrays' finances. He began with Halcyon Days Investments, an IBC registered in St Lucia. Using that, he opened a $3 million account at the Canadian Imperial Bank of Commerce. Two months later, he emptied the account and carried a cheque for the full amount to the Caymans where he deposited it in the Guinness and Mahon Bank. He topped up the account there and when it reached $5 million, he wired it out to a bank in Philadelphia. From there it went to Manufacturers Hanover Bank in New York, to the Bank of Bermuda and finally to the Swiss American Bank (SAB) of Antigua. The money was held in the names of two IBCs, Rosebud Investments and White Rose Investments, until

Fitzgerald transferred it out of the companies' accounts and into an SAB account in the name of a shell bank registered in Anguilla. By then, $5 million had became $7 million.

While this was going on, Murray got busted. He was sent away for ten years, served three, went home and got involved in a domestic dispute with his estranged wife. He lost the argument when she shot him.

Eventually, Fitzgerald was also arrested. Deciding that co-operation was better than a lifetime behind bars, he did whatever the Feds asked, which included signing over the $7 million in Antigua. Unfortunately, before anyone could get to the money, Fitzergerald died. It then took the Americans until 1994 to file the necessary paperwork in court. Once that was done, the Justice Department's Asset Forfeiture and Money Laundering Section wrote to the appropriate office in Antigua effectively saying, please send us our money. But no one in Antigua was anxious to do that. It took two years before the Antiguans happened to mention that, just before the American request was received, SAB had transferred $5 million to a government account. The bank then wrote off the remaining $2 million against fees incurred. Regretfully, came the Antiguan lament, nothing's left.

Several stern 'give us back our money' demands followed, all to no avail. Ultimately, the Justice Department sued Swiss American Bank, Swiss American National Bank, Swiss American Holding Company of Panama and the Bank of New York–Inter–Maritime Bank of Geneva, which had affiliations with Swiss American through a mysterious character named Bruce Rappaport. To press the case, certain documents were necessary, but repeated requests for them also fell on deaf ears. After all, it wasn't in Antigua's interest to hand over this money. So, the State Department dispatched Jon Winer to Antigua to collect it. He was, at the time, Deputy Assistant Secretary for International Law Enforcement Affairs. As such, he got all the way up to the Prime Minister.

Winer explained the case to Lester Bird, and politely reminded the PM, it's our money and we want it back, so please give us the documents.

That's when Bird asked if he'd heard about the big hurricane.

Winer didn't understand and asked what big hurricane?

Bird explained that there'd been a big hurricane in the Caribbean the previous week and bank records had been destroyed.

Winer wondered if a bank had been destroyed.

No, Bird told him, 'The big hurricane destroyed those documents.'

Winer was dumbfounded. 'You're telling me, there was a big hurricane which destroyed the records pertaining to a single account? Everybody else's accounts are fine, except this one? A big hurricane destroyed the documents we want? Just those documents?'

And the Americans never got their money.

The twin island nation of Antigua and Barbuda was first visited by Christopher Columbus in 1493. Ruled briefly by the Spanish, then the French, it became a British colony in 1632.

The creation of a 13-member legislative body in 1951 was the first step towards independence, and brought to power a local union activist named Vere Cornwall Bird. As first minister, he negotiated increased autonomy in 1959 and renegotiated for more autonomy in 1967. Although he was unseated by the opposition in 1971, he returned to power five years later, and became Antigua's first prime minister on independence in 1981. He ruled as the last of the great old-style Caribbean autocrats until 1994, when he stepped down and his son Lester succeeded him.

The year following independence, Antigua passed the International Business Corporation Act, turning itself into an offshore financial centre. It allowed the creation of IBCs, offshore banks, trust and insurance companies, and gave them a 50 year tax exempt status. It also gave the anonymous owners free rein in just about anything they wanted to do. There were no capital requirements, no exchange controls and no statutory audit requirements.

For the payment of a fee, the government of Antigua was now in the business of selling licences to steal. And over the next decade and a half, they didn't even pretend that banks chartered there were legitimate. During the early to mid-1990s, at least a dozen Russian banks were licenced, many of which proved to be largely fraudulent. In just two years, 1994–6, Antigua authorized the formation of 27 offshore banks, four of them Russian-owned, one Ukrainian-owned. This at a time when the government was steadfastly denying that it was encouraging or otherwise tolerating money laundering.

Such claims had been falling on deaf ears in Washington and London for years, but decidedly came back to haunt Lester Bird when, in 1994, Antigua chartered the world's first cyberspace financial institution,

European Union Bank. Like Hanover Bank, and most of those Russian banks, EUB wound up on the scrapheap, making a joke out of Antigua's offshore financial services sector. After all, an offshore bank chartered to do business in cyberspace raises several questions: where is cyberspace?; and, which jurisdiction has the authority to investigate wrong doings there? What's more, the reported theft of the bank's assets were not, under laws then in force, a crime in Antigua.

The Bird government talked a good game about cleaning up the mess, but, if they did anything in direct response to the EUB scandal, it was merely to change the window dressing.

'It is not certain,' a United Nations panel determined, 'that there have been any fundamental changes. The authorities in Antigua have attempted to play down the European Union Bank case while also suggesting that they have taken measures to prevent future occurrence of this kind. What they have not explained adequately, however, is how a country with a population of between 65,000 and 70,000 can develop the capacity for adequate supervision of the myriad and complex financial services and institutions available on the island. Until there is such a capacity, the changes in Antigua will be merely cosmetic.'

A similar warning came from Washington attorney Jack Blum, a severe critic of the island's record on financial due diligence. When Antigua announced it was investigating the EUB affair, Blum reminded the world, 'The last time the government was involved in this kind of investigation – an investigation of weapons going to the Colombian drug cartels on an Antiguan end user certificate – no one was caught, no one was punished, and the American lawyer hired to do the investigation was never paid for his services. In short, do not expect much.'

Around the same time that EUB made headlines, Swiss American Bank of Antigua came under suspicion as part of the Bank of New York fiasco. That's the same Swiss American Bank that once held and then dispersed John Fitzgerald's $7 million worth of marijuana money.

That bank was founded by the Swiss-based entrepreneur, Bruce Rappaport. Owner of Antigua's influential West Indian Oil Company, he was once described by the *New York Times* as, 'A Swiss banker who has had brushes with governmental investigators.' Born in Haifa in 1923, Rappaport's name surfaced in the press during the Iran–Contra affair of the 1980s. He was said to have been linked to a $10 million payment from the Sultan of Brunei to Colonel Oliver North which North later insisted he never received. Rappaport sternly denied any involvement in the missing money. His name popped up again during the BCCI scandal over his alleged business relationship with a Middle Eastern shipping magnate who'd been financed by BCCI. Rappaport, who has never been charged or prosecuted for any crime, was a golfing partner of the late CIA director, William Casey. His friendship with the Bird family earned him the status of Antigua's honorary counsel to Russia.

When the BoNY scandal broke, Rappaport's name came up in connection with Inter-Maritime Bank in Switzerland which he'd owned and had sold, in part, to BoNY. A statement issued by his office denied any involvement in the BoNY-Russian relationship. It noted that BoNY had held a 28 per cent stake in Inter-Maritime since 1996 and that Rappaport, who at one point owned 8 per cent of BoNY, then held less than 5 per cent. His position in BoNY-InterMaritime was that of non-executive chairman. The statement emphasized that Rappaport did not refer clients to the bank, had never brought any business to BoNY, was not involved in the day-to-day affairs of the bank and had nothing to do with Russian money laundering. Rappaport insisted he had no personal or professional dealings with any of the people or any of the companies named in reports of the affair.

Three years later, the US House of Representative Banking Committee called hearings on the BoNY scandal. Among the people asked to testify — because the Committee believed he had 'material knowledge of these matters' — was Bruce Rappaport. A man who has spent most of his life arduously staying away from any sort of publicity, he declined.

Rappaport no longer has anything to do with Antigua's financial services sector. His holdings there — the offshore Swiss American Bank, the onshore Swiss American National Bank, and the Antigua International Trust — have all been sold to local interests. Confusing the issue, however, is that when his entities were licensed by Antigua, SAB and SANB were both owned by Swiss American Holding Company, a Panamanian company. Furthermore, Swiss American Holding Company appears to have been owned by a Bermuda IBC which in turn is owned by a charitable trust that is said to be controlled by Rappaport. So, he may no longer have nothing more to do with Antigua's financial sector or, perhaps, he does. This is not a place where total transparency is encouraged. Rappaport's Panamanian and Bermuda interests, sources in Antigua say, are Mr. Rappaport's own business and not related to anything in Antigua. He is no longer the island's honorary consul to Russia, and apparently hasn't been on the island in quite a while.

A US Senate report critical of Antigua and aware of Rappaport's interests, found that, 'Throughout their (Antigua's) history, these banks have been troubled by controversial leadership, questionable practices by bank officials, and accounts that were repositories of funds from major financial frauds and other illegal activities.'

Senate investigators went on to allege, 'Swiss American Banking Group has a history of involvement in controversial and questionable financial dealings and banking activities.' In addition to accounts that held funds from frauds and other illicit activities, those investigators reported Antigua's reluctance to co-operate with law enforcement looking to seize these proceeds of crime. 'More recently, SAB has serviced accounts that are related to Internet gambling, an activity that is vulnerable to money laundering.'

Despite such accusations, and a series of scandals that mangled the island's reputation, the Bird government kept doing business as usual. For more than 50 years, their power has turned the twin islands into, what one critic describes as, 'a family estate'. They largely control the media and, through wealthy and loyal friends, have real power over many of the most important businesses in the country. Family members have survived claims of corruption, accusations of involvement in drug trafficking and a scandal involving covert gun shipments to the Cali cartel. Through it all, the prime minister has incessantly denied that Antigua does business with drug traffickers or money launderers. But the opposition party takes issue with that, in keeping with what opposition parties usually do. One Bird family political critic claimed, in the mid-1990s, that without narcodollars, the economy would be in trouble. The government maintains that wasn't true then, and is not true now.

Still, so much money has washed through Antigua over the years that whatever credibility the financial sector there lays claim to, in reality, most of it long ago went down the drain with the dirty water.

One man who found himself at the centre of the island's ruined reputation was William Cooper. A Californian who'd relocated there, he'd helped Rappaport organize Swiss American's interests by signing SAB's licence application as Vice-President of Rappaport's Panamanian holding company. A member of SAB's board of directors, Cooper was general manager of the banking group from 1981–1984.

In 1990, he turned up running American International Bank (AIB). Registered by him for some people in Florida, when the original owners decided they no longer needed or wanted the bank, Cooper purchased it. He capitalized the bank at the minimum required $1 million by forming a company called AMT. That company borrowed $1 million from AIB, allowing Cooper to use the $1 million in paid-up shares of AMT to back his bank. Next, he formed AMT Management, AMT Trust, and a company called Ship Registry Services, uniting them with the bank under the umbrella of American International Banking Group. Eventually he added American International Bank and Trust which was registered in Dominica.

Within five years, Cooper would claim, his banking group had 8,000 clients and held assets of $100 million. What really happened during those five years was that AIB laundered millions through correspondent accounts in the US. New clients were brought into the bank by way of a shell company, emphasizing confidentiality. The group also incorporated offshore banks for clients and AIB served as the correspondent for more than 30 of them, none of which had any physical presence anywhere. Included among the banks that AIB represented were Caribbean American Bank, Hanover Bank and Overseas Development Bank and Trust.

Cooper was able to link those banks and the fraudulent activities of their clients to AIB's own correspondents, among them: Jamaica Citizens Bank Ltd (now Union Bank of Jamaica) in Miami, the Toronto Dominion Bank in New York, Bank of America, Popular Bank of Florida (now BAC Florida Bank), Chase Manhattan Bank, Norwest Bank in Minnesota, and Barnett Bank in Florida. The banks Cooper formed also had correspondent relationships with Privat Kredit Bank in Switzerland, Toronto Dominion Bank in Canada, Midland Bank in Britain and Berenberg Bank in Germany. On top of that, AIB had a relationship with Antigua Overseas Bank, which in turn had correspondent accounts at Bank of America, Chase Manhattan Bank and Bank of New York.

He'd built himself a complex but very competent laundromat. At the same time, he ran a suspect investment scheme called 'The Forum'. Described by the SEC as a glorified chain letter, investors were lured in with the promise of huge returns on highly speculative investments, most of which never got off the ground. A lot of his investors' money was funnelled through Antigua to a highly suspect operator, then operating out of Panama, named Marc Harris.

An accountant by profession, the 25-year-old American-born Harris had his licence revoked in 1990 after he audited a mutual fund and failed to disclose that he both owned and ran it. He left the States shortly after that. Eight years later, his Harris Organization claimed to operate banks, insurance companies, a trust and a brokerage. Harris said he employed 150 people, was the largest offshore service provider in the world and managed over $1 billion in assets. Although, it appears that Harris never bothered to get proper licences for many of these services and was managing only around $40 million. At the same time, he was carrying huge liabilities.

In March 1998, articles published in the newsletter *Offshore Alert* accused Harris of stealing clients' funds, of laundering money and of being broke. Harris sued publisher/journalist David Marchant for libel, claiming damages of $30 million. The British born, Miami-based Marchant stood his ground. The trial took place in Miami, in July 1999. Harris did not appear, possibly fearing that his arrival in Florida would be met with subpoenas from the SEC, who'd already served two Harris employees with them. Harris lost the case, appealed and then lost the appeal. Three years later, Harris was evicted from his offices in Panama, supposedly for non-payment of rent. He left for Nicaragua where he changed the name of his business to avoid any association with his own reputation. That firm, Mitchell Astor Gilbert Trust, was registered on the island of Nevis, where the word 'trust' can be used in a company name even if it isn't a trust.

According to people who attended seminars Harris held for prospective clients looking to evade taxes, his plan was called 'The Octopus'. At the heart of it was a Panamanian shell. Branching out from there were a series of seemingly unrelated trading companies, banks, insurance companies, trusts and leasing firms registered throughout the offshore world. The sole purpose of those IBCs was to generate tax deductible expenses. The monies paid to them accumulated in the Panamanian shell. Secrecy laws in the various offshore jurisdictions made it impossible for anyone to link the various companies to the Panamanian shell and from there to the person evading taxes. Over an 18-month period, investigators estimate, the Forum-Cooper-AIB-Harris circuit moved $100 million for 30,000 clients through 1,600 banks and IBCs in the Bahamas, Antigua, Nevis,

Panama and St Vincent. In May 2003, Harris was arrested in Nicaragua and sent back to Miami when he today sits in jail awaiting trial on all sorts of charges, including fraud and money laundering.

While Harris was plying his trade in Latin America, Cooper was also at the centre of another money laundering scam, this one dubbed 'Risky Business' by the US Customs officers who investigated it.

Over a six year period, from 1991–1997, eight hardened criminals working in Florida, Canada and Britain – including a convicted murderer who'd once been sentenced to life in prison – duped more than 400 people around the world out of more than $60 million. Using advertisements in the *New York Times*, the *Wall Street Journal*, *USA Today* and the *International Herald Tribune*, the gang offered venture capital loans to finance businesses. Entrepreneurs, lawyers, doctors, sports' stars and entertainment figures – including singer Dionne Warwick and Star Trek's William Shatner – were lured into the scheme with the bait of seductively attractive interest rates. Warwick signed on and reportedly lost $100,000. Shatner wisely backed off.

Anyone answering the ads was invited to a series of interviews over the course of many months. By creating what appeared to be a selection process, the victims' desires to be chosen for the loan heightened. At each meeting, the 'executive' handling the matter was higher up the chain. Ostensibly, the meetings were to establish the victims' needs, to determine access to available funds and to set out a payment plan for the 'processing fees'. At each step, victims were told they were getting closer to obtaining their venture capital. By the time they reached the contract stage, they'd been so expertly set up that they willingly handed over cashier's cheques to settle the fees. Signed contracts set into motion the next stage. A clause obliged them to obtain a letter of credit or bank guarantee – ranging from $2 million-$20 million – which was required by the 'board of investors'.

Obviously, no bank would guarantee that kind of money without collateral. If the victims had enough collateral to raise that kind of money, then they wouldn't need to deal with these crooks. So, at the end of the deliberately brief period allowed for acquiring a bank guarantee – usually five to seven days – the victims would have to admit that they'd failed to raise the money. At that point, someone in the syndicate would explain how, regretably, they were now in breach of the contract, that the deal was cancelled and that their processing fee would be forfeited to cover expenses.

Some victims got angry and went away. Others believed the person they were dealing with when he said there might be a way around the problem. Those victims would then be introduced to various 'facilitators' and 'underwriters' – others gang members – who professed to be in a position to help them get the necessary guarantees. That, of course, entailed additional up front fees, usually $10,000–$35,000. When that inevitably run into problems, more facilitators and underwriters were brought in, incurring more fees. The most stubborn victims wound up paying as many as six fees, a few losing as much as $2 million.

Their money ended up in two shell banks in Antigua – Caribbean American Bank (CAB) and Caribbean International Bank (CIB) – both of which were formed by Cooper under the umbrella of AIB. At one point, Cooper was looking after as many as 16 such brass plate banks. The story is all the more perverse because shortly after Cooper set up CAB and CIB, Russian criminals arrived with funds to wash.

To accommodate his Risky Business clients, Cooper established shells for each of them, then issued gold Visa cards through Caribbean American in the names of those shells. That allowed the various gang members to spend their money freely, without otherwise being associated with it. One gang member, who ran up bills of $23,000 a month, used his gold Visa card to pay for plastic surgery, gambling junkets to the Bahamas and lingerie from Victoria's Secret. He also bought a car for a woman he'd met the night before in the Bahamas.

In March 1998, a federal grand jury in Gainsville, Florida indicted eight people for their part in Risky Business. Customs officers arrested members of the gang and successfully froze several accounts at Caribbean American. In a last ditch effort to save his stake, one member of the group tried to hire lawyer Vere Bird, Jr, the prime minister's brother. According to court records, the gang member offered Bird Jr 20 per cent of the frozen funds if he could unfreeze them. Bird Jr backed away from the case when that gang member was arrested.

Within three years, everyone associated with Risky Business was doing time in a federal penitentiary. Except Cooper. He was alive and well and safe in Antigua. The Americans tried to extradite him but Cooper denied involvement in the matter and fought extradition. By this time he was a citizen of Antigua, which meant that in order for the Americans to get him onto a plane, his crime in the States had to be a crime in Antigua, too. Local attorneys acting for the Americans tried various tactics, only to fail. The court ruled that based on the

Extradition Treaty with the US signed in 1996, the crime of money laundering – for which Cooper stands charged in the States – was not a crime in Antigua at the time of the requested extradition. Antigua's Parliament only outlawed money laundering in 1998.

Before they can resubmit the extradition request, the Americans need to link Cooper to an offence recognized by the Antiguans during a specific time period. Supposedly to help them do that, in early 2003, Antigua's director of public prosecutions arranged to have 'certain documents' handed to the Americans and invited them to sit down with Antigua's attorney general to review what the islanders now recognize as, 'the Cooper problem'.

Halfway through Bill Clinton's second term, the idea began to brew that new anti-money laundering banking regulations were necessary.

Specifically, the Federal Reserve Board and the Office of the Comptroller of the Currency wanted to impose much stiffer 'know your customer' (KYC) requirements. They were looking to oblige banks to categorize customers and report irregular activities. For example, anyone who did not normally make large cash deposits or withdrawals would be reported if they did; anyone who'd never wired money overseas, would be asked for an explanation if they attempted to. Proponents argued the regulations were a necessary step in keeping dirty money out of the US financial system. Opponents said such regulations would add to the cost of doing banking while, at the same time, would turn financial institutions into policemen.

Battle lines were drawn in Congress and the powerful Senate Banking Committee, led by Texas Republican Phil Gramm, promised that the new regulations would never get past him.

Around the same time, Representative Jim Leach, a fairly moderate Republican from Iowa who oversaw the House Banking Committee, co-sponsored the 'Money Laundering and Financial Crimes Strategy Act'. It gave the president the authority to implement a national strategy to combat money laundering and related financial crimes. The House passed it and, because it was fairly benign, the Senate passed it too. On the back of that, Leach championed the House version of a much stricter anti-money laundering law. His intention was to put the trafficking of dirty money into the same league as the trafficking of drugs. One result would have been to make it almost impossible for US banks to deal with offshore havens where secrecy was one of the products on sale.

The offshore world could not afford to let this happen, so their lapdog in the Senate – Gramm – was dispatched to the warpath. That he's from Texas is no coincidence. The most vociferous critics of legislation aimed at penalizing banks for handling dirty money have, traditionally, come from George W. Bush's home state. Banks there have, for years, been a favourite repository for Mexican fortunes, both clean and dirty. Texas money and Texas mouthpieces were not going to allow some northerner from Iowa to change that.

Representative Ron Paul, another Texas Republican – and, like Gramm, a full-fledged stooge of the Texas banking lobby – rallied the dissenters with: 'This is basically twenty-first century gunboat diplomacy. Because they're never going to use it against a major trading partner, they're only going to pick on small states.'

His opposition was backed up by words and money from several concerned parties, including officers and directors of two powerful border banks – the International Bank of Commerce of Laredo and the Laredo National Bank – plus the Stanford Financial Group, a $14 billion Houston-based company with serious interests in Antigua.

The CEO of Stanford Financial is R. Allen Stanford, a dual national holding American and Antiguan passports. He owns the onshore Bank of Antigua and the offshore Stanford International Bank, which is the country's largest offshore bank. He also owns a local newspaper, a local airline and the island's largest property development company.

According to the watchdog group, Public Citizen, Stanford Financial, which had never made a federal campaign contribution prior to this, now dumped money into political action groups on both sides of the aisle. Between February 2000 and June 2001, Stanford gave Republicans $208,000 and Democrats $145,000. But he didn't stop there. As is his right, another $95,000 was sent to the political action committees (PACs) of Democrat Senate Majority Leader Tom Daschle, Democrat House Caucus Chairman Martin Frost, and Republican Senate Minority Leader – and fellow Texan – Trent Lott. That Stanford opposed these bills is understandable, as they would have severely damaged Antigua's ability to operate as a tax haven.

At no time has anyone suggested that any of this is unlawful. It is not. Stanford's contributions are perfectly within his rights as a citizen. Anyway, Stanford was hardly alone. The Texas banking lobby had no intention of letting this bill pass, and soft money poured in to stop it. Some of the money came 'laundered' through the lobby from offshore jurisdictions intent on protecting their own interests. British and Canadian banks also contributed. As did major US financial institutions with offshore interests, such as J.P. Morgan Chase, which has a big presence in Texas and a strong lobbying arm on Capital Hill.

In the end, Gramm did as he was told. He shamelessly refused to take up the Senate version of the bill, which eradicated any chance of it becoming law. There was some talk of trying to get a full House vote on the bill, which would have put pressure on Gramm to take it up again, but Gramm and his Texas Republican cronies – Dick Armey and Tom DeLay – made certain that never happened. Later, Gramm would, disgracefully, brag that he'd killed it, 'Single handedly'.

What the public didn't realize at the time, was that Gramm might have had a hidden agenda through connections to Enron, the Texas energy company now in bankruptcy. The public did not yet know the extent to which Enron was dependent on the offshore world to defraud investors and the IRS; that Enron was pouring money into this fight, too; or that Phil Gramm's wife, Wendy, had been a member of Enron's board of directors for eight years.

She sat on the very same Audit and Compliance Committee that was supposed to have exercised oversight of Enron's offshore frauds. Public Citizen reports that Wendy Gramm earned between $915,000 and $1.8 million a year in salary, fees, dividends and stock options over an eight year period.

Her husband was the recipient of $97,350 in campaign and soft-money contributions from Enron from 1989–2001.

For 17 years, starting in 1982 when Antigua dove head first into the offshore business, the island's financial services industry was wildly unregulated. For three of those years in the 1990s, Allen Stanford held a seat on Antigua's financial services regulatory authority. From there, he could bolster the offshore sector against assaults by foreign tax authorities. Acutely concerned with the island's standing as a financial centre, there's no denying that he's worked hard to bring Antigua up to his version of world-class standards. But certain people close to Lester Bird clearly believed that they had too much to lose if the government cleaned up Antigua's dirty money industry and, in 1997, powerful forces inside Antigua passed amendments to the existing money laundering and company formation laws. The amendments effectively limited law enforcement's ability to police the sector, strengthened bank secrecy and impeded international co-operation.

Officials at the US Treasury chastised 'a prominent US offshore banker' for 'using financial and political clout' to take over the financial services regulatory agency.

Jon Winer, at the State Department, described the situation as, 'A leveraged buyout of Antiguan regulation by a private-sector person.'

The Americans had repeatedly warned Antigua that it would not tolerate an expansion of the country's haven status, but those amendments displayed Antigua's intention's to go its own way. After fruitless negotiations with Antigua, the Americans and the British issued official warnings to their own financial institutions to view with suspicion all transactions to, through and from Antigua, plus, transactions involving any of its nationals. Even the French, whose own Caribbean interests included Saint Martins – a centre of increasing transnational organized criminal activity – voiced concern about Antigua.

So did the G-8 Finance Ministers by convening the Financial Stability Forum (FSF) and inside that, the Working Group on Offshore Financial Centers. They divided the offshore world into three categories: Group I (deemed to be co-operative in anti-money laundering activities and well supervised) included Switzerland, Hong Kong, Luxembourg and the Channel Islands; Group II (potentially co-operative but with low quality supervision) featured Bahrain, Bermuda, Gibraltar, Malta and Monaco; Group III (non co-operative and with low quality supervision) took in Liechtenstein, Nauru, Niue, Vanuatu and most of the usual suspects in the Caribbean, including Antigua.

That was followed by an FATF review which named, and tried to shame, 15 jurisdictions that were to be considered non co-operative in the fight against money laundering. They were: the Bahamas, the Cayman Islands, the Cook Islands, Dominica, Israel, Lebanon, Liechtenstein, the Marshall Islands, Nauru, Niue, Panama, the Philippines, Russia, St Kitts and Nevis, and St Vincent and the Grenadines. Although Antigua escaped that list, FATF included 14 other jurisdictions under the heading of 'deficient': Belize, Bermuda, British Virgin Islands, Cyprus, Gibraltar, Guernsey, the Isle of Man, Jersey, Malta, Mauritius, Monaco, Samoa, St Lucia and Antigua.

Removal from the various lists required Antigua to implement 40 recommendations from the FATF, plus 19 recommendations from the FATF's regional offshoot, the Caribbean Financial Action Task Force

(CFATF). Combined, they outlined the role of a supervisory authority plus minimum standards for record keeping and co-operation with law enforcement. They helped to create an environment in which a serious attempt to deter money laundering can thrive. But fulfilling the recommendations, and getting serious about money laundering, are often two different things.

The world lined up against Antigua, limiting the island's options, and the Bird government had little choice but to give in. Legislation was proposed and passed, nullifying most of the objectionable amendments of the 1997 law. Banking licenses were revoked. Owners of IBCs were put on notice. Bilateral and multilateral co-operation in law enforcement was increased. And two new treaties – Extradition and Mutual Legal Assistance – were implemented with the United States.

Then came 9/11.

Within a month of the atrocities, no fewer than 30 nations conceded that it was time to get serious about the offshore world, at least in relation to terrorist funds. The Bush administration had already answered the call of the Texas banking lobby by announcing earlier that year that it would take a blind-eye approach to tax havens. But 9/11 had such profound effects on every aspect of life in the West, that Bush simply could not ignore certain offshore realities.

The greatest fear of every money laundering sink in the Caribbean was that, somehow, somewhere, Al-Qaeda money would pop up. Lester Bird didn't need to be reminded what would happen if it did, and chose to make a first strike. Within weeks of the terrorist attacks, he pushed through an anti-terrorism finance bill, making Antigua the first country to respond that way to 9/11. Using that law, Bird ordered every bank on the island to review the US and UK lists of suspected terrorist-related organizations and individuals. He warned that any bank making a false declaration would have its licence revoked and its principals sent to jail. When the reports came back, Bird was able to assure the Americans and the British that none of the listed terrorist-related organizations or individuals had a presence in Antigua.

The Americans responded by pointing out that charities and non-profit entities were still a problem, so Bird moved to close that loophole. In 2002, Antigua created a new office, the Financial Services Regulatory Commission (FSRC), with overall authority to regulate offshore banks, IBCs, insurance and trusts, plus Internet gambling.

Antigua insists that it's serious about cleaning up dirty money.

Though actual prosecutions are almost non-existent, the country has made at least one very public stand. They charged former Ukrainian Prime Minister, Pavlo Lazarenko, with money laundering, froze $83 million that he allegedly stashed in the offshore European Federal Credit Bank (Eurofed), ordered it forfeited, then shut down the bank.

Lazarenko, who'd served his country from 1996 to 1997, was accused by his own government of stealing $2 million and stripped of his parliamentary immunity. He fled to the States, hoping for political asylum. Instead, he got arrested on charges of laundering $114 million, of which $70 million was supposedly washed through Antigua. According to the indictments, the money came from bribery, kickbacks and illegal oil and gas sales. Ironically, these days, Eurofed's old website transfers automatically to an online casino.

That's an area where, despite their claims, Antigua still lacks credibility. They dove head first into Internet gaming, much the way they did with banks and IBCs all those years ago. Online casinos and sports betting have been placed in a virtual free trade zone. But where online casinos are concerned – as opposed to sports betting – there are serious doubts that any of them, worldwide, are legitimate.

Putting aside the obvious question – why would anyone in their right mind trust a roulette wheel that he can't see except on a PC? – some law enforcement officers who track these casinos suggest that none of them are legitimate. They say that, not only is there a 100 per cent possibility that they cheat by rigging games, there is an almost-equally high probability that any given online casino might be involved in some form of money laundering.

'I have maintained from day one,' says Detective Sergeant Dave Taylor of the Ontario Province Police in Canada, 'that Internet gambling is nothing but money laundering. There are some people who actually get on and play. But during numerous investigations, we've found that online casinos almost always lead to organized crime.'

A recognized expert on Internet gambling, Taylor has logged onto hundreds of online casino sites in an undercover capacity. He says, some are not set up to pay out, many don't have legitimate bank accounts, and some actually run their finances through convenience stores.

'We've watched money from street-level operations funnelled offshore, moved through the islands, then brought back as winnings. It's supposed to look like honest gambling, but we know full well that they've not established anything of the kind.'

It's not uncommon, Taylor says, for casinos to offer new players a credit as an incentive to sign on. Some of those credits can be as high as $500. But, he suggests, those credits can be just another form of laundering.

'What's to prevent them from creating 30,000 players? They can get lists of names from anywhere in the world. They buy a mass mailing list, or get credit card generators, and put down a name saying he's gambled $250 dollars. But that person never touched a computer and doesn't know that his name is being used. Or, they can get on a hacker's site, and within five minutes download lists of valid Visa and Mastercard numbers. They put them on a database of clients, credit/debit the cards on their database and move the money back and forth. Now the casino has a set of business records that shows all these people have played. It looks like a legitimate paper trail. What's a regulatory authority going to do, ask every name on the list whether or not he lost $250? I doubt it'.

He notes that every gambling licence he's ever investigated leads to a lawyer's office on some island. 'We have instances where one of the company's lawyers is the attorney general of the island. These groups connect to the islands simply to avoid jurisdictional problems. When they get found out, they jump to another island. They go to wherever they get the least hassle'.

Included in the list of islands he sees most often are Antigua, and St Kitts and Nevis. Australia and New Zealand also show up fairly frequently, as do Niue and Nauru. The more obscure the place, the more difficult it becomes to follow a money trail. A tortuous process, even at the best of time, it relies on Mutual Legal Assistance Treaties (MLATs) which depend, in large part, on the goodwill of any given jurisdiction.

'Typically,' Taylor explains, 'that can add three years to the process. Antigua and the Caymans are infamous. There are piles of MLATs waiting to be processed. We send an MLAT asking for help, and pray. We're never sure if, at the end of the day, we'll ever get anything back. In the meantime, the bad guys have switched banks and jurisdictions four times.'

In February 2003, the CFATF awarded Antigua a 'Grade A' rating for its anti-money laundering initiatives. The island had been lobbying for the upgrade for some time. It was earned, they say, because Antigua is now fully compliant with all the recommendations of the FATF and the CFATF.

Sir Ronald Sanders is Antigua's representative to the CFATF, a long-time friend of Lester Bird, and the government's High Commissioner to the UK. He is also the choirmaster in charge of singing the island's praise.

While the CFATF upgrade came out at a time when Sanders was Vice-Chairman of the group, and about to be named Chairman, he does not see a conflict of interest. 'Absolutely not. My taking over the chairmanship, in itself, should tell you something about the way in which the 30 countries which are members of it regard Antigua. Had they not thought that we were serious, I don't think I would have been elected to that position.'

Nor does he see fulfilment of the FATF and CFATF recommendations as mere window dressing. 'I don't think that's true. We've changed everything. You can't bring a dollar into Antigua and get it into a bank'.

All too well aware of Antigua's reputation – he corrects, 'former reputation' – Sanders says he was ashamed of accusations, like those levied in 1996 by *US News and World Report*. The magazine said Antigua was a unique money laundering sink, and noted that no other jurisdiction extended as warm a welcome to dirty money, having constructed a virtually unregulated banking industry built on secrecy and no reporting requirements. But Sanders insists, 'The situation has changed radically. The island is on its way to becoming spotlessly clean. I'm not saying we've got all the answers, but we are trying every day to do better.'

Significantly, bearer share IBCs are no longer for sale. The idea that a company belonged to whoever physically possessed the share certificates was a concept that dated back to an era in European history when religious doctrine dictated that discretion in financial affairs was virtuous. In modern finance, there is absolutely no legitimate use for bearer shares. The only reason anyone ever bought a bearer share IBC was to keep beneficial ownership of the IBC from being discovered.

Antigua outlawed them, in keeping with the trend throughout the offshore world. They've been banned by: the Bahamas (where there are around 47,000 IBCs), Jersey (30,000) and Hong Kong (500,000). The jurisdictions which still allowed them as of 2003 were: Panama (370,000), Liechtenstein (75,000) and Luxembourg (68,000).

The Isle of Man (24,300) announced its intention to abolish bearer shares, while the Caymans (45,000) and BVI (360,000) came up with a way to 'immobilize' them. They require bearer shares to be held by a registered third party. Ownership can be transferred, but not secretly. Gibraltar (8,300) also went with the flow, allowing bearer shares to be issued, but requiring the beneficial owner to be registered. The shares must then be deposited in a Gibraltar bank. Transfer of ownership cannot occur without permission from Gibraltar's Financial and Development Secretary, effectively nullifying any advantages.

In Antigua, where bearer shares were involved in just about every money laundering scandal the island ever saw, anyone purchasing an IBC now must register the names and addresses of the beneficial owners and directors with the authorities.

But like so many things in Antigua's history of money laundering, what you see is not always what you get.

One problem lies in the 13,500 IBCs already licensed. Beneficial owners and directors were required by law to register their names. Any IBC not compliant – perhaps because the beneficial owner doesn't want his identity known – has been struck off. But the actual number of cancelled licences is small. For the remaining IBCs, there's nothing more than hope that the beneficial owners and directors have complied honestly. If a scandal breaks and the registered names are not real, the law provides for criminal charges. But, by that time, the crooks will be long gone and Antigua will never knew who they were.

It's different with bank accounts. Antigua now provides that banks must know the true identity of account holders, must verify the nature of the account holder's business and must identify the source of the account holder's funds. Because the banks' directors are known, if the banks don't fully comply, the directors will pay the price. And where there were once nearly 60 banks on the island, there are now only 15.

'The number has been so severely reduced,' Sanders says, 'because the government closed some and others simply could not meet the new criteria, which includes physical presence. Banks must now have an address, books and records at the address, and mind and management there, as well. The people who are managing the operation have to be physically present there.'

Could Hanover or EUB happen again? Sanders hopes not. 'Anything is possible in any jurisdiction, but if it happens now in Antigua, people go to jail.'

That would include, he says, Mr Cooper. 'Certainly. And anybody else who operates in that way.'

He acknowledges that the country got itself into a mess, and puts it down to laxity. 'When offshore banking services began in Antigua, there was no real regulation. There was one man who was the supervisory authority. People applied to him and he issued a licence. In fact issuing licences was all he did. Nothing changed until people like me began to say, we've got to make sure that this reputation which we've earned doesn't continue.'

Internet gambling, however, is another problem that hasn't gone away. Besides being illegal in the United States, and the subject of legislation that could seriously affect all offshore jurisdictions offering online casinos, there is the matter of washing dirty money through the sites.

Here, Sanders takes the standard view. 'Our regulations on Internet gambling are stronger than anybody else's in the world. That's a fact.'

Granted, where there used to be more than 100 registered Internet gambling sites operating out of Antigua, by mid-2003 there were only 32. But saying you are policing an industry that is, at best, mostly dishonest, and actually being able to police it – especially when that industry only exists in cyberspace – are two different things. Antigua already went down that route with EUB.

Perhaps, not surprisingly, Sanders doesn't see it that way. He says Antigua is taking a long-term view. 'I'm for putting an end to money laundering in any form that it exists. I'm for Antigua's reputation being strong. We are cleaning up our act, not because of what the offshore sector is worth today, but what it could be worth.'

What the offshore sector is worth to today is easily calculable. The 15 banks pay Antigua a licence fee of $15,000. That's $225,000. The 13,500 IBCs pay $300. That's $4.05 million. Double that for the trusts, insurance companies and online gaming sites, and you're in the neighbourhood of $10 million. Most of that, he notes, goes to the cost of regulation.

'So what else do we get? Employment. Rental of buildings? After that, you're scratching. But, my contention has always been that there is more money to be made by building it legitimately. You cannot sustain employment, or your country's development, or anything on dirty money. It may come for a time, it may have a boom, but after that it's going to bust, and when it busts you're going to have people unemployed. You're going to have revenue disappear. Your economy is going to sink. It's not sustainable. The only thing that is sustainable is honest, clean, hard-working money. And that is what Antigua must go after.'

At the time Sanders made those remarks in 2003, Antigua was still on the US State Department list as, 'A Jurisdictions of Primary Concern' for money laundering. That assessment was not based on co-operation in the fight against money laundering, but rather, on an evaluation of financial institutions engaging in 'transactions involving significant amounts of proceeds from serious crime'.

So, whatever Antigua's good intentions, it takes more than that to put an end to dirty money.

The nation may be in line with FATF and CFATF recommendations, but it has also turned itself into a free-trade zone of deception on the Internet.

In this case, full compliance with those recommendations might do little more than to prove the old adage, you can indeed fool some of the people some of the time.

CHAPTER SEVEN

Smoke and Mirrors

Only the little people pay taxes
– Leona Helmsley, tax felon

Some 27 miles southwest of Antigua, the island of Montserrat is 12 miles long, 7 miles wide and, suffers from the nasty temper of an active volcano.

In July 1995, Soufriere Hills erupted for the first time in recorded history. Seismic activity continued for several years, culminating in 1997 in a major disaster. Entire villages were destroyed, plumes of ash reached heights of 40,000 feet and nearly 80 per cent of the buildings in the capital city of Plymouth were destroyed or badly damaged. More than 6,000 people – out of a total population of 10,000 – fled the island. Many never bothered to return.

Before the volcano erupted, Montserrat boasted a gaggle of 350 banks. Some of them had vaguely familiar names – Prudential Bank and Trust, Deutsche Bank (Suisse), Chase Overseas – and there was even one called World Bank. Of course, none of them had walls or a roof. They were merely brass plaques on the door of some company formation agent. Although the owner of one called Zurich Overseas bragged that his bank did have a physical presence, of sorts. He held court every day at a local bar.

Such was the demand for banks on the island that a thriving cottage industry of wholesalers developed. They advertised Montserrat as a 'bullet proof jurisdiction', offering folks the chance to, 'make exorbitant profits absolutely legally'. They issued credit cards, 'in the name of the offshore bank, to give you the peace of mind you want'. And invited clients to, 'place your assets out of reach of greedy tax collectors and governments, IRS, FBI, CIA, ex-wives, vicious relatives or anyone wishing you bad. Your own offshore bank will have various overseas properties, investments and assets while you are maintaining your anonymity'.

For an additional fee, they provided a mail-drop address in major cities to make your offshore bank appear to be domiciled onshore in say, London or Hong Kong, giving your bank an added patina of respectability.

Not that anybody on Montserrat cared who you were or what you did with your bank. It was yours to play with, as long as you submitted what looked like a legitimate business plan – wholesalers provided a template where you merely filled in the blanks – pretended that you were capitalized at $500,000, could came up with a formation fee of $3,000, and paid the annual fee of $8,000. Once you did that, as one wholesaler boasted, 'You have arrived at the invisible world where secrecy, privacy and freedom are of the greatest concern.'

The secrecy, privacy and freedom of Montserrat were what Panamanian laundrymen wanted when they came ashore to wash funds for the drug cartels and Manuel Noriega. Same thing for Israeli Mossad agents in the mid-1980s who used their bank on that island to launder money in a weapons deal with Colombian drug barons. Montserrat was also the island of choice of Robert Graven. He called himself Brother Eduardo of the Circles of Light Church, and somehow convinced 30,000 North Americans to send $3 million to the island's First American Bank to help him feed the poor. When it turned out that he was the only poor guy being fed, the FBI convicted him of fraud.

The situation eventually got so out of control on Montserrat that Britain could no longer delude itself into thinking problems didn't exist. Parliament was forced into the unprecedented step of amending Montserrat's constitution, removing responsibility for the financial sector from local control and placing it under the authority of the British appointed Governor General.

Given those powers, the first thing the Governor General did was to revoke 311 banking licences.

No discussion of Montserrat would be complete without a hearty mention of the self-proclaimed world's greatest living authority on offshore banking. Because Jerome Schneider – an American who, for the past several years, operated out of Vancouver, British Columbia – is the man who sold many of those 311 now defunct banking licences.

Sometime in the mid-1970s, as the offshore banking boom gathered momentum, Schneider hit on a neat money-making idea: help people avoid taxes by selling them their own bank. He wrote a bunch of books explaining the concept and organized thousands of high priced seminars which promised, 'Information that only an elite few enjoy.'

His seminars became the prototype for dozens of competing 'protect your assets' and 'create wealth' conventions that are held regularly throughout the offshore world. Typically, they're constructed around the notion that people looking to cheat on their taxes will pay large fees to hucksters who tell them what they want to hear – that it's easy to swindle the government if you know how to do it. Such seminars often take place in conjunction with meetings of medical and dental associations. It seems high income clients have proven especially susceptible to the erroneous assumption that by owning an offshore bank you aren't tax liable on any income the bank generates, even though you're the bank's only customer.

Schneider relentlessly played off that and, in those early days, flogged more than 200 banks in Montserrat. One of his clients was Marc Harris in Panama who operated several banks there, including: Fidelity Overseas, which took fees from clients without performing any services; First City, which doctored its own financial statements; and Allied Reserve, which operated in the United States without a banking licence.

Not surprisingly, given his relationship with Harris, Schneider's name came up during Harris' unsuccessful 1999 libel suit against David Marchant and *Offshore Alert*. In testimony for the defence, John Shockey – doyen of the US Office of the Comptroller of the Currency, having served there for 53 years – revealed that Schneider had once spent time in prison for a computer-related crime. Oddly, his conviction has since been sealed.

That Schneider's past was unknown to his clients is one thing. That the concept on which Schneider based the sale of those banks was fallacious, is more serious.

There are, perhaps, as many as 75 jurisdictions around the world with offshore banks for sale. But using them to defraud the taxman – or to launder money – isn't as easy as promoters like Schneider make it sound. To begin with, some offshore jurisdictions have no credibility whatsoever. Besides Montserrat, banks in Nauru, Niue, Vanuatu, Bodrum (a Spanish-Moroccan haven), Campione d'Italia (on the eastern Turkish border), Tbilisi and Montenegro aren't going to impress many people. Then, all the paperwork, bizarre trust structures and layers of shell companies, which you must buy from the people peddling these offshore banks, do not automatically offer protection for tax purposes. In the States, for example, the IRS takes the view that banks formed in jurisdictions where effective regulation is non-existent, or banks that do not perform regular banking business, or banks where the owner is the only client, are not considered banks for the purpose of tax law. Other countries share those views, labelling them 'Controlled Foreign Corporations', which nullify tax advantages.

That said, it did take the tax man a while to work out Schneider's tricks, especially the most sophisticated of all, 'decontrol'.

Describing himself as, 'the senior financial consultant' for Premier Corporate Services in Vancouver, Schneider touted a scheme to side-step the 'controlled foreign corporation' trap. For a fee of $15,000–$60,000, he'd buy an offshore bank for you. In recent years, he mostly chartered them in Nauru, but occasionally purchased them in Tonga, Vanuatu and the Marshall Islands. For an additional fee of $15,000, Schneider's partner – California attorney Eric Witmeyer – would detach the bank from your control by selling 51 per cent of it to what is called an Independent Foreign Owner (IFO). In principle, that's a neutral third party. More often than not, the Schneider–Witmeyer neutral third party came complete with a mail-drop address in Hong Kong.

Except, there never was a sale and there never was a neutral third party. Witmeyer supplied paperwork that merely created the semblance of that. Nor did any money change hands. Instead of receiving a check for the sale of your bank from that non-existent IFO, you'd get a promissory note for a substantial sum of money that Schneider and Witmeyer simply made up. The remaining 49 per cent of your bank would be converted into a Shareholder Purpose Trust. That, Schneider claimed, meant you didn't have to declare your ownership of the bank. Therefore, any monies earned by the bank had nothing to do with you for tax purposes.

Next, the foreign bank, which was supposedly no longer in your control, would open an account at a major bank in Canada so that you could conduct all of your banking business through Canada. In most cases, that meant obtaining a loan for anything you wished to buy – boats, planes, houses, country club membership, art, jewels, etc – which was secured against the funds held by your decontrolled foreign bank.

Schneider and Witmeyer sold the scheme to their seminar clients as being foolproof. But the US tax authorities weren't so sure. And after ABC Television sent their news magazine show '20/20' to cover a Schneider seminar in Cancun, Mexico in 1997, Schneider's and Witmeyer's world started to come unstuck.

Using a hidden camera, 20/20 extracted an admission from one of the seminar speakers, 'If you don't have a big mouth and are smart, your chances of getting caught are next to none.' They caught Witmeyer in a lie about the banks in Nauru, and caught Schneider in a quasi-admission that decontrol didn't mean a thing.

Over the next five years, the IRS made several undercover contacts with Schneider by putting agents into his seminars. In 1999, they got themselves inside a deal with Schneider for the purchase of a bank. During those negotiations, Witmeyer repeated to the undercover agents something that Schneider liked to say: 'We put all the documents in place. Then we turn the lights out. We create it in the full light and then just disappear into the background.'

In February 2001, the IRS raided Witmeyer's home and office, taking away files and computers. At the same time, under the mutual legal assistance treaty with Canada, the RCMP raided the Vancouver office of Schneider's twin companies, Premier Corporate Services and Premier Management Services. The Mounties conducted the search with two IRS agents as 'observers'. Under Canadian law, after a warrant is executed, it's up to the court to decide what evidence, if any, gets released under the terms of the treaty. Schneider's lawyer argued that the Americans had not been mere observers, that they'd been participants, that they'd helped to direct the search and that they're illegally inspected documents on site. One of the IRS agents then admitted he'd copied some documents before the court gave its permission. Schneider's lawyer petitioned the court, Washington refused to allow the IRS agent to testify, and the British Columbia Supreme Court ruled that, under those circumstances, they would not allow the Americans access to the documents obtained during the search.

Schneider's win in Canada wasn't enough, however, to stop him from being charged in the States. In 2003, he and Witmeyer were indicted on one count of conspiracy to defraud the Internal Revenue Service, 14 counts of wire fraud and eight counts of mail fraud. The 51-year-old Schneider pleaded not guilty. But the 48-year-old Witmeyer, facing the possibility of going away for 115 years, gave up. After explaining to the court how Schneider promised taxpayers that their purchase of a bank, and how the decontrol process that followed was sufficient to protect their assets from the taxman, Witmeyer pleaded guilty to conspiracy to defraud the IRS and agreed to testify against Schneider.

It is fair to say that the firewalls put up by offshore banks and shell companies – the stealth sold by men like Schneider, Witmeyer and Harris – serve no legitimate purpose. And where insurance fraud is concerned, the smoke and mirrors of the offshore world are custom-made for crime. Consider, for example, a group of Mexican politicians who, while Schneider and Witmeyer were working their 'decontrol' gimmick, were working one called the 'Dutch sandwich'.

Money from bribes were laundered through an offshore trust set up in the Netherlands Antilles, hence the 'Dutch' part of the sandwich. Those funds, moved through a shell bank, were used to purchase three savings and loans (S&Ls) in Texas, which had fallen on hard times. The S&Ls were on the block because their loan portfolios were over-burdened with non-performing mortgages.

No sooner had the Mexicans taken over the three S&Ls, than they bought a small domestic insurance company in Arizona which they paid for with loans from the S&Ls. Next, they took the non-performing mortgages from the S&Ls and swapped them for good bonds held by the insurance company. That meant, the S&Ls were now collateralized with profitable paper, making them very attractive, and the insurance company was sitting on a portfolio of non-performing mortgages.

To get their money out of the insurance company, the group formed an offshore re-insurance company. The Arizona operation wrote off 94 per cent of their premiums to the re-insurer, which went straight back to the offshore trust. The S&Ls were sold for a handsome profit – that money also went into the trust – while the insurance company was allowed to go belly up. The Mexicans walked away with $300–$400 million.

Many entrepreneurs look at money as merely a way of keeping score. By that definition, the Mexicans won bigger than a Connecticut-based geek named Martin Frankel. But size isn't everything, and Frankel's $200 million theft earned him a place in the history of offshore fraud.

From 1990–1999, Frankel siphoned funds out of seven American insurance companies in five states. With the help of a disbarred lawyer, who had several convictions for securities fraud and money laundering,

Frankel laid out an elaborate scheme that centred on a Luxembourg shell – through which he bought those seven insurers – and several other offshore shells that looked like re-insurance companies. Whatever money Frankel didn't spend on his own bizarre lifestyle – cloistering himself in a huge Connecticut mansion with women he met through ads in sex magazines – was wired through those offshore re-insurers to Switzerland.

Some people now believe that Frankel's use of the re-insurance shells was skilful enough to get away with the money, and that he would have, had it not been for two things: there was too much money in the game; and Frankel was too greedy. Had he stolen a mere 10 per cent of what he did, it's conceivable he'd have walked away with a life of luxury. Instead, he was arrested in Germany in 1999 and, three years later, pleaded guilty to racketeering, conspiracy, wire fraud and securities fraud.

It's a common syndrome. The same greed that brings victims into a scam, often traps the scammers. It happened to Frankel. It happened to Alan Teale.

A British conman who'd once been secretary of the Lloyd's Insurance Brokers Association, Teale was running the now-defunct Miami Insurance Exchange when he came up with a scheme that would eventually defraud 5,500 people out of $50 million.

He constructed a network of offshore shells that he fraudulently capitalized with non-existent properties and worthless shares. Known as 'the Teale Network', he then enlisted 90 co-conspirators to obtain re-insurance contracts. The companies that signed up with him believed they were protected. In reality, they were putting their own financial stability – and that of their clients – in severe jeopardy, because there was nothing behind any of Teale's re-insurance policies. By moving money through the Caribbean, Belgium and Ireland, he merely created the semblance of a thriving network. Unpaid premiums piled up quickly, families were ruined and eventually the cops moved in. The 61-year-old Teale was found guilty of 41 counts of various types of fraud, was sentenced to 17 years, and died in prison after serving only two months.

The ramifications of the Teale Network are still being felt. A substantial portion of the world's insurance business – especially the re-insurance side of it – finds its way to jurisdictions with questionable regulation. The cycle may start at Lloyds of London and legitimately go through Bermuda, an insurance tax haven with relatively strict guidelines. But insurers and re-insurers are forever re-insuring – spreading their risk as widely as possible – and that business quickly seeks out less well regulated islands.

If due diligence has not taken place at every step along the way, if some re-insurance company in one of the islands doesn't have the assets and backing it claims to, should that company be permitted to sell re-insurance? History says, no. But those smaller, less well regulated islands, don't have the resources to carry out extensive due diligence. And the bigger, better regulated jurisdictions – London and Bermuda – don't necessarily have any way of knowing what's really going on at the bottom of the food chain.

In Los Angeles in 1993, during the riots which followed the beating of a black man, Rodney King, by white policemen, a number of Korean groceries were destroyed by fire. They were insured by a company sitting in the unregulated British Virgin Islands. When they tried to collect on their policies, there was no money to pay out.

The nature of the offshore world is such that no legitimate insurer can ever be totally certain that there is, in fact, enough money down the line to back the original risk. Even before the ink on the Teale matter was dry, one of his disciples used precisely the same scheme to rip-off $31 million in insurance premiums.

Still, when it comes to sheer nastiness and lives being ruined, not even Teale comes close to the Bramson family. Their insurance scam is pretty much a textbook case of how to use the offshore world to commit long-term fraud and ruin the maximum number of lives.

Norman Bramson, a foul-looking character born in the Midwest in 1923, was a dentist by trade who, instead of filling cavities, ran a pharmacy in Skokie, Illinois. The father of five children, two of his sons – Leonard and Marty – followed him into the business. Except, by that time, his business wasn't running a pharmacy, it was insurance fraud on a gigantic scale. Both sons were lawyers. The 6 ft 5 in Leonard, was a gruesome fellow. Marty was a little smaller, and looked something like Groucho Marx.

The family first appeared on law enforcement radar screens in 1980 when regulators in Illinois discovered that they were selling inadequate policies in an unsatisfactory way. They were targeting podiatrists – a particularly lucrative source for medical malpractice insurance due to the number of operations they perform – but the State felt they were not providing adequate protection. The regulators ruled that the Bramsons were delinquent and issued a cease and desist order.

Six years later, the family popped up again. The RCMP in Canada had observed Norman on several occasions, crossing the border to the US, carrying suitcases filled with cash. They decided he was a drug money launderer. So a specialized drug unit set up a sting operation, intending to grab him with the cash. But the surveillance team got compromised – Norman somehow found out about them – and the smuggling stopped for a while. The Mounties eventually concluded that this was not, in fact, a drug case and moved the dossier over to a fraud team. That group tipped off US Customs, who waited until Norman was moving cash again, then grabbed him at the border red-handed.

What neither the Americans nor the Canadians realized at the time, was that the Norman had simply moved his illicit medical malpractice insurance scam beyond the reach of Illinois regulators. He'd set up a boiler room operation in Toronto and was still targeting podiatrists. By now, he'd also set up an offshore insurance company in the Bahamas, International Bahamian Insurance (IBI). He ran ads in newspapers and professional journals offering IBI's medical malpractice insurance at 20–30 per cent below the rate that legitimate carriers were charging. The way he could afford to do that, was by never paying out any claims.

Norman listed PO boxes and phone numbers in Chicago that automatically forwarded mail and calls to Canada. To create jurisdictional confusion, money collected there was deposited in the Royal Bank of Canada in Toronto and another bank in Windsor, Ontario, then immediately wired to Citizen Bank in Miami. That bank had a correspondent relationship with the New World Bank in Anguilla, which Norman owned.

It was nothing more than a storefront in a strip mail. But there, a young woman manning the New World Bank phone, cleared funds through a correspondent account at the Caribbean Commercial Bank in St Martins. The funds were then wired from St Martins to the Cantrade Bank in Zurich, Switzerland.

During much of this time, Marty had been running Norman's pharmacy in Skokie. But he'd got his father's licence revoked by dispensing drugs without prescriptions. When that happened, Marty applied for a job as a Chicago police officer. He enrolled in the police academy and, a few days before being sworn in, got arrested for having sex with underage girls. He moved to the Washington DC area, opened another pharmacy, got arrested again – this time for selling controlled drugs – and was sent to prison. When he got out, he went to law school. At the same time, Leonard had just graduated law school and was working in the State's Attorneys office in Chicago. Only later was it discovered that while Leonard was an assistant state's attorney, he was also listed as the president of Norman's fraudulent insurance company.

It took a while but once the Illinois insurance regulators cottoned on to the rip-off that Norman was running from Toronto, they issued injunctions against him. As usual, Norman stayed one step ahead by setting up new insurance companies with different names in different islands. A few of the state's insurance investigators came to believe that Norman was using the insurance scam to launder Chicago mob money. But they could never get the local US Attorney's office interested in him. As far as the Justice Department was concerned, this was a matter for the Canadians. In Toronto, the cops saw it as a case that really needed to be dealt with in Chicago. If Norman was, in fact, washing the Mob's money, no one ever proved it. Anyway, he and the family soon moved to Baltimore and started working their scam there. That's when a pair of seriously determined FBI agents set out to stop them.

Jim Vaules and Don Wadsworth are now both retired and run the National Fraud Center outside of Philadelphia. But, in those days, they were operating out of Atlantic City, New Jersey, where Vaules was special-agent-in-charge. Being a gambling town meant that Vaules, Wadsworth and the other agents kept busy trying to sort out the Mob's influence in the hotels and at the gaming tables.

Back in Washington, some senior managers at FBI headquarters decided to launch a somewhat lonely campaign to encourage agents in the field to go after white-collar criminals. That white-collar crime didn't have the glamour attached to it that organized crime does, goes without saying. And inside white-collar crime, insurance fraud had a fairly low priority.

The way the Feds usually looked at it, the insurance industry is regulated by the states, so that insurance fraud is ordinarily a state matter. The FBI only gets involved because state jurisdiction stops at the state line. And insurance fraudsters play off that. They work one state until they get into trouble, skip across the line and set up in another state. When they're ordered to cease and desist in the second state, they move on to a third. The problem often is that, by the time the Feds get into the game, if they bother at all, it's late. The damage has been done and the smart crooks are long gone.

What made Vaules and Wadsworth unique was, they didn't see it that way. Both of them had a strong background in white-collar crime, and both of them understood the kind of damage that white-collar criminals can inflict on unsuspecting citizens. So, when the Deputy Attorney General for the State of New Jersey – who headed the insurance fraud group – brought the Bramson case to them, they jumped on it.

The Deputy Attorney General told Vaules and Wadsworth that a dormant company, Preferred Indemnity Insurance (PII), had just been bought out. Normally, that wouldn't raise any suspicions. But, PII was licensed to provide property and casualty coverage, and the people now running it were selling high risk coverage to companies in asbestos removal and oil tank cleaning. Those lines were not authorized. Nor was PII's coverage backed by sufficient reserves. He said that the people running it were simply stealing premiums and getting the money out of the country as fast as they could.

Vaules and Wadsworth moved quickly, linking PII to an address in Columbia, Maryland where, they learned, the people running this company had once been affiliated with an insurance company in Chicago that had been forced out of business by state regulators. Following those leads, they soon found that seven companies were involved, and all of them pointed to Norman, Leonard and Marty Bramson.

Two of the companies were operating out of Canada, one was in New Jersey, one was in Maryland, one was in Indiana and, bizarrely, two were based in Guam. Looking more closely at those seven, Vaules and Wadsworth were able to identify four more offshore shells that also led back to the Bramsons.

The office and phone number for PII was a storefront address of convenience. Call forwarding re-directed calls to the Associated Insurance Company in Columbia, Maryland. A courier stopped by twice-a-week to pick up mail, delivering it to a company called Metropolitan Support Services in Greenbelt, Maryland. One of the people working at the rent-an-office admitted to the agents that whenever a state insurance regulator made an appointment to stop by, they hung a PII plaque on the front door, so that the regulator would think he was visiting a legitimate office.

Looking at what they knew was manifest deceit, Vaules and

Wadsworth now found several other companies tied to the Bramsons, including one called Legal Defence Support Services Ltd, which was registered in the Federated States of Micronesia (FSM). That's a four nation alliance sitting out in the middle of nowhere in the Pacific Ocean.

Notes Vaules, 'If you're running a big fraud and want to beat the taxman, you set up offshore shell companies so that you can bill your own companies for the operating costs. A lot of the shells the Bramsons created were done specifically to bill themselves for services. They were attorneys, so they had to have legal defence support services, they needed to send invoices to their companies and show a cost of operation. By the time we'd located 16 companies, we could begin to recreate the paper trail.'

When the agents were able to determine who served in what capacity with which company, Marty Bramson was conspicuous by his absence. His name wasn't listed on any official documents, although, the names Hans Martin and B. M. Martin turned up frequently. The agents eventually found logs from meetings with state insurance regulators that Hans Martin had attended, and were able to established that both Hans Martin and B. M. Martin were, of course, Marty. As a convicted criminal, he was otherwise ineligible to be licensed by any state as a beneficial owner of an insurance company. So he invented aliases.

Another company they stumbled across was called Trans-Pacific Insurance, which caused Vaules and Wadsworth to do a double-take because there happens to be a legitimate company operating with that name. But the legitimate company is spelled Transpacific, no hyphen, and this one had a hyphen. It was based in the FSM. As Wadsworth later explained, 'They tried to stay as close as they could to legitimate names. It's a trick all fraudsters use. They need to be able to pass the smell test.'

By now, the Bramsons had branched out from podiatrists and were selling insurance throughout the medical profession, shifting a lot of this new business to Trans-Pacific, which made the money trail that much harder to follow. One of their most important new clients was the American Organization of Healthcare Professionals (AOHP), through which the Bramsons were pretending to insure 68,000 nurses. As long as premiums were coming in, everything worked fine. But when a claim was filed, AOHP's members soon discovered that the Bramsons had built any number of escape hatches, to avoid paying out.

Each time they sent a policy to a newly insured client, it was deliberately one page short. The missing page contained a clause that said, if you don't pay your premium within 30 days, you don't have coverage. So every claim that came in, prompted a letter going out, quoting a clause on page 15 – the missing page – that said, if the premium isn't received in 30 days, it is no longer valid. As the company hadn't received the premium within that time frame, regretfully, they had no choice but to consider the policy as lapsed.

The insured person would write back that he or she didn't have a page 15. So the Bramsons would send them the master policy, which included the missing page.

If the insured person didn't give up there, the next step would be to acknowledge the error. The Bramsons would say, all right, we believe you paid on time, it's obviously an oversight. All you have to do now is send us $2,000, we will reinstate you and we will then cover the claim. Here the Bramsons were supplementing insurance fraud with advance fee fraud.

If the person continued to argue about it, the Bramsons would simply shut the door. If the person sent the money, the Bramsons would use it as a retainer to hire an attorney to fight the claim against the insured person, which gave the appearance of covering the policy.

With the lives and livelihoods of so many innocent people now at risk, Vaules and Wadsworth hatched a sting to stop the Bramsons. The FBI maintained a terrific apartment overlooking the ocean in Atlantic City, which was wired for sound and video for just such occasions. But to lure one of the Bramsons to the apartment, they would need a story.

Through the New Jersey insurance regulators office, they were introduced to a legitimate insurance executive who'd been approached by the Bramsons. The family had been trying to sell him a much-too-low discounted product, and he'd reported his suspicions. This man agreed to put the agents together with Marty.

The story was that Vaules, playing the bad guy, was looking to dump some phoney insurance on an association of physical therapists, but needed a legitimate company behind him. Marty said he could help, and came to Atlantic City for a night on the town. There, with what Vaules describes as 'all the props' – food, booze and the casinos – Vaules explained his scam. Marty reacted by spilling the beans on how the Bramsons' operation worked.

That's when Vaules knew that Marty had taken the bait. 'He figured me for a guy running a scam and he was going to run a scam on the scammer. He smelled our money and figured he could get it and then move it offshore.'

With that part of the operation falling neatly into place, Vaules and Wadsworth targeted some former Bramson employees, and were able to develop one into an informant. The key fact they gleaned from him was that the Bramsons' entire banking operation was run by Lenny, and that everything about it was on a hand-held Casio computer that never left Lenny's side.

The informant also helped them to lure Lenny to a meeting at Fort Lauderdale Airport. As soon as the agents spotted him there, and knew they could take him, word was sent back to an FBI command post to hit the other targets. Agents went through the doors at the Bramsons' offices in Maryland, and other agents arrested Marty at home. Norman was nowhere to be found. But they took Lenny and, most importantly, grabbed his hand-held Casio.

The FBI lab was able to break Lenny's codes and, as a result, Vaules and Wadsworth got the Bramsons' entire banking network. Startlingly, it consisted of 314 accounts held in Canada, Japan, the Cayman Islands, Anguilla, Panama, Denmark, Switzerland, Liechtenstein, Luxembourg, Germany, the Netherlands, Israel, Greece, the Federated States of Micronesia, the Commonwealth Nations of the Marian Islands (CNMI), the Solomon Islands, and Saipan. Surrounding those accounts were at least 53 different shell companies, registered throughout the offshore world.

Marty and Lenny were both charged and released on bail, and both subjected to an electronic monitoring device. The court ordered that neither were to move any money from any of their accounts. But within a matter of days, a call came in that Marty was looking to get his hands on some money. Vaules and Wadsworth rushed back to court and had the brothers' bail revoked. Marty cut his electronic ankle bracelet and made it out of town. Lenny tried, but he was too slow and spent the next 9 years sitting in a cell.

Hoping to get a lead on the father and son fugitives, Wadsworth approached the television show, 'America's Most Wanted'. The producers liked the idea and ran a big feature on the family. Within hours of the broadcast, a tip came in on Norman.

A little old lady in San Diego was watching the programme when she recognized the man she liked to dance with. She couldn't believe it. There was a social club at the apartment complex where she lived, and the fellow she now saw on television was the best dancer. She picked up the phone and, within an hour, the best dancer at the social club was in custody. In his room, police found currency taped under drawers and an indication that Marty was in Mexico.

Following that lead, Vaules and Wadsworth learned that Marty had arranged with a former prison cellmate to ship a boat – called *The Escape Clause* – from Buffalo, New York, across the country by lorry, to Monterrey, California, where it would be put into the water and sailed to Mexico. Money was hidden inside the boat. The Bureau intercepted it and confiscated the money. But Marty still had a stash somewhere, because when they finally located his whereabouts, he'd bought a nightclub. The FBI asked the Mexicans for help, but by the time the cops showed up at the nightclub, Marty was off to Europe.

An Interpol warrant was issued for his arrest.

Some months later, a border guard in Liechtenstein pulled over a shiny new Mercedes on its way from Austria into Vaduz. It was just a routine stop because he didn't like the look of the two guys in the car. He opened the trunk and found a duffel bag filled with 16 one-kilo bars of gold bullion, and neatly wrapped stacks of yen, pounds, dollars and Swiss francs. The total came to $5.6 million. Along with it were records indicating the location of several safe deposit boxes.

Marty was one of the two men. The other was his brother Carl, who'd flown to Europe to help Marty pick up all the cash the family had hidden there.

The United States wanted the Bramson brothers sent back home, and duly applied for their extradition. Marty decided he'd rather stay in Liechtenstein and spent $2\frac{1}{2}$ years fighting deportation. His attorney was a member of parliament who was close to the Prince and, in the end, the government refused to honour its extradition treaty with the US. The State Department put out press releases about Liechtenstein not playing by the rules, and a minor diplomatic row ensued. Wadsworth flew over to see what he could do. One night, after Marty's attorney left the cell in Liechtenstein where Marty was living, some local cops shoved Marty into a car, drove him to the Swiss border and, unceremoniously, turned him over to the police there. Within three weeks, Marty was on his way back to the States.

Receivers were put into the various Bramson companies. They uncovered 1,212 insurance claims outstanding, amounting to $66.5 million. Assets amount to only about $11 million. Some doctors who'd insured with the Bramsons were forced into bankruptcy. One attorney who worked for them committed suicide.

'These guys ruined a lot of lives,' Wadsworth says. 'Lenny got nine years. Marty got 10. Norman served very little. We seized what assets we could, but the correspondent banking relationships and the offshore shell companies made it very difficult. We got a lot of bank accounts in all those countries, but don't know how many accounts we didn't find. We don't know what other assets we missed. Without the correspondent banking relationships and the offshore shell companies they never would have made it as far as they did. Without the offshore connections, they never could have made it work.'

CHAPTER EIGHT

Ponzi's Ghost

All scams are basically the same,
and the people running them are typically not very bright,
but they're brighter than their victims,
which is all they need to be.

– David Marchant, investigative journalist

Carlos Bianchi left Italy in the waning hours of the nineteenth century, arriving in the New World to change his name from Carlos to Charles and from Bianchi to Ponsi. By the end of World War I, he'd not only served time in a Montreal jail for cheque forging, he'd changed his name again, this time from Ponsi to Ponzi.

Around 1919, looking for greener pastures, Ponzi left Canada for Boston where, one day, he received a letter from someone in Italy containing an international postal reply coupon. Still in existence today, it's a simple method of paying for postage in one country with the currency of another – if you will, the global answer to self-addressed stamped envelopes. Because someone in, say, Glasgow, can't buy stamps to pay for return postage for his correspondent in, say, Vancouver, Canada, he buys one of these coupons from his local post office. Worth a fixed amount, the fellow in Glasgow sends it to his correspondent in Vancouver who exchanges it at his local post office for a stamp which covers the postage back to Glasgow.

What caught Ponzi's eye was that the coupon he received from Italy had been purchased in Spain. He soon learned that while international postal reply coupons were priced at fixed rates of exchange, actual currency rates fluctuated to the point where this particular coupon had cost only about 15 per cent of the value of the US stamps he could buy with it. In other words, coupons bought in Spain and cashed in the States represented an instant profit of nearly 660 per cent. So Charles Ponzi promptly announced his entry into the international postal reply coupon business.

However, instead of funding the venture himself, which might have been legal and would have been profitable, he invited investors to join him. As he outlined the plan, he would personally travel to Spain to buy tens of thousands of coupons, bring them back to the States where he would exchange them for stamps, and then wholesale the stamps to businesses. Promising 40 per cent profits in just 90 days, he reinforced investor confidence with the old trick of forming a corporation with a legitimate-sounding name: 'The Securities and Exchange Company', which, of course, abbreviated to 'S.E.C'.

For the first few months, money trickled in slowly but steadily. It's when he upped the promise to 100 per cent profits that the floodgates opened and, on good days, hundreds of thousands of dollars arrived at his S.E.C. In fact, he got so rich so quickly that, within six months, he purchased a large stake in a New York bank and a Boston import–export firm. The only problem was, his fortune wasn't based on postal reply coupons, he was simply spending his investors' money.

Towards the middle of 1920, the *Boston Post* newspaper began asking questions. Reporters canvassed post offices all over town, only to discover that Ponzi couldn't possibly be buying as many coupons as he claimed because that many coupons hadn't been cashed in. The newspaper articles brought investors to Ponzi's front door demanding their money back. While fervently praising the scheme, he obligingly returned investors money, plus interest, paying them with the money sent in by new investors. Robbing Peter to pay Paul worked for a while but by August, the Boston Post was claiming that Ponzi was millions of dollars in debt.

Maintaining a calm and reassuring exterior, Ponzi did what conmen typically do when faced with the truth – he sued the messenger. He filed a $5 million claim for damages against the *Post* and then, in the next breath, announced a $100 million international investment syndicate. Before he could get it off the ground, the Massachusetts State Banking Commission closed down his bank. Newspapers across the country jumped on the bandwagon, reminding the public of Ponzi's earlier scuffles with the Canadian authorities, while auditors finetooth-combed his S.E.C'.s books. They quickly discovered that legitimate transactions were negligible. In fact, the grand total was a mere $30. It meant that Ponzi never even bothered with his international postal reply coupon idea.

His house of cards crumbled to the tune of $3 million. Ponzi went to jail for a few years in Massachusetts, was allowed out on parole, skipped and headed for Florida, where he set up a real estate scam which earned him another trip to prison. At the time he admitted, 'Only a fool would have a trusted a crook like me.' Around 1930–31, he was deported home to Italy. From there he made his way to Brazil, where, eventually, he died penniless.

His legacy is the 'Ponzi scheme', and his ghost blithely lives on.

Gilbert Allen Ziegler, whose legacy is the misery and financial ruin he's inflicted on thousands of people who trusted him with their life savings, did Ponzi proud.

Born in Seattle in 1951, the heavy-set and balding Ziegler tells people he grew up in the Pacific Northwest, but is deliberately vague about much of his background. He claims to be a university graduate, but doesn't easily cough up the name of the school. It turns out that he attended Green River Community College in Auburn, Washington. He claims that in the 1970s he was the president of a business college, but doesn't name that school either. It turns out to be defunct. He also claims to be an ordained minister, and while he admits he never attended any sort of theological seminary or had any formal training, he doesn't go into the specifics of who ordained him. His CV also lists a Master of Business degree and a doctorate, both unsourced.

By the 1980s, Ziegler was living in Hillsboro, Oregon, employed in what he describes as 'religious activities', apparently a reference to a short period as a church administrator. At various times, he notes, he was a precinct committeeman for a local Democratic Party, a ballot status adviser for a local Libertarian Party, and a precinct committeeman for a local Republican Party. He claims to have taught economics, history of economic philosophy, advertising and journalism. He says he was a partner in a Mexican fast-food restaurant, the founder and creative director of an advertising agency, a concert promoter and the founder/president of a non-denominational organization of Christian fellowships. He was also the architect of what the State of Oregon suspected was securities fraud.

In the early 1990s, Ziegler began soliciting investors for an offshore newsletter. The special $150 'subscription' fee included the right to sell additional subscriptions for which investors would be paid a commission. New subscribers could then sell subscriptions to newer subscribers, *ad infinitum*. It was a typical pyramid scheme, but with a macabre twist. Ziegler would deposit all commissions in an offshore account on the Caribbean island of Nevis where the money would be invested until the subscriber died. At that point, the account would be liquidated and paid to the subscriber's heirs. Some people fell for it. But the Oregon Attorney General's office didn't and the scheme was taken apart. Ziegler was investigated for various violations, though no formal charges were lodged.

By then, he was unsuccessfully running the Hometown Mortgage Corporation. A brokerage business, it failed and toppled him into bankruptcy. Court records show he'd amassed personal debts of $1.14 million owed to 148 different companies. His assets were $28,440 including $20 in cash, $10 in a saving's account and $10 worth of Hometown shares. At the time he was driving three cars and owed $320,000 in back taxes. His explanation for the debacle puts the blame squarely on someone he names as 'Revd Gregory Peck'.

According to him, Revd Peck told the cops that Ziegler was running a fraudulent investment programme because one of Ziegler's mates – whose wife was a Revd Peck parishioner – had taken up with another woman and she wanted revenge. To help her, Revd Peck duped the cops because Ziegler refused Revd Peck a directorship in a bank he wouldn't form for another two years. If it sounds convoluted – typical Ziegler-speak – that's because he always lays the blame for everything on someone else.

Leaving Oregon under that cloud, and now with two failed marriages behind him, Ziegler pitched up in Hawaii where he bought an existing offshore bank licence and changed the name of the company to Fidelity International Bank. Naming himself executive director, he abbreviated the name to 'FIB', the play on words being totally appropriate as the bank was chartered in Nauru.

A Pacific island nation of less than eight square miles and barely 10,000 people, until the mid-1990s Nauru's most important export was phosphate. But they foolishly mis-mined it and the country tumbled perilously close to bankruptcy. They needed a new export, so the government opted for fraud.

Nauru's offshore banking sector was designed to be conman friendly. In principle, licences were to be granted only to persons of sound financial standing with good reputations and sufficient expertise. In practice, they were granted to anyone willing to pay an initial fee of around $50,000 and keep up the annual payments of around $1,000. For an extra twenty grand, they would throw in an 'investor passport', meaning citizenship for foreign clients. Thousands of passports were sold until international pressure so humiliated the government that the practice was stopped. But banking licences continued. No local directors were required and if you asked nicely they'd throw in an insurance licence at no extra charge. Minimal capitalization was set at a lowly $100,000 with two years after the licence grant to raise the money. Then, you didn't have to show it to anybody. All Nauru required was an auditor's statement that it had been paid up. Any word processing programme and cheap ink jet printer solved that problem.

There were annual reporting requirements but, again, no one in Nauru cared who audited your accounts as long as the letterhead looked real. Applicants also had to provide a reference from an accountant, auditor or financial associate who could affirm that the applicant had a net worth exceeding $250,000 in unencumbered assets. In this case, the person applying for the charter – Ziegler – was bankrupt.

In 1998, the Russian Central Bank reported that $70 billion had been laundered through Nauru by Russian organized crime groups. At one point, more than 400 non-resident banks were registered there, all sharing the same maildrop address. Around half were reputedly managed in the old Soviet bloc. Correspondent relationships with Nauru banks have turned up in criminal investigations throughout the former Soviet Union, especially Belarus, Chechnya and the Ukraine. Just over one-third of the banks registered in Nauru were said to have been managed in the sub-Continent and the Middle East, raising serious questions about Nauru's role in the funding of terrorist groups.

If there ever were any legitimate offshore banks in Nauru – a big if – they could be counted on one hand. In 2003, the government ran out of money and the lights on the island were turned off. They've since revoked all the banking licenses, and recalled all the passports they sold. Yet Nauru's well-deserved reputation as a money laundering offending nation means that anything and everything chartered there must be considered 'extremely suspect'.

Ziegler's FIB was hardly ever going to be an exception. He claims that within a year, the bank's net worth had exceeded $200 million. But records show that Nauru licensed FIB on 3 July 1996 as a Class B bank, which meant that it could not legally function until it had a suitable correspondent relationship with a Class A bank somewhere else in the offshore world. Ziegler shopped around to set up such a bank in Belize, Barbados and Antigua but was turned down by all of them. It says a lot about Ziegler that even Antigua refused him, considering that government's lack of shame and the mass of inanities they have licensed.

Eventually he noticed a shiny new welcome mat in Grenada. The Caribbean 'spice island' nation of 90,000 people was open for business. And by then, he'd met a man who knew how to make that business work.

Robert Earl Palm also claims to be an ordained preacher. Operating out of Victoria, British Columbia, he tells people he represents a coalition of Christian philanthropists, oversees some European trusts and has advised both the Thai and Saudi royal families. Two years older than Ziegler, he too has been a bank director. But his United National Republic Bank (UNRB), which is supposedly based in Moscow, doesn't seem to be based anywhere. The Russians say they never heard of it, and in an official warning, Canada's Office of the Superintendent of Financial Institutions (OSFI) describes UNRB being of 'unknown jurisdiction'. As neither a licensed chartered bank in Canada nor a registered representative office of a foreign bank operating in Canada, OSFI says 'it may be operating in Canada in contravention of the Banking Act'.

Palm and UNRB hit the headlines in 2003 when the Supreme Court of British Columbia finally caught up with them for a 12-year old matter. In 1991, using a company called Advance Capital Services Corp and with UNRB as guarantor of the deal, Palm purchased $300 million worth of potatoes and wheat flour from a consortium of Polish farmers. He said it was to send to Russia as humanitarian aid. The Poles shipped $37 million worth which promptly disappeared. Two years later, still waiting to get paid, a Polish agricultural co-operative sued Palm, his partner Jason Dallas and Advance Capital Services. Palm was charged with criminal fraud in Poland but extradition from Canada never happened. Dallas, however, was extradited, convicted for fraud and spent $4^{1}/_{2}$ years in prison.

By the time the Poles had their day in court in Canada, Dallas was in jail, Advance Capital Services had been struck off the companies' register and, according to the judge, UNRB was not a normal licensed bank and had never operated as one. That left Palm to stand alone. The judge ruled he'd used Advance Capital Services 'to effect a fraudulent purpose and to convey fraudulent misrepresentations', and ordered him to pay the Poles their $37 million.

Press reports in Canada allege that Palm has been the object of investigations for more than ten years by the Mounties, Revenue Canada and police agencies in the States and Europe. Apparently, there is an ongoing racketeering investigation in the Ukraine over a $40 million roubles-for-dollars swap. A similar investigation for a similar currency swap is said to be underway in Finland.

To set up his deal in Poland, Palm and UNRB offered to lend $11 billion in hard currency to the Guangxi Trust & Investment Corp in Southern China. In return, the Chinese handed Palm some 200 letters of credit, including $80 million written on an obscure Chinese bank on the island of Hainan. The Chinese never got their $11 billion but Palm used $1 billion worth of this paper to guarantee the potato and wheat flour sale. Scotland Yard has since discovered 22 of these letters of credit, worth another $1 billion, in various scams. That leaves $9 billion in Chinese paper still floating around the offshore world.

The same people who have been investigating Ziegler for years, allege – but have not proven – that Ziegler paid Palm $2 million for 'business advice'. If so, his lessons on 'how to use phoney paper to borrow assets which you put on the bank's books disguised as real assets against which you borrow real money', turned out to be worth the price.

In Grenada, those politicians and businessmen who had just turned the country into an offshore financial centre reckoned it was a great way to cure all that ailed them and ensure economic health. They intended to licence a few companies and banks, then sit back and watch the money pour in. To manage it, they established the Offshore Financial Services Division of the Ministry of Finance and installed Michael Creft to run it. A crony of Prime Minister Keith Mitchell, Creft had been educated in Canada, worked for Agriculture Canada in Regina and then spent 15 years with Manitoba's Department of Highways. His qualification for being named Grenada's first Registrar of Offshore Services was that he'd come home and needed a job.

When he spotted Grenada, Ziegler could hardly believe his luck. Here was an island of foolish amateurs perfectly ripe for plucking. Single-handedly, he was about to turn the place into the poster child for what happens to an offshore financial centre when the people running it don't have a clue what they're doing.

He waded ashore, introduced himself as CEO of First International Bank and gave them a song and dance about creating jobs. He promised to bring wealth to the island by folding FIB into a new entity which he would call, First International Bank of Grenada (FIBG), or

First Bank, for short. And, just in case anybody in Grenada thought
for a moment that he was legit – which, obviously, they did and
which, clearly, he wasn't – he arrived sporting a passport issued by
the Dominion of Melchizedek.

A self-proclaimed 'ecclesiastical state', unlike Nauru with its
designer-fraud 'investor passport', this is an utterly fake entity.
Melchizedek's first address was the Isla de Malpelo, a rock in the
Pacific that just happens to be owned by Colombia. Next, Melchizedek
moved to Karitane, an island 1,000 miles south of Tahiti, claiming
to have purchased sovereignty from the Kingdom of Polynesia. Except
the kingdom doesn't exist and anyway, Karitane is most of the time
30 feet under water. Other addresses have included Antarctica,
Clipperton Island in the north Pacific, Solkope Island off Rotuma in
the south Pacific, and Taongi Atoll, an uninhabited rock barrier owned
by the Republic of the Marshall Islands.

Over the years, Hong Kong police arrested fraudsters trying to pass
checks drawn on Melchizedek banks; Texas issued cease and desist
orders against Melchizedek insurance companies; British cops raided
a company flogging a Melchizedek investment scheme backed by the
German Weimar Republic; Philippines police arrested three people,
including a British lawyer, for selling $1 million worth of Melchizedek
passports at $3,500 each; 2,000 investors in Singapore, Portugal and
the Caribbean lost millions of dollars in a fraud perpetrated by Credit
Bank International of Melchizedek; and the SEC filed fraud charges
against a lawyer and his investment advisory firm for running a
Melchizedek bank Ponzi.

The creation of David and Mark Pedley, a father–son team of multi-
convicted felons, Melchizedek first appeared in the late 1980s, when
Mark Pedley, disguised as Consortium Finance Corporation, began
selling banks chartered there. He added passports to his product line,
then formed International Auditors, bogus chartered accountants, to
provide fraudulent financial audits for those banks. He invented an
embassy in Washington – the address is a mail drop, the phone number
is an answering machine – and 40 others around the world, professing
accreditation to the United Nations, Canada, the Vatican, eight countries in Europe, five in the Pacific, five in Africa plus Oklahoma,
Kansas, Missouri, California, Chicago, a sovereignty called 'Europe'
and another called 'Central America.'

'Everything about Melchizedek is fraudulent', notes John Shockey,
the legendary fraud expert from the US Office of the Comptroller of

the Currency. 'Here you have a phoney government consisting of fraud-sters creating phoney citizenships, ambassadorships, embassy and lega-tion offices, issuing diplomatic passports, registering financial aid, granting business licences and creating a stock exchange. There is absolutely nothing legitimate about Melchizedek.'

Ziegler's Melchizedek passport introduced him as, 'Ambassador-at-Large to the Caribbean.'

To capitalize FIBG, Grenada's banking laws required Ziegler to put up $2.2 million. Needless to say he didn't have it. But knowing that the regulator wouldn't look too closely, he produced documentation that suggested he could substantiate a claim to $500,000 cash and $17.25 million in publicly traded securities. Those turned out be collateral for a loan that never happened and had simply never been returned. But even Ziegler must have been stupefied when regulator Creft didn't question the bank's biggest supposed asset – a $20 million, 10,000 carat carved ruby called 'Boy On Water Buffalo'. Ziegler listed it on FIBG's books at the 'fire sale' value of $15 million.

The only problems were, Ziegler didn't own it, didn't have any rights to it, and never saw it.

What he provided to Creft was a photocopy of an appraisal for the ruby. Not the actual appraisal, which was suspect enough, but a photo-copy! No original documentation has ever been produced by Ziegler, or anyone else, to support either the valuation of the stone or the assignment of it to him. In fact, when the FBI located the real owner of the ruby, they established beyond any doubt that the man had owned it for more than two decades, still owned it, had never given up any interest in it and had never heard of Ziegler.

Besides that, a ruby is not a liquid asset and, under Grenada law, could not be used as initial capital. Yet, on 9 October 1997, Michael Creft licenced FIBG as Class I Offshore Bank #005.

Having reinvented FIB, Ziegler's next step was to reinvent himself. In addition to companies and banks, Grenada was also, in those days, dealing in one of the more shameful aspects of the offshore world, the sale of national sovereignty. Under the guise of 'economic citizenship', Ziegler was allowed to buy a Grenadian passport. It cost $50,000 – a $22,000 fee to the treasury, a $17,000 donation to a government approved project and an $11,000 fee to an approved agent. Then, instead of having it issued to Gilbert Allen Ziegler – after all, he was already known as that in the States and in Melchizedek – he legally gave himself a new name, Van Arthur Brink.

The same people who have been investigating him for years, the
ones who link him to Robert Earl Palm, say that what happened next
clearly points to the influence of someone like Palm. And while
Ziegler/Brink might think of himself as intelligent, they insist he is
not smart enough to come up with the intricate rip-off that is FIBG.

First, he set up the International Deposit (re)Insurance Corporation
in Nevis. Known as IDIC, the name is purposely similar to America's
Federal Deposit Insurance Corporation (FDIC), inferring a relationship and/or suggesting that this is even better than the FDIC because
it is the International version. He next announced that, as a result of
'arms-length negotiations' – his own words, which were plainly untrue
– FIBG had entered into an agreement with IDIC to insure FIBG's
depositors. In other words, your money is perfectly safe because IDIC
says so. He claimed that as FIBG was holding over $200 in deposits
for every $1 insured, IDIC had awarded the bank it's 'AAA Rating'.
Needless to say, the rating was as worthless as IDIC's insurance because
Ziegler/Brink simply made it up.

After that, he established a series of IBCs throughout the Caribbean,
opening accounts for them in other jurisdictions, such as Jersey and
Austria, to create the mirage of business activity and to obliterate
money trails. To induce people to invest with FIBG, he established
the 'Given In Freedom Trust' (GIFT), a re-creation of the subscription pyramid he'd worked in Oregon. He would ultimately claim that
GIFT benefactors had accumulated $1 billion in the trust. It's not
true.

Once that was done, he concocted the World Investor's Stock
Exchange (WISE). It was, he said, 'An opportunity to create a market
for venture capital in which the risk factor is reduced to negligible
in order to help small businesses achieve seed capital and mezzanine
level financing in a world that is increasingly inhospitable to business formation and development financing.'

Whatever that means.

In truth, WISE was yet another hollow promise of more insurance. Shares purchased through WISE were guaranteed by FIBG and
IDIC, so that if the price fell below what the investor paid, IDIC
would reimburse the loss. Besides the fact that there was never a
secondary market for companies listed on WISE – meaning that once
you bought shares there was no place to sell them – the companies
he was flogging were described as 'emerging', which means they probably couldn't get funding any place else, which says a lot about what

these companies were emerging from and what they would end up emerging into.

At the same time, he began constructing a franchised network for his frauds. He helped his 'agents' set up sub-banks of FIBG, many of them chartered in Grenada with the aid of a company he formed there to act as a government agent for company licensing. The idea of the sub-banks was to create a conduit for income derived from frauds that would flow into FIBG where the proceeds could be disguised as legitimate accounts. Most of FIBG's nearly two dozen sub-banks – such as Wellington Bank, Cambridge International Bank & Trust, Crown Meridian Bank and Sattva Bank – were run by alleged fraudsters, previously convicted fraudsters or since convicted fraudsters.

Ziegler/Brink also took a valuable lesson from Las Vegas. Like casinos that invite gamblers on all-expenses-paid junkets just to have a shot at their bankroll, he brought potential victims to Grenada. He put them up at a good hotel, wined and dined them, dazzled them with white sand beaches and scuba diving, confirmed their worst fears about oppressive government tax regimes, set up accounts for them and helped himself to their money. He pledged that, in addition to IDIC's insurance of their funds, FIBG maintained cash, cash equivalent instruments and gold held at various international banks, including gold bullion certificates of deposit (CDs) from Union Bank of Switzerland. The documentation for the UBS gold turned out to be photocopies of photocopies. And in any case, banks do not issue gold bullion CDs. Nevertheless, he bragged, 'I know of no other bank in the world which operates with First Bank's underlying financial strength in support of its obligations to depositors.'

Sadly, in that regard, he was very wrong. The offshore world is filled with banks whose underlying support of its obligations to depositors are just as fraudulent as his.

Sadder, too, during a 25-month span – from March 1998 to April 2000 – Ziegler/Brink was able to pull off one of the most spectacular financial rapes in the history of the offshore world.

His game was nothing more than basic 'Prime Bank' fraud.

Estimated by the US government to be a $2.5 billion a year global scam – thriving and flourishing offshore – it's based on the totally bogus assumption that certain banks and governments will pay other banks and governments annual interest rates in the 100–500 per cent range for well-kept-secret reasons.

A typical script goes like this: The government of Japan, realizing that its largest commercial banks are about to go bankrupt, has put together a pool of 15 major international banks – so-called prime banks – to rescue the economy. Through them, Japan is offering $12 billion worth of financial instruments, at a guaranteed 12.5 per cent interest per month. That's 150 per cent a year. However, while the Japanese stand firmly behind the debt, and the 15 prime banks are entitled to a tightly regulated 2.5 per cent monthly commission on every $10 million instrument they sell, there are two important restrictions legally placed on any banks' participation. First, no bank can sell any of these instruments to any entity other than a foreign government or another prime bank. And second, no bank or government involved in this can ever admit publicly that these financial instruments exist.

With that in mind, an offshore bank makes it known through its agents onshore that it has miraculously tapped into this lucrative market and obtained a portfolio of these ultra-high interest notes. Understanding how the average investor cannot possibly pay $10 million for one, the offshore bank has subdivided each parcel into $100,000 tranches. After it takes a mere 1 per cent commission per month, investors are invited to reap $9,000 monthly interest on each $100,000 investment.

It goes without saying that anyone with half a brain should instantly question 9 per cent monthly interest on anything. But, by combining a 'risk free' element – each investments is guaranteed by IDIC – and the aura of something clandestine, even a mediocre conman can erase common sense with greed.

You must remember, comes his caveat, that the secrecy clause forbids governments and banks from acknowledging the existence of these unique and exclusive investment opportunities. And even if they were allowed to tell you about them, they wouldn't because they don't want you in on it. Various governments and prime banks have conspired to keep this for themselves. Therefore, if you pick up the phone and ring a prime bank, or if you ask a government agency about this, they will go blue in the face telling you it doesn't exist. They will probably even try to frighten you away by saying it's nothing more than a con game.

As unlikely as it sounds, thousands of people fall for variations on

this absurdity every day. They phone a bank, ask about ultra-high
yield interest investments, are assured by someone that they don't
exist and instantly conclude, the guy at the offshore bank who offered
this unique and exclusive opportunity to me was right, governments
and prime banks are covering up, so obviously this stuff does exist.

For every site on the net warning the public about prime bank
fraud – Offshore Alert (http://www.offshorebusiness.com); the
Metropolitan Police (www.met.police.uk/fraudalert/prime.htm);
the US Securities and Exchange Commission (www.sec.gov/divisions/
enforce/primebank.shtml); Quatloos(www.quatloos.com/cmprime/
programme14.htm); the Royal Canadian Mounted Police (http://
www.rcmp-grc.gc.ca/scams/primeinvest.htm); and the Office of the
Comptroller of the Currency (http://www.occ.treas.gov) – there are
literally thousands of sites that offer investors the opportunity to
lose their money.

At least in the beginning, Ziegler/Brink targeted his marketing to
members of evangelical churches in Canada and the States, showing
a special affinity for pensioners. He shamelessly played off their financial insecurities and religious beliefs, claiming, as he did in one video,
'God means for everyone to have the kind of freedom that comes with
wealth.' Before long, he turned his attention to other groups, ultimately abandoning all of them to take money from anyone at all
foolish enough to give it to him.

He also turned double-talk into an art form. In a lengthy exchange
of e-mails with journalist John Greenwood of Canada's National Post,
Ziegler/Brink displayed considerable skills, explaining how FIBG
could offer such ultra-high interest rates on deposits.

It came down to, 'Understanding what you can do and by lever-
aging'. He wrote, 'I discovered that there are holders of major assets
(in the hundreds of millions of dollars and in the billions of dollars)
that are willing to deed those assets to a bank for a price, the price
including a joint venture contract on sharing the profits that could
be achieved by the effective utilisation of those assets.'

His formula for success was: '(1) create credit lines against the assets;
(2) utilize the credit lines to achieve a profit; (3) do it some more.'

To acquire $200 million in deposits, he stated, it might cost
$500,000 in special service company formation and operating
expenses, $500,000 in bank operating expenses and $1 million in
acquisition costs. 'As a result, the bank has achieved an enormous
amount of potential leverage for its initial investment. I use the word

potential because it is unrealized gain at this point. If you do nothing with the asset, you still haven't realized a cash-in-hand profit (although you have an enormous paper profit).'

With that $200 million, Ziegler/Brink promised, he could easily achieve an 80 per cent loan against assets, producing $160 million. 'I know mortgage brokers in Oregon who do nothing but buy and sell first and second mortgages and earn not less than 70 per cent per annum on their working capital.'

This from a mortgage broker who went bankrupt.

Earning 20 per cent per annum on the $160 million, he claimed, produces an income of $32 million. Paying $16 million as cost of the credit line, then splitting the rest with a joint venture partner leaves $8 million. Paying 200 per cent interest to his depositors, claiming this represents the initial $2 million, takes $4 million out of the pot, leaving $4 million as 'net-net-net profit'.

It is, of course, unadulterated bullshit.

Enter now the Ponzi element.

If the risk-free investment isn't paid out early on, word spreads that the whole thing is bogus. Ziegler/Brink needed to take care of the first people in, paying them the published high interest in order to entice new pigeons into the game. The faster the game gets — the more Peters that sign up, in principle creating more money to pay Paul — the slower the payments are to those who are actually getting something out of it. Excuses about faulty wire transfers and mistakes by distant correspondent banks fend off people looking for their money. By the time most of them open their eyes to the scheme, the bank has folded and the culprits have gone to Uganda.

Which is exactly what happened.

If you believe in fate, then it's easy to assume that David Marchant's path in life was always destined to cross Ziegler/Brink's because while Ziegler/Brink was learning his trade as an offshore conman, Marchant was learning his as an investigative journalist who hunts down offshore conmen.

Born in south Wales, Marchant studied journalism in Cardiff and began his reporting career in the Welsh valleys, covering the violent miners' strikes of the 1980s. Ten years later, in search of new stories and better weather, he emigrated to Bermuda where he spent six years annoying officialdom by exposing their follies. He wrote about local businessmen stripping Bermuda Fire & Marine Insurance of $40 million before the company went belly up. He exposed dubious share listings on the Bermuda Stock Exchange. He wrote about Bermuda's best and brightest and hung out their dirtiest financial laundry, until he'd finally upset so many people that the government lifted his work permit.

In 1996, he pitched up in Miami, started a newsletter called *Offshore Alert* – and a sister publication called *Inside Bermuda*, because he's not the kind of guy to let go that easily – and is still pissing off a lot of people. Being an equal opportunity offender, he fearlessly takes on crooked banks, phoney shell companies and corrupt governments throughout the offshore world.

Marchant was the first journalist to target Ziegler/Brink. And predictably, when Ziegler/Brink fought back, Ziegler/Brink lost.

'It wasn't exactly the greatest piece of detective work in the world,' Marchant admits, 'you know, figuring out that Van Brink was running a scam. I mean, come on, he was offering 250 per cent interest rates. What was ingenious about it, however, was how he used FIBG as a marketing ploy, how he obtained banking licences for his mates and set up those sub-banks. He understood that by franchising his fraud, the brokers who owned the sub-banks would double their efforts to raise money for him because they were also doing it for their own bank.'

Within days of Marchant's first expose of Ziegler/Brink, a major Florida law firm filed a $100 million libel suit against him. On behalf of Ziegler/Brink, they accused Marchant of, 'deliberate lies, innuendoes, unsubstantiated allegations and misleading statements.' They also tried to injunct him from further exposing their client, but the court refused to grant them a hearing on that. Just as Ponzi had tried it on with the *Boston Post* – and Marc Harris had with Marchant, as well – Ziegler/Brink was using the courts as a truncheon to beat up a journalist. The conman's gamble is that most journalists can't afford to defend a suit and learn to steer clear. But Marchant stood his ground and a court date was set. Ziegler/Brink did not file his action on time and never appeared. Inevitably, his attorneys advised Marchant that the action would not be pursued.

Ziegler/Brink now accuses Marchant of being in the pocket of the FBI, and/or the CIA, and/or competing banks, and/or unnamed evil doers who were determined to put him out of business. In his own head, conspiracy theories abound.

Sifting through the massive amount of self-aggrandizement that Ziegler/Brink has posted on the Internet, you find stories laced with secret meetings, mysterious go-betweens who have sought his advice on how to solve all the world's problems, and mistaken identity. Someone called Gil Ziegler who was once involved in a gold scam is not him, someone called Zig Ziegler who was selling a suspect investment scheme is not his brother Zig. He rationalizes his perpetual victim-mode with pure Ziegler-speak. Just because he has a caring heart, he says, and just because he simply wanted to help the common man, the big banks despised him, the press lied about him, the auditors hated him and governments deliberately set out to get him. When it was discovered that the hard-drive of his laptop computer in Grenada was bookmarked with Internet porn sites, he needed the world to understand that those bookmarks were put there by some poor kid he'd kindly hired to teach him how to use the computer.

He says his current troubles began in 1999. 'Less than 30 days after writing and widely circulating a paper highly critical of the Organisation for Economic Cooperation and Development (OECD) Council's report on "Harmful Tax Competition", I became the target of a well-financed Florida internet writer determined to smear First Bank and me with (seemingly plausible, but wholly unsubstantiated) allegations of being a fraud and operating a Ponzi-scheme (can't be the case, since total deposits are less than one percent of the bank's retained earnings/net worth) or money-laundering (also can't be the case, since it is impossible for private international banks to absorb cash deposits – all funds must come in by way of wire transfers or checks drawn on commercial banks which "know" their customers and are satisfied as to the non-criminal origin of funds).'

Marchant just laughs. 'He's always got someone else to blame. Sure, everyone's out to get him because he attended a conference and submitted a seminal paper on how the countries of the world are ripping everyone off. Come on, he was perpetrating one of the crudest frauds imaginable and ruined a lot of people's lives. But, don't forget, he never could have managed it had the government of Grenada not let it happen. Someone told me you could literally put your right hand on FIBG's front door and put your left hand on the regulator's office door.'

It is possible that certain people on the island believed Ziegler/Brink was an original thinker who could work magic in the global economy. It is more likely that certain people on the island had a relationship with him that constituted a conflict of interest. Prime candidate for villain-in-chief is the former regulator, Michael Creft.

A soft spoken man who is embarrassed about the scandal and clearly not comfortable discussing it, he says there's no question that, if he had it to do all over again, Ziegler/Brink would never have been granted a licence. 'But, remember, Grenada had just started, just come into this business, we didn't have enough experience.'

Oddly, Creft states that when Ziegler/Brink filed for FIBG's licence, he asked the FBI for a background check. In all the paperwork on the matter, there doesn't seem to be any mention of the FBI's involvement in Grenada's fledgling regulatory due diligence. But Creft insists it was done. He also says the report sent back from Washington, 'Wasn't bad, it wasn't damning'. As far as he can recall, it made no mention of Ziegler/Brink's bankruptcy. 'They did say he had some problem in Oregon but they didn't say bankrupt.'

When you mention David Marchant's name to Creft, he comments, 'Marchant was a fellow who was just after us.' Then, he thinks about that for a moment, and backtracks. 'Certainly Marchant caused us to do some hard thinking on this whole thing.'

But hard thinking didn't happen until late in the game and Marchant was writing about the bank right from the beginning. He exposed IDIC – which was publicly claiming to provide up to $100 million in coverage – pointing out that it was not licensed in Nevis as an insurer. Certainly the regulators on that island did some hard thinking because they started asking questions about the word 'insurance' in IDIC's name.

Ziegler/Brink took Marchant seriously also, telling the regulators in Nevis that IDIC was not an insurance company but an administrator of assets for member banks. When asked to name the member banks, he refused, citing secrecy agreements. The truth of the matter is, he couldn't name them because there weren't any, besides FIBG and the sub-banks. No legitimate bank was ever found to be a client of IDIC, which is hardly surprising, considering that IDIC was nothing more than a garden variety shell company with no offices and no employees. But FIBG's clients didn't know that, Ziegler/Brink wasn't going to tell them and Michael Creft didn't seem to want to find out for himself.

To keep the regulator in Nevis happy, Ziegler/Brink changed the name to International Deposit Indemnity Corporation. Even then, IDIC would still be in violation of Nevis law if indemnity meant insurance. Which it clearly did. So on 26 January 1999, the Nevis Ministry of Finance shut it down. Ziegler/Brink arranged to reopen it in Dominica. When Dominica said no, he brought it to Grenada.

On 29 January, Marchant's *Offshore Alert* detailed more wrong doings at FIBG, WISE, IDIC and other parts of Ziegler/Brink's empire. Four days later, Creft faxed Marchant: 'No company registered and/or doing business under the Laws of Grenada has been involved in any alleged wrong doing.' Creft cleared both WISE and IDIC of illicit dealings, despite the fact that IDIC had been put out of business in Nevis for illicit dealings. Creft concluded, 'We have no complaints or allegations of wrong doing made by offshore investors in the State of Grenada.'

On 12 February, Creft wrote a letter to Marchant, re-confirming what he'd already said. As far as he was concerned, FIBG was operating wholly within the law. 'This office has not received one substantiated complaint concerning its banking operations.'

That the bank was deceitfully capitalized and running a massive prime bank fraud somehow slipped past Mr Creft. Still, he reiterated that he did not see any proof of wrongdoing at IDIC, and was somewhat surprised that Nevis had taken such drastic action. He said, if real evidence of fraud or misconduct were to be forthcoming, he would act according to law. However, he warned, 'Reckless smear campaigns hurt not only offshore companies but also the Government and the people of Grenada and casts aspersions on the integrity of our jurisdiction.'

Tellingly, this letter was not mailed to Marchant on the stated date, but faxed to him at 5 o'clock in the morning from a fax number – which appears on the top of each page of Creft's letter – registered to FIBG. The suggestion is that Creft never intended it for Marchant's consumption. Instead, it was for FIBG to file with their court documents as part of Ziegler/Brink's law suit against Marchant.

Creft was aware, by then, that FIBG was offering unrealistic interest rates because he was quoted as saying, 'I don't know how they do it.' He now says that FIBG's ultra-high interest rates did, indeed, worry him at the time. 'I was very concerned'. But he never showed much concern. One suspects that a serious regulator faced with transparent fraud might have made some inquiries. Instead, on 24 February, Creft wrote that he had never received any complaints from depositors of First Bank, or any other parties with a financial interest in First Bank. 'First Bank has not engaged in any such wrong-doing or suspicious circumstances and therefore has never been investigated.'

Yet, Nevis had shut down IDIC, the Comptroller of the Currency in Washington had issued an official warning that First Bank was illegally soliciting deposits in the United States and the Financial Institutions Commission in British Columbia had issued a cease and desist order against FIBG, IDIC, and several sub-banks.

Much later, in e-mail correspondence between Ziegler/Brink and some of FIBG's directors, it would be revealed that, '$30,000 was loaned to purchase a new car for Michael Creft's significant other who called in desperate need for many months running.'

Creft gets very nervous when that subject is broached. Taking 'significant other' to mean wife, he categorically denies it, noting that his wife lives in Canada and never had anything to do with FIBG, Ziegler/Brink or a car loan. Translating 'significant other' to mean girlfriend, brings the response, 'I heard about the loan, somebody asked me, but I don't know anything about that'. Eventually he remembers, 'There was a friend of mine I knew who used to work with Van Brink. She's the one . . . nothing to do with me. She worked for Van Brink.'

By March 1999, FIBG was late in submitting its accounts to the government. Lauriston Wilson, whose local accounting firm served as the bank's auditors, was having trouble getting information out of Ziegler/Brink. He became so frustrated that he voiced his concerns to the Prime Minister. Keith Mitchell said he wanted something in writing, so on 26 March, Wilson wrote a letter to him questioning Creft's competence and honesty, and urging the PM to remove Creft from office.

Mitchell now phoned Wilson at home. Transcripts of Wilson's conversations with the prime minister were lodged in court. According to them, Wilson told Mitchell that FIBG's accounts led him to believe that the bank was capitalized at just $2, and that FIBG lacked proper internal controls and accounting systems. Wilson said he had evidence that Ziegler/Brink was cooking the books by listing depositors' funds as revenue. He says he told the PM that the operations of the bank 'are bogus and fictitious'.

Wilson also accused Ziegler/Brink of refusing to provide details of the bank's assets, and of seriously obstructing the audit. He explained

that, after reviewing FIBG's bizarre roster of assets — including
Egyptian antiquities, pre-Ming Dynasty vases, $8.7 billion worth of
suspect gold certificates and photocopies of paperwork valuing the
$20-million ruby — he asked Ziegler/Brink to show him the actual
assets. Instead, Ziegler/Brink handed Wilson photographs and photo-
copied appraisal certificates.

After insisting that the bank was in complete violation of several
provisions of Granada's Offshore Banking Act — including a purported
$200,000 campaign donation to Mitchell's New National Party —
Wilson told the PM that everything had taken place with the full
knowledge of the Registrar of Offshore Financial Services. He accused
Michael Creft of failing to take the necessary corrective action, maintained that Creft's demeanour betrayed total ignorance of his responsibilities, and concluded that Creft is, 'Apparently corrupt'.

Mitchell was utterly shocked, although not utterly shocked enough
to fire Creft because his Party executive saw Creft as a loyal member.

Instead, Ziegler/Brink fired Wilson. He also demanded that Wilson
return the bank's accounts. Wilson later claimed that the PM expressly
asked him to hold onto the accounts, so that the government could
investigate them. The PM denies it. Ziegler/Brink sued and the court
ruled that Wilson had to return the accounts. By the time the liquidators arrived, important documentation — which Wilson says was
returned by him to Ziegler/Brink — was long gone.

As all this was played out publicly, Creft could no longer deny that
accusations had been lodged against FIBG by someone in a position
to know the truth. He now suggests, 'I did speak to some FBI people
then about this. Sometime around that time. But after that, we became
very suspicious of everything.' He persists, 'I was asking him
(Ziegler/Brink) serious questions and I threatened to revoke the licence
because he was not complying with some of the regulations.'

Still, the bank stayed open for another 16 months. 'That's true,'
Creft agrees, 'but remember, things here . . . we don't do things quickly
here. There were lots of communications asking for information and
asking . . .' He stops, then indicates, 'It wasn't just me, there was a
board, and I was asking directions of the board about what to do.'

With Wilson no longer his auditor, Ziegler/Brink needed someone
to sign off on the bank's accounts. He approached several firms, but
they all turned him down. He then sought the advice of an acquaintance 'who used to be a CPA'. According to Ziegler/Brink, after the
used-to-be CPA admitted he'd served time in prison for bank fraud,

he introduced Ziegler/Brink to a man named Kenneth Nelson Craig, another used-to-be CPA, whose licence had been revoked in California in 1996. The two used-to-be CPAs prepared the report together. It's Craig's name that appears on two similar versions of FIBG's 'un-audited' annual report for 1998. Issued on the same day, one comes from Craig personally, still representing himself as a CPA with an address in Nevada, the other comes from Kenneth Craig and Associates, with an address in Guadalajara, Mexico.

The report is unmitigated fiction, mis-stating and misrepresenting the capitalization and assigned assets, and referring to trading that never took place. One declared asset is shares of an unlisted stock. The cost is put at $850,000. The current value is put at $507 million, a figure pulled out of thin air. Another asset is listed as $3.8 billion in cheques drawn on Dai-Ichi Kangyo Bank. Except they weren't cheques, they were photocopies of cheques, and a set of the same photocopies were later found at another insolvent bank in another jurisdiction. The City of London Fraud Squad reports that these Dai-Ichi cheques are forged and have been showing up in fraud cases for years. Best of all, in the report, Ziegler/Brink claims to have increased the bank's capital from $110,000 to $14 billion, and states that net income had reached $26 billion. The assertion is so outlandish that, had it been true, FIBG would have been in the same class as Chicago's Bank One Corp, the fifth-largest in the United States. But no one in Grenada challenged this.

On 23 July 1999, with David Marchant tenaciously on the case, after months of relentless allegations about the bank, and despite Wilson's warnings to the PM, Mitchell proclaimed FIBG to be sound. He said his government had asked the FBI to look into the operations of FIBG and, based on correspondence he'd received from them, there was nothing irregular about the bank. 'We had not received any indication as to any illegality on the part of the bank at this particular time.'

Three days later, a press release was issued in the names of FIBG, IDIC and WISE entitled 'First Bank Says Thanks'. In it, Ziegler/Brink redefines irony with, 'It is nothing short of breath-taking how some people will try to exploit someone's unfortunate situation for their personal gain.'

Later, misquoting the Prime Minister, Ziegler/Brink told at least one journalist, 'The FBI had concluded that there was no evidence of money-laundering or other criminal activities on the part of First Bank.'

By then, Ziegler/Brink was already planning a hasty exit stage left, creating an infrastructure for himself in Uganda, using FIBG's fund to purchase more than $4 million in properties. Presumably, he was also stashing money somewhere as well. To help smooth his landing in Africa, he called on Creft.

In a 27 July letter, written on the official stationery of the Registrar of Offshore Services, Creft told the Chairman of the Parliamentary Committee on the National Economy for the Republic of Uganda, 'According to audited financial statements submitted by the bank (FIBG), it is in a healthy financial state.' That Creft would have written the letter to begin with is odd. That he misrepresented the facts by saying that FIBG's accounts were 'audited' is sinister.

'In retrospect,' Creft says, 'I wouldn't do that again. They had . . . up to that time, while I had a lot of misgivings, concerns about Van Brink and his operation . . . there were people in Grenada who . . . I didn't have enough . . . I wouldn't do that again. That was a mistake.'

Marchant was now screaming that the jig was up. 'First International Bank of Grenada makes a mockery of the island as a legitimate financial centre.'

In a desperate effort to feign legitimacy, Ziegler/Brink offered to guarantee depositors' funds by posting a $50 million bond with the government. The financial instruments he proposed to put up were drawn on an obscure Chinese bank on the island of Hainan.

Shades of Robert Palm.

Ziegler/Brink resigned as CEO and some of his henchmen stepped in to run the day-to-day operations. And still the island authorities clung like rats to this sinking ship. Creft wrote to Ziegler/Brink – again on official letterhead – that the US government had cleared FIBG of any wrongdoing. 'The FBI carried out an investigation into the activities, procedures and associations of First Bank. They also made inquiries and checks with respect to the source of many deposits. I can confirm that the result of this investigation has exonerated First Bank regarding the allegations. The procedures adopted by First Bank with respect to all deposits are more than adequate to ensure that all deposits received into the Bank are clean funds and from legitimate sources.'

Three weeks later, the US Justice Department informed the island's authorities that they were still investigating FIBG for fraud, had seen evidence that supported the claim, and offered FBI assistance in raiding FIBG's offices. The raid never took place because the government wouldn't allow it.

On 14 December 1999, the pressure on Creft was so great that he finally asked Ziegler/Brink to respond to the general tone of the allegations which had appeared in the press throughout that year.

Already in exile in Uganda, Ziegler/Brink's answered with a 26-page rambling monograph entitled, 'Overview of the Quasi-Facts Used to Support the Allegation that Van A. Brink and/or First International Bank of Grenada Limited is Operating a Ponzi Scheme, an Illegal Pyramid Scheme and/or a Money Laundering Facility.'

Besides laying the blame for injurious and unfounded allegations squarely on a conspiracy between the FBI, the SEC and David Marchant, he announced that FIBG, 'Has now accumulated over $60,000,000,000 (not a typo, $60 billion) in profits held in cash equivalent instruments issued by top 100 banks.'

His parenthesised 'not a typo, $60 billion' claim, suggested that FIBG had somehow made an additional $34 billion in just nine months. That too went unchallenged by the Grenadians. Ziegler/Brink supported this absurdity with the explanation that the increase in net income came about thanks to a secret side of Grenada's banking system, one that other banks purposely hid on their balance sheets. He wrote, 'First Bank has a cash equivalent base equal to over 600 times the total amount of its liabilities to depositors.'

He also hit out at Marchant's allegations. 'A Ponzi scheme? No. Just a bank that chose to report accurately on its balance sheet those matters other banks long ago decided to keep on an 'off ledger' basis. Naive, perhaps, but not dishonest, unethical, immoral, unlawful or illegal.'

Undoubtedly, Ziegler/Brink saw the big cash crunch finale waiting in the wings and desperately tried to finagle $3.8 billion from Malaysia to pay for humanitarian projects in something he referred to as the G-77 countries. The proposed collateral were two financial instruments drawn on an Asian bank. When that didn't happen, he went shopping for $21.6 billion, this time for a free-trade zone and health centre in Uganda, Soya products in Brazil and a buffalo ranch in Canada. This time the collateral would be, 'Top rated cash-equivalent instruments that have been deeded to First Bank.'

As his various associates began to flee, others took their place. A man described as, 'a little-known chartered accountant from Yorkshire', came along to do an audit and a report issued in his name – but without his signature – brands the bank, hunky-dory.

Marchant shot back that the audit, 'triggers disbelief'.

To secure his own financial future, Ziegler/Brink tried to buy a co-operative bank from the Uganda government. But his arrival in the country had been greeted with the local newspaper headline, 'Conman On The Run', and he was turned down on the grounds that he was not qualified banker. Ziegler/Brink claimed to have negotiated an $80 million deal with a Congolese rebel leader for control over mineral resources in an area that the rebel group controls. He also claimed to have negotiated a $16 million deal with another rebel leader who agreed to appoint Ziegler/Brink to run the nation's central bank, should the rebel group come to power.

By April 2000, the flow of funds from FIBG had come to a halt.

Throughout that spring and summer, the authorities in Grenada refused to believe they'd been had. When they assigned the former accountant general as interim administrator, he reported that millions of dollars were missing and that several millions had been transferred to Uganda.

At the time, the annual jazz festival was taking place on the island, sponsored in part by FIBG. So the government – finally conceding defeat – politely waited until the jazz festival ended before putting the bank out of business.

Apparently someone thought it would look bad if they did it while the music was still playing.

For years, the Eastern Caribbean has been a sink for dirty banks and suspect shell companies. Grenada dragged the region's reputation to a new low.

At one point, in one of the most dim-witted decisions in the history of offshore finance, the government of Grenada actually agreed to grant a new licence to the people running FIBG, calling the Mark II version, First International Bank of Grenada 2000.

Somehow, better advice prevailed. They revoked Ziegler/Brink's citizenship and a Grenada court formally accused him of stealing $150 million.

The government then set about making substantial reforms to their offshore industry. Seventeen banks directly affiliated with FIBG were shut down. A few months later, they closed six more. Most of the rest of their offshore banks have been shut one by one. Only a couple of the original 29 remain. The government revoked the law which allowed

them to sell economic citizenship, amended their banking and companies acts, accepted Michael Creft's resignation – he announced he was
doing it for purely personal reasons, so that he could pursue other interests – and established the Grenada Industrial Development Corporation
to put in place a more serious regulatory infrastructure.

Finally, hoping to salvage something out of this mess, the government turned to someone who actually knew what he was doing. They
appointed Marcus A. Wide, of PricewaterhouseCoopers, to be official
liquidator. Enormously experienced in the ways of the Caribbean, Wide
recognized immediately, 'FIBG was a sham from its inception.'

In three well documented reports, Wide describes the fraudulent
chaos in which the bank operated. He says that Ziegler/Brink's only
intentions were to mislead depositors and to use their funds to line
his own pockets. He says that depositors were subject to fraudulent
misrepresentation with respect to investment opportunities, and that
funds received by FIBG should now be considered proceeds of crime.

As of mid-2003, Wide has found less than $500,000 in assets,
although he calculates that the bank took around $125 million in
deposits from about 6,000 victims of Ziegler/Brink's criminality.

'Brink was indiscriminate about who he sucked money from. Many
of his victims were pensioners who were just scraping by, and put
their life savings into this looking for a better lifestyle. Now they
have absolutely nothing. And Brink doesn't give a shit. He's a
disgusting man. He's the worst of the lot. He's repellent.'

The only reason that Ziegler/Brink is not in jail, Wide says, is
because he's in Uganda and there's no extradition. But he promises,
'It's just a matter of time. Sooner or later, we will get him.'

At the end of 2002, Wide obtained a judgement in Grenada against
Ziegler/Brink for theft of $125 million. In February 2003, a court in
Uganda recognized that judgement, which allows Wide to go after
properties there. 'He says he doesn't own them, but we've got the trail
that clearly says he does. We've now frozen them, so he can't sell
them.'

Wide also believes that Ziegler/Brink has stashed money somewhere
and can't get to it without tipping his hand, or that he's deliberately
staying away from it for the time being. 'He did such a good job of
raping and pillaging, and a great job of putting blinds in the way,
using payment centres through which money flowed, that it's very
difficult to trace the money. We figure he probably got away with
$20 million.'

Expressing some sympathy for the islanders — 'They didn't appreciate the extent to which they were opening doors to the crooks and thugs and liars and cheats' — Wide concedes they were done in by a masterful scheme. 'Out of the 30-something banks that I'm involved with down there, as a liquidator and receiver, this is the best scam I have seen, by far.' Wide is not convinced, however, that Ziegler/Brink came up with it all by himself. 'The guy's not that smart. He was nothing but a petty fraudster from way back. I think he learned a lot of this stuff from someone else.'

Whether Ziegler/Brink, or anyone else, ever goes to jail for this is up to law enforcement. With the agreement of the courts in Grenada, Wide has made all of FIBG's records, and all of the records of the subsidiary companies, available to the FBI.

Hiding in Uganda, Ziegler/Brink clearly hopes he's out of reach. Just in case, he married a local woman half his age which, blissful love aside, means he can't now be extradited. Along with his bride comes the possibility of an Ugandan passport. But then, Ziegler/Brink apparently doesn't see any reason why he might be extradited. He maintains that he wasn't the owner of FIBG, just the guiding spirit.

In yet another protracted e-mail to John Greenwood at the National Post, Ziegler/Brink waxes lyrical, 'Isaac Newton may have not legally owned the Law of Gravity, but when he spoke of it and wrote as concerning it and made recommendations to others as pertaining to it, people tended to listen. He was looked up to as a father, legal ownership notwithstanding . . . I was looked up to as a father, legal ownership notwithstanding.'

He steadfastly maintains that he's not to blame for anything, that everybody else is out to get him and that, obviously, they did because he's penniless.

When conmen get caught out, many of them run a second scam off the back of the first. As long as there are enough defrauded investors clamouring for their money, it's not usual to see someone pop up with an investors' reclamation group. True to form, Ziegler/Brink is doing just that in various Internet forums, hiding behind the alias Ira M. Samuels.

Introducing himself as a fellow investor who's lost money, Samuels explains that he's organizing a team of private detectives, lawyers, accountants, butchers, bakers and candlestick makers — he never gives specifics and refuses to name names — in order to help get everyone's money back. Ever altruistic, he's doing this for the common good of the human race, and has recently been assured by his team that they are ready to pounce. Like-minded defrauded investors who want to share the booty, are invited to split expenses with him.

Which means, send money.

Writing in the same forums under his own name, Ziegler/Brink berates Wide, constantly proclaims his innocence, sings the praises of Ira M. Samuels, and swears that he is ready, willing and able to do whatever he can to see that First Bank's creditors get their money back. One email even contains his firm promise that he would happily return to Grenada to sort out the problems if someone would simply cover his expenses.

Marcus Wide heard about that and quickly took Ziegler/Brink up on his offer.

But safety in Uganda remains the better part of valour.

As Ziegler/Brink explained it in his answer to Wide: 'I have to devote on an average of 10 hours a day to generate a living. I have yet to take a 20+ hour airline commute to a destination, spend a day or two there and return 20+ hours and not be sick in bed for the following week (and that is flying business class, not economy class – I think in economy class I would require hospitalization on both ends of the flight). Therefore, financially and for reasons of physical health, I say "No, thank you".'

CHAPTER NINE

Cabletrap

Without bank secrecy, the Cayman Islands
would be a fishing community again.
— Former Caymans' banker, John Mathewson

Gordon Ryan owned a hotdog cart on a street corner in downtown Jersey City, New Jersey.

One dog with sauerkraut and mustard, please . . .
It was called Gordon's Hotdogs.
. . . one Dr Pepper . . .
And for a while, business really boomed.
. . . oh yeah, and a pirate cable box to go.

The Grenadians were pure amateurs who learned some expensive lessons at the hands of Ziegler/Brink. Instead, they should have taken a few classes in the Caymans, where learning to fly below the radar is a required course.

John Mathewson had served in the US Marine Corps and, afterwards, ran his own construction company in Chicago. Closing in on his 52nd birthday, around 1980, Mathewson decided he'd made enough money to retire. After all those Midwest winters, it's understandable why he chose some place warm like the western Caribbean. But there was more to his choice than just sunshine and scuba diving. He had it in his head to start a second career. This time he was going to be a banker. And the Caymans was a very good place to do just that. Little did he know when he moved there that, one day, a New Jersey hot dog would ruin his life.

The first thing Mathewson did after buying a shell bank called Argosy was look around for a more suitable name. He settled on Guardian Bank and Trust Company because there were at least 11 other

banks around the world called Guardian and he knew that by creating
a bit of confusion, it would be that much more difficult for someone
to trace any transactions back to his Guardian.

'This was a key concern,' he said later, 'because offshore banks in
small jurisdictions, by necessity, conduct most of their transactions
through international payment systems and need to find ways to minimize detection and disclosure of client information.'

Unlike many other companies and banks registered in the Caymans
in those days, Guardian did have a physical presence, renting office
space on the second floor of a downtown low-rise building. The law
obliged that his clients be foreigners, but that wasn't a problem because
he'd always intended to go after a European clientele. Yet, owning a
bank was one thing, bringing customers in was another and no matter
what he did, he couldn't secure enough European business to stay open.

Worried for his own investment, he turned to the North American
market, advertising heavily in US and Canadian in-flight magazines.
His ads hinted that he could help make income tax 'an optional matter'.
Though he never came right out and said, we'll help you evade taxes,
he didn't have to. He couched his sales pitches in the usual lingo of
'asset protection'. And it worked. By 1990, Mathewson would claim
to hold $350 million in deposits. More than 90 per cent of his clients
were American, of whom 95 per cent were there specifically to evade
taxes.

'Without US clients, there wouldn't be a banking industry in the
Cayman Islands,' he said later. What's more, 'it is ridiculous to think
that anyone would establish an offshore account without tax evasion
as the motive.'

Long before Mathewson invented Guardian or Gordon started selling
hotdogs, America was wiring-up for cable television.

Even though it took more than a decade, and even though most
of the rest of the world opted for satellite, by the 1980s an abun-
dance of sports, movies, cooking, all news channels and all-night-
porn – but especially CNN, HBO, ESPN, Cinemax, Showtime,
pay-per-view events and porn – assured an abundant flow of customers.
However, there was a serious flaw in the business. Like the little
Dutch boy who needed to keep his finger in the dyke to prevent the
sea from flooding his village, cable service providers were constantly

wrestling with the way their scrambled signals were so easily stolen.

The problem lay in the chip. Unlike, say, a mobile phone where the computer which allows you access to the network is at the phone company, the cable box which descrambles the television signal lives in your house, usually right next to your set. Given untethered access to the box, anyone intent on stealing service merely has to open the lid, pull out a 28-prong chip, put in a modified chip and screw the lid back on. People who can't work their own VCR are able to manage this trick in less than 30 seconds. Cable service providers blame equipment manufacturers for making signal theft too easy. Manufacturers blame advancing technology which is readily available to anybody who wants it.

As long ago as 1984, Washington recognized that cable piracy was a serious problem, tried to help but only made matters worse. Under that year's Cable Act, Congress ruled that the crime was stealing the signal, not buying, owning or selling a descrambler. Unlike drugs, where possession counts, the weight of the law fell on the use to which you put the pirate cable box. Technically, you can buy and use one without risk of penalty, as long as you pay the cable operator for what you're watching. Therefore, it's been argued, the only person who can break the law is the end user, not the people who build or sell the decoders.

Based on that ruling, pirate descramblers poured onto the market throughout the 1980s. Cable box pirates emerged from the underworld and into the shadows of the legitimate world, in large part abetted by the industry itself which charges clients per television. If you're paying for cable on a livingroom set and you decide you'd also like to hook up your bedroom set, service providers claim the right to add a fee for that second television. Consumers, feeling hard done, argue that because it's not illegal to own a pirate box, if you're already paying for cable on one set, connecting a box to a second set is not theft of services. If it's anything, it's just an inexpensive way to beat the cable companies at their, arguably, greedy game.

And so cable piracy donned the cloak of a perfect crime.

Pirates, seeing this as a high return, low risk venture, advertised in prominent magazines and newspapers. The public assumed this must be legit or the pirates wouldn't be permitted to publicize it. Accordingly, well into the 1990s, more and more product was fed onto the market to meet ever increasing demand. With the advent of the Internet, pirates headed *en masse* to cyberspace, offering ready-made boxes online. Today, there are sites with instructions for hobbyists who want to build their own. The parts cost around $13 and are cheerfully available in electronics stores found in most shopping malls.

As a result, cable theft has become so widespread that it's said to occur with one in five subscribers. These days, the American cable business is worth around $24 billion a year. Piracy accounts for roughly $7 billion of that. It's hardly surprising then, with so much money at stake, that cable pirates employ professional marketing people and top class engineers and spend enormous sums on research and development to stay one ahead of the legitimate chip manufacturers.

Understandably, cable operators are very aggressive when it comes to protecting their market. So when a senior executive at the service provider in Jersey City heard that a hotdog vendor was moving pirate boxes, he alerted the FBI in nearby Newark. Because taking a hotdog seller off the streets isn't quite like shooting it out with John Dillinger, the job went to the lowest guy on the Totem pole.

Bill Waldie had been with the Bureau just three years. A New Jersey kid who'd originally been assigned to the Washington DC field office, he'd recently transferred home. His supervisor handed him the short straw. As far as the Bureau was concerned, this was a case of low priority signal theft. As far as Waldie was concerned, his desk was already piled high with grunt work.

'Gordon was selling Oak Sigma boxes,' Waldie begins, 'which seemed to be the most interesting thing about the case because prior to this, nobody had been able to descramble an Oak Sigma box. Everybody did General Instrument and Scientific Atlanta boxes, but Oak was the tough one. I figured I was looking at two days work, tops. I'd eat a few hotdogs, do a couple of controlled buys and take this guy down.'

Waldie went to look at Gordon, where hotdogs turned out to be the easiest part of the deal. Lunch came with no questions asked, but Gordon demanded answers before he'd even discuss cable boxes. He wanted to know how Waldie knew he had boxes for sale. He wanted references. Of course, Waldie told Gordon what he wanted to hear and once Gordon was satisfied that this customer was legit, Gordon asked, 'Suburban or Jersey City?'

That sparked Waldie's interest. If Gordon could offer Oak boxes with different chips, Waldie wondered about Gordon's suppliers. It's one thing to stick a chip in a box, it's another to provide for variations in the same market. Legitimate cable boxes are worth around $35. Adding a $5 pirate chip to it puts the price up to $250–$350.

Gordon was asking $450 for the Oak Sigmas.

'Where I made my mistake,' Waldie admits, 'was thinking, this guy is too low level. He was selling hot dogs for a living. It just didn't figure that he could be dealing a lot of boxes. But it was obvious that Gordon's suppliers were running a sophisticated operation. I didn't know how many more Gordons there were, but I was less interested in them than I was in finding the next guy up the ladder, then following the ladder all the way to the top. That's where I made my mistake. Instead of working this case for a few days, I turned it into four years.'

Along the way, Gordon got shut down.

But more than ten years after that first hotdog, a lot of people a long way from Jersey City are still getting indigestion.

As a young man, Philip Deming spent five years with the Bureau of Alcohol Tobacco and Firearms. Although he left ATF to set up as a security consultant to the telecommunications industry, he never stopped thinking like a street cop. It all came back to him in 1993, on hire to General Instrument, then the world's largest manufacturer of cable boxes. Reporting directly to Stan Durey, GI's head of security, Deming had been scouring the country, investigating the major pirates. He'd identified a Lebanese family in Nebraska named Abboud and had approached the FBI in Washington hoping they'd help him shut these guys down, but the Bureau hadn't shown much interest.

That's when Durey received a call from a former employee looking to move a load of boxes into South America. It's a critical market for manufacturers because that's where they sell excess descramblers. With newer, more advanced models tempting American consumers to upgrade every few years, out-of-date models sold south of the border represent a significant revenue stream. The former employee told Durey that he and a business partner had a deal to place $4–$5 million worth of older boxes in Brazil and wanted Durey to supply them. He was very persistent and Durey didn't want to risk losing the sale, but something about it made him uncomfortable. Durey asked Deming to find out more.

Deming quickly suspected that the former employee was working some sort of scam. But rather than cancel the deal outright, Deming suggested that he and Durey meet with the former employee and his partner to find out exactly what was going on. The encounter was arranged for the US Airways lounge at New York's LaGuardia Airport.

'At the time,' Deming recalls, 'that was the only airline lounge at LaGuardia inside the security loop. You had to go through the metal detectors to get there. I wanted to make sure these guys weren't wired, that they couldn't use any information against us at a later date. I also wanted to be sure they weren't armed.'

Arriving at the club early to make certain that no one could bug the conference room, he wasn't there long before a character in his early 40s appeared, looking as if he'd just walked off the set of *The Sopranos*. Dressed in a black suit with a black shirt, and sporting a signet ring that no one could possibly miss – the initial 'F' was made out of eight one carat diamonds – this guy was also casing the place.

When the former employee showed up, he had a brief conversation with the man in black, then left him alone until Durey arrived. The former employee greeted Durey, who introduced Deming and those three went into the conference room. Only after they settled in, did the man in black join them.

'His name was Frank Russo,' Deming says. 'And he clearly wanted everyone to think he was seriously connected. We found out later that he'd beaten up a few people and done some loan sharking, but nothing more than that. He was on the periphery, just someone who liked wiseguys. But we didn't know that then. He spent the whole meeting smoking and drinking scotch. I kept thinking that he was exactly the kind of guy who would show up wired and armed. He made us very ill at ease.'

Frank was introduced as the president of a start-up company looking to move boxes south. Durey went to great pains to explain that General Instrument, like all legitimate cable equipment suppliers, kept tight control of boxes specifically so that pirates couldn't get their hands on them to re-chip them. He warned that the company vetted everyone they sold boxes to and before they could make any sort of deal, they'd need to run background checks on Frank and his company.

Frank's answer to that was, 'Okay, what's your price?'

Durey was stunned.

But Frank was prepared. 'Two million to facilitate the deal.'

With only $4–$5 million up for grabs, a bribe that size made no sense. But Deming immediately saw this as his way in. 'The first thing I did was get Durey out of there. I said to Frank that Durey had to leave the room, that he represents a publicly held company and that there's no way he could be party to anything like this.'

Durey followed Deming's lead, stood up and walked out.

Now Deming turned to Frank. 'Okay, tell me more. If I'm interested, we'll cut Durey out of the deal.'

Frank said that sounded good him and outlined his plans.

The following day, Deming briefed General Instrument's lawyers on the deal Frank was proposing. When they agreed that this was a case of commercial bribery, Deming rang his FBI contacts in Washington and explained what had transpired. Suddenly, they seemed interested in what Deming had to say.

What he didn't yet know was that back in Newark, Bill Waldie was making big plans.

The deeper Waldie got into 'the hotdog case', the more expansive the web of players became.

The more mobbed up the players became, too.

Waldie now sat down with Assistant United States Attorney Donna Gallucio – a fireball prosecutor who is one of the last people in Newark that defence lawyers volunteer to tangle with – and the two of them started talking 'big picture'. The presence of the Mob meant this had the potential of a major, nationwide case. But Mob presence also raised the risk of danger. A case against them would require a lot of 'backstopping' – physical backup, established safety measures, evidence gathering systems securely in place. If they were going to do it right, Waldie and Gallucio decided, they'd need to commit 'assets'. And that cost money. So Gallucio and Waldie put together an elaborate game plan, seeking permission and the funds to go 'Group One'.

For the sake of definition, when a cop does a 'buy-bust' – goes undercover and wears a funny hat and a wig to purchase something from somebody on a street corner – that's a 'Group Three' undercover. When a cop spends a couple of days being somebody else to get evidence on tape, and there is also a danger element, it slips into the category of 'Group Two'. But when an operation covers the scope of this one, when there is a heightened element of danger, when human resources are committed and assets are required – 'toys' such as registered corporations, leased offices, penthouse apartments, helicopters, jets, Ferraris, gold chains, silk suits, speed boats – then 'Group One' rules apply. For that, a special board is convened by the Justice Department in Washington to approve or disapprove the plan, then to amend the plan, set parameters, establish timing, supervise the backstopping and fund the operation.

What started with a couple of hotdogs soon became six months of dreary paperwork and cheerless administrative battles simply to secure Washington's approval. But the case they made for going Group One was sound, the board said yes, and as soon as that happened, everything else moved at lightening speed. Waldie rented a warehouse with a loading bay in an industrial park in Kenilworth, New Jersey. Bureau technicians wired it for sound and video while Waldie purchased furniture for the office, got stationery printed, got invoices printed, got phones and computers installed, and even got himself a forklift truck. He obtained a supply of cable boxes from one of the manufacturers, had them secretly stamped to identify them as evidence, installed a young agent named Jim Kay at the front counter and, just like that, went into business as Prime Electronics. The only thing he didn't have were any customers.

That's when Philip Deming came along with Frank Russo.

'This was the perfect point to introduce our company into the game,' Waldie says. 'Everything fitted together. Prime had boxes to sell and Deming had Frank Russo to buy them.'

They played him like a fish. Deming told Frank there was no way General Instrument would authorize him to be a dealer but said he'd located a company willing to act for him. Deming promised that he could get his friend Jim at Prime Electronics authorized, waited a reasonable amount of time before ringing Frank to say that Prime had GI's blessings and within days Jim was moving cable boxes to Frank. To keep Deming sweet, and make certain that Prime wasn't a bunch of cops, Frank put Deming on the payroll at $10,000 a month, cash.

'We started with the people selling this stuff', Gallucio says. 'From there we moved on to the distributors. When we saw how they were getting boxes, we moved up to the wholesalers. Before we knew it, we were doing business with people all over the country.'

Cable piracy had never been a priority for the FBI and nobody could recall a cable case initiated by the Bureau. But 'Cabletrap' got so huge so fast that it became a 7-days-a-week, 18-hours-a-day venture. Gallucio soon needed help so another Assistant US Attorney was brought on board.

His name is Jim Carney. 'The hotdog guy was a mope. What made this case exciting, what Bill and Donna did, was go from one guy on a street corner in Jersey City to multi-million dollar companies operating throughout the States, Asia, Malta, the UK and other parts of the world. Prime moved boxes by the thousands, all the time developing and processing a staggering amount of evidence against an ever expanding network of people.'

To convict them, Gallucio and Carney would have to show 'intent'. Because Prime was dealing in raw, unchipped boxes, the prosecution would need to demonstrate in court that the people buying those boxes from Prime intended to turn them into pirate cable boxes which would allow their clients to steal signals. So with surveillance cameras running, Jim Kay began telling some of his customers, I'll get you 100 raw boxes but need you to send 10 back to me chipped because I've got some friends. And just like that, chipped boxes started coming back to Prime.

In one instance, Kay didn't have to do anything because the bad guy did it by himself. He swaggered into the warehouse, sat down in front of a hidden camera and lectured Kay, 'The FBI can't catch you unless they know you're stealing, and we know we're stealing but they don't.'

Another genius chipped a bunch of boxes in front of Waldie and Kay, not realizing that he was being taped or to whom he was bragging. 'The only way the FBI is going to catch me,' he said, 'is if they're standing here right now watching me do this.'

From the start, Frank Russo was moving so many boxes that he was always going to be Prime's biggest customer. But what made Frank even more interesting was his partner, Joe Russo. The two were not related but shared a Hollywood, Florida company called Leasing Ventures. They also owned a company called Cable Box Services and had several large warehouses in Port St Lucie, Florida through which they moved pirated boxes.

Where Frank was a poser, Joe was the real thing, a major player hooked into the Gambino mob. The man behind Joe – his silent partner who backed several large purchases of raw boxes – was John 'Johnny Black' Trematerra, an ageing and respected wiseguy with the Luchesse crime family. It was Joe who elevated Cabletrap into the big leagues.

The Russos bought boxes when they could get them and stole boxes when they couldn't buy them. Hand in hand with Joe's connections came guns and violence. When Joe heard about a thief named Willie Pagan who'd stolen 40,000 boxes from a warehouse in Baltimore, Joe moved in on him. Willie had been so adept in lifting the $5 million worth of boxes that the company didn't even know it had been ripped off until Bill Waldie told them. But Willie made a critical mistake while moving the boxes to a fellow in Florida who was, in turn, selling them to Frank and Joe. He'd accidentally left the original labels on a few. Joe tracked the labels back to Willie and, accompanied by one of his leg breakers, informed Willie that from now on he was selling to the Russos direct. Joe also decided how much he would pay for the boxes, which was considerably less than the Russos were already paying. Willie became the Russos' new supplier and, every now and then, Frank Russo would sell some of Willie's stolen boxes to Jim Kay at Prime.

'These guys didn't care who they did business with or how,' Waldie points out. 'They robbed everything they could, and even robbed from themselves. Frank and Joe set up a company called Greenhouse Electronics in order to rip off John Trematerra. They used Greenhouse to buy stuff, which they'd mark up, then sell to Leasing Ventures at the higher price. Leasing Ventures paid for it with Trematerra's money and the mark up got split between Joe and Frank.'

Joe's legbreaker friend and Willie Pagan were not the only sleazebags to stroll into Cabletrap with the Russos. The legbreaker introduced his mate 'George The Animal' into the circuit and George sold stolen boxes to Prime, which Prime sold on to Frank Russo, who often commented on tape that he knew the boxes were hot.

'These guys are not exactly what you'd call intellects,' Waldie continues. 'But they're streetwise. Their problem is, greed blinds them. It's about money. How much can we make? How much more can we make? They become pigs. They don't trust each other and rightfully so. They do backdoor deals. There were times when Frank would say to us, don't tell Joe because he doesn't know about this so you've got to get me cash, send the money to my house.'

With tens of millions of dollars pouring in, Frank bought himself a Mercedes convertible. Joe decided he wanted one too but still had a year left on the lease of his Lexus. To get rid of it, he arranged to have the car stolen, then trashed. Unfortunately, he reported it stolen the day after it was recovered. And every bit of this was recorded on tape as the guys bragged to Jim Kay.

Also on tape was the Russos' benevolence to Deming. Once, when Deming went to Florida to collect his monthly ten grand, Frank pulled a stack of fresh $100 bills out of the dishwasher.

Before long, Deming announced that he wanted more. 'We were moving boxes by tractor-trailer loads. One of the things that concerned me was that the sums of money changing hands wouldn't mean much if we went to trial in Newark. Think about someone sitting on a jury

from a working-class neighbourhood downtown, and you tell him that
the defendants are doing millions of dollars worth of business. He sees
a businessman and figures that's what businessmen do. So I suggested
to the Bureau that we needed to show the jury that these weren't ordinary businessmen, that they paid their bills in extraordinary ways.
The FBI agreed and so I asked Frank for a Porsche Carrera.'

Keeping Deming happy made sense to Russo, who paid $52,000
for the car in Florida and delivered it to Deming in New Jersey.

'It was beautiful,' Deming says with a tinge of anguish in his voice,
'but the FBI wouldn't let me keep it. I tried to convince myself that
I shouldn't be too disappointed. I rationalized the whole thing away
by saying, anyway, it's an automatic.'

Feeling his pain, the Bureau let Deming drive it – once – and then,
like everything else collected in the case, the Porsche was stored as
evidence. Later Russo offered Deming a cigarette boat, but the operation got closed down before he could drive that, once, too.

Mathewson always held his clients' hands as he walked them each
through the same routine.

He started by selling them a shell company and into the shell went
whatever bank and brokerage accounts the client wanted. To access
their money, he gave them a gold Visa or MasterCard – always in the
name of the shell – and a spending limit that could go as high as $1
million a month, depending on how much the client had on deposit
with the bank. He also coached them to sign the back of the card
with a signature that was 'reproducible but hard to read.'

Clients wishing to deposit cheques were instructed by Mathewson
to make them payable to a Guardian owned shell – they had names
like Fulcrum and Sentinel and Tower – and warned never to endorse
the cheques. Instead, he told them to send the cheques with their
Guardian account number written on a separate plain sheet of paper.
In turn, Guardian stamped each check for deposit in the name of a
correspondent bank, without any reference to the Cayman Islands.

Guardian's correspondents included: Credit Suisse in Guernsey;
Cayman National, Bank of Bermuda, and Butterfield International in
the Caymans; Sun, Popular, Capital, First Union National, EuroBank
and Bank of New York in the States; and, Royal Bank of Canada, Toronto
Dominion, Credit Suisse and Cannaccord Capital in Canada. Guardian

also had correspondent relationships with brokers, including Prudential, Wheat First, Smith Barney Shearson, Charles Schwab, and Richardson Greenshields.

According to Mathewson, none of those correspondents requested any information about Guardian's clients. As far as he could tell, 'I don't think any of them ever attempted to monitor the account.'

If funds were being wired in, Mathewson told clients to use a non-US correspondent bank, so as to keep documentation held in the States to a minimum. Again, no personal information was to be included. Clients would simply phone Guardian to advise them of the transfer.

The easiest way to get money out of an account was with the credit card. But clients who wanted chequebooks could have them. They were usually issued by one of the correspondent banks, either with the word Guardian printed on the top – but without any address or phone number – or, with nothing at all printed on it, except the number of the Guardian account at that correspondent bank. Furthermore, Guardian also maintained its own current accounts with correspondent banks, which did not identify Guardian, so that any client wishing to make a large purchase without leaving a trail could have Guardian pay the bill, writing as many cheques as it took to skirt any reporting requirements. That meant cheques were usually written for sums under $10,000.

Doing business with Mathewson was not cheap. Guardian's charges were $5,000 to open an account, and $3,000 annually to maintain it. Clients paid an additional $5,000 for a standard shell company – they only cost Mathewson $500 to buy from the local authorities – and $12,000–$16,000 if they needed an 'aged' shell. That's a company incorporated several years before which allowed clients to back date invoices and create fictitious trading records. The required nominee shareholder for each shell was often a Guardian subsidiary, for which there was a fee. Mathewson also supplied company directors – usually another Guardian subsidiary – for another fee. On top of those, he charged $100 per wire transfer, sent or received.

Additional services included invoices in the name of any company to help clients defraud their own companies with transfer pricing scams, and shell companies incorporated in the Netherlands to work back-to-back loans disguised as mortgages. Mathewson's fees for transfer pricing ranged from $1,000 an hour to a flat sum of $25,000 per year, plus a percentage of the cost of the product invoiced. His fee for the back-to-back loan scam was $30,000.

It all added up to a lot of money, but Mathewson knew that whatever it cost, it was still cheaper for his clients than paying taxes. 'Why would any citizen wish to go through the time and expense required to establish an offshore account unless it was for the evasion of taxes or the hiding of funds? Even when an offshore account looks innocent, it very probably has a hidden agenda.'

Bill Waldie's investigation of the Russos — which included Frank's wife and son — soon caught the attention of an FBI team in Florida. Together they went up on wire taps to target a load of new people.

Around the same time, the FBI finally turned its sights to Deming's Lebanese pirates in Nebraska. The Abboud family was among the most visible of the cable pirates. They advertised and were active in a pirate cable consumer's association that held regular meetings in Las Vegas. There pirates openly lectured on how to avoid forfeiture by the FBI, what to do if you got caught with cable boxes and how to hide pirate goods. Trailing the Abbouds, agents also showed up at conventions, took a lot of notes and added names to the target list.

One of them was William S. (Trey) Prevost, III. Something of a cult hero in the trade, the 29-year-old owned and operated several businesses in Sun Valley, California including two pirate cable firms, Novaplex and Gage Systems Group. Prevost had run up against the police before, in the early 1990s, when he was raided and the cops seized 3,500 cable boxes. The judge put him on probation, ordered him to stay out of the business and to pay $2.75 million to the southern California cable operator he'd defrauded.

The quarter of a million dollars worth of boxes that the cops seized from Prevost wound up in a Los Angeles Police Department evidence facility, which happened to be a used jail that they occasionally rented out to television and film production companies. Somehow, Joe and Frank Russo found out where that was and, along with a connected guy in LA whom Joe knew, convinced the LAPD that they were an MTV crew. They rented the jail for a music video, arrived in an empty van, located the boxes, cut the bars, filled the van and drove off.

As if stealing evidence from the LAPD wasn't audacious enough, they came back two more times, until they had all 3,500 boxes.

Needless to say, when Prevost found out who did it he was extremely annoyed. He knew he'd never get the boxes back from Joe and Frank, but reckoned he could get something out of it from the LAPD. So he sued the cops, claiming that the police had a responsibility to safeguard his possessions while they were being held in custody. It was a good try, but didn't work.

The Russos sold some of Provost's boxes to the Abbouds, and the rest to Prime. Frank Russo even explained to Jim, unknowingly on camera, how he'd cooked up the perfect alibi. He said he had receipts proving that he'd purchased the boxes from a fellow named Ken. Making the alibi watertight, Frank declared, 'Ken's fuckin' dead and dead men can't talk.' To which he added proudly, 'I thought of that all by myself.'

In the meantime, Waldie's investigation of Prevost revealed that he was still very much in the business and therefore, in violation of his probation. He had a 50,000-square-foot warehouse filled with 17 articulated lorry loads of pirate cable boxes. He'd also formed a consortium with Joe, Frank and a group of other guys, called 'Cable Box Central', which served as an umbrella under which they concealed several companies, their own identities and a great deal of illegal activity. They brought components into the country from the Orient addressed to aliases and sham corporations, sneaking past Customs with false declarations. They also hijacked an articulated lorry carrying cable boxes. While law enforcement in California and Arizona investigated the thefts, Waldie watched the stolen cable boxes arrive at Prime's front door. He added interstate transportation of stolen property to the growing list of charges eventually brought against both Russos.

Targeting Prevost also led Waldie to the computer nerd who masterminded the chip technology. For his services, Prevost was paying him more than $1 million a year.

'It was a huge web,' Waldie continues. 'All the big players were intertwined. They all dealt with each other. They were each other's competitors, but they all needed raw cable boxes and Prime became the centre of this. It got so hectic that Jim Kay and I were in the warehouse every morning by 6, sometimes seven days a week, sometimes staying there 18 hours a day.'

There were days, he says, when a load would come in with a couple of thousand boxes. They'd have to unpack them, micro-stamp each one so they could be used as evidence, then repack them and ship them. In summer it was 110 degrees inside that warehouse.

'Prime was making money hand over fist and we weren't even the ones who were chipping the boxes. We were selling raw boxes in big numbers. Nobody walked in off the street to buy one or two. In fact, unless you knew us, you couldn't even get in the front door. Frank Russo would show up to buy 2,000 boxes. That might be a $135,000 deal for us, he'd flip it for $250,000, somebody would chip them and retail the load for $350,000. Everybody made money.'

Including the FBI.

'Once we got this thing off the ground, we were self-supporting. We didn't use any Bureau money. Prime paid for the entire investigation, all four years worth. Our warehouse, our travel, our food, our buy money, everything we did, got paid for out of the profit from Prime. Then, when it was all done, we sent the Bureau something like a million dollars that we still had in the bank'. Waldie thinks about that for a moment, then jokes, 'Of course, when you break it down, Jim and I were working for a buck an hour.'

With so many cable boxes moving out of Prime and so much money coming into Leasing Ventures, the Russos started to worry about protecting their stash. They wanted to put their money somewhere safe, where no one could find it. Should the day ever come when they got busted, they needed to make sure there'd be no money trail to follow.

It was Joe Russo who knew about Guardian Bank. He told Frank, who mentioned it to Jim Kay, and that's how the Bureau first heard about Mathewson. Frank's idea was to move all their banking to the Caymans and run everything through Guardian. He wanted to use false invoices to justify payments, and to pay Deming's monthly ten grand with a credit card on a Guardian account. So a trip to the island was planned. Originally it was to be Frank and Joe – who'd make the introduction to Mathewson – Kay and Waldie, plus a few other people from Leasing Ventures. But Joe pulled out at the last minute and the rest of them had to walk into Guardian cold.

Not that Mathewson would have turned them away. If someone had money to deposit, he didn't particularly care who they were or where their money came from. He set the Russos up with a shell company called Hanson. Frank put $20,000 into the Hanson account and Mathewson issued credit cards, including one to Deming. From that moment on, the Russos paid Hanson, Mathewson supplied invoices to justify the payments, and the Russos used the invoices to deduct those deposits as business expenses on Leasing Venture's books. From that moment on, as well, Mathewson and Guardian were placed high on the list of people the FBI intended to indict.

Waldie and Kay now started working Mathewson, bringing cash to him, always making certain that Mathewson understood the money was the proceeds of unlawful activity. Mathewson happily accepted it and even advised Waldie how to get large amounts of cash out of the United States, in direct contravention of US laws, and into the Caymans, in direct contravention to Caymanian law.

'Mathewson knew all the tricks,' Waldie says. 'He warned us, don't wear a lot of jewellery to attract anyone's attention, and don't put any cash in your bag. Instead, wear cowboy boots. Which is what I did. I filled each boot up with cash, about fifty grand worth, and walked right through the detectors. They did the wand on me, and I stood there thinking to myself, if they find the money, I'm going to get arrested. That would probably blow the case. We definitely didn't want to do that. So I stood there with tens of thousands of dollars stuffed in my boots while they inspected me and, frankly, I was in a little bit of panic.'

But no one ever found the money and Mathewson never suspected he was being set up.

In January 1995, seven months after Mathewson incorporated Hanson for the Russos and inadvertently opened the door to the FBI – and just two months before Waldie, Kay, Gallucio and Carney planned to take down Cabletrap – the Cayman Islands government surprised everyone by shutting Guardian.

The Caymanians claimed the bank was going under and that they needed to step in to protect the depositors. Mathewson's version is very different. He insists that a bank regulator demanded a $250,000 bribe and, when he refused to pay it, the regulator launched an investigation for some vaguely stated malfeasance. Regardless of which version is true, the government sent in the liquidators. Shortly thereafter, Mathewson left the island with his Caymanian wife and three children, settled in San Antonio, Texas and started planning his comeback, this time with a bank in the Bahamas.

After recording more than 3,000 conversations, and going up on nearly as many wiretaps, after spending months listening to all those tapes and all those wiretaps, and after compiling all the evidence gathered by Waldie and Kay, prosecutors Gallucio and Carney obtained sealed indictments against dozens of conspirators in four states. The charges were mail fraud, wire fraud, bribery, receipt and sale of stolen property, money laundering, unauthorized use and unauthorized reception of cable television services, various types of conspiracy and interstate transportation of stolen goods.

Waldie now needed to co-ordinate a massive, national take-down. 'We had 60–70 subjects spread out over the country. I can't tell you how many dozens of search and seizure warrants we had to put together but the paperwork was massive. We planned a simultaneous hit on 24 locations across the country.'

Thinking he might be able to turn Frank Russo against Joe Russo and some of the others, Waldie and Kay plotted to bring Frank to New Jersey on the same day that the arrests were happening. So ten days before the takedown, Jim called Frank to say that there'd been another hijacking and that 2,000 of the hottest new boxes were coming onto the market. He asked, 'Do you know anything about the hijacking?'

Frank said he didn't but begged Jim to get those boxes, "Cause I need 'em like blood.'

Jim promised to try. Frank started ringing back every few hours, pleading with Jim for the boxes. When Jim announced that he could get them, but that the price was $150,000 for the load, Frank haggled him down to an even $100,000 cash, and agreed to pick them up on the appointed day. But at the last minute, Frank announced that Joe was coming with him and Waldie knew his chance to turn Frank was gone.

The Russos arrived at the warehouse with one hundred grand in cash just as 300 FBI agents were spreading out across the country serving warrants and locking up suspects. The two men were sitting with Jim, talking about the deal, when Prime's front bell rang. Jim opened the door and eight agents wearing FBI vests – including Waldie – burst in with weapons drawn. There was a lot of screaming, 'Freeze, freeze, gets your hands up, freeze . . .'

Frank and Joe looked at each other, looked back at the agents, looked at each other again then simply put their hands on top of their heads. Waldie separated Frank and Joe, then introduced Frank to FBI

Special Agent Jim Kay. Frank couldn't believe it. Waldie explained that not only was Jim an agent, but Deming was working with them too.

Frank kept saying, 'No way, no way.' Waldie confirmed that it was true. Eventually Frank said, 'Let me get this straight. Jim is an FBI agent? And Philip . . . Philip's a prick!' There was a long pause before Frank shrugged, 'I guess this means I don't get the new boxes?'

Waldie assured him, 'No new boxes.'

Still, Frank gave it one last try. 'Come on guys, we can make a lot of money.'

And that was the end of Frank Russo.

Being the real thing, Joe played it cool. He lied right from the beginning and kept lying right to the end, insisting that he had nothing to do with any of this, that he was simply Frank's accountant.

Waldie insists, 'Joe can't even spell accountant.'

Joe also denied knowing anything about the suitcase filled with cash that the two of them had carried into the warehouse. He swore it wasn't his. Of course, Frank said the same thing. But neither had any wiggle room because it was all on video.

The Russos were in handcuffs by the time all the other warrants were served. Some 40 premises were raided and around 50,000 cable boxes were seized. The Bureau also got computer and electronic equipment, vehicles and cash. The sting had been so well put together that five of the targets gave up and pleaded guilty right away, and some of them, like Frank Russo, quickly turned coat to co-operate.

In June 1996, 14 people were additionally charged by the FBI with stealing and selling millions of dollars' worth of illegal decoder boxes. Among them were Frank and Joe, sharing 71 counts that included conspiracy, wire fraud, interstate transportation of stolen property, theft of cable television signals and money laundering. Both of them went to jail. Further indictments followed, including a laundry list of charges against the Abbouds. They pleaded, assets were seized, fines were imposed and the family business was, to all intents and purposes, dismantled. It would later come to light that the Abbouds had banked at Guardian, as well, moving around $27 million through the Caymans. Records would reveal that they'd also transferred funds to Venezuela, which opened an entirely new line of investigation.

Prevost, who was originally charged with 93 counts, had been enjoined by a California court to stay out of the cable business. But he'd violated the order by establishing a sham company in Ireland, called Hazeltown Trading, with a maildrop address in London's Knightsbridge. When his customers wanted pirated chips, they paid Hazeltown and that money was moved by one of the Big-Four British banks to Malta. From Malta, some of it came back to the States, and some of it disappeared into a void. Now, at his Cabletrap hearing, when asked about Hazeltown, Prevost swore under oath, that he knew nothing about it.

Comments Waldie, 'Frank and Joe Russo were pigs and they were dumb. But Trey was smart. He had a very sophisticated set-up. His problem was that he allocated in court that he wasn't Hazeltown, which was really stupid, because we knew he was.'

Released on bail, when Prevost heard he was about to be re-arrested for lying to the court, he fled the country. He was located living in Costa Rica under an assumed name. The FBI 'invited' him to return to the States, and in May 1998 he surrendered to federal agents. Now he was charged with flight to avoid prosecution, new counts of money laundering, false reporting and criminal conspiracy. He worked out a plea agreement, was fined $500,000 and sent away for five years.

And still there was unfinished business.

The FBI banged on John Mathewson's door early one morning in June 1996. He was pushing 70, had a heart condition and now faced the prospect of spending the rest of his years in prison. He was petrified. Right away, he waived his right to counsel, fessed up and agreed to co-operate fully. He asked, what can I do to keep from going to jail? The agents told him the truth, that there was probably no way he could avoid jail time. He pledged to help them. They said they doubted there was much he could do at this late stage. How about, he wondered, if I had copies of the bank's computer back-up tapes and was willing to hand them over? Before that day was out, Mathewson and the FBI had found room for discussion.

The following day he turned over the tapes, containing 14 months of transactional activities for around 1,000 Guardian clients in 1,600 accounts. All but 73 of the clients were American. In addition, Mathewson gave the FBI his electronic Rolodex which linked the shell company listed for each account with the name of the beneficial owner. The only problem was, the tapes were encrypted.

The FBI asked the Caymanians to help decipher them. The island authorities flew into a rage, vehemently refused, announced that the tapes had been stolen, insisted that they rightfully belonged to the Cayman Islands Monetary Authority and demanded that they be returned. When the FBI reminded them there was no chance of that happening, the bank's liquidators – obviously with the encouragement of the local government – filed suit in US federal court demanding their return. The liquidators also asked the court to prohibit the United States government from publishing, communicating or otherwise acting upon the information contained on the tapes. They insisted that the information needed to be protected to preserve client confidentiality, to safeguard the integrity of the Cayman banking system, and to stop the Americans from embarking on 'a fishing expedition' for tax evaders.

Gallucio and Carney responded that the Caymans' position had no basis in US law, was disingenuous and otherwise pretty silly.

Up to this point, the Cayman authorities regularly asserted that their reputation as a money laundering sink was based largely on, 'a media stereotype', rather than 'objective reality'. The bank's tapes proved them dead wrong, and plenty of islanders understood that. If the tapes were decrypted, officials wrote, it would have, 'a significant negative impact on the integrity, confidentiality, and stability of the financial services industry of the Cayman Islands.'

In other words, this had nothing to do with protecting clients, this had to do with protecting themselves. In one court brief it is clearly stated, 'The Cayman Islands and, indeed, the economy of the territory, could suffer irreparable injury.'

Those concerns are echoed in confidential correspondence between the liquidators' attorneys, the liquidators themselves, other lawyers and the Royal Caymanian Police, making it very clear what the government was really worried about.

Attorney John Rodger, acting for the Caymans, wrote in one letter, 'In the likely event that the Federal authorities share the information they obtain from the disks with the Internal Revenue Service, we would anticipate widespread investigation and possible prosecution of Bank clients.'

The Guardian bank liquidator, Christopher Johnson, further warned the police, 'I believe these events will be potentially very damaging to the wider public profile of the jurisdiction and the reputation of its banking industry.'

These days in the Caymans, they contend that Mathewson was

always suspect. The official line from the government is, 'We got rid of him because we didn't like what he was doing.' The Bankers Association maintains that the liquidators were justified in trying to block American access to Guardian's records and steadfastly affirms that tax evasion is not why people deposit money there. They say they were shocked to have found themselves on the FATF blacklist and, in response to that, tightened their statutes on criminal money laundering. They say they've taken steps to become as transparent as commercially possible, which obviously pleased the FATF sufficiently to remove the Caymans from the blacklist.

In 2001, the island's authorities accepted the argument that they needed to allow investigations of fiscal wrongdoing when criminality is evident both internationally and in Cayman itself. Accordingly, they announced that they would sign a tax treaty with the Americans which, once and for all, would end any ambiguities as far as US tax evasion goes. Under certain conditions, the Caymans would now turn over banking and corporate information to US tax authorities.

For a while, it seemed as if Mathewson's rebuke – 'The Cayman Island government is knowingly aiding and abetting tax evasion' – was a thing of the past. That is, until 2002 when the government announced that, in fact, they would not be signing the tax treaty.

Looking back, John Carney finds it difficult to believe how two-faced the Caymanians have been through the Guardian saga. 'While they were saying publicly, we have no idea what the bank and its clients were doing, their correspondence shows that they knew damn well why these banks existed and why people banked in the Caymans.'

Mathewson was charged with money laundering, aiding and abetting the evasion of income tax and conspiracy to commit wire fraud. He pleaded guilty and asked the court for leniency. 'I have no excuse for what I did in aiding US citizens to evade taxes, and the fact that every other bank in the Caymans was doing it is no excuse.'

Gallucio, Carney and Waldie went to bat for him, telling the judge that the nature and extent of his co-operation had been tremendous. To his detriment, Mathewson had never much cared with whom he did business. In addition to abetting fraud, theft and tax evasion, drug money and organized crime money also moved through Guardian. Still, US District Court Judge Alfred Lechner Jr agreed that Mathewson's assistance to federal authorities was 'unparalleled', and that saved him from prison. Noting that he'd received an extraordinary number of requests for leniency, the judge sentenced Mathewson to six months of house arrest, five years probation, a $30,000 fine and 500 hours of community service.

He showed less sympathy to the Caymans. The judge decided that possession of the tapes by the US Government was lawful and that the liquidators had no right to seek their return. 'The interest of the Cayman Islands in maintaining confidentiality of records protected by the Cayman Confidential Relationship Law, while vital, does not overcome the interests of the United States Government in investigating violations of its criminal laws.'

Unwilling to abide by spirit of the Judge Lechner's ruling, the liquidators did whatever they could to keep the tapes from being decrypted. They threatened the foreign software company that had written the programme, and threatened Mathewson, as well. Suitably intimidated, the software company told the FBI they wouldn't co-operate. But Mathewson did and, with his help, the Bureau broke the code. The FBI then handed the Guardian client list to the IRS.

'There are so many people,' confessed one IRS agent working his way through the Guardian cases, 'I don't know if we've got the manpower to handle them all.'

The IRS rounded up a conman who'd transferred $25.3 million through the bank as part of a gigantic credit card fraud, and a doctor who'd filed false returns, saving around $22,000 in tax. They fined a lumber broker $30,000 for illegally diverting corporate funds to his account and sent a man to jail for 46 months for defrauding the government out of $14.6 million. They charged a video producer with evading $40,000 in taxes, and charged the owner of a computer retail chain with evading $2 million.

Hundreds of cases have been prosecuted and hundreds more are awaiting court dates.

The IRS estimates they will still be working on Guardian's files well past 2005 and expects to have collected nearly $300 million in back taxes and penalties.

Not a bad return for the price of admission.

One dog with sauerkraut and mustard, please . . . One Dr Pepper . . . Oh yeah, and a pirate cable box to go.

CHAPTER TEN

Pump-'n-Dumps and Other Games

If you're a guy who runs pump-'n-dumps,
and you're not channelling your money offshore,
you're committing malpractice

– Wayne Carlin, attorney,
US Securities and Exchange Commission

As a kid growing up in Cranston, Rhode Island, back in the 1960s, Stephen Saccoccia bought gold coins from his school friends – after encouraging them to steal the coins from their parents – and sold them to dealers, making so much easy money from petty theft that he decided, when he grew up, he wanted to be a substantial thief.

Finishing high school in 1973, he opened his own gold and coin shop and, within a few years, had built up such a huge cash business that he was able to swindle gigantic sums from the tax collector. Although it took the IRS until 1985 to bust him, when they did they sent him away for three years. As soon as he got out, he went straight back into gold and coins, turning Trend Precious Metals and Saccoccia Coins into one of the world's most important drug money laundro-mats. His clients were the Medellin Cartel of Pablo Escobar and the Cali Cartel of the Orejella brothers. As testament to his abilities, Stephen Saccoccia is the only laundryman ever to do business with both groups at the same time.

Money laundering is essentially a simple process and his method was fairly straightforward, even rudimentary by modern standards. Drug cash was collected at jewellery shops in New York and Los Angeles, bundled as gold shipments and crated to him in Rhode Island. He converted the cash to cashier's cheques, backed by false invoices and sales receipts to explain the sudden increase in turnover, then deposited them into his own company accounts. From there, the funds were wired out to phantom offshore companies and, eventually, to Colombia. For the service, he charged his clients a flat 10 per cent commission.

In 1991 the Feds finally said enough was enough, but before they could handcuff him, Saccoccia bolted. Months later, he turned up in Switzerland. He was arrested, fought extradition, lost that battle, was shipped back to the States and lost the next battle, too. Convicted on 54 counts of money laundering and conspiracy, he was fined $15.8 million, subjected to a confiscation order for $136.3 million – the documented amount of his drug money laundering – and sentenced to 660 years in prison.

When he heard the sentence, he demanded of the judge, 'How am I supposed to serve that long?'

And the judge responded, 'Just do the best you can.'

While dissecting Saccoccia's Colombian connections, the government stumbled across his relationship with the Patriarca crime family. From that, they discovered, he'd also been handling contract money laundering for New York's Genovese clan. Following those money trails led investigators to Britain, Austria, Switzerland and back into the Caribbean. But the closer the Americans looked at those money trails, the more they saw new players, most of whom did not have drug connections. And that confused them. It hadn't yet dawned on many cops that dirty money is dirty money, regardless of how it got dirty. It hadn't yet hit home that money laundering is a business and that the laundrymen who work in that industry don't particularly care where their product comes from.

It was Stephen Saccoccia's money that would rewrite the textbooks.

Way back in time, in those Dark Ages when people only had land-line telephones and there was no such thing as the Internet, boiler room fraud was one of the biggest games around and Canada was the world capital.

Canadians had been exporting telemarketing scams to the States for decades, and still do. It flourished because the phone system was good, the market to the south was lucrative, and the police were singularly inefficient in shutting it down. All anyone needed was a basement with a lot of telephones, a lot of phone books, a high pressure selling script, and a lot of people willing to work under terrible conditions for a small percentage of a whole lot of money.

Dozens upon dozens of folk sitting in airless rooms for ten to twelve hours at a stretch, would cold call one name after another – typically targeting the elderly and inexperienced investors – to flog financial instruments, low interest credit cards, land investments, subscriptions of all kinds and shares in obscure companies listed on the woollier stock exchanges, like Vancouver and Alberta.

As in all scams, this one too plays off greed and the lure of high returns for very little risk. In the beginning, the scripts were mono-logues for the cold caller who was ordered to stick to the pitch word for word. But as the scams got more sophisticated, so did the scripts. Instead of one call, now there were a series of calls. The initial contact man would hand off to the expert, who would quantify the potential for profit, who would hand off to an executive, who had special powers to authorize a special deal for you.

And time was always of the essence.

I've only got 15 minutes left to sell these because this market closes early and if I don't sell them now I've got to toss them back into the pool which means the instant profit will be lost so you've got to let me know yes or no right now and if it's yes you make the 7 per cent I told you about when I explained how the spread on these things works and you'll double your money in three months but if it's no it's lost forever and I won't be able to get you in on it.

These days a lot of the same nonsense spreads through the Net. The new technologies, especially the global explosion of e-mail, have made it much easier for criminal groups to run their business while hiding in the anonymity of cyberspace. But the Net is a long way from replacing phones and the easy availability of satellite communi-cations has seen phone-based boiler rooms thrive in faraway places like Thailand.

The Canadians remain high up in the major leagues of telemar-keting fraud. But back in the 1970s, Canada and telemarketing fraud were synonymous. They owned the game outright. It wasn't until European phone systems disengaged themselves from state owned post office monopolies and modernized, that new markets opened for tele-marketers. By far, the most attractive was the Netherlands. So Canadian conmen colonized the Netherlands. They loved the Amsterdam stock exchange because it was a free-for-all, appreciated the fact that the country came equipped with built-in island laundromats – Aruba, Sint Maartens and Curacao – and could employ locals because the Dutch speak English. Best of all, the fraudsters wallowed in the lax Dutch laws which meant, even if they got caught, there wasn't much anybody could do.

An added bonus was the confusion created by the Netherlands's drug trade. Banks there were used to taking cash, while the cops were generally too busy worrying about heroin, coke and even marijuana to care about a telemarketing scam. The drug wars distorted law enforcement on all levels, rearranging prerogatives and monopolizing international police relationships. Every time a foreign cop travelled to the Netherlands to ask for help in busting a drug trafficker, white-collar crime was demoted another notch on the priority table.

It remained that way until the 1990s when stock markets boomed. With fraud squads everywhere fighting for their budgets, two things occurred to change the landscape. First, the cops in New York orches-trated the demise of the Mafia's $50 million control of the Fulton Fish Market, clearing out rackets that had been going on for more than a hundred years. Second, around the same time, they smashed large chunks off the Mobs' $500 million rubbish-hauling cartels, a racket they'd been working since Prohibition. A severely wounded Mob needed to find a new act. They looked around, spotted oppor-tunities in the booming markets and limped over to Wall Street.

The Russians were already there. Particularly clever at staying below the radar, they've tended to work off-market scams – private place-ments and unregistered offerings. Sometimes the company they're selling is a start-up but has no functioning business or any real prospects. At other times it's a completely non-existent company. Cold callers in boiler rooms tell you how well the company is doing and how you can get in on the ground floor now because there's going to be an initial public offering. They invite you to buy shares for $6 a unit, a golden opportunity and really cheap because in three months the company is going public for $20 a share. When you finally realize you've been had your money is in Cyprus, Vladimir has changed his name to Grigori, and the boiler room has moved down the block.

Of course the five New York LCN families had worked Wall Street before. But in the 1990s there was so much money flying around and the excitement of a racing bull market was contagious. What's more, they felt the pickings would be easy because law enforcement was forever struggling with drugs.

At the Securities and Exchange Commission, they're fast to tell you that white-collar crime and boiler room fraud have never been low ticket items for them. They've been on the case since 1934 when Congress passed the Securities Exchange Act and President Franklin Roosevelt appointed Joseph Kennedy – JFK's father – as the SEC's first chairman. Prior to that, regulation of the markets was a non-starter. There wasn't a government in the world that cared. But the stock market crash of 1929 changed that. Roosevelt needed to restore investor confidence. Unlike Britain, where until recently the City had conned Parliament into allowing self-regulation – leaving the City wide open to decades of astonishing abuse – the SEC has always been a humourless, no-nonsense sheriff. It goes into any area of the financial industry to investigate insider trading, manipulation of the market, theft of investors funds and the illegal sale of securities. Though its remit is strictly civil, many of the 400–500 actions that the SEC brings each year are in tandem with federal, state or local law enforcement.

'If I had 30 more people I could keep them fully employed,' explains Wayne Carlin, a regional director of the SEC's New York office. 'But I was saying the same thing three years ago, and saying it six years ago, too. There's always more that comes to our attention than we can adequately pursue. Does that mean that if something significant comes to our attention we won't pursue it? No, it never means that. When we need to go after someone, we do.'

Once the SEC sinks its teeth into a company, or the people behind the company, it doesn't tend to let go. One of the keys to the Commissions success lies in hiring young lawyers who are especially ambitious and particularly aggressive. SEC recruiters troll law schools for the best, the brightest and the most combative, offering young lawyers a unique opportunity. Their pitch goes something like this:

Many of you are dreaming of walking into a Wall Street firm and earning a cool three-mil a year. But no one's going to pay you that kind of money unless you've got a three million dollar reputation. So, come to work for us and we'll help you get that reputation. We'll pay you less than you could earn as a first-year attorney on Wall Street, but we'll give you the powers of a federal officer, we'll introduce you to some FBI agents with guns and hand-cuffs, and we'll let you round up all the crooks you can find. Then, once you make a name for yourself as an exceptionally vicious good guy, if you really want to, you can cross over to the dark side of the courtroom and defend bad guys and earn yourself three-mil, because by then the people you've been terror-izing will pay you whatever it takes to have you on their team.

It clearly works, because each year the SEC brings in a new crop of sharp young lawyers and turns them loose on Wall Street. They never earn anywhere as much as they could in that other world, yet many of them stay because rounding up bad guys is, as one of them explained, 'Almost as good as sex and you never have to buy them a drink.'

In this respect, the SEC stands apart from other regulators, like the City's Financial Services Authority (FSA), which takes a much more gentlemanly approach to regulation. The SEC puts the fear of God into people while the FSA, doing the best it can with limited resources and weak laws, is effectively little more than a minor annoyance.

'We don't do raids and shout hands up, stand where you are,' Carlin explains. 'But our examiners show up unannounced and when we want to see something, we want to see it then and there. We'll be polite if someone says, have a seat while we get our lawyers. But we'd better start seeing things in the course of that morning or we go into federal court for an order. No, we don't barge in and yank open file drawers. But when our examiners show up, it's too late to turn on the shredders and cart out boxes of documents.'

Although the SEC does not have the power of arrest, it does have the statutory authority to walk into any brokerage or any investment house or any mutual fund and demand to see whatever they want to see without a search warrant. It's a different game, however, when the people they're looking at are mobbed up. That's when they show up with their FBI friends bearing guns and handcuffs.

'Be careful not to overstate the presence of the Mob on Wall Street. Our view is yes, there is an organized crime presence. But it's confined to a very small segment of the securities marketplace. Their activities, in general, are pretty much limited to the bulletin board market. That's not to say that when you find it, it's not tremendously egregious. It's awful conduct. But it's a very small slice of the market.'

Still, it's the SEC's close partnership with the police and criminal prosecutors that makes it a force to reckon with. In the end, battling the SEC on its own is much less worrisome than battling the SEC and the FBI and the US Attorney's office at the same time.

Carlin agrees. 'We can get an injunction from a federal judge that says don't do it again. We can get a judgement that says pay back your profits. We can get a judgement that says you have to pay a civil penalty in a large amount. But when it comes to some people, if you're not able to put them in jail, they're not going to be real worried about you. For certain people, the only thing that's really going to get their attention is the threat of incarceration.'

Just as white-collar crime was once considered low priority by the police, criminal prosecutors historically showed very little interest in

securities fraud. Besides the fact that securities fraud is usually complicated and document intensive, cases are often filled with unexciting
accounting issues. The last thing a criminal prosecutor wants to do
is put a jury to sleep. Which is one reason why criminal prosecutors
weren't interested in the SEC's 1996 case against Salvatore Mazzeo.

Five years previously, the 43-year-old Mazzeo and his partners
opened Westfield Financial Corp in the Seagram Building on Park
Avenue in midtown Manhattan. The address was impressive. Their
intentions were less so. Mazzeo had set up Westfield to look like a
dealer-brokerage but underneath, it was a brokerage-laundry. He was
using the markets to wash funds through 16 offshore shell companies
that a British lawyer had registered for him in Moscow, Gibraltar and
Liberia. He was also bulking cash to Europe in suitcases. In the four
years that Westfield operated, Mazzeo and his partners made around
$17 million for themselves.

The SEC only happened along after Westfield was out of business.
They never knew about the cash and anyway, they weren't looking at
Westfield for money laundering. They wanted Mazzeo and his partners for four specific violations of Regulation-S of the Securities Acts
of 1933.

Known simply as Reg-S, it's a set of rules designed to make it
easier and less expensive for small companies to raise capital through
special sales of shares to foreign investors. Because they take place
outside the regulated securities markets, companies don't have to file
all the usual statements or make all the various disclosures they would
otherwise be obliged to in a registered offering. The thinking goes,
as long as these shares are sold into another jurisdiction, it should be
up to that jurisdiction to regulate the matter and protect its own citizens. The major restriction placed on Reg-S sales is a holding period
– originally 40 days, it's since been changed to one year – during
which time the offshore buyers cannot resell the shares onshore in the
US markets. That's mainly so that companies can't use Reg-S to get
around US reporting requirements.

However, because Reg-S shares are sold at a deep discount offshore
and because the buyers can resell them in the US markets after the
waiting period – meaning that there's a potential for immediate profit
– Reg-S sales can involve foreigner buyers acting clandestinely for US
sellers. That's patently illegal. And that's what bothered the SEC about
four of Mazzeo's Reg-S deals.

In March 1993, Mazzeo and Westfield sold 50,000 unregistered shares of a woman's footwear company called Candies at a discount to a foreign entity in return for a short-term, unsecured promissory note. Mazzeo negotiated the sale directly with the foreign purchaser's attorney in London. The attorney provided a $150,000 unsecured IOU for the shares. Forty days later those same shares were sold by Mazzeo on behalf of the foreign buyer and the money from that sale paid off the IOU. Two months later Mazzeo sold 727,272 shares at a discount for $2 million to four foreign entities. One of them was a Liberian shell whose address was listed as, 'P.O. Box 26, Moscow 117049'. No other information was provided. The same London attorney handled the deal for the buyers and, again, IOUs were used. When the 40 day period was up, the sale of the shares in US markets grossed $2.8 million and the IOUs were paid.

Two more Reg-S discounted sales followed, using the same formula. There were 25,000 shares of Candies' stock discounted for $75,000 and 600,000 shares of a company called Response USA – manufacturers of personal emergency response systems – discounted for $1.5 million. The same lawyer in London acted for the foreign buyer in both instances, bought the shares with IOUs and paid off the IOUs when the shares were sold 40 days later in the US market.

The SEC ruled that these were illegal side-steps to avoid properly regulated sales and, therefore, a Reg-S violation. Mazzeo was ordered to cease and desist and was suspended from being a broker, dealer, investment adviser, investment company or municipal securities dealer for a period of five months. The SEC moved on to fry bigger fish and Mazzeo let out a huge sigh of relief.

As a direct result of the demise of the Fulton Fish Market and the Mafia's rubbish hauling rackets, offices all over Wall Street and in the backwater financial neighbourhoods, too, got turned into boiler rooms. And boiler rooms were being made to look like offices. The new game became microcaps – minutely capitalized, thinly traded companies that you find swimming along the bottom of the smaller, less regulated, murkier exchanges. Because microcap companies are not required to submit audited reporting to the SEC – some do but most don't – it's often impossible to find out what the company does or what it's really worth. Combine that with totally fraudulent sales methods and it's easy to understand how prices can be manipulated, how investors can be duped and why the Mafia loves this.

The crooks behind these deals feed the shares into boiler rooms where the telemarketers, disguised as brokers, pump up the price by moving shares to the unsuspecting – and bribe and intimidate other dealers to do the same thing – until the share price is high enough, at which time the crooks dump whatever they're holding onto the unwitting market. Investors lose everything while the crooks conceal their profits offshore and move on to the next microcap swindle.

Mazzeo had managed it, for example, with a microcap called Guardian Technologies International. A bullet-proof vest manufacturer founded by Oliver North, whose own money laundering exploits were highlighted by the Iran–Contra scandal back in the 1980s. Thanks to Mazzeo, his 16 shell companies and his ability to manipulate share prices, Guardian Technologies jumped $12 on the first day. He then dumped shares on unsuspecting investors and the price sank like a stone to a few cents.

He got away with it because his was common, every day Reg-S stuff at a time when criminal prosecutors were looking for big deal, mobbed-up operators. Which is how the SEC, the FBI and the Manhattan District Attorney's office came to bust Meyers Pollock Robbins.

Operating out of New York, Las Vegas and south Florida, Meyers Pollock Robbins ran a standard pump-'n-dump on more than two dozen microcaps, swindling 16,000 clients out of $176 million. Sitting at the heart of the scams were the Genovese and Bonanno crime families who not only backed certain deals but handled the 'incentive' side of the business – the bribes and intimidation.

The Manhattan DA's office followed the money trails and located $1.5 million in Guernsey. Some of the sham companies Meyers Pollock Robbins used had also been registered there.

No sooner had the SEC and their criminal prosecutor pals put Meyers Pollock Robbins out of business when they joined up again to bust another mobbed-up microcap dealer-brokerage, A.S. Goldmen.

The 1988 brain child of brothers Anthony and Salvatore Marchiano, those two decided that if their business worked, they'd be worth their weight in gold. The A and S of the firm's name were their first names – Anthony and Salvatore – the Goldmen part was what they hoped to become. The brothers opened offices in Naples, Florida, New York and New Jersey and by the mid-1990s had more than 300 brokers and 50,000 customer accounts. In just one of their fraudulent offerings, the Marchianos moved three million shares of a microcap called Millennium Sports Management. They walked away with $7.5 million. They spent a lot of it on their own lifestyles, but also dumped a lot into offshore accounts. It would later turn out that the Millennium offering was financed by some Genovese mobsters.

In total, A.S. Goldmen moved ten microcap companies into the world, bilking investors of $100 million. Some of that money went through the Bahamas. Some of it turned up in the same places that Meyers Pollock Robbins money did. But then, there was a lot of cross-over between the two firms, with many brokers moving back and forth. Like Meyers Pollock Robbins, A.S. Goldmen was shut down and people went to jail. Anthony got 10–30, Salvatore got 5–15.

Before long, the SEC and the FBI came down on DMN Capital Investments. That firm was backed by the Bonanno and Gambino families with some participation of all five LCN families. DMN had fraudulently traded in the shares of 19 companies and in the private placement of 16 others. There was also racketeering and physical violence. A ten-month investigation resulted in a round-up that saw 600 FBI agents and police officers grab 120 people in 13 states. Investors had suffered losses of up to $50 million. Some of it has been found in the Caribbean. Some of it is still hidden offshore.

'There's always an offshore connection somewhere,' Wayne Carlin maintains. 'If you're not offshore, you didn't go to the right school, you didn't have the right mentor, you just don't get it. Offshore makes the task of tracking you down that much more difficult. It doesn't mean you can't be tracked down, but when you're offshore it takes longer and it is much more difficult.'

He notes that all the usual suspects show up all the time – Switzerland, the Bahamas, the Caymans, Liechtenstein, Antigua – but adds that he also sees many jurisdictions that he describes as, 'not on the all-time hits list', such as Gibraltar, Cyprus and phoney operations in the Pacific like Nauru and Niue.

'We see them all. And we try to go after it all. But don't assume for a moment that when we come knocking on their door they're necessarily very helpful. There was a judicial decision not long ago in Switzerland that was decidedly unhelpful. The Supreme Court there narrowed our ability to obtain financial evidence. I think it's fair to say that the most popular places for dirty money continue to be popular, and the places that are the least helpful when it comes to letting us in to look for dirty money, continue to be the least helpful.'

Policing the investment world, Carlin adds, is a continuous juggling act. 'We watch activity in the market. We have informants. We listen to complaints. We conduct field audits. Our guys are very good at realizing what they've walked into. Many times it's not by accident that they're going into a certain office. When a share suddenly blips 300 per cent in just two hours, we want to know why. There's all kinds of surveillance that goes on. We have all sorts of ways of spotting activities that shouldn't be going on.'

There's no doubt that, while they come up with the goods very often, they didn't in 1996 with Sal Mazzeo.

What they didn't know was what happened when Mazzeo learned that the SEC was sniffing around Westfield's crooked Reg-S deals. He panicked. He couldn't afford to have the SEC looking too closely at the offshore companies that had purchased the Reg-S shares because, if they did, they'd also see the money laundering. So he decided to make the ownership of those offshore shells disappear. He wanted to find someone who would stand up and lie, 'We own those companies.'

The one man he knew he could count on was the lawyer in London who'd set up those 16 shells for him. He was the same lawyer in London who'd worked the foreign end of those Reg-S deals. Mazzeo rang him for help and the lawyer assured Mazzeo it would be no problem to supply a beneficial owner for the shell companies. Even better, the lawyer claimed, the person he had in mind was a minor Liberian diplomat and, minor or not, his diplomatic status would provide a certain immunity to the whole business. As a diplomat, he couldn't be called on to testify in court.

Mazzeo thought it was perfect.

If it wasn't for Stephan Saccoccia, it might have been.

The Americans knew that some of Saccoccia's money had gone to Europe but didn't know how much he'd stashed away there or where he'd hidden it. However, they had a pair of names in the UK who might know something about it. So they asked Britain's Southeast Regional Crime Squad (SERCS) for help.

Details of the UK side of this investigation are revealed in an official confidential report begun in 1991 and continually updated through throughout the decade. It explains that one of the two men was Robert Dick, a stocky 53-year-old who claimed to be in the film business, at times telling people he was a producer, at times telling people he wrote screenplays. The other was John Joseph O'Carroll, a

35-year-old workaholic who'd made a fortune in commodities during the boom days of the 1980s.

SERCS officers interviewed the pair separately. Both categorically denied laundering Saccoccia's drug money. However, both men admitted to having met Saccoccia. Dick acknowledged that he'd been holding £50,000 for Saccoccia and handed it over to the police. O'Carroll, who said that Saccoccia was a minor acquaintance, divulged that he'd helped Saccoccia obtain a safe deposit box at Selfridges Department Store on Oxford Street, in which the police found £357,000.

According to the report of those interviews, both men denied knowing anything about Saccoccia's funds outside the UK. But the FBI had intercepted telephone conversations between Saccoccia and O'Carroll, suggesting that the two were more than simply minor acquaintances. Anyway, accounts had already been discovered in Austria, opened on Saccoccia's behalf in 1988. One of Saccoccia's American attorneys had shown up in Vienna and had tried to withdraw funds from an account that the Austrians had already frozen. The attorney was arrested and found to be carrying papers relating to another code-named account in Vienna, this one, the report says, registered to O'Carroll.

The attorney was prosecuted in Vienna for his involvement in laundering Saccoccia's money but, against the odds, was acquitted by the bench. The trial judge later received a reprimand from the Vienna High Court, the acquittal was overturned and a re-trial was ordered. By then the American attorney was back in the States and not planning on ever visiting Austria again.

That's where the British inquiry ground to a halt. No charges were lodged against Dick or O'Carroll. The officers who'd been working the case moved on, and the matter lay dormant for nearly nine months. Then, in November 1994, Gordon Hutchins was assigned to SERCS.

A rugged Metropolitan Police detective, he'd been chasing murderers and organized gangs when the team he was on decided to follow a money trail left by some drug traffickers working around London's King's Cross Station. That was his introduction to financial crime. When Hutchins came to SERCS, he went straight to the money laundering team and the first case he picked up was Saccoccia.

Several inquiries abroad hadn't been answered. Over the course of the next 13 months, he discovered a bunch of offshore companies that opened new lines of inquiry. One of them, registered in Ireland but administered in Jersey, was called FRM. Hutchins tied that company to O'Carroll. Records showed that $8 million had passed through FRM's account at the Bank of Ireland branch in Jersey. The money was a consolidation of wires from stockbrokers in the States addressed to other shell companies. Most of $8 million was then wired back to the States, addressed to six different recently registered shells – two in the British Virgin Islands (BVI), one in the Isle of Man, one in Liberia, one in Panama and one registration was unknown. Four of the six were managed out of Guernsey.

An FRM payment that did not go to the States was the $89,000 transfer to a Bank of Ireland account in Jersey in Dick's name. Looking at that account, Hutchins saw two deposits in a two-month period – one for $54,096 and another for $130,000 – which Dick wired on to Barbados.

Hutchins was also able to establish that of the six recently registered shells, the two BVI companies and the Liberian company had been receiving monies from FRM in Jersey. Those three had, in turn, made some substantial payments to a third BVI company, this one administered Guernsey with accounts held there by the Royal Bank of Scotland.

From the account of this third BVI company, a payment was made for $1,631,000. Around the same time, a payment for $1,950,000 was made from FRM in Jersey. A third payment, this one for $200,000, came from the Liberian company. The recipient all three – totalling $2,151,631 – was a company in California called Scorpion Technologies.

While Hutchins was nosing around the accounts in the Channel Islands, the SEC – without knowing about the British investigation – was nosing around Scorpion Technologies.

A Colorado-registered company with offices near San Jose, California, Scorpion's business was computer software conversion systems and imaging processing technology. But business wasn't good. Scorpion's shares were flat on the basement floor at 48 cents. The company's president and CEO, Terry Marsh, knew they were about to go bust. Drastic measures were needed, so Marsh and others plotted to save the company and, at the same time, to save themselves.

Marsh hired a man named Barry Witz. It's not clear whether Marsh approached the 25-stone Witz looking for help, or if Witz came along

on his own offering to solve Marsh's problems. But Witz was clearly a
man who knew how markets functioned in the real world. A lawyer by
trade, he'd worked at both the SEC and the New York Stock Exchange
and, for a while, was employed by corporate takeover specialist Carl
Icahn. In any case, it was Witz who took Scorpion to Reg-S.

The day after Witz joined the company, Marsh announced that
newly developed imaging software would generate $12 million in
revenues. The Reg-S issue followed that. Almost overnight, the
company's shares shot up, going as high $7.59. A lot of people made
a lot of money very quickly and Scorpion duly reported revenue of
$12.5 million. Except, $10 million of that was a sham.

Within 18 months, the FBI had raided the company, the NASDAQ
had halted trading on it, and the share price had sunk to 19 cents.
The Bureau's investigation revealed how Marsh and others in the
company used bank accounts and shell companies in 20 countries to
generate fraudulent sales and trading figures. After pumping the price,
Marsh and others dumped 22 million shares onto the market. Foreign
buyers in the Reg-S offering illegally split their profits with Scorpion,
which now moved money back into the company, creating a cash flow
that made it look as if Scorpion was actually selling software.

Federal prosecutors would eventually lodge fraud and money laundering charges against Marsh and eight others. And Marsh would go
to prison for that. According to depositions filed in the case, it was
alleged that Witz had bribed brokers to pump Scorpion's share. Witz
denied it and was never charged. However, a pair of class-action civil
suits brought by Scorpion's shareholders followed the criminal case
and in one of those Witz is named as a defendant.

When the SEC unravelled Scorpion's Reg-S scam, they found that
two shell companies were listed as buyers. One was registered in the
BVI, the other in Panama. Both were owned by O'Carroll. The
Panamanian company, Mayfair Financial, had purchased four million
shares offshore and had unloaded them quickly through a small New
York brokerage. The BVI company had purchased four million and
unloaded them through the same broker – Westfield Financial Corp.

It meant that O'Carroll and Witz both knew Mazzeo.

And Witz knew O'Carroll.

Hutchins' investigation in the UK revealed payments from

O'Carroll's FRM to several shells that Witz was involved with in the States.

By now, the UK investigation had grown too big and too complex for one man, so two more detectives joined Hutchins in the search. Neil Jeans had been a PC in uniform working out of a central London police station. But he'd also once been a stockbroker and when Hutchins heard that, he requested that Jeans be assigned to SERCS. Along with him came a young general CID detective, Martin Woods.

'Neil and Martin came along,' Hutchins explains, 'because the investigation had broadened out so much and I needed help. I'd got stacks of details from Jersey that showed all sorts of stock trading, but I didn't understand what it was all about. Neil, having once been a stockbroker understood it immediately. That's when we identified some $2.2 billion going through one of the companies. These were stock trades by Mazzeo at Westfield Financial. One company, for instance, issued one million shares and wound up trading 93 million shares. In other words, here was a company that sold itself 93 times.'

It was at this point that the Brits, looking at Saccoccia's money, and the SEC lawyers, looking at Scorpion, became aware of each other. The SEC had filed a request for mutual assistance with the UK Department of Trade and Industry (DTI). They wanted to find out more about O'Carroll, about Mazzeo's lawyer in London, and about whatever dealings Mazzeo and Westfield Financial had with either of them. The request included a long list of companies, among them FRM, Mazzeo's shells and at least one in which Witz was involved. After scrutinizing the SEC's request, the DTI discussed the matter with senior managers at SERCS. Companies and names on the SEC list matched companies and names that Hutchins, Jeans and Woods were looking at.

Of particular interest was O'Carroll's Panamanian company, Mayfair Financial. Hutchins, Jeans and Woods learned that he'd first tried to register it in the BVI, but the name wasn't available. Wondering why he needed that specific name, the Brits found that six weeks before the company was registered in Panama, Scorpion Technologies had already noted in its Reg-S subscription a sale of one million shares to Mayfair Financial. In other words, the shares had been assigned before the company was formed. The Scorpion paperwork, which declared both O'Carroll and Mayfair Financial as non-US citizens which therefore made them eligible for the Reg-S offering, was signed by Barry Witz.

Those same folks showed up again with a BVI company called Saturn Enterprises. O'Carroll appeared to be the beneficial owner of it, and the only reason for the company's existence appeared to be the purchase of Reg-S shares in a firm called Osicom Technologies.

That company was the creation of a man called Parvinder Chadha. Publicly held, Osicom made personal computers but had been struggling for years. In 1992 it looked as if it was going under. Until Barry Witz came along. He said he knew an overseas investor willing to buy a piece of Osicom's floundering business. Saturn Enterprises acquired Osicom's UK subsidiary for $1.25 million worth of shares and $2.5 million of debt. The next thing that happened was that Scorpion Technologies acquired Saturn. When the SEC looked closely at that sale, they suspected it was part of Scorpion's Reg-S fraud. They believed the deal was done in an effort to make Osicom look profitable and augment Scorpion's balance sheet.

The SEC was also concerned about the paperwork they saw supporting the deal. In one document, Saturn's president – a Bolivian national – signs his name, Mario V. Andrade. In the other, identical to the first, the president's name and signature is said to be O'Carroll's. Sworn depositions by at least one of the defendants in the Scorpion Technologies case, names Witz as the power behind FRM and Mayfair Financial. Witz answered that it wasn't true and that his only dealings with O'Carroll were to represent him as his lawyer. O'Carroll has steadfastly maintained his innocence and has never been charged in any of these inquiries. Nor has Witz.

Worryingly, some of the money from Scorpion's Reg-S sale was wired into Bolivian bank accounts associated with a company in La Paz apparently run by a man also Andrade. When the FBI looked at that they couldn't find any reference anywhere to the company, but did recognize the name. They informed the British officers that there were open drug inquiries on several Bolivians named Andrades. The three British investigators never found out whether or not the Andrades involved with Saturn were the same ones being looked at by the Americans for drug trafficking. But according to the Americans, two Bolivians named Andrade had been caught in a sting in Los Angeles, instructing undercover agents to deposit large amounts of drug cash into bank accounts in London and Switzerland.

That sting was part of the Saccoccia investigation.

So now Hutchins, Jeans and Woods looked again at the relationship between Witz and O'Carroll, and Mazzeo kept showing up. That brought Hutchins, Jeans and Woods straight back to Mazzeo's lawyer in London.

At least one of the companies that the lawyer in London had incorporated in Liberia for Mazzeo, was managed in Jersey for the benefit of Westfield Financial. Some of the deals that were moved through that account were Reg-S sales that tied back to Witz. From there, Hutchins found one of Mazzeo's BVI companies, set up by his lawyer in London and also managed out of Jersey. Then he found another Liberian company. Then he found a Dutch company. And then he found several bank accounts where large sums moved in and out very quickly.

The more the three British officers thought they were looking for Saccoccia's drug money, the more they kept seeing what appeared to be the proceeds of securities fraud.

Dozens of companies popped up all over the offshore world – but especially in the Channel Islands, the BVI, Antigua and Ireland – many of them linking back to one another. As the ties between those companies grew more complicated, the officers started seeing commercial paper, including a $10 million note signed by Mazzeo that related directly to the drug laundromat BCCI. Then they started seeing Russian money moving through companies that used false addresses and would eventually link back to the Bank of New York.

Senior managers at SERCS soon decides that the Americans would have to handle that side of the inquiry because they wanted to focus on Mazzeo's London lawyer.

Andrew Warren was born in 1946, had practised law at a solicitor's firm called Rutherfords, and was now with one called Talbot-Creggy. His partner there was Stuart Creggy, born in 1939. But Creggy was not only a practising solicitor, he was also a sitting magistrate at the North Westminster Petty Sessions court.

If Warren was bent, the police worried, his partner might be as well. And if Magistrate Creggy was bent – putting criminals away for the same crimes he was committing – then the ramifications for the British judicial system could be enormous.

CHAPTER ELEVEN

When Parallel Lines Meet

You'll only ever have two friends in life,
your mother and your bank balance.
— advice to her son from Stuart Creggy's mother

W hile the British were starting to investigate Andrew Warren
and Stuart Creggy, John Moscow had worries of his own.

In the mid-1990s, with markets going wild and organized crime
taking full advantage of confusion bred in greed, Manhattan District
Attorney Robert Morgenthau put Wall Street on notice that microcap
fraud would not be tolerated, and put the Mob on notice that they
were not welcome on Wall Street. His point man was Moscow and
there was plenty to keep him busy.

Broker-dealer Stratton Oakmont made $28 million in illicit profits
on five microcap offerings. Broker-dealer D.H. Blair excessively
marked-up on 16 microcaps. Broker-dealer GKN Securities excessively marked-up on eight microcaps. Broker-dealer Sterling Foster
made illicit profits exceeding $50 million on three microcap under-
writings.

There was market manipulation at La Jolla Capital and at Hibbard
Brown and at Chatfield Dean and at H.J. Meyers. A four-year probe
of Mob activities on Wall Street brought indictments to 19 people,
including six LCN guys and some Russians, for running multi-million
dollar scams. At Globus Group, 18 Russians were indicted on 22
counts of securities fraud and conspiracy to commit murder.

Along the way Moscow busted A.R. Baron.

A small-time bucket shop pretending to be a legitimate broker-
dealer, A.R. Baron was run by an aggressive young conman named
Andrew Bressman. Over the five years that Baron was in business —
July 1991 to July 1996 — Bressman and his cohorts managed to steal
more than $75 million from 8,000 investors. The National Association
of Securities Dealers (NASD) caught up with them in July 1995,
fining Baron $1.5 million for excessively marking up on clients.

Restitution was ordered, and some executives, Bressman included, were given a slap on the wrist with minor suspensions. It was, nevertheless, the NASD's largest enforcement action that year. A year later, Baron was in such terrible financial difficulties that liquidation became inevitable.

The company was later described by Robert Morgenthau as a place, 'Where every conceivable form of dishonesty was used. It was created and it existed for no other reason than to line the pockets of its executives and employees at the expense of unsuspecting members of the public.'

In July 1997, Moscow convened a Grand Jury which handed down a 228-page, 174-count indictment against A.R. Baron and 13 employees, Moscow charging them with enterprise corruption, grand larceny, a scheme to defraud and other crimes. Bressman was charged with the theft of $8.5 million.

The SEC now ordered Bressman to return $6,038,412 to his clients. In response, he filed for bankruptcy. Some people believe that his money remains hidden offshore. Bressman owned some Liberian shell companies in Jersey and had hidden illegal profits in an entity called Mid-Ocean Trust which was registered in the Pacific backwater of Rarotonga, Cook Islands.

Confronted with the overwhelming evidence that Moscow had gathered against him, Bressman pleaded guilty to enterprise corruption and grand larceny. Facing 25 years in jail, he agreed to co-operate with the authorities while sentencing was pending.

At the same time that Moscow was busting A.R. Baron, Gordon Hutchins, Neil Jeans and Martin Woods back in London were trying to build a case against the lawyers Andrew Warren and Stuart Creggy.

The three officers had identified funds going back and forth between the US and the UK, and knew that some of those funds were the proceeds of crime, specifically securities fraud. But under UK law, as it was then in force, to pin money laundering on Warren and Creggy, they needed a predicate offence in the UK. And in those days, Parliament was still foolishly insisting that money laundering was a crime only when the predicate offence was drug, terror or major fraud related.

In search of that predicate offence, the detectives spent three entire months putting names into various databases, desperately hoping to find one little shred of evidence that would allow them to nab the two lawyers.

'It was very frustrating,' Hutchins recalls. 'The more we looked the more difficult it seemed to become.'

Exasperated, one lunchtime, Jeans left the office and headed down the block to buy a sandwich. As he approached the local news kiosk, he noticed a story in that day's *Evening Standard*: 50 investors, including Sir Anthony Pilkington, chairman of the family glass company, and the late Duke of Atholl, had been victims of a fraudulent securities dealer in New York named A.R. Baron.

Jeans recognized those names and bought the paper. Then he spotted Andrew Bressman's name. He knew that Bressman was a Creggy client and that Creggy had set up some Liberian companies for Bressman in Jersey. He rushed back to the office and, within an hour, Hutchins was on the phone with Clark Abrams, a bright, go-getter lawyer he knew at the SEC.

Hutchins told Abrams about the Creggy-Bressman connection and asked if he knew John Moscow. Abrams said he didn't, but promised to call Moscow to see if he was interested in knowing more about this British connection. Within an hour of speaking to Abrams, Hutchins was on the line with Moscow. And when Moscow heard what Hutchins had to say, he responded, 'Come to New York.'

Hutchins and Jeans flew out a few days later to lay out their case. 'We were selling, not buying,' Hutchins says.

It was apparent that the cases on each side of the Atlantic were parallel. But being parallel, they were also separate. Moscow now included Creggy and Warren on his list of people to look at, while questioning Hutchins and Jeans about the lawyers' links to Russians who were showing up in the Bank of New York money laundering investigation.

One of the companies that Hutchins, Jeans and Woods had spotted in Jersey was tied into a second offshore company, controlled by Russians living in the United Kingdom. Those Russians were connected to some Russians already under investigation by Moscow in the BoNY case. One money trail led directly to Benex and Becs International. Another pointed to Semion Mogilevitch, the Russian accused of being at the heart of the YBM Magnex scandal which fed into BoNY.

Over the course of three days in New York, the parallel lines moved closer together. By coincidence, at one point during those three days, Moscow mentioned that he was hiring staff. Hutchins put in a bid for his pal Abrams. Not long afterwards, Moscow hired him away from the SEC.

Hutchins and Jeans returned to Britain but the phone and fax lines to Moscow's office stayed open and active. Moscow expanded his BoNY investigation to Europe, particularly to the Channel Islands. Hutchins, Jeans and Woods continued to focus on Creggy and Warren. A few months later, when they felt they had sufficient evidence to take a crack at Creggy and Warren, the British officers obtained search warrants for their offices.

The law firm of Talbot-Creggy was at 38 Queen Anne Street, a block north of Wigmore Street in London's West End. Creggy's office was on the first floor of the building, Warren's on the second floor.

The search warrants were written specifically to permit access to all materials concerning 20 named offshore companies, like the ones in Jersey, and to several named people including Bressman, O'Carroll, Witz and Mazzeo. Hutchins handed a copy of it to Creggy, who looked down the list and said that none of the names meant anything to him. Hutchins then went upstairs and presented a copy to Warren, who looked down the list and admitted to knowing Mazzeo. Warren also said he had some documents in the office relating to some of the named companies and provided the officers with 21 files.

Many of the documents the officers obtained that day duplicated documents they'd already acquired in the Channel Islands. Of the ones they hadn't already seen, some added substantially to what they knew about Sal Mazzeo and Westfield Financial. But one file in particular would stand out. It contained copies of correspondence and faxes to and from a lawyer in Montreal, Canada named Harry J.F. Bloomfield.

One of those faxes, dated 6 April 1994 and addressed to Bloomfield on Talbot-Creggy letterhead, had obviously been returned by Bloomfield because it had a handwritten note at the bottom of it.

The original message from Creggy to Bloomfield read: 'Dear Harry, we have the need of the services of Charles again. Could you be kind enough to fax through a phone number where we can make contact with him (if necessary), although I do not think it likely. So that we can have it just in case. Or would you like his phone number to be yours? Could you please reply to my partner Andrew Warren in my absence.'

The handwritten note back from Bloomfield read: 'Dear elder

colleague, Wilson 613-830-6901. I have advised him of a possible call. Send dollars, dollars.'

The 'Charles' and 'Wilson' in question turned out to be a minor Liberian diplomat with that name, then stationed in Ottawa, Canada. He was the same minor Liberian diplomat who'd signed off as the beneficial owner on Sal Mazzeo's 16 shell companies. Those were the same 16 shell companies that Mazzeo had asked Andrew Warren for help with when Westfield Financial was being investigated by the SEC for Reg-S fraud.

Harry Bloomfield moved in rarefied circles.

Born in 1944, he was a Queen's Council and senior partner in a Montreal law firm that bore his name, Bloomfield Bellemare. His father Bernard was a high profile businessman and philanthropist. His uncle Louis Mortimer Bloomfield was a lawyer with ties to the Bronfman family, owners of Seagram's whiskies and spirits. Louis had served during World War II as an officer in the British Special Operations Executive – a euphemism for the spooks – and afterwards, was chairman of a decidedly shady operation called Permindex. Conspiracy buffs link Permindex to nefarious goings on and criminal intrigue in Cold War Europe, all of it managed on behalf of some spy service somewhere. From there they tie Permindex and Louis to the same organized crime guys in New Orleans who eventually form part of the conspiracy buffs' endlessly mutating DNA of the Kennedy assassination.

Various reporting suggests that Louis, through Permindex, was associated in money laundering – again, supposedly at the behest of a spy service – with Tibor Rosenbaum's Banque International de Credit (BIC). One unconfirmed report has it that, as a young man, Harry Bloomfield worked for a time at BIC.

Bloomfield was president of a private charity, the Eldee Foundation, a director on several company boards and had been an unsuccessful parliamentary candidate in Canada's 1980 election. Seven years after failing to win a seat, Bloomfield's friend Prime Minister Brian Mulroney appointed him to the board of the Business Development Bank of Canada (BDBC), where he served as chairman of the audit committee for four years. He left the BDBC board in 1996.

Described by one Canadian newspaper as, 'a man who collects titles like lesser mortals collect postage stamps', Bloomfield comes by it naturally. His father was Honorary Consul General to South Korea and Uncle Louis had some sort of unofficial status as an adviser to the opposition party in British Honduras, now Belize. Harry also had a diplomatic relationship with the Government of Belize and appeared to have an honorary title from Djoubouti.

But the title that really mattered, the one that Uncle Louis also had, was Honorary Consul General to Liberia.

Sal Mazzeo moved in less rarefied, decidedly more dangerous circles.

In 1994 two young men who'd briefly worked at Westfield Financial stepped into his midtown office and one of them shoved a pistol into the side of his head. The man with the gun was Albert Alain Chalem, a French born broker who'd made a name for himself pumping micro-caps. The other, was Maier Lehmann, a similarly dodgy broker and Chalem's sidekick. Chalem nervously reminded Mazzeo that he and his pal were still owed money, and because Mazzeo had been warned before, and because Mazzeo didn't take those warnings seriously enough to pay up, they intended to settle the debt their way.

Mazzeo somehow managed to calm them down, then slowly talked Chalem and Lehmann out of doing something stupid then and there. Eventually, he persuaded them to leave. The instant they were gone, Mazzeo phoned someone who could guarantee his safety. He had a lot of those connections. But whomever it was that he begged to inter-vene with Chalem, that man needed credibility because Chalem was personally close to Phil Abramo, a DeCavalcante crime family 'capo'. The two had been buddies in Florida at A.S. Goldmen where, among other fraudulent deals, they manipulated Osicom Technologies shares during that Reg-S offering.

Whether Mazzeo had markers he could call in, used family connec-tions which he definitely had, or simply paid in cash, it worked. The Chalem problem went away. But another serious problem would soon manifest itself – the identification of Charles Wilson and his fraudu-lent claim to being the owner of Mazzeo's 16 shell companies.

And John Moscow wasn't going to let anyone make this one disappear.

The prosecutor moved on Mazzeo and his two partners at Westfield Financial, George Carhart and James Cohen. By then, Westfield was out of business and Mazzeo was running a small gourmet food shop on Long Island. Moscow charged Mazzeo with attempted enterprise corruption. At the end of October 1997, Mazzeo pleaded guilty to illegally obtaining over $17 million from investors. Based on his evidence, his partners Carhart and Cohen were also arrested and charged. But before anyone could discover that Mazzeo had turned, Moscow sealed Mazzeo's plea. He kept it secret for nearly nine months, specifically to allow the officers in Britain time to work their end of the investigation.

In March 1998, Hutchins and Jeans returned to New York to interview Liberian diplomat Charles Wilson, who was now attached to his country's delegation there. As a result of conversations with Wilson, the parallel lines were about to meet.

On 23 June, Moscow unsealed Mazzeo's plea. The following morning, in London, Stuart Creggy and Andrew Warren were arrested.

Mazzeo's sentencing was delayed another ten months. Under normal circumstances, it happens relatively quickly. When it's put off for any real length of time, it's usually because the prosecutors want access to that person. The reason why is, generally, because that person has something to say. Mazzeo was free, awaiting sentencing for 19 months, until July 1999, when he was found dead.

Officially he died of natural causes in his sleep at home. But not everybody believes it because 41-year-olds don't usually die in their sleep of natural causes. Anyway, this was a man who moved in circles where death is one way of doing business. There are even a few people who believe Mazzeo is not dead at all, that he was able to fake it. His death certificate was signed by a relative. Limited toxicology was done by the Coroner's office. The photo of his body on the medical examiner's table is inconclusive and may or may not be him. Cremation took place before the DA's office was informed that Mazzeo was dead.

Far-fetched, perhaps. But certainly not the first time that such things have occurred to people who move in the same circles as Sal Mazzeo.

On the night of 25 October 1999, Albert Alain Chalem and Maier Lehmann were found dead in Chalem's home in New Jersey. In this case there's no doubt that they're dead. Or, that someone wanted them dead. The cause of death was multiple gunshot wounds to their heads.

In June 1998, new search warrants had been issued for Andrew Warren's office, for Stuart Creggy's office, and also for an office in Brighton where the police believed other documents might be. On the morning of 27 June, only hours after Moscow unsealed Mazzeo's plea, Hutchins, Jeans, Woods and other officers from the National Crime Squad raided Talbot-Creggy. They were joined by a couple of people from Moscow's office in New York, including his chief investigator, Andrew Finan. Also accompanying the raiding party was a technical team from Scotland Yard for the computers, and representatives from the Law Society because searching and seizing documents from lawyers' offices is a delicate matter. The client-attorney privilege of people not involved with the case needs to be protected.

Another group of officers raided the Brighton premises.

But when Hutchins and his team arrived at 38 Queen Street, they were in for a surprise. The brass plate that bore the name Talbot-Creggy had been removed from the front of the building and there were signs that the place was not fully occupied. Asking inside, Hutchins was told that Talbot-Creggy was no longer practising at that address. A hasty discussion took place on the sidewalk as the officers tried to figure out what to do next.

As luck would have it, that's when, Andrew Warren happened along. So what Hutchins did next was arrest him.

The officers brought Warren inside, read him his rights, and started bundling documents. While this was going on, Warren gave Hutchins a phone number for Creggy. Hutchins dialled it, Creggy answered and Hutchins explained that the police were in the midst of executing a search at Queen Anne Street. Hutchins invited Creggy to join them there. Creggy said he knew about the raid because he'd already got a call from his staff in Brighton but, unfortunately, he could not attend because he was on his way to the airport to fly out to the States.

Hutchins asked for his new office address, which Creggy gave him. As soon as they hung up, Hutchins and Jeans jumped in their car, got to Creggy before he left for the airport and arrested him.

More officers now showed up at Creggy's new office and documents were seized there, too.

'With the first search warrant,' Hutchins explains, 'we believed we were investigating money laundering. As a result of the additional information we managed to obtain, it now became obvious to us that we were also looking at conspiracy to defraud.'

During the move to his new office, Creggy had shipped a large portion of his files to a garage lock-up in another part of the country. The officers found out about that, obtained access to the garage and seized those files too. In all, the police acquired seven full pallets of paperwork from Creggy and Warren, an estimated half million documents. It would take them a year just to begin to realize the full extent of incrimination these documents held, how relationships had come together and where the money trails would lead.

Among the documents was a wealth of correspondence between Bloomfield and Creggy. Much of it refers to Wilson's services as their for-hire diplomat. One letter, dated December 1994, mentions a Liberian honorary consulship on sale in Germany for $25,000. Another, dated September 1995, has Bloomfield explaining how he's been selected as an 'Approved Immigration Consultant' by the government of Belize and is now in a position to help people buy citizenship in that country. The price he quotes is $75,000 plus fees, for which a new passport can be issued immediately. He asks Creggy if he has any potential clients.

Some of the documents opened entirely new lines of inquiry. In one file, Martin Woods stumbled across a Times Law Report that discussed aspects of offshore company ownership as raised in a 1993 case called 'El Ajou v Dollar Land Holdings'. Creggy sent the report to one of his clients in Canada, who was a defendant in that suit. Woods contacted the lawyers who'd represented El Ajou and learned how their client lost $12 million in the deal. The lawyers told Woods that several Canadians had perpetrated this fraud, including one who could be tied directly back to Meyer Lansky. The lawyers also described the money trail in the case – starting in Geneva, going to Gibraltar then on to Panama, back through Geneva and finally to London. The more Woods found out about the Dollar Land Holdings case, the more he saw unmistakable similarities with the Creggy and Warren case. Several new areas now needed to be looked at.

In another file, a Canadian suspected of fraud was linked to Creggy. When Creggy was first asked about this man, he said they'd met in 1993. But this file proved they'd met as early as 1989. That caused the officers to look again at other relationships Creggy had denied. And other inconsistencies began appearing.

In an offshoot from information discovered in these files, a gentleman in Canada was stopped with an attaché case containing CD$200,000. The police wanted to know what this money was. The man explained that he'd just withdrawn it from his account at a Swiss bank in Montreal to pay for a new kitchen. The Mounties seized the money, pending their own inquiries. But when officers interviewed employees at the Swiss bank, they were told that no such withdrawal had taken place. It subsequently turned out that the money had been brought into Canada from the Bahamas. When the police confronted the man with that fact, he denied it. So the Mounties decided to hold onto the money until the man was able to satisfy them that this was not somehow tied to the proceeds of crime. Rather than expose himself to the inquiry, the man simply walked away from the two hundred grand.

Also among the papers found in Creggy's files were copies of false export documents that he'd supplied, either to Bloomfield for a Canadian company or directly to the Canadian company, so that the company could fraudulently reclaim taxes and duties on goods it hadn't exported. Further documents led to a Canadian boiler room operator set up in England seemingly with Creggy's help. The money from that scam was shipped off to Malta, a matter still being investigated.

In a particularly bizarre twist to the story, documents were discovered indicating that a company called Panavest UK, which was registered in Gibraltar, owned several shell companies registered in Guernsey and Luxembourg which in turn owned an historic church in Toronto. But in 1995, St Paul's Trinity United burned to the ground. The matter is still officially listed with police as a $5 million unsolved arson.

Panavest UK had obtained the church in 1992 to redevelop the property. During the ensuing investigation, a fire marshal looking into the possibility of arson received threats to his family which the police say they took seriously. Creggy told the police that Panavest UK was owned by two Israelis and two South Africans, whom he would not name. Creggy, himself, was once managing director of Panavest UK. Insurance investigators in Canada say the company was secretly owned by a Canadian and that the Israelis and South Africans are fronts set up Creggy, the same way he used Wilson. That investigation also continues.

However, it was in New York that the Creggy and Warren files really had an effect. Through them, Moscow was able to tie up several loose ends involving Mazzeo, to open several new lines of inquiry in the Bank of New York matter and to begin putting together a case against Creggy, Bloomfield and Warren.

In June 1999, a New York Grand Jury indicted Andrew Warren on 78 charges, including enterprise corruption in connection with the offshore companies and false documentation to conceal Westfield Financial's criminal activities in the United States. Warren refused to come to New York to answer the charges and extradition proceedings were opened against him. Warren chose to tough it out. His defence was that he was mentally too depressed to stand trial. In March 2003, a British court ruled that it was up to the American courts to decide whether Warren could stand trial, and ordered him sent to the States. Whatever happens there, the investigation against him continues in the UK, with inquiries into front companies that link him with Benex, Becs International, certain Russians and the Bank of New York.

While Warren was fighting extradition, a Grand Jury in New York also indicted Bloomfield and Creggy on 22 counts of criminal conspiracy. Bloomfield presented himself to the New York authorities. Creggy was invited to New York but refused. Instead, he planned to hole up in his condo in south Florida. His lawyer implored him, 'For God's sake, don't go to America.' But Creggy was a guy who believed he was fireproof.

John Moscow's guys proved he wasn't, and arrested him there.

Eighteen months later, the Manhattan DA's office faced off in court with Bloomfield and Creggy. Because Bloomfield and Creggy knew they'd lose in front of a jury, they requested and were granted a bench trial. It would be left to one judge to hear the evidence and decide their fate.

From the beginning, certain people involved with the case found an unsettling arrogance about Bloomfield and Creggy. Spotting Bloomfield coming into the courtroom one morning, one of the detectives who'd investigated him told the Canadian, 'I like your tie.'

Bloomfield stopped, looked at the detective and promised, 'When, not if, but when I win this case, I'm coming back to New York to give you this tie.'

Having seen the evidence stacked against Bloomfield, the detective shook his head. 'When you lose, I'm going to ask you for your shoelaces and belt, too.'

Moscow handled some of the courtroom work, but most of his time was taken up with work on the unfolding Tyco case and the $600 million looting of that corporation by its senior executives. So responsibility for the day-to-day lead fell to Clark Abrams. Together with Kenneth Chalifoux and Rebecca Roiphe, the three assistant DA's went at Bloomfield and Creggy with everything they had, turning the job into 18 hour days and seven day weeks.

Abrams, Chalifoux and Roiphe, with Moscow to backstop them when he was needed, laid it all out for judge. Their case was that, from around January 1980 until mid-March 2001, Bloomfield and Creggy had conspired to falsify business and banking records, and to forge securities to assist their clients in violating the law. Specifically, Bloomfield and Creggy had agreed to establish and operate offshore companies and offshore bank accounts for which they'd misrepresented the identities of the owners and directors of those companies and bank accounts. By going offshore, the conspirators were deliberately trying to prevent anyone from discovering the true owners of the companies and bank accounts. By using a diplomat as a front, they were counting on immunity from subpoena or any other legal inquiry into the actual owners of the companies and bank accounts.

In one instance, Bloomfield had a friend in Canada who'd built up a chain of nine pharmacies. Over the years, the man had squirreled away $400,000 in an offshore bank account. Because Revenue Canada didn't know anything about it, he couldn't just repatriate the money and spend it. On his behalf, Bloomfield and Creggy invented a scheme that involved a Declaration of Trust in the name of two Creggy clients from Cyprus. This was 1995. Creggy agreed that the paperwork should be dated to coincide with the formation of an offshore trust in 1979. Creggy even cooked up the story that his Cypriot clients had met Bloomfield's friend in 1979, decided that Canada was a wonderful place to invest their money and that their investment was still sitting in that offshore trust all these years later.

Bloomfield told Creggy it would be helpful to have the Declaration of Trust, 'Drawn up in October or November of 1979, just prior to the opening of the account in early December of 1979.' He also wanted a letter written by the Cypriots confirming the arrangements plus, 'One or two letters over the years that you might have sent him (Bloomfield's friend) to his office asking whether or not investment opportunities were foreseeable.'

A few days later, copies of passports and bank references for the Cypriots arrived. So did a draft copy of the Declaration of Trust dated 1 December 1979. It turns out that neither of the people whose names Creggy was using were aware of the transaction. But then, neither Bloomfield nor Creggy ever imagined the two would find out about it.

There was, however, a problem that seriously worried Bloomfield about the paperwork Creggy supplied. 'Your draft appears to have been produced on a word processor.'

Creggy realized that if this stuff had been written in 1979, a word processor would not have been used. He faxed Bloomfield, 'We do have a typewriter. It (the draft) was sent to you in great hurry, as and when it will be typed on the old fashioned typewriter.'

Needing to make sure that Creggy had his dates and places correct, Bloomfield reminded him that one of the Cypriots, 'travelled to Zurich in May of 1976 and stayed at the Hilton Hotel. He also visited Interlaken, Geneva and Montreux. Of course he was also in Nassau in December of 1979 and I am sure he could have met you in Canada or Florida at different times over the years.'

Bloomfield wanted Creggy to make sure that it would be obvious to any authorities reading the phoney paperwork that his friend had maintained contact with the Cypriots throughout the intervening years. 'I therefore again suggest that you look at my October 10 letter for guidance on correspondence that would be in your file, e.g., a letter by which the Cypriots suggested to (Bloomfield's friend) that they stay in touch through you; and one or two letters over the years where you state that you are aware that the funds are accumulating, but no suitable investment has been found, the funds are still not large enough, etc.'

The address Bloomfield supplied to Creggy for his friend was where he'd lived in 1979.

Over the course of the prosecution's case, it was shown how Bloomfield and Creggy were doing this sort of thing for loads of people. When a New York plastic surgeon saw one of his patients die on the operating table, he decided to put his assets off-shore to render himself judgement-proof. It was Creggy who supplied everything the man needed. Creggy did the same for a heavy weight New York criminal, setting up an offshore network for 'Spanish' Raymond Marquez, the man who ran Spanish Harlem's biggest numbers racket.

In yet another example of fraudulent deception, Bloomfield knew a man named Matthew Snyder in New York who was concealing from his employers at Chemical Bank, the bank's regulators and presumably the IRS, money he was receiving from a client at the bank. Snyder needed Bloomfield to help him hide it, so Bloomfield went to Creggy who decided to set up a Liberian corporation called Bloomfield and Bloomfield Investment Management Limited (BBIM). But when Creggy tried to open a bank account for BBIM at Butterfield Bank, Bermuda, he was informed that, under the money laundering laws in force in Bermuda, the bank would require details on the beneficial owner of BBIM. Bloomfield didn't want to put his own name to the account, nor did Creggy. Knowing that it would defeat the purpose to use Snyder's name, Bloomfield asked Charles Wilson for the use of his name. Wilson agreed and supplied photocopies of his diplomatic passport. Bloomfield sent Wilson $3,000.

Two months later Creggy forwarded paperwork to Bank Butterfield falsely claiming that Wilson was the owner of BBIM, reminding them that 'the gentleman is a diplomat'. Still, to comply with Bermuda's laws, Bank Butterfield insisted that a reference come from a bank and a lawyer in order to open the account. Instead, Creggy opened an account for BBIM at Barclays Bank in Jersey. To be sure that the paper trail was covered, records for the Liberian registered BBIM, with a bank account in Jersey, were held in Gibraltar. Snyder's money was deposited in Jersey, then regularly wired in amounts of $5,994 to his personal account in New York with the reference, 'Consulting fees re: BBIM'.

Shortly after that, in April 1994, Creggy told Bloomfield he needed Wilson again. This is when Wilson was asked to sign the documents falsely declaring that he was the beneficial owner of the 16 shell companies set up by Warren for Mazzeo and Westfield Financial.

Seven months later, Creggy called on Bloomfield to supply Wilson's signature on the share certificates of the fund Concord Capital Growth. Wilson was already listed as President of the corporation.

By now, Wilson was growing concerned that he was being asked to do something illegal. He needed reassurances. He reminded Bloomfield that he did not want to be, 'tangled into any unlawful and illegal business'.

In November 1994, when Bloomfield and Creggy asked him to sign more papers, Wilson repeated his anxieties. 'About two years ago when you requested I sign some papers for you to open an account for yourself, I raised the concerns that I did not want to be tangled into any unlawful and illegal business. You immediately assured me that this was not the case and in our relationship you will never mislead me nor talk me into anything illegal. As you are aware, I appreciate all the assistance you have granted me but I am concerned if these documents will not eventually be used for that purpose. You are equally aware that I have a family that depend on me for support that would not like to see me fall into problems. I need your reassurances if possible, written, before I can proceed further. Please understand I am trying to protect myself from problems.'

Bloomfield answered Wilson, 'Creggy assures me that these are regular business accounts. I know him and trust him. Be assured that we will always try and protect your position.'

When originally asked about all this correspondence, lawyers working for Creggy and Bloomfield attacked the letters as fakes. Later, when shown the correspondence in which Bloomfield admits to asking Wilson to claim, deceitfully, that he is the beneficial owner of the 16 shells, Bloomfield's lawyer acknowledged his client might have asked Wilson to do that, but insisted, 'Bloomfield had zero to do with the fraudsters.'

In court, Bloomfield's attorneys painted a picture of an innocent man unwittingly seduced into a scheme that he knew nothing about. Wilson had been representing his country in Canada when civil war broke out in Liberia. The government in Monrovia could no longer afford to pay its overseas diplomats and Wilson had a family to support. He needed an income. Bloomfield was simply helping Wilson get through those hard times.

Not true, Abrams, Chalifoux and Roiphe countered. The defendant was, 'Borrowing, then renting, and then essentially stealing Charles Wilson's identity.'

No longer a diplomat at the time of the trial, and therefore no longer shielded by diplomatic immunity, Wilson's testimony painted a different version of events from Bloomfield's and Creggy's. Wilson claimed that when Bloomfield first contacted him in 1993 about using his name and signature on certain documents, it wasn't for shell companies but for a Swiss bank account that Bloomfield wanted to open to put money away for his children. 'He said that because I was an accredited diplomat, I didn't have to pay taxes in Canada.'

As a result of the civil war, Wilson said, Liberia stopped paying foreign service workers and he was left penniless in Ottawa. He had five children to feed and was also coping with health problems. The money from Bloomfield was a great help. But Bloomfield, he swore, had assured him it was not illegal. 'I trusted his judgement . . . He said I was not breaking the law.'

Wilson was not charged in the matter.

But when the judge added everything together, he found Bloomfield and Creggy guilty on 16 of the 22 charges. Moscow, Abrams, Chalifoux and Roiphe were all hoping the judge would now do the right thing and send Bloomfield and Creggy away for a couple of years. Hutchins, Jeans and Woods were hoping for that, too. They'd all put in a lot of work, and the condemnation of guilt, branding

Bloomfield and Creggy convicted felons, was the cake. Sending them to prison would be the icing.

However, lawyers for Bloomfield and Creggy had one last card to play – Creggy's health.

At the sentencing hearing, in February 2003, they made a passionate plea to the judge that their client was in remission from leukaemia. They begged the judge to understand that jail would be detrimental to his health. Moscow vigorously reminded the judge that medical facilities in prison were just as good as they were outside prison, and that the State would look after Creggy's condition.

In the end, staggeringly, the judge fell for the emotional appeal.

He sentenced Creggy to treble-fives – five years probation, a trifling $5,000 fine and 500 hours of community service. He then turned to Bloomfield, who maintained his freedom only by clinging desperately to Creggy's coattails. The judge said he felt it would be unfair to send Bloomfield to jail when Creggy was equally or more culpable in the offshore shell scheme. So Bloomfield got the same treble fives.

After 21 years of aiding, abetting and laundering money for fraudsters, Creggy went back to Florida, to fight deportation to Britain where an arrest warrant is waiting for him.

And Bloomfield went home to Canada, along with his tie, considerably freer than he might otherwise have been.

CHAPTER TWELVE

You Gotta Have A Gimmick

You gotta have a gimmick if you want to get ahead.
   – career advice given to legendary stripper, Gypsy Rose Lee

Cole Bartiromo, who sometimes called himself Tom Manning, spent most of spring 2001 hunched over his bedroom computer manipulating the share price of 15 publicly traded companies. With an initial borrowed stake of $60,000, he purchased several million shares – in some cases as much as 50 per cent of the day's volume of his target company – posted as many as 6,000 false messages on Internet bulletin boards touting the company's prospects, waited for the price to rise, then unloaded the shares at a profit. He salted away a lot of money in offshore accounts before, apparently, quitting for the summer.

That autumn, he was back online, this time with a website called 'Invest Better 2001'. Bartiromo, as Manning, promised investors huge returns on 'safe bets' that he was making – or, at least that he said he was making – with an online sports bookie. He claimed he'd cracked the secrets that Las Vegas gamblers employed 'to make billions' and was now employing those 'guaranteed' and 'risk-free' methods for everyone else's benefit. If investors wanted to join him, he pledged to repay them anywhere from 125–2,500 per cent of their stake over a period of three days to a month. The minimum in was $50. There were no maximums.

Yet again, P.T. Barnum was right – 'There's a sucker born every minute'. The money poured in, thousands of dollars at a time, with the unwitting help of the Internet's most popular digital money exchanges – PayPal, Evocash and E-Gold. All Bartiromo had to do was move it electronically to banks in Curacao, Dominica, Bermuda and Panama, and from them into his account at an online gambling site in Costa Rica. By Christmas, he'd bilked 3000 investors out of more than $1 million.

What he didn't know was that the Securities and Exchange

Commission monitors the Internet all the time, that they'd stumbled across his 'Christmas Miracle Investment', that they'd refused to buy into the metaphysical aspect of it or, for that matter, his use of the word investment, and that they were coming to get him.

Dogged persistence and skilful detective work led the SEC to Costa Rica. There, with the co-operation of the offshore gambling site that Bartiromo was using, they followed the money trail back to Mission Viejo, California. The SEC not only put him out of business but reclaimed a large portion of the money he'd stolen.

Yet, Bartiromo's ability to move money over the Internet and through the offshore world demonstrated how Cyberspace and the offshore world are made for each other, how the Net provides a highly effective, easy to use tool for fraud, and how the offshore world is a purpose-built firewall. The ease with which Bartiromo manipulated the Internet made the offshore world look like a place where even a kid was welcome.

Which is exactly the way it was because, at the time, Bartiromo was just 17.

Liberian shell companies should have been a giveaway to anyone looking into the affairs of Messrs Bloomfield, Creggy and Warren. For three men who doubtless considered themselves intelligent, their raw stupidity could not have been more apparent because the offshore world is filled with much better gimmicks than Liberia. That they staked so much on such a patently dumb ploy reinforces the notion that common sense and greed are mutually exclusive.

In the end, they turned out to be a bunch of dull-witted crooks who failed to comprehend what the offshore world does best: it creates confusion, so that real secrecy is mistaken for acceptable privacy.

The Merriam-Webster Dictionary of the English language defines privacy as, 'the quality or state of being apart from company or observation; freedom from unauthorized intrusion'. The same dictionary defines secrecy as, 'the condition of being hidden or concealed'.

While the two sound as if they are the same, in practice they are anything but. Privacy is what you expect in your bedroom with your spouse; secrecy is what you count on at a motel with your lover. Put another way, your income is secret to your neighbours but merely private as far as the government is concerned. The inference being that your neighbours can't get to your secrets but the government is permitted to breach your privacy.

Peddling secrecy in the guise of privacy is what makes the offshore world effective and profitable.

The Ansbacher Bank scandal is a perfect example. The biggest money laundering and tax debacle in Irish history, it featured evasion on a huge scale and was littered with prominent business and political figures, not least of whom was the former Prime Minister, Charles Haughey. It didn't do much for the reputation of the Caymans, either.

The story starts with Desmond Traynor who, as an old man in the 1990s, was described as taciturn, respected, trustworthy, fiercely loyal and one of the leading figures in the Irish business community. More than 40 years previously, he'd been articled to Haughey at the chartered accounting firm of Haughey Boland where a life-long friendship began.

While Haughey climbed his way up the political ladder of the Fianna Fáil party, Traynor stayed at the accounting firm until 1969, when he was named a director of the bank, Guinness & Mahon (Ireland) Limited (G&M). A few years later he was named Deputy Chairman and, in effect, Chief Executive of G&M. An accountant who clearly understood the desire for secrecy in a banking environment that merely permitted privacy, one of the first things Traynor did when he took control of the bank was to open a tiny investment company in the Caymans and turn that into a bank called Guinness Mahon Cayman Trust Limited (GMCT).

His man in the Caymans was John Furze, an ex-pat banker who'd been there since the mid-1960s working for Canada's Bank of Nova Scotia. Furze knew every offshore trick then in the book, having cut his teeth helping the Bank of Nova Scotia earn the money laundering reputation that would dog it for much of the 1970s and 1980s. Traynor, recognizing talent when he saw it, named Furze managing director of GMCT in 1973. Furze then set about designing the various discretionary trusts that Traynor used to help wealthy people in Ireland hide their money. To all intents and purposes, G&M in Dublin and GMCT in the Caymans functioned as a single unit. Traynor became a one-man money laundering sink, personally accepting deposits and getting them into the system, while Furze controlled everything in the Caribbean.

The system went through a series of name changes, but for two decades it remained essentially the same. In 1984, GMCT was sold to Guinness Mahon & Co in London, parent of Traynor's Dublin bank. The following year, it was sold again, this time to a private group headed by Traynor and Furze. They unloaded 75 per cent of it to the London bank Henry Ansbacher, who changed the name from GMCT to Ansbacher Limited, then changed it again to Ansbacher (Cayman) Limited. It was later sold to the First National Bank of Southern Africa.

Traynor and Furze offered clients three essential services.

First was a discretionary trust. That's an offshore account so constructed as to appear that the beneficial owner is independent of his money and, therefore, not liable for taxes on the income. The specific gimmick Furze used was the same that made Liechtenstein famous as an offshore centre – 'Red Cross Trusts'. Money is held for a named charity. No taxes are therefore due. But that's followed with a 'letter-of-wishes' in which the beneficial owner secretly informs the trustees that the charity will only receive a peppercorn and then lists the real beneficiaries. It's the ploy that tycoon Robert Maxwell was using when he announced to the world that his family were not the beneficiaries of his wealth, held in trust in Liechtenstein.

Second was a facility through which people could deposit and with-draw offshore monies in Dublin, as if their account was onshore. Traynor, presumably at Furze's suggestion, established two shells – Amiens Investments Limited and Amiens Securities Limited – both of which held non-resident accounts at G&M. Deposits and with-drawals in Dublin would be credited and debited against funds in the Caymans, skirting the usual Irish resident-account requirements of tax and exchange controls.

Third was back-to-back loans. Traynor's clients could use their own money on deposit in the Caymans as security for a loan from a bank onshore. This allowed them to make large purchases without the tax man realizing they were actually repatriating their own funds.

It is now believed that perhaps as many as 200 tax-liable Irish residents moved as much as £38 million through 400 shells to hide their money in the Caymans. And it is just possible that none of this ever would have come to light, had it not been for a Dunne family feud.

In 1992, Ben Dunne, then the chief executive of Dunnes Stores and one of the wealthiest men in Ireland, got into a fight with some of his relatives about lifestyle matters and during it, they discovered that he'd been writing cheques to Haughey. The press got wind of it

– these didn't appear to be political donations – and the stories that followed forced a board of inquiry. The investigation established that, around 1987, Haughey had run into personal money problems. His friends decided they would ask half a dozen folks to offer £150,000 each to ease the prime minister financial pain. Dunne was approached. He is said to have retorted, 'Christ picked 12 apostles and one of them crucified him', and volunteered to pay the full amount himself. Over the course of the next couple of years, he reportedly gave Haughey £1.3 million.

The most interesting thing about the payments was the way Traynor and Furze handled them. The official report on the matter reveals that the first cheque from Dunne to Haughey, for £205,000, was given to Traynor who sent it for collection to Guinness Mahon & Co in London. Four days later in Dublin, before the funds cleared in the UK and were credited back to the Irish bank, the equivalent amount in Irish punts was wired out of an anonymous GMCT account for the benefit of Amiens Investment Ltd. Two days after that, the money deposited in London was wired to Dublin to fill the hole left in the GMCT account.

Flash back now two weeks prior to the cheque from Dunne. Records show that the same sum, in Irish punts, was withdrawn from that Amiens Investments account and deposited into a special loan account at the Agricultural Credit Corporation to be applied against monies allegedly owed to them by Haughey. A decidedly convoluted process, it served to obliterate the trail, separating Haughey from any association with Dunne's money.

Further payments were moved through Haughey Boland clients' accounts, a Swiss trust company, Credit Suisse, a bank on the Isle of Man, Barclays, Royal Bank of Scotland in London and the Irish Intercontinental Bank in Dublin.

The discovery of the Dunne/Haughey money sparked an investigation into the way Traynor, Furze and their banks were assisting in tax evasion. Irish authorities petitioned records from the Cayman Islands which, of course, prompted a lot of excuses from the island as to why they couldn't possibly be helpful. Dublin put pressure on Ansbacher hoping to force disclosure, but account holders objected. After all, they were paying for secrecy and expected Ansbacher and the Caymans to live up to their end of the bargain. The case wound up in court.

Cayman Chief Justice Anthony Smellie heard arguments for six days *in camera* before coming down with a ruling that showed the island to be co-operative without really co-operating. He ordered the bank to divulge account records to the Irish inspectors, but only after the names, addresses and any other descriptions of clients were removed.

As if to contend that privacy and secrecy were the same, Smellie justified his decision by writing: 'This court must stand ready to reject any request for disclosure which may proceed upon a presumption that the mere fact of doing business with a Cayman Islands financial institution points to some reproachable objective such as tax evasion.'

Inquiries followed in Ireland and little by little the story came out, much to the embarrassment of many of the protagonists. It would have happened sooner and more completely had the Caymans played ball, but that's not what the offshore world does. In the Caymans they actually declared Smellie's decision 'a win-win'. This, while much of the rest of the world decided the islanders had simply run true to form.

Plainly, for the Caymanians, the cost of making clear distinctions between privacy and secrecy would be high. But a situation now arose in the States that would send tremors through the entire offshore world.

Three people in Florida were targeted by the IRS in a criminal tax evasion case. They were clients of Ansbacher using a 'pass through account' (PTA), a variation on the two Traynor-owned Amiens accounts at G&M. Ansbacher was a client of Marine Midland in New York, giving Ansbacher's clients access to Ansbacher's PTA account there. They could make deposits and withdrawals, exactly as if this was Ansbacher, but without anyone at Marine Midland knowing offshore funds were involved.

When the IRS discovered that the three Floridians were using a PTA, they demanded that Marine Midland produce transaction records. Marine Midland objected and, not surprisingly, so did Ansbacher, arguing that the summons was much too broad because it would include records of people unrelated to the targets. The IRS argued that because of the way the accounting was done, they were entitled to see everything in order to do establish what their targets were up to. The court agreed with the IRS and ordered Marine Midland to turn over the records.

Suddenly, a US based bank was required by US law to give up offshore banking information that was otherwise protected elsewhere. The only way the offshore world could get around this was by eliminating any business which left traces in a US bank. So now, most offshore banks with PTA accounts in the States keep those records well outside US jurisdiction.

Keeping records outside US jurisdiction was at the heart of the Enron scandal.

The Texas energy corporation pinned a lot of hope on offshore secrecy. And Enron knew a lot about that because they'd been offshore since the mid-1980s. From 1985–1987, several Enron executives diverted $142 million in company funds to offshore shells and Panamanian banks. At the time, CEO Ken Lay claimed total ignorance of such fraudulent activities.

He can't say as much these days.

The company created 881 foreign subsidiaries, including 692 shells registered in the Caymans which were designed for no other reason than to fool shareholders and regulators into thinking they were legitimate companies. There were also 119 shells in Turks and Caicos, 43 in Mauritius and eight in Bermuda. Lay and his mates used their offshore empire to shelter profits, enrich themselves and avoid taxes to the extent that Enron paid no corporate income tax to the US government for four out of the five years between 1996–2000. As a matter of fact, thanks to sham accounting, during one of those years the company actually worked out a $382 million refund.

Much of what Lay was doing to avoid taxes was transfer pricing, moving onshore profits to an offshore shell where taxes don't count. But Enron took it to new depths of sleaze. For example, Enron had several negotiated deals to sell oil and natural gas to a company called Mahonia, registered in Jersey. Mahonia's bankers, Chase Manhattan – which later became JP Morgan Chase – financed the deals from mid-1998 to the end of 2000. On paper, when payments were due, Chase would pay Mahonia which would pay Enron. But the way it actually worked was very different. In a typical deal – this one dated 28 December 2000 – Enron sold a gas contract to Mahonia for delivery from April 2001 to November 2005 at an agreed price of $394 million. Off that came a discount for full payment up front, making the total $330 million.

So, Chase paid Mahonia which paid Enron. However, that same day, Enron agreed to purchase from another Jersey company, Stoneville Aegean, the same amount of gas for delivery during the same period of time. The price was $394 million but did not include the up-front full payment discount because Enron chose to pay monthly, which is standard industry procedure. Enron now had $330 million to put on their books as revenue, with a debt of $394 million due in the future. That worked out to a 55 month loan of $330 million at 7 per cent interest.

The Mahonia and Stoneville Aegean contracts were signed by the same man, who happened to be a director of both companies. But that's hardly a coincidence. Mahonia and Stoneville Aegean had the same address in St Helier, Jersey, which they shared with a local law firm, and the man who signed those contracts was a partner in that law firm. Company filings in Jersey show that Mahonia's shareholders were two shell companies, Juris Limited and Lively Limited. Those shells owned shares in each other. The local law firm also owned shares in Juris and Lively. Company filings in Jersey show that Stoneville Aegean's corporate structure was exactly the same. This is not to suggest there's anything untoward with the offshore governance of either company, simply that it refutes claims that the deals with Enron were unrelated.

The deals were structured in such a way as to keep up appearances, while allowing Enron to use the bank's money and still have the same amount of commodity on hand to sell a second time. Call it, 'commodity laundering' – a loan disguised as a trade. Over the years, Enron materially benefited by being able to disguise borrowings of $3.9 billion. Instead of listing that as debt, they added it to revenue. For some people at Enron, putting Mahonia and Stoneville Aegean offshore and keeping the records offshore too, was a good idea. These days, to much of the rest of the world, what Enron did looks exactly like fraud.

It was another Enron partnership where loans were disguised – a shell called Chewco – that came to light during a US Congressional hearing and lit the spark which became the Enron bankruptcy. Dissecting the corpse, it's blatant that none of this could have happened without three very important ingredients.

First, the company needed to be run by crooks. They designed a dishonest structure for their own benefit.

Second, it required the collaboration of hundreds of financial professionals. Enron's crooked management could not possibly have pulled this off without bankers, lawyers and accountants playing along. At best, those financial professionals were myopic. At worst, they were criminals.

And third, it had to be offshore. Without a place to hide, Enron could not possibly have perpetrated such a gigantic lie.

Unfortunately, in this regard, Enron is hardly unique. There's Worldcom, Tyco and more recently, the French oil company Elf Aquitaine which used the offshore world to throw bribes at every tin pot dictator in Africa with an oil well.

All typical examples, notes attorney Jack Blum, of what happens when people are allowed to say, I'm going somewhere else so that I can break all the rules. 'You want to understand the offshore world? Just look at what's gone on in the last five years. Corporations have reached a point where they cannot continue to compound earnings at 20 per cent. So what's the next step? They cook the books. Why? Because the board has stock options and the only way they can get the price up and steal more is if they cook the books.'

The place to do that, he says, is away from home. 'Because it's much more fun to play where there are no rules. That is, forgetting at the end of the day, that we could be rocketing towards a global catastrophe with absolutely no capacity to fix anything. The whole enterprise is based on, how do we get out from under the rules? The truth of the matter is that the rules are there for a reason. If you want to see where we are running without rules, look at Enron and Worldcom.'

Equally illuminating, look at the way some major tobacco companies have allegedly used the offshore world to deal with organized criminals and break UN sanctions.

In 2002, the European Commission filed suit in the United States against the RJR Reynolds Tobacco Company claiming that, for much of the 1990s, RJR knowingly sold cigarettes to Italian, Russian and Colombian organized criminal groups. The claim states that, to keep payments from those criminals secret, RJR directed, managed and controlled money laundering operations in several offshore jurisdictions. Furthermore, the EU says, the company violated UN trade sanctions by doing business with Iraq.

The suit outlines a criminal conspiracy, beginning with a company in Puerto Rico called Japan Tobacco (JT). Acting under licence of RJR, JT shipped 5,340 master cases of Winston cigarettes from the US factory to Valencia, Spain. There are 10,000 cigarettes in a master case, making for 53.4 million cigarettes in this shipment. That's enough to fill five 40-foot containers. The accompanying bills of lading showed the shipment bound for Cyprus.

When the containers got to Spain, they were offloaded from one vessel and onto another which sailed to Cyprus. There, the containers were unpacked, and the master cases were then repacked into new containers, with new bills of lading that showed the shipment bound for Russia. By changing the containers and the bills of lading, these cigarettes could no longer be identified as the same one that had gone from the States to Spain.

Leaving Cyprus, the vessel sailed first to Lebanon, then to Turkey. The cigarettes were unloaded there and trucked overland to Iraq. The EU maintains that RJR and Japan Tobacco knew the people they'd sold the cigarettes to and knew what those people intended to do with them. RJR and JT steadfastly deny this, insisting that any allegations of deals with the Mafia or terrorists or sanction breaking are absurd.

But that hasn't stopped similar accusations coming from other sources and, allegedly, RJR is not alone. A major investigation conducted by the Washington watchdog, The Center for Public Integrity, accused senior executives at British American Tobacco and Philip Morris of selling cigarettes to individuals directly connected to organized crime in the States, Canada, Colombia, Italy and Hong Kong. BAT and Philip Morris both deny the allegations.

Trade in black market cigarettes – product produced for one geographical area and smuggled into another to sell at a lower price – is gigantic. It's said that one out of every three exported cigarettes winds up on a black market somewhere. The cigarette companies disavow complicity, insisting that they do everything they can to stop it.

For every black market cigarettes sold, a cash register rings some-where in the offshore world. Italian criminals launder their cigarette money in Montenegro, an emerging sink on the Adriatic. Russian criminals launder their cigarette money through Cyprus. It's believed that some of it is then reinvested in Russian-Cypriot joint venture factories that manufacture counterfeit cigarettes for the eastern European black markets. In the Caribbean, the two major cigarette smuggling centres are Aruba and Panama, both of which come complete with built-in money laundering facilities.

The EU suit claims the criminals couldn't function without product from the big manufacturers. Notes Kevin Malone, a lawyer repre-senting the EU in its suit against the big companies, 'What you have is one big smuggling conspiracy. The cigarette manufacturers, their distributors, the money launderers, it's the same people doing the exact same thing.'

Again, the companies deny it.

A major test of Malone's theory came in 1999, when the Canadian government started an action in US federal court against RJR-Macdonald, RJR Reynolds and related companies. The Canadians claimed that the manufacturers had conspired to export and illegally re-import cigarettes into Canada, thus depriving Revenue Canada of taxes. It was happening, they said, along the border that Ontario and Quebec share with New York State, on land designated official territory of the St Regis-Mohawk Indians. Known as Akwasasne, organized gangs of native Americans living on the reservation have, for years, moved cigarettes north or south depending on the tax situation.

The manufacturers successfully argued the 'Revenue Rule'. That's eighteenth-century common law which says a court can refuse to hear a case if its judgement would only serve to enforce another country's tax laws. Appeals went all the way up to the US Supreme Court where, in November 2002, a decision came down for the manufacturers. By then, the Canadians had run out of appeals.

Next, a suit was filed in the US by the European Commission against Philip Morris and RJR. Their claim was that the tobacco companies had been running a global smuggling operation to deprive EU member states of tax revenue and had become a money laundering outlet for criminal organizations. This time lawyers for the cigarette companies convinced the judge to throw the case out on the technicality that the European Commission could not act exclusively on behalf of the member states.

So the European Union re-filed, now joining ten member states with the European Commission. That case was dismissed on the basis of precedents set in the Canadian case. The EU appealed and began reshaping its case, yet again, this time to play off the terrorist and money laundering aspects of the USA Patriots Act, which Congress had passed in response to 9/11.

At the same time, the EU filed a money-laundering version of its suit against RJR. The company has promised to take this one all the way, too. And the EU doesn't seem ready to let the matter drop, either.

In the meantime, the offshore world is gearing up to make it easier for big companies to function. It's part of the new image the big jurisdictions are polishing. For them, shell companies and private banks which cater to small-time crooks and tax evaders, are too much trouble. The big jurisdictions – notably Hong Kong, the Bahamas and the Caymans – seem intent on getting out of what might be called retail money laundering because the wholesale side of the business is safer and more profitable. They see their future in tax structuring, in multinational financial chicanery. It's no longer about the Cali Cartel, it's about tomorrow's Enron. It's about catering to companies like Halliburton and Bechtel and the Carlyle Group, huge multinationals with massive global investments that need to be protected from the whims and fancies of any single government.

An added incentive for the big jurisdictions is reputational risk. If due diligence fails and drug money or Al-Qaeda money turns up, it's the jurisdiction that takes the heat. If due diligence fails and another Enron happens, it's the company's problem.

At least in the big jurisdictions, the days of small time crooks are numbered. Sure, there will always be some place else for them to go, but for multinational giants with money to hide, Hong Kong and the Bahamas and the Caymans are laying out the welcome mat.

Of course the big jurisdictions all talk the due diligence game. But the way the cards are getting shuffled, chances are nil that their due diligence will ever get in the way of: a cigarette company looking to move into an untouched black market; a pharmaceutical company looking to transfer price its drugs so that it never pays any taxes anywhere; an insurance company looking to run re-insurance around the offshore world to the point where it never has to pay on a huge disaster; or an Ansbacher-imitation helping people evade taxes because it satisfies all the requirements of being a legitimate bank.

That said, because the offshore world is a competitive business, while the big guys move to wholesale, smaller players will upgrade their retail side. For them, due diligence creates room in the game for small- to medium-sized players with street cred. Except, you can't always tell whose cred is cred.

Just ask Mark Edward Valentine.

Once the darling of Bay Street, Toronto's equivalent of Wall Street, Valentine was born in Brazil in 1970 where his father was a career diplomat. Douglas Valentine would go on to serve as Canada's Ambassador to Saudi Arabia and to Colombia. Mark attended Concordia University in Montreal before getting a job as an investment adviser. A loner at heart, his workaholic energy and money-making talents quickly turned him into one of Canada's hotshot dot-com brokers, a feat that did not go unnoticed by the otherwise venerable 50-year-old financial services firm Thomson Kernaghan (TK).

Where TK had prospered through strong and reliable research in some of the less exciting areas of investment – mining, power generation and machine makers – the firm was now old, tired and falling behind its younger, more vigorous competitors. The Kernaghan brothers, who were running their late father's company, wanted to breathe life into it and Valentine seemed like an exciting choice. He was less than half the firm's age when they hired him in 1994.

Within a year, Valentine's partners were so appreciative of the business he brought to the company, and the way he'd begun taking them into sexy hi-tech, that they gave him a thank-you Ferrari with the special licence plate, 'GIDDYUP'. Within three years, Valentine was making so much money for TK that the partners agreed to sell him 25 per cent of it and allowed him to turn the company into a technology specialist house. He moved the firm out of its dismal Bay Street offices and into shiny new ones around the block, then opened branches in Calgary and Vancouver. Before long, 100 employees became 200.

By 2001, Mark Valentine was chairman, but TK was on the verge of bankruptcy. They were over-extended in hi-tech at a time when hi-tech was heading south. Also, the Ontario Securities Commission (OSC) was investigating Valentine for the way he'd been financing certain deals. Their concern was a game called 'death spiralling'.

Simply put, a death spiral is a scheme devised to run a company's share price into the ground, while all the time selling shares to hapless investors who don't know the cards are stacked against them.

A variation on the pump-'n-dump, it begins with what appears to be a big investment into a thinly traded microcap. Because the company doesn't have access to large investors, when someone comes along with money to spend, it's willing to give up 'floorless warrants'. Those are guarantees that the investor can convert into shares at a later date. But unlike agreements that put a price on the shares to be issued to the investor, these put a value on the investment which means the number of shares fluctuate.

For example, with 'floorless warrants', if $1 million is the agreed investment and the shares are $1 each, the investor has the right to 1 million shares. But if the share price drops to 80 cents, the investor gets 1.25 million shares. In other words, as the value of the shares changes, the number of shares issued changes to match the investment.

Knowing that he has a guaranteed supply of shares, the investor starts pumping the shares to other investors, while all the time selling short, which means he's unloading shares that he doesn't yet own. He's betting that the price will drop which, as more shares come onto the market, it invariably does. By selling at 80 cents, when the price drops to 60 cents, he makes the difference. Of course, if the share price goes up to $1.20, then he has to buy them back at that price and winds up losing the difference.

Many brokers consider short-selling a mug's game because it's not an investment, it's a bet. But if you've got inside knowledge or can control the share price, then it's not really a bet, it's a sure thing. You're guaranteed a supply of shares all the way down, creating the financial equivalent of perpetual motion. The more you sell the more the price drops, the more the price drops the more shares you get from the floorless warrants and, consequently, the more you can sell.

Investors out of the know wind up holding worthless shares. The company that falls victim to this almost always goes bust. Players on the inside walk away with fortunes.

All the various securities commissions, like the Financial Services Authority and the SEC, are supposed to be on the lookout for this scam. They may know it when they see it but it isn't easy to prove. A source in Canada suggests that TK under Valentine made $2 billion in six years playing the death spiral game.

No one noticed because the action was funnelled offshore.

Valentine was connected in Bermuda to a fellow Canadian named Paul Lemmon, who owned the Voyager Group of financial services companies. The two guys intertwined their offshore entities. Valentine had a Bermuda company called Ashland Resources. Lemmon was listed as the trading authority for Ashland Resources and a fund called Hammock Account. Valentine was the controlling shareholder of Hammock and the agent for Hammock Group, which was actually registered in BVI. However, the address listed for Hammock was the same one in Hamilton, Bermuda that Lemmon listed for Voyager Group. Valentine also owned a company called VMH Management, in which he put a hedge fund called Canadian Advantage Limited Partnership, which had a sister incorporated in Bermuda, Advantage (Bermuda) Fund. He mirrored that with VC Advantage Limited, a company that managed a hedge fund called VC Advantage Fund Limited Partnership, and its sister, VC Advantage (Bermuda) Fund.

Enter here Valentine's pal and partner in the VC Fund, Cameron

Brett Chell. In a previous incarnation, Chell had been a salesman for a securities firm in Calgary but ran afoul of the Alberta Stock Exchange and, in 1998, admitted to violations. He was banned by the Exchange from acting in any capacity for five years, placed under supervision for two years after re-registration and fined $25,000. Now he ran the Chell Group, which owned an internet company called Jawz Inc. The OSC and TK investigations found that, in late spring 2000, Valentine and Chell worked a death spiral with Jawz. Valentine is accused of using TK to issue a buy recommendation on Jawz, while motivating other TK clients to sell. Valentine and Chell short sold as well.

It now appears that Valentine might have been working both sides of a trade with another Chell company, C-Me-Run. One of his hedge funds was buying C-Me-Run shares at the same time when several offshore entities controlled by Lemmon were selling. Funds held at TK lost $4.5 million, The offshore funds made $6.4 million.

Valentine always maintained that he did nothing wrong. But the movement of large blocks of Chell Group shares in and out of these funds – creating profits for Valentine at the expense of TK's investors – worried the OSC. The TK Management Committee mounted an inquiry which ended by ordering Valentine escorted from the building. The OSC then issued an order banning him from working or trading in the markets.

Ever intent on making money, Valentine turned his attention to Germany's poorly regulated penny share market. What he didn't know when he flew to Frankfurt in August 2002 was that, instead of coming directly home to Canada, he'd be detouring for a very long time through Miami.

A year and a half before, he and Lemmon concocted a deal with an investment office in Boca Raton, Florida to move over-priced shares through a UK-based unit trust run by a crooked manager, in return for a multi-million dollar kickback. It was a pretty good gimmick and they weren't the only ones working it. The owners of one company agreed to sell shares to the unit trust for $8 million – which was more than seven times the actual market value – for a $3.2 million kickback. Another company CEO offered to sell two million shares at $4 each – when the share price was 65 cents – for a $4 million kickback.

Because none of these transactions could be straightforward and on-the-books without regulators realizing that something was wrong, money and shares were moved through Canada and the Caribbean.

There were shells in the Bahamas, a bank in Barbados, a bank in the Caymans and, of course, Valentine's and Lemmon's companies in Bermuda.

There was only problem with the scam – it was a scam.

The UK unit trust didn't exist, the British fund manager didn't exist and the office in Boca was run by an undercover FBI agent. Called 'Operation Bermuda Short', it was a full-frontal attack on fraudulent penny share promoters. Along with the FBI came the RCMP, the SEC, the US Postal Inspection Service and the National Association of Securities Dealers.

By the time Valentine was ready to board his flight from Germany to Canada, the US Justice Department had unsealed indictments and issued arrest warrants for 58 people, including him. The Germans grabbed him and held him for nearly five weeks until US Marshals arrived to escort him to Florida. Valentine and Lemmon were charged with conspiracy to commit wire, mail and securities fraud. Valentine pleaded not guilty, maintaining his innocence and, as of mid-2003, is still fighting his corner. Lemmon took a plea to one count of conspiracy to commit wire and securities fraud, and agreed to testify against Valentine. Lemmon was sent away for 21 months.

CHAPTER THIRTEEN

Entangled Alliances

If we lose sight of the threat that organized crime poses,
even for a short while, it will take us years to regain all that we've
accomplished during these past five years.
– Chief Superintendent Ben Soave RCMP, crime fighter

Thanks to films like *The Godfather* and *Goodfellows,* over the past 30 years there's been a real interest in and increased understanding of organized crime. That's reflected in today's never ending diet of Discovery Channel, History Channel and Biography Channel insights into the Mob, Colombian drug cartels, the Russian Maffiya and the mysterious gangs of the Orient. But as public fascination grew, a small movement took hold among a close knit group of academics which, in the simplest of terms, denied the existence of organized crime.

While admitting that serious crime was happening, and that some of it was very well organized, and that most of it was economically motivated, and that all of it posed a threat to our communities, these scholars accused law enforcement and politicians of deliberately misleading the public. They refused to recognize a united conspiracy driven by a hierarchy seeking riches, and blamed law enforcement and politicians for camouflaging reality and misdirecting enforcement efforts.

The overwhelming response from law enforcement and politicians is that this bunch has a lot in common with the Flat Earth Society.

Yet, the revisionist theories of this group merely hardened with time. While they might have got louder, it's not clear that they've taken on many new recruits or, for that matter, influenced the public perception in any meaningful way. The popularity of *The Sopranos* suggests that whether or not a professor somewhere warrants that organized crime doesn't exist, the dysfunctional antics of Tony and his crew carry the weight of the argument.

This is not to say that the academics don't make some valid points. The problem is that being academics, they're too used to talking to each other, and for non-academics theirs is a foreign language.

For example, this from two of the group's chief cheerleaders, Dr Margaret Beare, director of the highly respected Nathanson Centre For The Study Of Organized Crime And Corruption at the Osgoode Hall Law School of York University in Toronto, and Professor R.T. Naylor, a recognized authority on enterprise crime, financial fraud, black markets and criminal justice enforcement issues who works out of McGill University in Montreal.

According to them: 'The danger is of course a self-fulfilling process whereby the police, believing in a national criminal conspiracy (in part because of the advantages in this interpretation), focused their attention on these groups and individuals. In police work, one tends to be able to verify the criminal involvement of those groups who are targeted. Over time, if the police focus on Italians, the police files would indicate a dominance of Italian organized criminals, thus confirming the initial belief in the existence of the LCN (La Cosa Nostra) model.'

If what they're saying is, just because you set out to look for trees and find some, you can't claim to have discovered a forest, they're absolutely right. But if you set out to look for trees, and you find a whole bunch of them clumped together in the same ecosystem, and after a while there are so many trees that you can't see where you started and you can't see what's on the other side either, well, most people would forgive you for calling it a forest.

Still, the academics remain particularly vociferous. Law enforcement has an agenda, they insist, which is to manipulate statistics and create a fear of criminal power in order to increase budgets and, consequently, their own power.

To recognize the validity of the point, the argument goes, you merely have to observe how law enforcement and politicians play on easy to understand images of, 'an assortment of bogeymen such as the Russian Mob, the Colombia drug cartel and biker gangs.'

Accepting the theory that increased threats – perceived or real – lead to increased budgets, it's still a stretch to deny the existence of organized crime.

Common ground, however, might be found in the recognition of 'networked crime'.

This is the concept that disparate individuals and groups are linked through their common interest in criminal enterprise. Without ignoring the vertical or ladder image of crime groups, syndicates, families, whatever you call them – from foot soldier on the street corner to godfather in a fortress – the 'networked crime' picture is laid out flat. You need to look down on it, the way you would a map of a ring road around a city.

You start at any point and follow it around until you get back to the beginning, and every so often there is a street or highway feeding off it to take you in another direction. These intersections represent those disparate individuals and groups as they go about the business of crime. But while they may appear at first glance to be totally independent of all the others along the ring road, they are in fact joined by it. The connection from the first to the second may be a banker, the connection from the second to the third may be a drug trafficker, the connection from the third to the fourth may be a money laundering jurisdiction.

Granted, when money laundering becomes part of this – as it inevitably does – the ring road will be multi-jurisdictional. That creates the problem of multi-jurisdictional co-operation. But the point is, when you join up all these individuals and all these groups with that ring road – when you find the common bits that network them – you have another target to attack. By identifying the network, then breaking into it at a few strategic points, by blocking off some the streets that feed off the ring road, you can cause such an enormous traffic jam that, effectively, you've brought the entire network to a halt.

Just like the old rhyme about 'the man who shook hands with the man who shook hands', you don't need six degrees of separation to spot the connections.

Start with Ken Taves, a man in his early 40s who, one day, decided to go into the Internet porn industry.

The web is so filled with sexually related material that, as a single category, it is believed to be the most visited and the most profitable. But designing a site and uploading a lot of hardcore does not automatically a porn king make. And the California-based Taves found that a few thousand subscriptions at $19.95 a month was not enough to retire on.

So he invented 900,000 more.

His bank, Charter Pacific, maintained a massive database of all its credit card transactions and, under the guise of fraud control, was willing to make that database available to certain merchants. In 1997, Taves paid Charter Pacific $5,000 for access to 3.7 million account numbers. He got through nearly a quarter of them, submitting the account numbers to the merchant's service he used with instructions to charge each account $19.95 a month. In the credit card fraud business, that's known as 'cramming', and by the time the Federal Trade Commission (FTC) clamped down on him, he'd crammed himself $37.5 million.

Understanding that he would, eventually, get caught – after all, he had to expect that a lot of the 900,000 people he was defrauding monthly would question this recurring bill on their credit card statements – Taves turned for help to the Cayman Islands.

He opened an account there with Euro Bank, one of the less reputable financial institutions still in business at the time. On his behalf, Euro Bank incorporated a company called Benford Ltd in Vanuatu. That's the island chain in the south Pacific a couple of thousand kilometres north-east of Brisbane, Australia that used to be called New Hebrides. Its status these days as an offshore centre is highly suspect, right up there in the league tables with Nauru and Niue.

Within hours of incorporating Benford for Taves, Euro Bank opened an account in the company's name at European Bank in Vanuatu with a wired $100,000. In all, European Bank would eventually move $7.5 million from the Caymans to Vanuatu.

Although it took the FTC two years to investigate the thousands of complaints that were filed against Taves, his wife, their friends and all of their companies, when the agency finally lowered the boom, it was to put them out of business. The FTC filed a civil suit in Federal Court against Taves and the others for deceptive trade practices, and successfully proved that this bunch had used at least five different merchant accounts and four totally fictitious businesses to steal people's credit card numbers and bill them for services they had not subscribed to.

As a consequence, the court appointed a receiver to go after Taves assets and repay his victims. They ordered Taves to disclose all his financial interests and to repatriate any offshore assets. They then barred him for 10 years from having anything to do with any business that handled credit or debit card accounts.

Taves, who sometimes used the name Kenneth Till, had been in trouble before, involved with counterfeit cheques, fraud and even attempted murder. In 1980 he was arrested for hiring someone to kill a conman who'd swindled him out of $100,000. But the case dried up when the hired gunman, who'd agreed to testify against Taves, was killed in a car accident.

This time too, Taves seemed to be side-stepping criminal prosecution. His victims were spread out across 22 countries – including the UK, Ireland and Canada – and many of them would never be able to testify against him. What's more, in places like Japan, thousands of victims were so embarrassed about being bilked by a porn site that they refused to complain.

However, Taves got stupid and did his victims an enormous favour when he lied about his financial interests. He didn't tell the court about the $23.5 million sitting in Euro Bank. Or about Vanuatu. Or about any of the shell companies he owned, such as Satmax Family Limited Partnership and Coastal Holding Limited, which owned a $3 million mansion along the Pacific Coast Highway in Malibu. Not only was this his home – a fact he also neglected to mention in court – but when the judgement came down against him, he rushed to move the property out of those companies and into a Canadian shell called Trans Global Development Corporation. He also started moving his offshore money around to make it safe.

It was about this time that the authorities in the Caymans decided they'd had enough of Euro Bank and, using the Taves matter as an excuse, shut it down.

By now, too, the receiver was all over Taves' offshore holdings. But Taves was fighting back. Lawyers in Vanuatu and more lawyers in the Caymans put up hurdles to keep anyone from getting inside the various accounts, especially those at European Bank in Vanuatu. According to papers in the Cayman Islands, European Bank in Vanuatu had known for some time that Euro Bank was, 'open to business when other doors are closed to it, very much lower end of the local banking business, dubious, 3 months ago there were rumours that they might fail, not well respected, advise caution when dealing with them.'

Furthermore, the papers continue, reputable banks such as Barclays would not accept a reference from Euro Bank and, 'would certainly not do business with them.'

One reason why the bankers in Vanuatu might have chosen to ignore the warnings was that Taves' Benford account was too big to lose, representing about 15 per cent of European Bank's total deposit base.

As soon as Euro Bank was forced into liquidation and it became obvious that the Benford monies were proceeds of fraud, European Bank transferred the Benford money into a non-interest bearing account and froze it, so that neither the US receiver nor the Euro Bank liquidators could get their hands on it. Without advising their correspondent bank in New York that the funds were dirty, European Bank left them there on deposit in a high interest bearing account for the benefit of European Bank.

In February 2000, authorities in the Caymans took the big step of charging three Euro Bank officials – and Euro Bank, too – with money laundering in connection with the Taves' case. It was the first time the Caymans had ever brought a money laundering prosecution against a bank or bank officers based there. Similar charges were also lodged against Taves and five other people involved with him.

Realizing now that Taves had lied about his assets, the US receiver went back to Federal Court in August 2000 to have Taves ruled in criminal contempt. Taves further aggravated his situation by refusing to reveal his assets and the judge tossed him into jail until he did.

In the Caymans, where Euro Bank had been a local embarrassment for quite a while, secret banking laws prevented foreigners in civil actions from getting to the bank's records and laying claim to any funds there. Yet once the liquidators stepped into Euro Bank and the Taves case became a criminal matter, everything changed. The US receiver put in his claim for Taves' money and the bank's liquidators agreed to it. But the attorney general of the Cayman Islands didn't. He placed a restraining order on the funds, claiming that the bank was now a defendant in a criminal matter on the island. The US government quickly applied to exclude the Taves' money from the restraining order and the attorney general just as quickly opposed the motion. However, the Caymanian court noted that because this was a criminal matter the funds could be repatriated and ruled in favour of the Americans.

From that point, it became much easier to establish a fairly reliable money trail. It showed that, from mid-1997 until late-1998, Taves moved $25.3 million through four different companies to Euro Bank where it wound up in two Taves-controlled accounts. From there it was moved into other Euro Bank accounts, including one in Taves' parents' names. Records in the Caymans reveal that Taves owned property in the name of a shell company, and had accounts at Barclays Bank, the Bank of Nova Scotia and the Cayman National Bank. In addition, he maintained investment accounts at Morgan Stanley Dean Witter and the Royal Bank of Canada. Through Euro Bank there was also an investment account in Germany.

Money was moved from the Caymans to Vanuatu to Citibank Australia and then to Citibank, New York; to a lawyer's client account in the Bahamas and from there back to the States; from the Caymans to Jamaica; from the Caymans to the account of a Taves' company called Global International Media at Landesbank in Liechtenstein; and from the Caymans to the Toronto Dominion Bank in Victoria BC. Furthermore, Euro Bank had issued Taves a MasterCard that worked off one of the accounts so he could spend money in the States without the IRS finding out. In just under two years, Taves ran up nearly $300,000 on that credit card.

He has since pleaded guilty to what is now believed to be the biggest credit card fraud in history and is spending a considerable part of the rest of his life in a federal prison.

While the US receiver was chasing Taves' money and the Feds were building a case to put him behind bars, Brian Gibbs in the Cayman Islands was working for too many masters.

A sturdily built man in his fifties, Gibbs had joined the Metropolitan Police in London in 1964 and had spent the next 22 years working on any number of squads, investigating all sorts of criminality, including organized crime. In 1986, he was asked to form the Met's first Drugs Profit Confiscation Unit, which is how he got interested in money laundering. Three years later an opportunity came up to live in the Caribbean, seconded to the Royal Cayman Islands Police (RCIP), and he took it. There, he set up the island's first drug money laundering unit and although he retired from the Met in 1994, he remained on the Caymans' force, rising to the rank of detective chief inspector. He continued running the money laundering squad until the end of 2000 when the Caymans, in order to comply with FATF requirements, established a Financial Reporting Unit (FRU). Gibbs and his money laundering team were slid sideways out of the RCIP, renamed and placed under the auspices of the attorney general.

From that point on, money laundering cases on the island were dealt with by the FRU. The unit established its own intelligence sources, analysts and investigators, and had direct access to prosecutors.

'The reason it was taken away from police,' Gibbs explains, 'is because it consists of civilians and police officers and attorneys and the whole idea was to make it independent of everybody. It wasn't a political situation and the politicians don't like it.'

A confidential unit that, he points out, was 'charged with maintaining confidential information in confidence', the FRU was designed to operate as a closed unit right from the beginning. That meant, among other things, it had to be totally detached computerwise from any other arm of government so that whatever came in – reports, intelligence, evidence from confidential sources – would not be available to any other authority on the island or in anyway compromised. But because the attorney general has overall control of the FRU, it appears as if the executive council now has its own police force.

It's a situation that hasn't sat well with at least one well-known critic of the system who claims, 'It is dangerous to have more than one commissioner of police.'

The jury is still out on how independent the politicians actually permit the FRU to be. Proof of the pudding will come when, one day, the relationship between a politician and a local bank gets closer than arm's length. By then, the wisdom of taking the FRU away from the police might be called into question.

Still, the Caymanians shut down Euro Bank. When they did, the publicly stated reason was money laundering and the Taves fraud. But behind the scenes there were other, more sinister concerns.

The bank was started in 1981 and, right from the beginning, maintained a physical presence on the island. This wasn't just another brass-plate operation, there was an office and there was staff on the island. The reason was that certain people needed it to be a real bank.

Several men with banking backgrounds were behind it. One of them was a Canadian accountant with residence in the Caymans and Monaco named Donald Fraser. He had a connection to Saudi arms dealer Adnan Khashoggi who'd spent most of the 1970s encouraging rumours that he was the richest man in the world. Although he never was that, by the time Euro Bank was up and running, Khashoggi was one of the more amusing ultra-rich Middle Eastern eccentrics running around the world making money, flaunting money and marrying rather gorgeous women.

Along the way he'd established a business relationship with a Canadian wheeler-dealer, Peter Munk. While it's clear that the two did a number of deals together, less clear is the extent to which Khashoggi helped Munk get his company Barrick Gold off the ground and then keep it off the ground. Depending on whom you believe – Barrick's official version of events denies this – Khashoggi rescued Munk and Barrick on at least one occasion and, at least for a while, owned a controlling share in the mining company. Again, it depends on whom you believe and there are several versions of the story around, many of them contradictory, each of them suspiciously serving the person telling it. But what is known for certain is that Khashoggi was holding Barrick shares in 1985 when he got involved in the Iran-Contra scandal.

This was a concoction of the then CIA director, William Casey, who'd envisioned a way to sell arms to Iran and use that money to support the paramilitary Contras in their revolution in Nicaragua. His guys on the scene were a bunch of CIA refugees from the Nugan Hand Bank in Australia, which itself had been an offshoot of Paul Helliwell's Castle Bank in the Bahamas and Caymans. Star player was Marine Lieutenant Colonel Oliver North, then on assignment to the National Security Council. He was the man most directly involved in the day-to-day arms dealing and money laundering.

But it was Casey, in his role as puppet master, who pulled most of the strings. It was Casey who brought in Khashoggi, having access to him through their mutual friend, Kamal Adham, the Saudi intelligence chief.

Never one to play the shrinking violet, when he was invited into the conspiracy, Khashoggi promised Casey he could deliver the goods, which in this case was missiles. But when it came time to do just that, Khashoggi discovered that he'd need to come up with $15 million. He found $5 million from one source, then called on his mate Donald Fraser to help with the rest. Euro Bank loaned Khashoggi the money. Khashoggi's collateral was his shares in Barrick.

Of course BCCI was involved in this too, and BCCI was also in the Caymans. Yet by 1986, as Khashoggi and Fraser were sighted together all over the Caymans, some people came to believe that Khashoggi was also one of the original investors in Euro Bank. In fact, his reason for hanging out there was that his wife Saroya was in the midst of dumping him and needed some place safe to stash his money so that her lawyers couldn't find it.

Until then Khashoggi had used banks in Liechtenstein. Now he re-registered his Triad Holding Corp in the Caymans and packed a lot of his real estate wealth into a Cayman's Trust. He also incorporated a company there called AK Holdings for his toys — his plane, his yacht, his cars — the kind of stuff his ex-wife's lawyers would have loved to get their hands on.

So throughout the Iran-Contra days, money was moving through Euro Bank to the Contras. US Senate investigators also discovered in

1991, that there were dozens of transactions between Euro Bank and BCCI. But other people were moving money through there as well, including at least one American fugitive from justice, prompting the local inspector of banks to complain quietly to the management that too many bad people were associated with the bank.

There's no doubt that drug barons were among the people washing money through Euro Bank. Nor is there any doubt that, in the wake of 9/11 – given its pedigree – certain intelligence agencies around the world had an interest in who walked through Euro Bank's doors. One of those intelligence services was Britain's MI-6.

And their guy on the ground in the Caymans was Brian Gibbs.

Surveillance of the bank and its clients was codenamed 'Operation Victory'. To manage it, Gibbs had a source inside the bank. He was Edward Warwick, codenamed 'Warlock'. The two had met some years before when Warwick was working at Finsbury Bank on the island. Gibbs and his unit at the RCIP investigated Finsbury for drug money laundering and the government shut it. Gibbs maintained contact with Warwick, who came to be considered a high-value source by MI-6. According to documents in the Caymans, there were several people Warwick spoke with Gibbs about over the years.

One was Donald Stewart. Before coming to Euro Bank, Stewart had been country manager at the Royal Bank of Canada. While there, Gibbs had served Stewart with a production order to hand over certain bank documents in connection with a drug case. According to Gibbs, Stewart did not fully comply and withheld information.

Another was Brian Cunha, a Euro Bank officer who'd previously been manager at First Cayman Bank. Gibbs had served him with a production order in a case involving David Namer, a now convicted fraudster out of Tennessee. Namer had been laundering his proceeds of crime through the Caymans, and working Reg-S fraud with Meyers Pollock Robbins, the mobbed-up brokerage that the SEC and John Moscow had busted.

Warwick was also a source of information about David Bockius, a man running insurance fraud out of Pennsylvania. Bockius was laundering funds through an investment account at PaineWebber in New York, and was also using the casinos in Atlantic City to wash some cash. The rest he merely carried with him to the Caymans. On his initial trip down, using the alias Louis Middleton, he stashed half a million dollar into secret compartments of his suitcases. He formed a shell called Little Mermaid Holdings and through that, with some of his cash, bought himself a house. He intended to put the rest of the cash into Canadian banks, making multiple deposits of under $10,000 to escape reporting requirements. But either some of the banks flatly refused him, or he found out that the others would probably report him anyway. At Euro Bank they welcomed him and his cash.

A certain Russian whose name popped up frequently during the 1990s involved with offshore scams was also brought to Gibbs attention this way, although intelligence on that person was coming from several sources at the same time. Gibbs wrote in a report about this Russian, 'The matters on record concerning (name omitted) were ongoing not just from Mr Warwick, but from the National Criminal Intelligence Service UK, press reports, City of London Police, FBI and other sources.'

As outlined in a confidential report written by a New York investigator, this particular Russian was an intermediary in the purchase of certain financial instruments by a small Moscow bank. The money was being run through three shells in the Caymans, all of which had accounts at Euro Bank. The first two deals, totalling $9.7 million, worked fine. But the third, for $4.75 million, went missing. The Moscow bank asked Euro Bank for the return of the money, but Euro Bank refused.

On further investigation, it was determined that monies had been moved out of Euro Bank in various directions. A large sum was sent to an account at Citibank, New York for credit to Bank Von Ernst et Cie in Zurich. Another large sum was sent directly to BankVon Ernst. The supposition was that the Russian intermediary had ordered the transfers and controlled both accounts.

But the Russian intermediary claimed that the two transfers were forgeries. Investigators in New York, the Caymans, Switzerland and London didn't accept his excuse at face value and were continuing to look into the Russian intermediary's business affairs. One area of interest to all of them were associations he might have with certain people involved in the Bank of New York laundering scandal.

Two other names that were brought to Gibbs' attention by Warwick were Jay Bartz and Patrick Smythe. Both of them were stock-piling money at Euro Bank, and both of them would be the next stop along the ring road of networked crime.

But Brian Gibbs wouldn't be around to do anything about that.

The Caymans brought charges against Euro Bank and some of its officers – including Stewart and Cunha – and took the case to trial.

Back in London, MI-6 grew increasingly nervous about the possibility
that its position might be exposed. Paranoid about publicity anyway,
the last thing it wanted was for evidence to be presented in court
which would require it to 'neither confirm nor deny' an active presence in the Caymans, expose Gibbs as its agent, compromise any of
its on going inquiries, or expose 'Warlock'.

Early on in the trial, when the defence attorneys and the judge
began to realize that certain documents had not been made available
to them by the prosecution, attention focused on the FRU and Gibbs.
The prosecution pressed Gibbs about the documents, too. There were
then discussions with London about possibly sanitizing the missing
information, loading it onto Gibbs' computer and making some excuse
about having misplaced it until now.

That's when word came to Gibbs that the RCIP was about to raid
him. If that happened, MI-6's work in the Caymans would be
destroyed. So the decision was made to shred certain documents. When
the judge discovered this – and was led to believe that MI-6 might
even have been bugging his phones – he castigated Gibbs and tossed
the Euro Bank case out of court. He declared all of the defendants
not guilty.

Gibbs quickly resigned from his post at the FRU and left the
island.

In 1990, the financial position of the National Heritage Life Insurance
Company, a subsidiary of LifeCo Investment Group, became tenuous
as a result of a series of bad deals, and the company's future was at
risk. The Delaware Insurance Department, which had oversight
authority, threatened the company that unless they raised additional
capital, the department would take regulatory action. But instead of
bolstering the company's bank accounts, several directors of LifeCo
decided to sacrifice National Heritage in favour of their own bank
accounts.

Over the course of the next seven years, Patrick Smythe, then president and chief operations officer of LifeCo, together with a group of
corporate insiders and at least one professional fraudster, ran through
a series of scams to embezzle $440 million from the company.

Among the scams was one revolving around non-performing mortgages. Smythe announced that he was in the midst of negotiating a

$200 million reinsurance deal and that National Heritage would have to come up with the money to fund it.

One of his partners-in-crime, Lyle Pfeffer – who served on LifeCo's board – moved the National Heritage money to other associates who, in turn, sheltered it away in various shells. That money was then used to buy a portfolio of non-performing mortgages which were eventually grouped into another shell company. Bonds, with grossly exaggerated values, were issued by the shell company holding the essentially worthless non-performing mortgages, for which National Heritage paid $118.3 million.

Smythe's second partner-in-crime was Jay Bartz, whose name had come up along with Smythe's at Euro Bank. He was an attorney in Arizona who also sat on LifeCo's board and served as Smythe's laundryman. Bartz's primary task was to make money safe, which he did for Smythe by moving $2.2 million first to the Channel Islands and from there to the Caymans. In the end, Bartz was put in prison for three years and disbarred.

Two other men now come into play.

The first is Michael Blutrich, a New York attorney and convicted paedophile who, through his friendship with Pfeffer, was brought into the LifeCo swindle. Blutrich helped Smythe and Pfeffer divert $47 million from National Heritage by creating a ruse that made it look as if the money was being spent on capital investments.

With their share of the money, Blutrich and Pfeffer bought themselves a strip joint and turned it into Manhattan's first lap dancing club, Scores. Not only was this a place where they could hang out, but they'd worked out a way to help their friends at LifeCo launder money through the business. What neither of them understood, however, was that in New York the five LCN families had long ago divvied-up the strip club market. It's one of many traditional businesses where one of the families is always a silent partner. In this case, the Gambino family, then run by John Gotti, moved in with Blutrich and Pfeffer at Scores.

At the same time, the Gambinos were laundering drug money through an up-market strip joint in Atlanta called the Gold Club. The man running it for them, Steve Kaplan, had turned it into a hot spot for celebrity athletes which he easily did by pimping some of the dancers. At his trial, stories of sex at the Gold Club came from NBA stars Patrick Ewing and Dennis Rodman and Atlanta Braves baseball player Andruw Jones.

Kaplan, who was looking to move up in the world, tried to convince his masters in the family that he could work the same routine at Scores. So pressure mounted from at least one faction of the family looking to install Kaplan. Blutrich never liked the idea that the Gambinos were setting the terms of his own business. They were skimming wherever they could, in addition to over charging him for booze, rubbish collection, doormen, bouncers and the girls. Now they wanted to run him out. Blutrich realized he needed some help and turned to the Feds. He let them wire the club in their effort to target Gotti.

Push came to shove when Blutrich fired the Gotti-installed manager. Kaplan wanted a showdown and the only way Blutrich could save his business was to ask for arbitration. John Gotti Jr agreed to hear both sides, and ruled in Blutrich's favour. He then sent Blutrich a bill for $200,000 for settling the matter.

When the LifeCo case came down, Blutrich pleaded guilty to 18 felony counts of racketeering, conspiracy, wire fraud and money laundering. Along with Smythe and Pfeffer, the judge handed him 25 years. Rather than do all that time, Blutrich and Pfeffer offered to turn state's evidence against Junior Gotti, the Mob, Kaplan and the others at the Gold Club. They helped to expose what they knew about seven Mob controlled corporations and the money laundering apparatus attached to them.

It pretty much worked because Gotti and Kaplan and most of the rest went down. For their trouble, Blutrich and Pfeffer were made life members of a witness protection programme, were allowed to spend the next 17 years in the relative safety of solitary confinement. Eventually, if they live long enough to get out, they will be given new identities.

The other man who got involved in the LifeCo scam and went on to bigger and better things was Blutrich's friend, Shalom Weiss. A professional fraudster, he was the genius behind the non-performing mortgage rip-off. It was his shell company that acquired the mortgages and another of his shell companies that sold them.

When the cops came looking for him, however, Weiss decided it would be a good idea to abandon his wife and children in New York, and spend time with his girlfriend in Brazil. He went on the lam for more than a year, until he was found in Vienna and brought back to the States to stand trial. Ordered to pay a fine of $123 million, plus restitution of $125 million to National Heritage's policy holders, Weiss was sent away for 845 years.

Previously convicted of mail fraud, Weiss had been working Reg-S scams for several years and had close ties to various Russian mobsters also working securities fraud in the States. There are connections through those Russians to the Gambinos.

Weiss is also linked to Phil Abramo, of the Decavalcante crime family. The same Phil Abramo who'd once worked at A.S. Goldmen in Florida with Albert Alain Chalem – the man who'd threatened Sal Mazzeo – and had helped manipulate the Reg-S offering of Osicom Technologies.

Weiss and Abramo also showed up together in an investigation in Vancouver. The British Columbia Securities Commission (BCSC) spent two years investigating a local brokerage house, Pacific International Securities, which had been named in three US money laundering indictments. As a result, several brokers were arrested for dealing with mobbed-up clients. In a press release, the BCSC even announced some of the names of the mobbed up clients. High on the list were Weiss and Abramo.

Slightly lower down that list was a convicted stock manipulator from Las Vegas named Barclay Davis. He'd been involved in a series of fraudulent microcap offerings that were moved through several brokerages in Vancouver. Among the promotions complained of were Systems of Excellence, Combined Companies International Corp. and Bio-Tech Industries Inc. which was originally called Twenty First Century Health.

A Davis comrade in at least one of the fraudulent offerings out of Vancouver is Thomas Clines. And he brings the ring road back to the beginning.

In 1990, Clines was convicted for income tax evasion for failing to declare $260,000 that he made in arms' shipments to the Nicaraguan contras as one the CIA refugees working the Iran-Contra scandal for William Casey and laundering money through Euro Bank.

CHAPTER FOURTEEN

A Better Mousetrap

Build a better mousetrap
and the world will beat a path to your door
– Ralph Waldo Emerson

There was a time when drug money laundering was a fairly straight-forward business. You gathered up all the cash from street corner sales, walked it around to lots of banks, dumped a little bit here and a little bit there, then consolidated the accounts, wired the whole stash out of the country and hid it in some secret jurisdiction. That's the way Stephen Saccoccia did it.

That's also the way Gary Henden did it, although this legendary Canadian laundrymen had a variation on the theme. Instead of having the money delivered to him, he used a delivery boy to take it to the banks – a 15-year-old on a bicycle.

It was basically the same method for the drug trafficker who bragged when he was arrested that he employed an army of 'Smurfs' – named for the cartoon characters – who could make up to 2000 deposits a day at 513 different banks.

Law enforcement figured out that approach pretty quickly and although it took politicians a while to catch up, eventually they passed laws making it more and more difficult to get cash into banks. So much so that Pablo Escobar, the late Colombian cocaine cartel boss, once had to write off $40 million because he couldn't launder it fast enough. The cash was found rotting in a California basement.

Without any doubt, when you get right down to it, cash is the most difficult problem that drug traffickers face. Holding on to it is dangerous and getting rid of it is clumsy. Because street sales are made in small denominations, cocaine and heroin can generate six to ten times their weight in banknotes. Smuggle 50 kilos of coke into the country and your street sales will net approximately 300 kilos worth of cash. Import ten kilos of heroin, and you've got to worry about 100 kilos in small bills.

As laundering became more difficult, traffickers looked to bulk money out of the country and import it into laundry-friendly jurisdictions. In many cases they used the same methods to get money out as they did to bring the drugs in.

Customs officers at Kennedy Airport in New York stopped a woman about to board a flight to Europe and asked her how much money she was carrying. She answered, $9,000. When they searched her luggage, they found $24,000 stuffed into shampoo bottles. When they examined her, they found she'd hidden six wads of $100 bills vaginally and had swallowed a dozen condoms with another 20-grand rolled in them. Their cohorts at nearby Newark Airport stopped another woman wearing a lot of clothes as she was getting onto a flight to Colombia. Underneath her dress, girdle and stockings she wore a surfer's wetsuit stuffed with $75,000.

Inspectors all over the world report money hidden in toys, sealed inside wax candles and stuffed inside re-sealed boxes of popcorn, pancake mix and sacks of rice. Some $695,000 was found by inspectors in biscuit tins and packages of baby wipes inside the luggage of a man boarding a flight to Egypt. Another $625,000 was located in plastic bags that had been professionally sewn into the lining of a comforter. Bulk cash has been found rolled into carpets, shoved inside laptop computers, packed into fridges and in one case, hidden inside a stuffed animal just back from the taxidermist. Cash has been found in vats of battery acid and toxic waste, and some years ago, $6.5 million worth was found at the bottom of drums filled with bull semen on its way to South America.

At Heathrow Airport, it is becoming more and more common to see HM Customs officers with specially trained 'cash sniffer' dogs doing spot checks of people flying out of the country. Not long ago, a team with dogs was checking people leaving on a flight to Miami. When the team leader was informed by a nosy passenger that he was wasting his time, the officer wondered why. He was told that he'd do better to check flights going to Canada – where laundering cash was more viable – because no one in Miami wanted cash. Instead, every laundryman in Florida was paying over the odds to get rid of cash.

Either the HM Customs officer refused to believe it, or he didn't understand which, in either case, says a lot about Britain's war on dirty money.

Although sniffing dogs checking the wrong flight do create a presence which might, if HM Customs gets lucky, have a knock-on effect in deterring some amateur money launderer from carrying cash through the airport, more effective methods can be derived from a deeper understanding of how creative money launderers need to be.

Brokers at the Wall Street firm, MLU Investments, were well aware that the Colombians had found a better mousetrap, because they were part of it, helping the Colombians move $8 million through the markets.

The president and chief laundrymen of MLU Investments was Ron Rose. Now in his mid-40s, athletically lean with bright eyes and a laid-back friendly smile, he grew up on Long Island, graduated from John Jay college in Manhattan in 1978 and got himself a job working in the Inspector General's office at the New York City Department of Finance. He wasn't there long before he realized what he really wanted to do was be a cop. So he signed on with the NYPD, did all the usual uniformed street patrol stuff and got himself interviewed for a detective's position. Transferred into plain clothes, he was assigned to the Organized Crime Control Bureau.

'It's really just the luck of the draw.' He recalls, 'I spent time working in Public Morals, the vice squad, doing gambling and loan sharking. I also worked traditional organized crime, racketeering cases on the Bonanno crime family and did a lot of cases going after the Colombo family. Then somebody asked me if I wanted to move into something new. They were setting up a money laundering unit. I didn't seek it out, didn't even know much about it. But one day I was working the Colombos, next day I was working the Colombians.'

In 1992, as Lieutenant Rose, he and his NYPD money laundering unit moved into offices leased by US Customs at the World Trade Center to become an integral part of a joint task force known as El Dorado.

Literally billions of dollars had been going through New York banks each month in a well organized, professional manner. The bad guys were frantic to get their cash out of the country, while the good guys were trampling over each others feet to try to stop them. The idea behind the 200-strong El Dorado team was to unite the 35 federal, state and local agencies that were working money laundering throughout the New York metropolitan area. The feeling was that the good guys were out-gunned, out-financed and out-lawyered, so that by combining forces – by putting law enforcement together with prosecutors, intelligence and analysts – they might stand a chance at interrupting the cash flow and reinvestment that the traffickers needed to keep their business flowing.

One of El Dorado's senior managers, US Customs agent John Forbes, believed that if El Dorado could target money remitters in some of New York's high density drug trafficking neighbourhoods, they could interrupt the money flows and, in turn, effect trafficking. Forbes wanted to target a Colombian neighbourhood in Jackson Heights. About a mile south of LaGuardia Airport, it's a lower middle-class section of Queens where, in those days, the average family earned about $20,000 before taxes. But so much money was going to Colombia that it averaged out at $30,000–$40,000 per family.

Forbes sold the idea to the then Under Secretary of the Treasury for Enforcement, Ray Kelly – later Commissioner of Customs, and then Police Commissioner for the City of New York – who signed a 'Geographical Targetting Order' (GTO). Among other things, this restricted the amount of money a person in Jackson Heights could wire to Colombia without filing certain forms.

The money laundering laws limited the amount to $3,000. The GTO reduced it to $750. And almost immediately, Forbes' idea proved right. Big sum wires to Colombia from Jackson Heights virtually ceased. At the same time, fees for a wire of under $750 to Colombia dropped from 7 to 3 per cent. Forbes, Rose and other managers at El Dorado suspected that the rate drop reflected increased competition, so now they went after the remitters.

These were, ostensibly, mom and pop businesses – beauty parlours, candy stores, travel agencies – which offered a remitter service in the shop. Some of them also sold mobile phones, and phone cards so that anonymous calls could be made. All of them advertised 'ENVIO' which meant they wired money. Along Roosevelt Boulevard, running through the heart of Jackson Heights for about a mile and a half, there were more than 175 ENVIOs and these places were moving $1.1–$1.3 billion a year.

Of course it was dope money and El Dorado started shutting the remitters down. Typically, whenever they closed one, two more would open up. After a while the traffickers understood that they were being targeted and the money being wired out moved across Manhattan, to Washington Heights on the upper West Side, where Dominicans controlled the drug trade. Forbes went back to Kelly and got another GTO to target the Dominicans. Before long, some of the action left town, heading south to Florida, which meant that El Dorado was having an effect.

Around 1998, disquieting news started coming out of their surveillance of the wire remitters. Instead of money moving to Colombia, the taskforce saw some Colombian drug money wired out to Pakistan. Forbes grew very concerned and went to his superiors to say, we need to look at this. No one up the ladder felt the same sense of urgency about it. Forbes simply couldn't get anyone to commit to it. That Colombian drug money was heading to the sub-continent – with all the ramifications of money moving through there to the Middle East – didn't seem important.

Three years later, when El Dorado's offices were destroyed by the 9/11 attacks, Colombian drug money going to Pakistan took on a whole new meaning.

El Dorado was still focused on Jackson Heights when Rose got a call from his boss at Police Headquarters saying that the Commissioner had met a couple of retired FBI guys with an informant who knew a couple of guys hoping to invest some dirty money. Rose was told to look into it.

The retired agents explained to Rose that their informant had connections with Mexico's ruthless Gulf Cartel and that this would be a way to land some heavyweight money launderers. Rose thought about it and decided he might be able to set up some sort of an investment firm to handle their money. If he worked it right, the money trail should lead to the cartel's investment brokers. But the more he talked to these guys, the less enthusiastic he was about dealing with them. They wanted to run the whole thing by remote control from another part of the country and Rose saw too many problems with that.

Undercover operations are inherently risky and Rose knew from experience that the stakes in this one could run very high. He decided he didn't want any part of it and explained to the Commissioner why he felt the NYPD should stay away. He returned to El Dorado, thinking that's the end of that. But a couple of days later, one of the retired FBI guys decided that he and his mate would be willing to do it any way the NYPD wanted to, so Rose's boss asked him to write up a game plan and cost it. He did, putting the price tag for the operation at around $100,000, and sent it up the chain of command.

Normally, proposals like this one get sent from office to office and a year later someone remembers to say yes or no. So Rose wasn't counting on anything happening for a long while. But two days later he received a call to say, go ahead.

He was shocked. 'Most of the time I couldn't get $10 out of them to buy batteries for a tape recorder, now in two days they're telling me to spend a hundred grand.'

The Commissioner wanted the operation run in conjunction with the New York District Attorney's office, which teamed Rose with Assistant DA Gilda Mariani.

Describing her depends on the circumstances of how you met. If you've been introduced by mutual friends, she is a charming, bright, sophisticated woman with a deep love of animals, whose mind and door are always open to new initiatives and new ideas. As chief of the NYDA's money laundering and tax crimes unit, Mariani is a genuine authority on money laundering and was one of the driving forces in getting an effective money laundering law implemented in New York State. If, on the other hand, you've been introduced to her by cops who have locked you in handcuffs, she is a tenacious and resolute workaholic who categorically will not quit until she gets the result she wants, which usually means putting you behind bars.

Rose and Mariani spent a year setting up everything they needed to go into business as investment brokers. It began with a lot of back-stopping that had to be put in place – undercover identities, drivers licences, credit cards, personal histories, credit histories and work histories. Because Rose and his guys were going into the markets, they needed memos of understanding with the SEC and the NASD. They also needed, and got, some professional training.

Next, Rose and Mariani had to form a company. They incorporated themselves and set up bank accounts as the MLU Investment Group Corporation. It was their little inside joke. MLU stands for 'Money Laundering Unit'.

'We had to assume,' Rose says, 'that we might come under a lot of scrutiny. If these people were actually going to trust us with their money, they would want to know who we are. We were going to do cash management and investment for companies that were cash inten-sive, so we wrote a business plan that showed us dealing with video arcades, amusement parks, video rentals, supermarkets. We then created accounts in the names of Lake Wholesale Foods, American Video, Funtime Arcade. Our story was that we could place their money in the bank. From there, we would send it wherever they needed it, and hold onto whatever they wanted us to invest for them. We set it up so that when some bad guy looked at us, he'd think to himself, these guys can wash our money for us and nobody will ever know.'

With backstopping place, MLU Investments needed an office. It had to be in the right part of town and it had to have the right look. At the same time, it had to be secure enough that they could run the undercover safely. They settled on a 22nd floor suite at One World Trade Center, a building where security had been seriously increased following the 1993 attack. Unless you had an ID card, you couldn't walk into the elevator banks and go upstairs. Anyway, the last thing Rose wanted, was someone just stopping by. To get upstairs, you needed to ask at the desk in the lobby and someone from MLU would come down to escort you up.

The MLU office was behind a secure door, with cameras guarding the entrance. Naturally, the place was wired for sound and video. It wasn't plush but it was typical and adequate. Rose filled it with 25-grand worth of furniture – cherrywood desks, high backed leather chairs – computers and market wires to make it look like a boutique investment firm.

Rose, case officer Joe Thompson and four undercover detectives would work the office. The rest of the crew – about 10 people – would handle surveillance and back-up. They also needed people to handle administrative support, which meant bookkeeping and accounting and someone to type transcripts when they were running wiretaps.

Once they had it all equipped, when Rose and Mariani and everyone else were all ready to go, Rose told the guys running El Dorado what was about to come down. Around that office, he was always pushing for equal footing, always reminding the Customs and IRS guys running it that the locals had to have an equal share. So he told them about his undercover and invited El Dorado to play a support role.

'They didn't know if they wanted in or out. They hemmed and hawed. I asked them not to tell anybody about it because it was under-cover and we weren't looking to advertise, and gave them time to think about it. I went to Puerto Rico on a job and while I was there I get a call from my boss at NYPD who said, your new case is in the newspaper. Except we hadn't done anything yet, we were still in the process of setting it up. We hadn't even started and it's already in the newspapers.'

Rose later learned that someone at El Dorado had mentioned the undercover to a friend at the US Attorney's office. The Feds like to think of Wall Street as their turf and don't necessarily like it when the New York DA's office plays there, too. On at least one occasion, District Attorney Morgenthau is known to have reminded a certain US Attorney, 'Last time I looked out my window, Wall Street was in Manhattan.' So when someone at the US Attorney's office heard about Rose's undercover, and realized that he was working with the DA's office, whoever that person was decided to remind the New Yorkers that the Feds were not to be ignored. The DA's office had locked up a woman for insider trading. Over one weekend, an assistant US Attorney visited her in jail and got to her to take a plea on federal charges. Essentially, the US Attorney's office stole the case. That person then leaked a story to the *New York Times* about how the Feds had scored some points, mentioning in the last couple of paragraphs that there was a dispute going on with the DA's office over an undercover investigation that the NYPD was running despite objections from the US Attorney's office.

That didn't please Rose and Mariani. And didn't sit well with the El Dorado hierarchy, either. They decided they didn't want to upset the US Attorney and opted out of Rose's undercover. They also ruled out any participation by anyone assigned to El Dorado. That placed Rose and his team in the middle of a power struggle between El Dorado's masters and the NYPD. So now, with everything ready to go, the NYPD simply pulled their guys out of El Dorado and went ahead with MLU.

They called it 'Operation Bluechip'. Right from the beginning, Rose put out the word that they weren't going to do street pick-ups. He wanted his customers to know that cash had to be delivered to his office. And not just to the lobby. Cash had to be brought upstairs to the office, and only after the person making the delivery was behind the locked office doors, would MLU take possession of the money.

'We did that for several reasons,' Rose goes on. 'Number one, it helped support our story that we were brokers and investment advisors, not just some slugs on the street. It showed them that we knew we had a lot to lose by doing it any other way. It showed them we didn't intend on getting robbed by some mutts. We don't do pickups, that's not us, we're not going out there. Number two, it protected my guys from getting ripped off. No one could set us up where one guy gives you the bag here and the next guy comes around the corner with a gun and takes it from you. Number three, we needed to protect ourselves from other law enforcement people out there. We didn't want to get arrested in a sting that someone else might be running. So our guys never touched anything until the money was handed to us upstairs, behind our locked door with our cameras running.'

Because attention to detail is always so vital in any undercover, Rose set up a system where the guys working in the office were not the same people who took the money out of the office to the bank. Nor did anyone taking money out use the same bag that brought the money in.

Yet with all their planning, and all the tension that had been caused by the *New York Times* article, and all the political problems with El Dorado, Rose and Mariani suddenly found themselves dressed to the nines with no place to go. They'd sent a Confidential Informant (CI) out into the world, seeded him with ten grand to spread around and only got promises in return.

They both understood how an undercover like this could produce major results, and they were determined to make it work. So Rose and Mariani tried to find someone who would authorize them to branch out. But the powers-that-be were nervous about that – branching out wasn't written into the game plan which meant the bosses wouldn't have their butts covered if something went wrong – and they kept coming back to Rose and Mariani with stuff like, give the CI a chance to deliver, hang in there, something will happen.

Except it didn't.

Months passed and the only thing they had to show for MLU was one guy who offered to sell them some phoney Paraguayan bonds.

Refusing to give up, Rose and Mariani eventually got permission to use their own contacts, reached out to certain people, and let it be known that MLU Investments was able to do stuff that no one else on Wall Street could do.

That's when a call came in from someone who knew someone who might be interested in doing business.

With Rose and Mariani in the background, Detective Jimmy Ricaurte, a Spanish speaking undercover, negotiated with the intermediary, who had a friend in Colombia, who had some money stashed at a wholesale clothing place in midtown Manhattan. The intermediary explained that if MLU wanted to do business with his friend the Colombian, MLU would have to pick up the cash.

Right away, Ricaurte explained that they didn't do collections. He told the intermediary, 'We're brokers, not guys who pick up bags of money.'

But the intermediary insisted and Rose knew that tapping into the Colombian could lead to bigger things. To facilitate the deal, Rose nodded to Ricaurte, who told the intermediary that he'd contract out the pick up, but just this once. What Rose and Mariani didn't find out until much later was that this particular wholesale clothing business was being watched by an NYPD narcotics team. Luckily, when one of Rose's guys made the pick up, the narcotics team didn't get in the way.

Once the money was moved, the Colombian himself – call him Jorge – phoned Ricaurte to say, I want to work with you but I don't know you, you don't know me so we have to meet before we can do anything else. Jorge suggested they get together in Colombia. That was out of the question for the good guys. Rose wanted Ricaurte to meet Jorge in the States. That was out of the question for the bad guy, who now suggested Panama. On Rose's advice, Ricaurte compromised by setting up the meet in Curaçao. The Dutch island off the coast of Colombia would be safe because Rose had law enforcement connections there. Curaçao is also an offshore banking centre, which gave Ricaurte the built-in excuse of being able to say that he needed to be there on business, anyway.

Jorge agreed and the meeting took place on schedule. He told Ricaurte that he was a money broker who got in the middle of other guys' deals. Rose and Mariani couldn't yet tell how important Jorge was because these guys always play themselves up to be a lot more important than they really are. But even a small broker was capable of moving tens of millions of dollars. And anyway, the MLU undercover didn't have anyone else to play with.

During the meeting in Curaçao, Ricaurte reminded Jorge that money moving wasn't their business, that they did investments but that he might be willing to do a certain amount of money moving for serious investors. Jorge became MLU's first client.

'Getting into Jorge was a big step,' Rose points out. 'These guys have associates who are always looking for outlets to move money. When they find one, they never tell their friends about it because then their friends can deal directly. Instead, they broker deals for their friends. We moved his money, he trusted us and his friends trusted him. Before long we were moving money with our guy for a lot of other people, wiring it all over the States and all over the world. Hong

Kong. Shanghai, Italy. London. This guy put us in the middle of a huge black market peso exchange.'

The black market peso exchange (BMPE) was, indeed, the better mousetrap.

Based on the same ancient system of barter that Middle Easterners and Asians call '*hawallah*', it was perfected in the Western hemisphere by smugglers who needed to do double-sided trades to thrive in the underground economy.

Simply put, it's a system where goods move and money stays put. Drug traffickers, faced with the increasing difficulties of shifting money, latched onto the idea in the mid-1980s. By 1990 they'd perfected the system to the point that Colombia's black market peso exchange was a $5 billion bazaar. Today, it's anyone's guess how much this market is worth, but estimates of two to three times as much as it was in 1990 could all be in the ballpark. One official Colombian estimate suggests that 45 per cent of the country's imported consumer goods are paid for through the BMPE.

The reason for the market's indisputable success is that money laundering doesn't have to be about money. In fact, these days, it seldom is. Money laundering in the globalized twenty-first century is about honey and diamonds, automobiles, tractors and stereos, charities and paperless networks like *hawallah* banking that you find throughout the Middle East and sub-Continent. Recently money laundering was also about sports memorabilia – a Mafia loan-sharking operation washed money through collectable baseball cards, Michael Jordan autographed basketballs, signed hockey pucks and a pair of Muhammad Ali's boxing gloves.

In its most basic form, a broker sitting in Colombia arranges to buy a trafficker's drug cash in Britain at a discount. At the same time, he takes pesos from a legitimate businessman in Colombia looking to import a product, say a large shipment of Scotch. The broker uses the pesos in Colombia to buy the drug trafficker's cash in Britain, then uses the drug cash in Britain to buy the Scotch for the businessman in Colombia.

Traffickers and legitimate businessmen both have to trust the broker with their money. But as he's in Colombia, if anything goes wrong, retribution is simple. So it's the broker who takes a risk by trusting associates outside Colombia to facilitate transfers, deposit cash and sometimes make payments. But then, these brokers frequently work like bookies, laying off parts of contracts to spread the risk.

The system flourishes because it is efficient. Whether the product is Scotch or household appliances, consumer electronics, cigarettes, used auto parts, precious metals, footwear, cars, boats, heavy earth-moving equipment, whatever, everyone gets what he wants. The trafficker winds up with pesos, which means his drug money has been laundered. The businessman get his goods and, because the purchase is outside normal channels, he usually beats the taxman. The broker has made money on the spread between buying and selling dollars and pesos, plus a commission on the deal. And the company selling the goods has probably made a sale it might not have otherwise made. Except that the company selling the goods has also laundered drug money – albeit unknowingly. Still, very few serious companies want to get caught doing that.

Just ask the folks who make Bell Helicopters.

In 1998 a man with links to drug traffickers and paramilitary groups in Colombia wanted to buy a Bell 407 helicopter. The company didn't know anything about his background or his business dealings. Nor was there any requirement for them to do so. This was simply a guy looking to buy a helicopter and selling helicopters is the business Bell is in. He agreed to pay them $1.5 million for the machine and nobody at Bell thought twice about it.

Yet, alarm bells should have gone off when Bell saw how he was paying for it. They received 29 third-party wire transfers from 16 different sources, in addition to a third-party cheque endorsed over to Bell from yet another source. None of those third parties had any sort of relationship with Bell. As it turned out, none of them had any sort of relationship with the man buying the helicopter, either. The third parties were following instructions from a BMPE broker who was moving drug money into negotiable paper, payable to Bell. The actual buyer had already put down $1.5 million in pesos in Colombia.

Bell's response was understandable. *How could we know this was drug money? If we'd known this was drug money, we'd never have done the deal.*

US Customs' response was then – and is now – *you should have known*.

But then, Bell was hardly alone in getting duped. The investigation which uncovered this sale led to investigations into half a dozen other companies that had fallen victim to the same ruse. In every one of those cases, the company denied intentionally taking drug money.

In some of those cases, the denials are believable. But it's not always easy to understand why a legitimate business wouldn't question payment methods which are so out of the ordinary.

That said, BMPE brokers count on the fact that most companies would rather have a strange sale than no sale at all.

And many of those sales are decidedly strange. Take for example, the order that arrived at the sales' office of a world-famous sporting goods company for $10,000 worth of soccer gear. It was to be shipped to Colombia. Payment was a pile of money orders but the envelope that it came in didn't even have a return address.

One US company, General Electric, instituted a very strict money laundering compliance programme in 1995 after getting burned by a BMPE broker buying a load of refrigerators. The programme was in place and effectively stopped another BMPE broker when he tried to pay for $40,000 worth of air conditioners with 35 money orders.

In October 1997, an anonymous BMPE broker went before a US congressional committee to name several international companies with whom she'd placed deals. Among them: Sony, Procter & Gamble, John Deere, Whirlpool, Ford, Kenworth, Johnny Walker, Swatch, Merrill Lynch and Reebok. As she explained, 'These companies were paid with US currency generated by narcotics trafficking. They may not have been aware of the source of this money, but they accepted payments from me without questioning who I was or the source of the money.'

By the mid-to-late 1990s, the volume of money moving through the black market peso exchange was so large, it's hardly surprising that Ron Rose and Gilda Mariani were not the people setting up a sting to get inside one.

In Operation Juno, the DEA and the IRS rented office space in suburban Atlanta to set up a stockbrokerage called Airmark. Although they never did any actual stock trading, they found some peso brokers who believed they were for real and contracted Airmark's undercover agents to make drug pickups. Juno was followed by a US Customs' sting called Operation Skymaster, where undercover agents arranged pickups for black-market peso brokers. Those two operations resulted in more than 250 arrests, drug seizures totalling more than eight tons and money seizures in excess of $36 million. Those two operations also exposed 34 US banks and 52 foreign banks to warrants, seizures and further scrutiny.

One of the banks that showed up in those stings, was the British Bank of Latin America (BBLA), a tiny offshore affiliate of Lloyds TSB.

Licensed in the Bahamas, it only had a couple of hundred clients, but they were all Colombian and all of them used this offshore facility to maintain dollar accounts. In turn, BBLA had correspondent relationships with Bank of America, Bankers Trust, Barclays Bank, Chemical Bank and Citibank, plus Lloyds in the US and in Panama. Towards the end of its life, BBLA had a strong working relationship with the Bank of New York.

Hardly surprising, BBLA maintained no anti-money laundering procedures and was subjected to no real oversight. The British, the Colombians and the Bahamians were all depending on one of the others to watch the bank. BBLA finally folded in 2000. By then, it had been operating as a sink for Colombian brokers for a good part of its 19 years.

Enter here Luz Mariana Gómez Alzate, a 5-foot-tall Colombian woman in her late 30s with bleached blonde hair.

Known to her friends as Patricia, she had a small business in one of Bogota's many illegal markets – they're called '*sanandrecitos*', named for the Colombian smugglers' island, San Andres – which is how she got to know Jorge. When he needed somebody to do pickups in the States, she moved her five kids to Florida – her first son Hernan was 20, her second son Andres was 16, and the other three were little – and decided to teach her boys the business.

She showed up at MLU with Hernan the first time he made a delivery for Jorge. The surveillance team in the lobby spotted this woman and this young boy immediately, but didn't know who she was. Hernan went to the desk to ask for MLU and Patricia stayed off to the side, waiting alone while Hernan went upstairs. She returned with him on his next delivery, and the delivery after that. It was Hernan who then happened to mention that his mother liked the way they did business. He asked if MLU was interested in dealing directly with her.

Rose answered right away, 'Who are we to say no?'

So now, Patricia became an MLU client. Jorge didn't know that she'd gone into competition with him. And she wasn't the only one. As in any business, word of mouth can be good business, and word quickly got out that MLU Investments could move money. Several people working for Jorge double-crossed him by going behind his back and doing deals directly with MLU. But none of the others was ever like Patricia. She became the exception to everything they did at MLU.

It wasn't enough that she was moving money through them, before long she announced that she wanted Andres to stay in New York to work deliveries, and asked Ricaurte to help find an apartment for him. This was not part of their original plan, but Rose decided it was a good idea to keep Patricia close, so his guys located a flat for Andres in a good neighbourhood in Forest Hills, Queens. They also got him a mobile phone and a pager, and of course put wires on everything so they could listen to his calls.

Through Andres' conversations with his mother, the team was able to learn about other deals being set up. They also listened as people working with Patricia in Colombia started ringing Andres, too. It gave Rose and the team access to both sides of these deals – the money side and the drug side. Which was important because they needed to tie the two sides together.

Mariani, who would take these cases to court, had to prove to a jury that the money they were laundering was drug money and that the brokers they were working for knew that this was drug money. In a few instances, it was easy. A bag of cash arrived at the office one day with so much coke on it that the counting machine jammed. But getting brokers and delivery guys to admit on camera or on a wire that they were dealing drug money, was another matter.

When money came in there was hardly ever any paperwork attached to it. Most of the time hundreds of thousands of dollars were simply handed over, just like that, by people who didn't know the guys at MLU and never expected to see them again. When there was a slip of paper with a total, the count was usually wrong. So Rose decided that they had to keep their clients informed. On the premise that MLU didn't want any trouble, the team rang every broker with a ball-park figure of how much money had been delivered. It was during those conversations that one of the MLU guys would say something like, we counted the money and my table was covered in white powder. Or, the guy you sent up here looked like he just sold crack on the corner. As the brokers talked about drugs, Mariani collected the evidence she'd need.

A couple of months into the sting, Jorge phoned Ricaurte to ask if he'd heard about a BMPE case that the IRS had taken down in Miami. Money was going through computer and electronics stores.

Ricaurte said he didn't know anything about it. But after the call he and Rose researched it and decided they could use it to throw back at Jorge. During their next conversation, Ricaurte warned Jorge, 'If you're involved in that case in Miami, we don't want any of this coming to us.'

Jorge assured Ricaurte that while he knew the people there, it didn't have anything to do with him. Ricaurte then faxed Jorge some newspaper articles about the case which really worried Jorge. He started pleading with Ricaurte not to throw him out. And all the time, he kept acknowledging that he was doing the same thing as the guys in Florida, which was a drug money case, which added to the evidence that Mariani was compiling against him.

Demand for MLU's services had grown to the point that Rose was able to do to other brokers what he'd just done to Jorge, throwing the entire undercover scenario on its head. 'Usually you have to prove yourself to the bad guys. They're always questioning you. They want to know, who are you, who do you know, how do I know you're not the cops? But when word got out about us, we started saying to them, who are you, who do you know, how do we know you're not the cops? We'd make them prove themselves to us.'

Before long, Rose goes on, they had a UN of crime going on. 'An arrangement was made through a Colombian broker for a guy to deliver money to us. He's a white Canadian guy of Italian descent, supposedly half tied into the wiseguys up there. He's wearing a blue windbreaker with Wayne Gretzky's number on it, is carrying $100,000 in a bag, and is wearing a fanny pack around his waist. Right away we figure he's an undercover DEA agent and that he's got a gun in the fanny pack. We take the money from him, then set up on him. We follow him to a meeting where he hands 40,000 Ecstasy pills to a Russian who takes the pills to Brooklyn. Meantime, the Canadian guy goes to Queens to hang with a Korean kid who turns out to be doing home invasions as part of a local gang. So here we are getting instructions from Colombians, taking money from a Canadian of Italian decent who's dealing Ecstasy with a Russian and hanging with an Asian gang guy.'

As it turned out, laundering drug money, setting up brokers and gathering evidence was only half the job. The rest of the time, Rose and the team were baby-sitting Patricia and Andres.

When Patricia lost $300,000 of the cartel's money, she was kidnapped – not once, but twice. The second time, some people in her office called MLU to ask what they could do to help.

Ricaurte had to remind them, 'Hey, we're brokers.'

Patricia's friends wanted MLU to forward some of her money to the kidnappers to pay her ransom. In the end, the Colombian police rescued her. She still owed a lot of money to people in Colombia and, feeling the heat, ran to Spain for a while. Rose figures she was dipping into the till, which is pretty common in that business for lower end brokers. It's also pretty stupid because the deal with the drug cartels is, you're responsible. If the money gets seized or stolen, that's your problem, you've got to make it up. If money is missing, you either pay the cartel back or work a bunch of deals for free. Patricia had got too deep in the hole and needed to put a little space between herself and some of the people she owed money to.

Then Andres lost $200,000 of the cartel's money. The story he made up was that some Dominican guys came to the apartment, pushed the door in and robbed him.

Rose knows that's not true. 'When we got him the apartment we told him, nobody comes here. His mother told him the same thing. Meanwhile, he's 16 years old with a nice apartment in Forest Hills that he's not paying for. So what does he do? He has everybody in the world partying there. He had that money in the apartment and I'm sure he got drunk one night and passed out and somebody found it.'

Adding to Rose's worries, Andres got himself kicked out of the apartment so they had to find him a second one.

The MLU guys didn't like it when Patricia suddenly showed up with her two youngest kids to live with Andres. They liked it even less when they overheard her telling Andres to forget about school and do a pickup. And they couldn't believe how stupid she was when she told Andres to show the younger kids how to count money.

Rose just shakes his head. 'Dealing with that family was a nightmare.'

Then came the pick up when someone offered Andres an unexpected gift.

The kid got a call to meet some really sharp people in Times Square. A surveillance team followed him. When Andres got to Times Square he received another call telling him to go from there to Second Avenue and 22nd Street and then ring a certain number. So Andres walked over there, phoned the number and was told, 'Halfway down the block is a pizza place. There's a blue car parked in front of it. The keys are in the car. The money's in the trunk. Keep the car.'

Andres didn't understand. 'What?'

The guy on the phone said, 'Keep the car. It's a gift from me to you,' and hung up.

Andres walked down the block, found an older model used car in decent shape, got in, found the keys and just sat there for 20 minutes because he didn't know what to do. Rose wasn't even sure if Andres had a driver's licence. Eventually, Andres phoned the number again and said, 'I'm going to take the car, drive around the corner, park there, take the money and leave the car.'

The guy told him, 'Keep the car. It's yours. It's a gift. Goodbye.'

Getting out of the car, Andres popped open the trunk – there was half a million dollars in a duffel bag – got back in the car and still couldn't figure out what to do. Rose's guys were watching this and so too, Rose assumes, were the people who owned the money. But they never showed their faces, nor did Rose's guys. The car was obviously bought for just this deal. The registration was in a phoney name.

After a very long time, Andres started the engine. He drove a couple of blocks, turned into a side street, then suddenly pulled over. He got out of the car, took the duffel bag out of the trunk – it was so heavy that one of the straps broke – and lugged it for several blocks, looking for the subway. He rode that home, abandoning the car. Later, he told one of the MLU guys, 'The whole thing was just like the movies.'

Throughout the operation, MLU Investments wired money offshore, mainly to the Caymans, Panama and Barbados. They also wired money to Sun Life Assurance of Canada, Eagle Star International Life, Kia Motors in Korea, Lineas Aereas Suramericanas, Tissot Watches, Avianca, Daimler Chrysler in Germany, the Dole Company in Chile, Dynamic Cassette International in Britain and to brokerage accounts at Merrill Lynch and Charles Schwab. Money was used to purchase textiles in Shanghai, car parts and electronics in the Orient, goods from import-export companies scattered around the world and gold jewellery businesses throughout Latin America.

MLU also wired money into personal accounts, including some held by diplomats. They also facilitated capital flight for wealthy Colombians who were looking to hide money, by selling pesos in the markets there and having the dollars in the States moved into investment accounts in New York or insurance trusts offshore.

Among the 100 banks to whom they wired money were: HSBC, Lloyds TSB, Royal Bank of Canada, Standard Charter, Sun Trust, Citibank, Bank of America, Chase Manhattan, Mellon Bank, Bank of Miami, Bank One, Republic National, Bank of New York, First Union,

Wells Fargo, Banco Santander in Spain, Banca Populare di Bergamo in Italy, Union Banque Suisse, Bank of Tokyo, Industrial Bank of Korea, Korea First, Thai Farmers Bank and Banco Do Brazil.

The nature of the BMPE being what it is, the various companies and banks to whom money was wired almost certainly had no direct knowledge that this was drug money, and their mention here should in no way be construed to mean that they knowingly engaged in any criminal activity.

'We sent money to some of the largest manufacturers in the world,' Rose says, 'and to small companies, and to individual accounts. We sent money everywhere. Europe. Latin America. Japan. Hong Kong. We even saw people using Latvian banks.'

As part of this operation, Rose says, MLU was asked to make pickups in Egypt. He declined. They were also asked, several times, to make pickups in Australia. He declined those as well. Rose thought about accepting some work in Spain, but when he learned how difficult it was to deal with the Spanish in an undercover operation, he said no. At one point there was talk about putting undercovers in place elsewhere in Europe. Rose refuses to go into too much detail, but says it didn't happen because they didn't need it to happen. However, there were meetings with officers from other countries and arrangements were made.

'Just getting that far couldn't have happened five years ago. That it happens now demonstrates how levels of co-operation between law enforcement in various nations have greatly improved'. Still, he adds, 'It's too bad we had to turn down so many opportunities, but a lot of countries in Europe aren't set up for undercover work. They can't do it legally or operationally. Yet tons of money is going through Europe.'

One of the first places Jorge asked them to go was London. He begged Ricaurte to do a $200,000 pick up there. But Rose wasn't ready to bring Britain into this. However, he did set up a company and some bank accounts in Amsterdam, just in case he needed to bounce money from New York to the Netherlands. He felt that, for the sake of appearances, it would look good if they had accounts all over the place. After all, they were moving a lot of money to a lot of different countries, especially Italy, Britain, Guernsey and the Isle of Man.

Startlingly, Rose says, while moving this money MLU stumbled across other law enforcement undercovers doing the same thing. 'We uncovered all sorts of other government operations laundering money.

And let me tell you, it's sad. Customs. DEA. Guys in Florida. Guys up north. Guys out west. You name it, they were doing it everywhere. What's really sad about it is that everyone is sending the money to the same places. They're all dealing with the same people, the same brokers, and nothing is co-ordinated, nothing is shared. So much information just goes down the toilet.'

Rose isn't sure how much of the money he saw had terrorism written on it, but he has his suspicions. 'There's a big Lebanese and Middle Eastern community in Colombia. A lot of those people are in the jewellery business and some of them are clearly facilitating. A certain amount of them are brokers. But whether any of them are taking some of their money and funnelling it back to terror groups, there's no way to know for sure.'

By Summer 2001, MLU was starting to wind down.

Dozens of indictments came down and arrests followed in the States and in Colombia. Several brokers were taken down and $6 million was seized. Another $1.2 million has since been seized as a result of leads developed during the case. MLU more than paid for itself by collecting around $1 million in fees from the bad guys. Patricia was sentenced to 4–12 years, while Hernan and Andres both got a couple of years. Other warrants are still outstanding.

When Patricia's arrest made the papers in Colombia, Rose pretty much figured that the operation was finished. He didn't know for sure if anyone had sussed that MLU was involved, but that hardly mattered now. He and Mariani had got inside a BMPE network – taken apart this better mousetrap – and no one had ever managed that before. There probably wasn't much else they needed to do. Still, Rose kept the MLU office open, anyway, just in case the phone rang.

On the morning of 9/11, the fellow who was supposed to stop in to check the answering machine was late getting to work.

CHAPTER FIFTEEN

Too Many Bagpipes

I used to love bagpipes.
But then there were all those police funerals.
And all those firemen's funerals.
And . . . and there were just too many bagpipes.
— Joe Webber, 9/11 hero

Joe Webber was in a staff meeting that morning, on the seventh floor at Six World Trade Center, when the first plane hit.

Many of the agents who worked with him at the New York field office of US Customs had been there during the 1993 bombing, and the instant the explosion rocked the building they knew what was happening. People began to evacuate very quickly. But Webber, as special-agent-in-charge of US Customs for New York, at first refused to go downstairs. Instead, the tall, solidly built Texan ordered everybody to reassemble at Seven World Trade – at the emergency command post that the City of New York maintained there – then ran through the various floors of Six World Trade to make sure everyone was getting out.

By the time he arrived at Seven World Trade, there was debris and panic and confusion raining down all over the block. The doors to the command post were locked. They couldn't get in. That's when the second plane hit. Webber and the others were right there, on the street below, with the fireball and destruction coming down.

Webber and the others rushed further along the block to a day-care centre where they commandeered phones and called headquarters in Washington to tell them what was happening. Some of the other senior agents announced that they were heading for the FBI Headquarters. Webber watched them leave, then went back to Six World Trade. He got into the building and raced upstairs to make absolutely certain that everyone was out and that his offices were secure. Electricity in the building was coming on, then going off, then coming on again. Alarm systems were going on and off, too, adding to the noise from all over the block. Many of the electronic locks were shut, keeping him out of certain rooms.

Going back like that nearly cost him his life.

Webber was just 30 feet from the North Tower when it crumbled. Fire ripped through the building, trapping him. He tried to make it down the stairs, but there was too much smoke. And the rooms around him were caving in.

From inside, Webber could see that fire fighters were trying to get in. Two men from Ladder Company 11 had managed to get up to a balcony on one side of Six World Trade. From there, they rigged another ladder up to the fourth floor. There was nothing Webber could do but brave the flames and the smoke and make one desperate dash down the stairs to the fourth floor.

Somehow, he made it. The firemen spotted him, grabbed him and dragged him down the ladders to safety.

Two weeks later, Webber and two of his agents went back inside.

It was around 2 a.m. Fires were still burning below ground and the air smelled of fire and destruction and death. Crews were working non-stop, still hoping beyond hope to find survivors, finding instead limbs and body parts and horrible reminders that 2,800 people had been murdered here.

Webber identified himself to one of the senior fire officers and explained why he needed to get back inside. It took some convincing, but for the men and women who were working there, Webber's request was one more remarkable gesture in a place where days and nights were replete with remarkable gestures.

The fire department launched a crane in front of what was left of the building. Joe and Customs agents Alysa Erichs and Tina Zimmerman bravely climbed into a cherry picker along with some emergency workers, and the NYFD lifted them up to the fifth floor. It was pitch dark inside. The fire department now raised up some flood lights and with long shadows cast against the eerie burnt out walls, the agents and the emergency workers made their way through each floor of what had once been US Customs – New York.

In the main seizure vault there were 3,200 pounds of cocaine, 983 pounds of heroin, and some Ecstasy. They got it out.

In another part of the offices, there were firearms, including a cache of fully automatic weapons and 1.4 million rounds of ammunition. They got them out.

There was cash in one safe and thousands of classified documents, confidential informant source files and case files in other safes. They got them out.

'We recovered about 96 per cent of all the controlled substances we'd had in the office,' Webber says. 'There's no evidence that any of the rest of it ever hit the street. We worried about that because it was all packaged and tied together with US Customs tape around it, and finding any of that back on the streets would have been terrible.'

His voice gets very quiet. 'You can't imagine what it was like. This had to be the crime scene of all crime scenes. In just one morning, 2,800 people were murdered. And the frustration of not being able to help, the sense of helplessness . . .'

Shaking his head, he stops for a few seconds. 'They started taking down the building, so we established a detail, working like everyone was, twenty four – seven, so that as the building came down, our agents were right there going through the rubble. We recovered guns, some of them still fully operational, some of them melted. We worked that detail for six months.'

Within three months of the disaster, El Dorado and US Customs were back in business in new offices uptown. Webber's big corner room is on the wrong side of the building to see downtown. He doesn't say if that's on purpose.

Then his voice gets quiet again. 'I used to love bagpipes.'

While Ron Rose and his team at MLU Investments were working Patricia, his old mates at El Dorado had stumbled across a group of Colombians – brothers Hermes and Luis Torres and Norberto Romero Garavito – whom they identified as BMPE brokers for Colombia's North Coast drug cartel.

Through relationships built up over time, the El Dorado agents were able to call on the assistance of Colombia's Departamento Administrativo de Seguridad (DAS) to set up an operation that would, for the very first time, take in both sides of a BMPE network.

Known as 'Operation Wire Cutter', it began in September 1999. With introductions arranged by informants in New York and Colombia, the El Dorado guys started doing cash pickups in New York. When the BMPE brokers saw that these guys could be trusted, the pickups extended to Chicago, Miami, Los Angeles and San Juan, Puerto Rico.

Once the cash was collected, the brokers would tell the undercovers what they wanted them to do with it. Some cash got bulked out by private air charter to Colombia. Some was deposited in banks – including Lloyds, HSBC and Deutsche Bank – some was handed off to other brokers, some was wired to shell companies. Money went to Singapore, Canada, and the UK. Some of the money was laundered through shares on the NYSE and NASDAQ. Some of the money went into purchasing merchandise. The shopping list included helicopters, fridges and electronics, everything purchased from manufacturers, wholesalers and distributors who were happy to accept cash or third-party payments.

While this was going on, undercovers in Colombia – from US Customs, the DEA and the DAS – were working with the brokers. The Americans spent a year with the Colombians, identifying the brokers in Bogota and trying to get inside the system that they would eventually dismantle.

'We had successfully done a number of BMPE cases,' Webber says, 'and we'd done loads of pickup cases in the City. What we had never done, however, was to take one case full cycle, to watch the monies picked up in Manhattan and watch that money come out the other end in Colombia.'

Over a period of 30 months, the undercover agents gathered evidence on eight BMPE brokers in Colombia and 29 brokers and money launderers in the States who were driving this BMPE.

The World Trade Center disaster got in the way, and the possibility of losing the evidence stored in the offices at Six World Trade jeopardized the case. All of the Wire Cutter evidence was there, including original tapes of wire taps, agent reports and transcripts.

Webber, Erichs and Zimmerman got them out.

Within a few days of 9/11, Webber says, they got a call from a citizen in Brooklyn who'd found documents in her backyard. To this day, he still finds that scary.

'It was a synopsis of wire taps we'd been running on the Mafia hitman Sammy "The Bull" Gravano. We got them back but it made us think about what else might have blown away. This stuff turned up 10 to 12 miles from the World Trade Center. It frightened us because we didn't know what else we might have lost. We were worried about losing prosecutions and about compromising our undercovers. But I think we got lucky and that turned out to be an isolated incident. What we did lose in the building were some surveillance photos. You know, "fenoo-lenoos".'

That's 'f-n-u-l-n-u' as in, 'first name unknown, last name unknown.'

When they brought down Wire Cutter, the 37 targets were arrested and more than $8 million was seized. So were 400 kilos of coke, 100 kilos of marijuana, $6^1/_2$ kilos of heroin and several weapons.

'All these folk wanted to do was move money quickly', Webber continues. 'I found it remarkable how, unlike legitimate business which is always about the bottom line, these people weren't interested in profit margins. Not at all. There's so much profit built into the drugs that they don't have to worry too much about cost at this stage. They'll pay whatever the price is because this isn't about profit, it's about how quickly they can place the money.'

Another surprise came in the methods they used. 'All of them. Whatever worked. They showed us that there's no single traditional way. And that was one of the problems we'd had in the past. We'd sit on one type of money laundering scheme and while we were drilling on down to the bottom of that we'd miss other stuff. These guys were all over the map.'

As often happens during one investigation, the good guys stumble across bad guys they don't know about and other good guys chasing bad guys they don't know about, either. Just a year into Wire Cutter, US Customs in Miami was working a major Colombian drug money laundering case of their own, looking at a BMPE network.

At the same time, Britain's National Criminal Intelligence Service (NCIS) had picked up word on the streets that large amounts of cash were being laundered through some bureaux de change around London. A surveillance operation was set up. Officers were able to watch cash coming into these storefronts and from there leaving the country. The money was either bulked out to South America – the ring had an Avianca air hostess carrying cash for them – or wired out to various places, including the US. This was the first time that the British had seen money laundering in this purest of forms, where the suspects where strictly laundrymen and not traffickers involved with drugs.

Several suspects were tagged for observation, but two names emerged at the top of the target list – Juan Miguel Solgado, who ran the Latin Linkup bureau de change in north London and Luis Edwardo Hurtado, who ran the World Express bureau de change in south London. Both were Colombian born, naturalized Britons. Codenamed 'Uproar', the operation sent 13 people, including Salgado and Hurtado, to prison for laundering more than $70 million, the proceeds of $2^1/_2$ tons of cocaine.

In the old days, it's likely that none of the dots would have connected. But in recent years, one of the major advances in law enforcement has been a recognition of the global scope of organized crime and terror, and an understanding of the need for law enforcement to think global, too.

The Brits gave the Americans a heads-up about how some of the bureau de change money was coming their way. Miami Customs took a real interest in it and discovered a connection between this money and some of the people Webber and El Dorado were dealing with in New York. They also spotted a connection with Ron Rose's MLU Investments.

The common link was the Isle of Man.

The 77,000 people who live on this self-governing British territory have had their own parliament for more than 1,000 years. This long independence has allowed them to create a financial services environment that, at times, has been wild and woolly enough to earn the island its offshore laundromat reputation. But eventually, some people on the island said enough was enough and they started to clean up their act. Today law enforcement has stepped into the fight and now actively co-operates with international investigations. There are no more bearer share companies, although by the beginning of 2003 they were still around 36,000 IBCs licensed there. That figure, however, was down 15 per cent from what it had been just four years previously. The island incorporates 50 per cent fewer companies each year than they used to and now requires strict due diligence. There are 59 banks on the island, 16 life assurance companies and about 160 collective investment schemes. Nearly £5 billion are managed through funds there and bank deposits total more than £28 billion.

Still, there was a time when money came onto the Isle of Man and no one there gave a damn where it was coming from, who owned it or what anyone intended to do with it. Change came slowly, but it came, and for the Americans – many of whom had been severely critical of Man – the first real sign of change came in 1999.

Cops in the States had been after a major fraudster named Robert Brennan for more than 25 years. His First Jersey Securities had bilked tens of millions of dollars from investors. The SEC filed civil proceedings against him, and in 1995 a $75 million judgement was lodged against him. Brennan elected to avoid paying up by declaring bankruptcy. And for a while, it looked as if he was still side-stepping the authorities.

Four years later, the NY District Attorney's office was actively seeking better co-operation from the Channel Islands. A real effort was being made to improve relations. After dozens of trips back and forth by prosecutors, as working friendships grew between New York and Man, results started coming in. The Americans were trying to gather evidence in several securities fraud cases. The authorities in Man helped them get it. Then Brennan's name came up. The authorities in Man helped the Americans file the necessary paperwork – as required by Manx law – then helped them find where Brennan had hidden several million dollars, money that had not been disclosed during his bankruptcy hearing. Brennan maintained a nominee account at the Bank of Scotland in Man, from which he used a Bear Stearns brokerage account in New York. At one point he had $22 million in three trusts there, but during the bankruptcy hearing, records show, he moved one of the trusts to Mauritius and, from there, to St Kitts and Nevis.

With the evidence they'd collected in Man, the Feds and the State of New Jersey – where Brennan lived – hustled him back into court and charged him with ten counts of bankruptcy fraud, money laundering and manufacturing evidence to cover up his crimes. The jury found him guilty and the judge sent him away for nine years and two months, without the possibility of parole.

Now the Americans started singing praises for the way the authorities in Man had co-operated. And the authorities in Man – especially those who'd been so reluctant to co-operate – decided that being a responsible member of the global financial world wasn't quite as painful as they'd imagined it could be.

The Brennan case turned out to be a prelude of what was to come.

Back in Miami, US Customs were putting a case together against several drug traffickers and their BMPE networks, one of whom was Rodrigo Jose Murillo. A trafficker on everyone's radarscope, he'd been indicted in San Diego for trying to smuggle 13-tons of cocaine into the US. Having shipped the drugs from Colombia to Mexico, he was then moving them north in small boats and over land. The guys in Miami were able, through various undercover operations, to target one of Murillo's money launderers – a small investment company that was using banks in Mexico, Hong Kong and one in Latvia to put money into a Murillo account at the Bank of America in Fort Lauderdale.

The Latvian connection was interesting because it's not one of the more glamorous money laundering centres. That said, more and more dirty money gets moved through Latvia, and the authorities there seem less than interested in doing much to stop it. In Murillo's case, $697,000 was transferred through a Latvian bank, where it was not considered suspicious enough to report because no one there knew anything about it. The bank manager would later explain that, because the bank had no information that would have linked this money to drug trafficking or money laundering, and had never heard of Rodrigo Murillo, he didn't bother flagging it.

Which, of course, is why the money was sent through Latvia in the first place. Then again, this was not the first time that the same bank had been used in a laundering scheme. In 1997, $1.2 billion was wired in from a bank in the Ukraine with instructions to wire the money out again right away, this time to a bank in Nauru. The Latvian bank did what was asked of it, because it had no reason to suspect that $1.2 billion they knew nothing about, especially going from the Ukraine to Nauru, was suspicious.

In this case the Customs guys in Miami knew better. What worried them was why some of Murillo's money was also coming back from the Isle of Man and was tied into insurance policies.

Miami contacted Man and, based on information they received from the Americans, Manx Customs and Excise officers started looking into their side of this money trail. What they saw worried them.

Over the next two years, active investigations were launched in Man (Operation Basking), the States (Operation Capstone) and Colombia (Operation Fan). The three countries shared information. What they uncovered was a highly sophisticated and well thought out plot by Colombian black market peso exchange brokers to launder drug money through the offshore insurance industry.

It worked off the back of investment-grade life insurance. These are policies that function very much like a unit trust. You buy a policy, then over-fund it. In principle, you're supposed to wait until the end of the term before recouping your investment. But you have the right to cash in the policy early, although there are penalties to discourage you from doing that. However, cashing in a policy bought with drug cash nets you cheque or money wired into your bank account that now looks clean.

Some of the money that wound up in Man originated from the Hurtado–Solgado network in London. Some of it came from Mexico. Some of it also came from MLU Investments in New York. Ron Rose's undercover brokerage wired $500,000 for three different cells to more than a dozen different accounts at Eagle Star International Life Services. Although that company was not charged in this matter, MLU Investment documents show that it wrote policies and accepted wire transfers from several third parties.

That these policies were coming in from, and being topped up by, third parties should have been a tip-off that something was strange.

The traffickers were putting these policies – worth as much as $1.9 million each – in the names of all their relatives and, in most cases, the relatives didn't know anything about it. That the third parties were then cashing in these policies, and paying 25 per cent penalties for the privilege, really should have sounded alarm bells.

From Man, money was sent back to the States – to banks in Florida, New Jersey, New York, Texas and Puerto Rico – but also to Spain, Portugal and Panama. Over the course of two years, it's estimated that traffickers laundered nearly $80 million through 250 insurance policies. Although on the Isle of Man someone hints, 'actually, it's considerably more.'

By early 2003, with parts of Capstone/Basking Fan still running, US Customs in Miami had seized $9.5 million and indicted five Colombians, including Murillo's launderers and his son. The amount of money seized in Man has been announced at $8.75 million. The DAS in Colombia arrested ten people and seized $20 million worth of insurance policies, bonds and cash. In Panama, $1.2 million was frozen.

Using the BMPE to wash money through offshore insurance caused a lot of people in post-9/11 law enforcement some sleepless nights because if the system worked for drug traffickers, it could work for terrorists. And at one point, a rumour started circulating around law enforcement and around the insurance world, too, that Osama bin Laden had moved some of Al-Qaeda's money through the offshore insurance world.

Authorities in the Channel Islands, well aware of about those rumours – and worried about them too – checked them out as best they could but found nothing to substantiate them.

At least, not yet.

Once upon a time, the Colombians controlled the product and their one product was cocaine. They might have turned it over to the Mexicans for smuggling, but before it hit the streets, the Colombians were in charge again.

No more.

Now they're doing what McDonalds does – they franchising. They've sold street-sale rights to Mexicans and Dominicans and even Vietnamese gangs, who work the retail side. In the meantime, the Colombians have diversified and increased the number of products they deal in.

For the 300 mini-cartels that picked up where the Cali and Medellin Cartels left off, it's no longer just coke on the menu, it's marijuana, heroin and there are some indications that they're also dealing Ecstasy.

'They're fully diversified,' Joe Webber of US Customs says. 'They're selling the product outright to the Mexicans, which means the Colombians aren't running the risks. With the brokers in Colombia, they're getting their money outright, so they're not even running those risks. They've positioned themselves as businessmen. Maybe they're not realizing the profit margins they once did because they're sharing the profits with the Mexicans and the peso brokers, but the risk is way down and the diversity of the product they're shipping means they're doing fine.'

The Mexicans are also making out better. Which means more bulk cash going to Mexico. While Customs and the DEA and local law enforcement keep trying to attack bulk cash on the Southwest border, Webber feels, there are better ways of going about it.

'You attack it in New York City and in Chicago, in Los Angeles, in Boston. You attack the cash where it's generated. The opportunity to attack it along the Southwest border relies on a cold hit, a lucky inspection or some inside information.'

Anyway, the Mexicans who move money are well prepared for whatever law enforcement has in store. They keep coming up with all sorts of new ways to hide cash – containers within containers within containers – and then they're very compartmentalized.

He goes on, 'A number of years ago we got six tons of cocaine in a warehouse in Los Angeles. If you dissect that case and dissect that organization, you see how they work. They'd moved cocaine across the border for years, one load at a time. Like an army of ants. There was one group who would pack the car and leave it somewhere. There was another group who drove it across the border and left it. A third bunch would pick up the car and take it to a warehouse. A fourth would move it to another warehouse. Even if you picked up one of those violators, he couldn't give you the whole picture because he wouldn't know it. You might get one load, but you weren't going to get the warehouse.'

It's the same with money, which is why, he reiterates, the best place to attack the money is where it's generated. And banks are an obvious place to start.

Webber explains, 'The banking community has a wealth of experience in moving money. If something attracts their attention, it's probably right on. I think too many banks are too concerned with their image being tarnished. Some banks are better than others. Some banks will close the account down instead of calling us because they're concerned with the bank's reputation. There's one individual whom we're looking at pretty hard, and four banks closed him out before we stumbled across him. Rather than call us, they sent him away. The banks were in compliance, but they just didn't want the controversy.'

Occasionally, though, banks can be extremely helpful. Valley National was, a few months after a US Customs' border team intercepted 500 kilos of cocaine concealed in a rolled-up carpet.

It was one of those fortunate inspections that happens every now and then. With luck still on their side, Customs was able to get some background information on the shipment. They passed it along to the DEA. In turn, that agency had contacts in Colombia who pointed to a fellow named Antonio Pires de Almeida. Watching him led the DEA to a bank account in Connecticut where they were able to seize $6.87 million, some of it associated with the drugs in the carpet. Exactly two weeks after de Almeida lost his money in Connecticut, he switched banks. The DEA told Webber's team about it and El Dorado couldn't wait to take a closer look at the way de Almeida was conducting his affairs at Merchant's Bank

His money was being handled by Maria Carolina Nolasco, a Portuguese born naturalized American in her early forties. She was an assistant vice-president for international and private banking, and the more they looked at her, the more interested they became, because Mrs Nolasco was a major player.

They watched her for quite a while, and kept an eye on de Almeida's accounts, too, until the bank was taken over by Valley National. When it was, Nolasco stayed on in her same role at the Madison Avenue branch, in midtown Manhattan. But the new management gave Webber and his crew a chance to get closer. Webber approached certain people at Valley National, explained what he wanted to do and the bank gave him permission to put someone inside the branch.

A female US Customs officer who spoke fluent Portuguese became Nolasco's assistant.

The extent of Nolasco's business now became clear. She managed some 250 accounts, the records of which – including identification documents and wire transfer instructions – were locked in a safe in her private office and not accessible to anyone else in the bank. Not only did no one else at the bank seem to know who her customers were, everything she did for the bank was in Portuguese. Nolasco was, manifestly, running a bank within a bank, keeping everything secret and putting every transaction in a language that no one else at the bank spoke.

Except the Customs' undercover.

She was quickly able to determine that 44 accounts that Nolasco personally handled were in the names of shell companies. They were all 'hold mail' accounts, meaning that none of them received statements. The undercover soon suspected that all of those shells were involved in BMPE payments.

Three of the shells – Sorabe SA, Harber Corp and Gatex Corp – carried the signature authority of Antonio Pires de Almeida, who was listed on the accounts as the representative of two South American companies. One of those companies appeared to be a bureau de change.

Nolasco accounted for a very large percentage of the branch's daily wires, but the wires didn't tell the story. They only showed money in and money out, leaving a lot of unanswered questions. However, based on what the undercover had been able to glean, the El Dorado team felt they had probable cause for a wiretap. A judge agreed and they were able to go up on Nolasco's office.

What they now saw was truly startling. Deposits into the three de Almeida accounts were either wire transfers from outside the bank or transfers from other accounts controlled by Nolasco. All of the withdrawals were also either transfers to other accounts or wires to Brazil. Reviewing hundreds of the outgoing wire transfers, the team learned that they were payments made on behalf of companies other than de Almeida's shell companies.

This was all drug money going through Nolasco's end of a BMPE.

For the period 4 May 2001 through 31 December 2001, Sorabe's deposits and withdrawals were negligible. Harber Corp saw $39.5 million come in and $39.7 million go out. But Gatex Corp had deposits of a whopping $136.5 million and withdrawals of and equally astonishing $137.3 million.

In fact, when they finally got to look at Nolasco's bank inside the bank, the 26 most active business accounts she handled, including Gatex and Harber, showed that for the same period, deposits exceeded $538.5 million and withdrawals exceeded $534.6 million.

Over an 18-month period, Nolasco had moved more than $2 billion through those accounts to Brazil.

As luck would have it, one of the other operations they were involved with crossed this one, and through a money launderer in Florida, El

Dorado was able to get an undercover in to meet with Nolasco about laundering some money. On one occasion she was handed $30,000 in cash by this undercover. She suggested that deposits be made in amounts under $10,000 to avoid reporting requirements. She agreed to deposit $9,000 immediately and hold the rest in her safe to be deposited over the next few days. She then asked the undercover how he brought money into the country. He told her he carried it on his body and in bags. She warned him that was dangerous and said she could put him in touch with money remitters in Brazil who could do it for him safely.

Eleven days later, the undercover brought her $50,000 in cash. Now she told him that she was worried this might be drug money and that if he was caught she might wind up involved in the case. She told him from now on he had to have it wired, and that she wouldn't take cash from him again.

The original intention was to continue surveillance on Nolasco for as long as possible, hoping to get inside the entire BMPE network – not only in the States but in Colombia and especially in Brazil – and dismantle it. The problem was they weren't sure about the Brazilian side of it, didn't know how secure it would be and began to worry that if they stayed up too long, the undercover might get compromised. That's when Nolasco announced she was going to take a trip to Brazil. And that's when the decision was made at El Dorado to take the case down.

They arrested her and seized 39 bank accounts with about $20 million.

If the same case came along today, El Dorado would certainly consider it, and the likelihood is that they would probably take it. But it's not given.

Since 9/11, the only given is terror money.

Joe Webber has since left New York and is back in Texas. But El Dorado is still in New York, and even in Texas, Webber's priorities remain the same.

'It's terror.' He insists. 'We haven't shifted resources away from drug cases, because we're still working those. But our priorities on September 10 are not what they became on September 11. Life as we know it changed forever that day.'

Pre-9/11, he says, if someone came in the office with a money laundering scheme that moved a total of $300,000, it wouldn't raise anybody's eyebrows. 'By the standards of this group, that's a Class III case and we really didn't have the time to be bothered with that nuisance. We were dealing in big numbers. If you came in with $3 million, then you'd have gotten my attention. Now, post-9/11, tell me there's $300,000 associated with a potential terrorist incident and that just became a Class I case with a number one priority.'

The heart of El Dorado is the huge, open plan office filled with desks and agents and chairs with bullet proof vests dangling over the back of them. Off to the side are huge tables. That's where they count the money.

'There's something special about seeing millions of dollars of stacked cash sitting on the counting table. It's a difficult feeling to explain. The guys have arrested people for their whole careers. Big dope cases, big fraud cases, they've arrested loads of people and sent them away. But there's something special about millions of dollars stacked on the table. I think the most I've seen there is six million. That's a lot of money.'

In the end, Webber knows, it's all about money. 'If you follow the money, you're going to back into every criminal scheme known to man, eventually. The money is the key to everything. The cartel members in Colombia may never touch the cocaine, never touch the heroin, but they will touch those pesos. That's the motive. So if you can attack the money, you get so much further. They can replace a mule, they can replace the product. The most disruption you can cause them is taking the money away. I would rather see a couple of million stacked on the counting table than the powder itself. Of course, I'd love to get the powder too. But the impact is greater when we take the dollars off the street.'

In that respect, drug dealers and terrorists are similar.

'The real key to dismantling some of these organizations,' he explains, 'is infiltrating the command and communications structure. We learned that doing pure dope cases. If we can identify their means of communication, if we can identify the command structure, infiltrate it through informants or Title 3s' – wire taps – 'that's when we have the most impact. The goal is to dismantle the organization. The old school of picking money up on the street corner is attacking the organization, and we continue to do that. But now we do that with an eye towards moving up. All too often in money laundering operations, people see attacking the money as an end, in and of itself. From our standpoint, especially looking at terror groups, that's just the beginning.'

The problem with many terrorist organizations is that, like modern drug trafficking groups, they're highly compartmentalized. Except more so. They are also more resilient and have an ability to change faster than drug groups.

'There have been instances where we've watched them collect money and forward it to support other groups in Pakistan, Indonesia, the Philippines. There's a steep learning curve here for us because they've demonstrated the ability to shift course very quickly. So we watched them, studied how they concealed bulk cash in a multitude of ways and then did a full court press to hit some bulk cash outbound. We hit FedEx and express courier packages and suddenly they switched to cheques. For a brief period of time we were seizing cheques. Within a matter of less than 30 days, they moved to bearer instruments. There were choke points we tried to focus on. But as soon as we had a few successes, they would dry up quickly.'

These terror groups also launder money through gold and honey and diamonds, and that makes it all the more difficult because they mask their laundering as a legitimate enterprise. They also use all the offshore tricks. 'We see shell companies everywhere. And charities. They do whatever they can to look like a legitimate business with money moving through them.'

And of course, there are drugs.

The Taliban were the largest heroin business in Europe and, until February 2001, they had a liaison office in New York not far from the United Nations. The Americans finally got fed up and demanded that they leave. There were indications that heroin proceeds were being handled by certain people associated with that office.

Webber won't talk about that, but he will say that heroin money and terror groups tie together. 'We're not seeing the heroin, just the money generated from the sales. I find that troubling. Seizures in New York amount to about half of all the heroin seized by the US Customs. So it's troubling when we see the proceeds of Afghan heroin sales and can't find the heroin.

Equally troubling is a new drug that's come onto the North American scene in recent years, khat.

A stimulant derived from the *catha edulis* shrub, it is strongest when the fresh leaves are chewed. Being perishable, it loses it's potency in a few days, but even then it can be made into a tea or chewed as a paste. The plant comes primarily from East Africa and the Arabian peninsula and is traditional in that part of the world.

The United Nations estimates that the international trade in khat is worth $50 million and notes that Kenya is the largest supplier to the international market. The UN also believes that khat sales have funded terrorist activities in the Horn of Africa. They are especially concerned with khat exports from Nigeria to Somalia where some tribal leaders are known to sponsor terrorism. In recent years, Somalia has become a transit point for terrorist groups.

Sold openly in ethnic shops throughout Britain at around £4 a bunch, khat is illegal in both Canada and the US. The RCMP says khat arrives in Toronto by air cargo aboard flights from the UK, the Netherlands, Germany and Kenya. In 2001, Canada Customs seized 11 tons of khat. In the States, the dope groups moving it are generally Ethiopian, Yemeni and Somalian. Between Newark and JFK Airports in the New York area, Webber says, they've seized 43.5 tons of khat.

Historically there have been very few prosecutions in North America. However, khat does generate an income for some groups, selling for around $350 a kilo in North America. 'This is not a drug used on college campuses or in the bar scene. The average street cop wouldn't recognize it. Khat has a unique audience and is clearly associated with a network of people we're interested in. We've had two cases where khat is mentioned, where money has gone through the system back to the Middle East. It's below the radar. We're concerned.'

His concern gets right back to money.

'In money laundering events that relate to terrorism,' he says, 'you don't find huge amounts of cash. And that can be a problem for us. So relying on those types of indicators are not always productive.' He pauses for just a second, then nods, 'If you look at some estimates that say the 9/11 event was funded with as little as $300,000, imagine what $6 million can represent to a terrorist. If we can take that money away from him, if we can get his six million . . .'

Webber nods slowly . . . 'That's twenty September 11ths.'

CHAPTER SIXTEEN

Blood Money

How much does a terrorist attack cost in Britain?
Of course, the answer is 2p.

– a conclusion reached by the FISAC

As the ferry arrived at Black Ball Terminal in Port Angeles, Washington that December night in 1999, a weary group of US Customs agents made ready to look at what they expected to be the usual assortment of Canadians heading south from Victoria, British Colombia, and the usual assortment of Americans coming home.

Christmas was still 11 days away, so traffic was light.

Cars pulled off the ferry. Some were waved through. Others were randomly stopped. Agents asked drivers a few standard questions – they weren't looking for anything in particular, just people who answer standard questions uncomfortably – and when the agents were satisfied with comfortable answers they sent those drivers on their way. But a female agent noticed a 33-year-old Arab man in a brand new rented Chrysler with Canadian plates and something about him bothered her. She motioned to him to pull over. He tried to run for it.

Agents chased him and grabbed him. Other agents opened the Chrysler's trunk. Inside there was a timing device, a substance used to make military-grade C-4 explosive and a nitro-glycerine equivalent in two glass jars.

The suspect was carrying cash, false IDs and the business card of someone called Dr Haydar Abu Doha in London. When he refused to give up his real name, the agents finger-printed him and within a few hours, they'd linked this man – Ahmed Ressam – to a terrorist 'sleeper' cell in Montreal.

His mission was to blow up Los Angeles International Airport in three weeks time. The millennium was about to happen and that's how Al-Qaeda wanted to celebrate it.

Within hours of his capture, cops in Canada were trying to find Ressam's pals in Vancouver and Montreal, cops in New York were grabbing some of Ressam's friends there, and cops in London were checking out Dr Doha.

Ressam came to Canada in 1994 with a false French passport. The first thing he did was apply for asylum. When that was refused and a deportation order was issued against him in 1996, he obtained a bogus Canadian passport and continued living in the country. It's known that he travelled on his Canadian passport because shortly after he got it he went to France. Authorities there have since tied him into some bombings. Back in Montreal he was arrested no fewer than four times for theft. At no point was Canada Immigration ever notified. In all, Ressam only served two weeks for just one theft.

He shared a flat in Montreal on Lacordaire Boulevard with Said Atmani, an active member of the *Groupement Islamic Armee* (Armed Islamic Group), otherwise known as the GIA. A small, violent bunch formed in 1992 specifically to destroy the secular government of Algeria, many of the original GIA recruits had fought against the Soviets in Afghanistan and trained with Osama bin Laden when he and the Taliban moved in. The GIA claimed responsibility for assassinating President Boudiaf in 1992 and for hijacking an Air France plane in 1994. Although their agents failed in an attempt to destroy the Eiffel Tower, GIA was successful in launching two series of nail bomb attacks in the Paris Metro which killed 11 and injured more than 100.

Atmani was one of GIA's document forgers. He'd been arrested in Canada in 1998 for credit card fraud and extortion and deported to Bosnia, despite the fact that there was an active arrest warrant for him in France. Three years later, peace-keeping forces in Bosnia arrested him and this time he was deported to France to stand trial for terrorist activities there.

Ressam's contact in Vancouver was Abdelmajid Dahoumane, another former roommate in Montreal. The two had met at Al-Qaeda's Khalden Camp training camp in Afghanistan. Dahoumane came to Canada a year after Ressam and he too sought asylum. Like Ressam, his request was turned down. By then Dahoumane had managed to enrol himself for welfare benefits and was receiving regular cheques at the same time that Canada Immigration was looking for him to deport him. Dahoumane was the subject of an Interpol 'Red Notice' – arrest immediately – for his ties to the training camp and the GIA.

In Vancouver Ressam and Dahoumane spent several days together at a motel making the explosives that were found in Ressam's car.

As soon as he heard of Ressam's arrest, Dahoumane fled. Fresh warrants were issued for him in Canada and the US, but Washington wanted him more and put a $5 million price on his head. The reward was substantially higher than most because the Americans had reason to believe that Dahoumane was close to a Muslim radical living in Calgary, who in turn was close to, and supposedly in daily contact with, Abu Zoubaida, bin Laden's so-called right-hand man. In March 2001 Dahoumane was arrested by Algerian Security Forces.

But the most interesting man to come out of Ressam's arrest was Abu Doha. Not only did Ressam have Doha's business card, but when the police searched the Montreal apartment they found a diary from a Swiss bank that contained names and phone numbers of several people, including Abu Doha.

When terrorist squad officers from Special Branch searched Doha's home, they discovered that his real name is Amar Makhlulif. They found passports and fake IDs in several names and documents that linked him directly to the timing device found in Ressam's car. And the timing device in the car was identical to timing devices used by bin Laden-trained terrorists in previous attacks.

The 37-year-old Algerian-born Doha/Makhlulif had been a senior officer at the Khalden Camp where he'd recruited Ressam and Dahoumane for their assignment in Canada. He moved to the UK in 1999 where he planned attacks on Strasbourg Cathedral and a market in that city. Neither happened. Since then, it is known he met with bin Laden in Afghanistan to negotiate a plan that saw GIA's international operations come under a loose umbrella arrangement with Al-Qaeda. He also maintained regular communication with a terrorist cell in Milan.

Suspecting Doha/Makhlulif of being both an operational chief and a financier, British police sat on him for more than a year trying to establish who his contacts were and where and how he was moving money. When it became clear in February 2001 that he was about to flee, they arrested him at Heathrow Airport. He was checking in for a flight to Saudi Arabia with a Spanish passport.

Based on an indictment against him for conspiracy to commit terrorist acts and for providing money, safe houses and other material support to terrorists, the Americans requested his extradition. A British court ruled in favour of the US, but Doha/Makhlulif appealed. A year after the court decision against him, he was still in Bellmarsh top security prison, desperate to avoid the trip across the Atlantic.

That Ahmed Ressam was trying to enter the States on the ferry from Victoria made sense, because the border stop there is notoriously easy. But the fact that he was coming into the States from Canada raised eyebrows in Washington, because the US intelligence services had been saying for years that Canada's immigration policy was dangerously lax and that the border was no longer safe. Canada could no longer claim that Canadian asylum laws were strictly a Canadian problem. The fact that anybody who could get into Canada could slip into the States – and try to blow up an airport – made it Washington's problem, too.

Eventually, the Canadian Security Intelligence Service (CSIS) conceded, with some embarrassment, that they'd identified 50 terrorist groups in the country comprising 350 people, and that the US intelligence services were right – Canada had become a haven for terrorists.

Because Ressam and the others in Canada needed to earn a living while plotting to blow up Los Angeles Airport, they turned to some of the trades in which they'd been trained – credit card fraud, identity theft, counterfeiting cheques, forging documents and breaking into cars to steal portable computers and mobile telephones. They lived quietly and what money they accumulated in excess of their living expenses was sent through an established network to finance other cells in France, Belgium, Italy, Turkey, Australia and Bosnia.

The big-money-trade they didn't get involved with was selling drugs. The reason why is simple – selling drugs get you noticed much faster than credit cards, forged cheques and stolen mobile phones. And for these guys, not getting noticed was also something they were trained to do.

So here were pre-9/11 terrorists, already installed in North America, doing what terrorists usually do when terrorist cells are 'sleeping' – working as criminals.

The difference between terrorist-criminals and non-terrorist-criminals is that one thieves for politics, the other thieves for profit. In Britain, the GIA thieves for politics, and makes so much money doing it that the group intentionally avoids violence. No one wants to kill the cash cow.

For years, nine cops banished to a lonely room to the end of the corridor of the Special Branch Intelligence office, SO-12, were just that, nine cops at the end of the corridor.

When you asked the others about them, when you spoke with someone at SO-12 who was busy spying on Irish terrorists or tracking down Turkish drug traffickers, he'd scratch his head and say, *I'm not really sure but I think those nine blokes at the end of the corridor might have something to do with the Internet, or maybe it's not the Internet, maybe it's banks but, like I said, I'm not really sure.*

The office where the nine worked was officially called FISAC – the Financial Investigation and Special Access Centre – and it did have something to do with banks. That was the financial part. It also had something to do with the Internet. That was the special access part. But most of the people who referred to them as the nine guys at the end of the corridor, couldn't have cared less.

The unit was made up of one detective inspector, two detective sergeants and six detective constables who, no matter how hard they tried, were never really an integral part of most investigations. Even when SO-12 started realizing that IRA cells operating inside England were supporting themselves with financial fraud, no one did very much about it.

The FISAC guys would try to remind the others, *we should find out how the IRA pays their rent, and where they buy their bombs, and how they pay their phone bills.* But everyone else worried more about bombs going off. How a terrorist paid his rent didn't seem terribly important if people were about to get murdered.

Then came 9/11 and someone in the States decided that Osama bin Laden had managed the whole thing for under $300,000. Around SO-12, senior management started wondering, how much does a terrorist attack cost in Britain?

The guys at the end of the corridor told them, *of course, the answer is 2p. That's what it cost someone to phone in a bomb threat and stop the Grand National at Aintree and cause millions of pounds worth of damage.*

Because that made sense to senior management, they listened as the FISAC guys explained how an act of terrorism is cheap, but life as a terrorist is expensive. After all, terrorists need to pay rent and buy food and recce targets. They need to sustain themselves and that costs money. So, now the FISAC guys asked the senior managers, isn't it about time we found out how terrorists make their money and how they spend their money, and isn't it about time we interrupted their lifestyle which might stop them from buying a bomb?

For all sorts of reasons, but mainly traditional-bureaucrat thinking, it took certain senior managers a long time to grasp the simple concept that money was at the heart of terrorism. But once they started to get it, they changed FISAC to NTFIU – the National Terrorist Financial Investigation Unit – and made certain that the NTFIU guys were in on every meeting.

Now everyone at SO-12 knows exactly what the guys at the end of the corridor do – they follow the money.

To get to their end of the corridor isn't easy. You have to go through security when you come into the building, and then you have to be escorted upstairs to a secure floor where 500 SO-12 officers make up Special Branch Intelligence. It takes a security check to get on the floor. Then to get anywhere near the front door of the NTFIU, you need to be vetted at a very high level. Few people get into their office. And nothing leaves their office, like paperwork, or laptops, or anything case related. That's how seriously they take this unit.

Once inside the double locked door, the office is a dump. It's a long room that was barely big enough for nine and now there are 20.

The windows are sealed shut, so it's baking hot in the summer and, they say, the heating doesn't work good in the winter, so they freeze. There aren't enough desks, there aren't enough cubby-holes and there aren't enough computers. Go to the loo and you lose your workspace. But there is enough work to keep twice as many people busy.

The unit is run by a superintendent, with a detective chief inspector as deputy. There are two detective inspectors, four sergeants, 10 detective constables and a couple of analysts. Of course, Special Branch is elite and it's customary that Special Branch units are staffed only with Special Branch officers. But the NTFIU is a little different because the management was brave enough to defy tradition and bring in two non-branch guys – both of them highly experienced financial investigators with 25-plus years experience. These are old fraud squad guys who know about money laundering and know how to work a financial case and aren't shy about banging on doors to confront people for answers, which is not necessarily the way investigations have always been handled at SO-12. But then, since 9/11, nothing's the same.

The likelihood of terrorist violence happening in the UK sharpened everyone's focus, the NTFIU became pro-active, and SO-12 began to look at several groups known to be operating on British soil. They include the Tamils from Sri Lanka – there appear to be some drug connections with them – Afghanis, Iraqis and the Algerian GIA.

Attention also turned to the man who'd led those attacks in France. He'd been granted political asylum in Britain several years before, which set the stage for the UK being used as a financial base for small groups of GIA members. The arrival of Abu Doha in Britain merely upped the importance of the UK as a money source.

Officers at the NTFIU believe there are around 50–100 hardcore GIA members in the UK at the centre of some very fluid groups with young soldiers on the periphery. GIA hasn't formed cells in the IRA sense, but work in ad hoc bands of four, five or six. A financier or manager from the hardcore group supervises the others, who are foot soldiers. They come together to work cheque fraud and credit card fraud in order to finance the GIA's activities abroad. Many of the hardcore group are Afghan veterans, men who are military trained and who fought for the Taliban.

These are not your normal burglars or robbers who are streetwise kids. These are men who have killed. And Special Branch operates on the assumption that they will kill again.

When a group goes out to work, their average take seems to be in the region of £15,000–£20,000. Then multiply that by 50–100. When you understand that these groups are going out on a very regular basis, you start to see the kind of money involved. Not long ago when Special Branch raided the house of one of the hardcore guys, they found several hundred chequebooks and cheque guarantee cards that controlled 52 bank accounts. In addition to what these guys steal through cheque and credit card fraud, many of the hardcore members are in the UK under the asylum laws, so there is also large-scale benefit fraud.

For these guys, opening a bank account in the UK is easy because British banks accept any ID from anywhere in the EC. And the EC is rife with stolen passports, counterfeit national ID cards and counterfeit drivers licences – all documents that UK accepts under the 'Know Your Customer' regulations.

On the rare chance that one of these guys arrives in Britain without a phoney ID, there are plenty of places where they can be bought. The police across the country have located cafes and bars where young foreign students hang out and where, just before they leave the UK to go home, they can sell their empty bank accounts and cash cards and passports, too. They're mostly French and Italian, but any passport will do. And there are plenty of places where new photographs can be put expertly into a passport or a drivers licence or a national ID card.

That, combined with a chequebook and cheque card, gives anyone in Britain access to the financial system.

You go to the bank and say you've moved house and need to change your address, and while you're at it, you say that you need a new chequebook. So the bank sends one to your new address. And after a while, you tell the bank you never got that one and ask for another. Over the course of a year, you stockpile chequebooks. During that time, you kite your accounts. You go to the bank and put money into your account, then go to an ATM and take the money out. You put money back in and take money out and put money back in again, so that when someone looks at your account, it's not only being used properly, it's responsibly kept in credit.

After a while, you visit your bank manager and ask for a small loan. The bank manager looks at the monthly figures, decides you're credit worthy and agrees the loan. You pay it all back within a few months, move more money in and out, and eventually return to ask for a bigger loan. The bank manager looks again at your account, likes what he sees and grants you the bigger loan.

When you've worked your way up to borrowing 20 or 30 grand, you empty your account. And that's the last time the bank manager ever sees you. In the meantime, you've stockpiled all those chequebooks, and along with a bunch of your mates, you start hitting the chain stores.

That's how the police first discovered Pierre.

An Algerian man in his late twenties had driven four younger foot soldiers – including Pierre – down to the south coast to work the major retail chains. The four went into the same store, each with one cheque and a cheque guarantee card, to buy something for under £99. The driver circled the block, waiting for a call on his mobile phone to say that purchases had been made. When he got the call, he picked up the team and drove them to the next retail chain store.

The group hit towns from Brighton all the way to Southampton, but that afternoon, they ran into a minor problem. Pierre tried to shop lift something from a store, got spotted on CCTV, the cops were called and he got busted. The others did what they were told to do in such a situation, they melted away.

At the police station, Pierre showed the young arresting officer a French passport. He didn't seem to speak English so they got a translator. But Pierre didn't seem to speak French either. The young arresting officer thought that was odd. Pierre got binned up overnight, was taken to magistrates' court the next morning. He pleaded guilty, was fined on the spot and released.

That might have been the end of the story as far as Pierre was concerned except that the young cop was still bothered about a French guy who didn't speak French. He kept thinking about it, then remembered seeing something that had come in a couple of weeks before from a unit in London called the NTFIU.

It was a 'heads-up' they'd sent across the country to say they were interested in knowing about any cases which fit this type of MO with these types of people. The young officer didn't know if anyone in London would really care about Pierre, but he wrote it up anyway and sent it off.

The NTFIU was very interested. They checked Pierre's address and examined the photocopies of Pierre's passport, the single cheque he'd been carrying and his cashcard. With that in hand, an NTFIU officer went to see Pierre's bank manager.

British money laundering laws require financial institutions to keep copies of whatever ID documents are used to open an account for six years after the account is closed. In the real world, however, the copies get lost, or they're filed offsite and take forever to retrieve, or the photocopies are useless. But one of the many assets that those two old time financial investigators brought to the unit is a network of helpful contacts in the financial industry. Of course, all necessary paperwork must be filed by the police. The NTFIU does everything by the book so that whatever evidence is collected can be used in court. But some bankers are more co-operative than others and the old timers know how to start with the helpful ones.

So the officer asked Pierre's bank manager about any other accounts Pierre might have and the bank manager came back with several. The officer threw Pierre's name and address into his computer system and discovered that the address matched for ten other people. At this point, the NTFIU brought in some experts to sit on the house and everybody in it, which is something that Special Branch really knows how to do.

'The expertise built up over 100 years of doing that kind of work,' says one Metropolitan police officer who has regularly seen them in action, 'is where Special Branch is the best in the UK. You could be the number one bugger in the UK, and you would never know you've got Special Branch up your bottom. They can get that close.'

Which is almost as close as they got to Pierre and his friends. They watched him for weeks, got to know the people he knew, and got to study their cheque fraud routine. Police officers tailed them as they went out on a daily basis, working one town after another, always operating the exact same way. They would buy goods for under £99 and fill up the car. After a few days of doing that, they would head up north and start returning things to different branches of the same store, handing sales staff the untouched item, producing the receipt, pointing out that this had been bought with a cheque, and getting a cash refund.

Pierre appeared to be one of the more senior guys in this crew. He was the one who controlled the lock up where the goods were kept.

As more people showed up in the surveillance and more names got added to the NTFIU list, mobile phone numbers were added too. But with this bunch, mobile phones were a nightmare for the police. Each phone would get passed around to someone else every few days. And SIM cards got moved, too. Tracking calls became next to impossible.

That said, it was clear that Pierre and his friends were working within a structure and that someone somewhere was pulling the strings. However, identifying this group was one thing, linking it to terrorism was the big leap.

Realizing that some of these men had fought in Chechnya, Afghanistan and Bosnia – they often reminded others that they were *jihad* veterans – the Special Branch guys sent pictures and names and addresses to Immigration to see what they knew. They also sent fingerprints of Pierre and all his friends to various law enforcement and intelligence agencies in Europe to see if any matches come back.

Sometimes you get lucky and this time they did. A file appeared from Immigration and a print match came back for that file, which identified Pierre – now they had his real name – and tied him directly into the Paris Metro attacks.

Knowing where Pierre's lockup was, they waited for the right moment to document what was in there. This is another area where Special Branch is among the best on the planet. A specialist team got inside the lockup, photographed it, video taped it, inventoried it and got out without leaving any sign at all that they'd been there. Not a single item was out of place. It's very specialized work and the only thing anyone at Special Branch will say about that team is, 'The people who do this for a living really know how to do this very well.'

What the people who do that for a living found were bags filled with merchandise waiting to be returned. There was so much stuff, that in order to keep track, Pierre had stapled the receipts to each bag. That would come in handy when it came to proving which cheque had bought which item.

With his lockup inventoried and his banking records in hand, the cops had a good sized evidence package and were ready to make an arrest. They got the necessary warrants and raided Pierre's home. Although he turned out to be a non-violent family man, the 'T' in NTFIU stands for terrorist, so the officers came suitably equipped and Pierre was immediately handcuffed.

Naturally, the first thing Pierre did was swear that he didn't know what this was all about. They explained it to him, and he still said he didn't know they were talking about. They kept explaining it and he kept denying it. While a few of the officers were interviewing him, one of the others found a key ring. Pierre claimed it was just an old key ring and that he didn't know what any of the keys were for. He was obviously lying, and one of the officers had a hunch. He left with the key ring and went to Pierre's lockup. One of the keys opened it, so he had another officer photograph the key in the lockup door. He came back to Pierre's house and showed the photo to him. The moment Pierre saw it, he broke down and cried.

The search of his house produced £15,000 in cash, chequebooks, ATM cards, diaries, address books, phone books and computer files. With all the money that passed through Pierre's hands, the officers were surprised to see that he was living in squalor. Where all the money has gone is a question they're still trying to answer. They know that some money was transferred out to Algeria. And there is a sign that some went to Tanzania. But at the other end, they don't know who picked it up or what it's being used for.

Pierre went to trial and got sent away, but only for two years. The judge was told about the Paris Metro connection, but didn't take it into consideration and, for security reasons, whatever information the unit had connecting Pierre to Paris was not brought up in sufficient detail to charge him for that.

While Pierre was getting used to his new accommodations, the NTFIU was working through all the leads they'd picked up when they arrested him. Some of it melded with information they were already holding. Patterns evolved and associations evolved. Half a dozen good cases came out of Pierre and those six have since led to others.

Although no one at the NTFIU will confirm that there are links, some very high profile cases have taken place since Pierre's arrest.

There was the raid on the Finsbury Park Mosque. There was the case of two Algerian men who entered Britain in 1997. Almost immediately they began collecting council tax benefits and housing allowances. They sustained themselves by defrauding banks and credit card fraud until they were arrested carrying false passports. They had direct links to the GIA.

There was the operation launched by Special Branch officers to round up 75 suspects, a vast majority of them Algerians, who'd entered the UK under the asylum laws. And in February 2003, an Algerian man was arrested at Waterloo Station getting off the Eurostar from Paris. He was widely believed to have had a connection to a plot to develop the deadly ricin toxin in North London.

'It is fair to say,' explains one of the NTFIU team, 'that a lot of these investigations do not end in simple fraud cases. That's absolutely true. The power of financial investigations has, at long last, been grasped by our senior management and the people who lead intelligence in the United Kingdom, and the NTFIU is being used the way it should have been used decades ago.'

And that's all anyone at the NTFIU will say about that.

Other terrorist groups have been just as successful in other parts of the world. In certain ways, they've also been more clever.

As long ago as 1986, the Abu Nidal organization demonstrated a real knack for earning money. It wanted to find negotiable instruments in the United States that it could hijack and turn into money to fund their war against Israel. The answer it came up with was right there staring back at them from the breakfast cereal box – 50-cents off your next purchase of cornflakes!

Discount coupons on cereal boxes and soap powder and the booklets filled with them that come with the Sunday paper, have been a popular marketing tool for hundreds of different products for a long time. The idea is to induce consumers to buy a product by offering a discount on the purchase. But the whole thing is based on trust. There's no way for the manufacturer to know for sure if the person cashing in the coupon actually bought the product. Retailers accepting coupons are supposed to be honest about it and only reward the customer when a purchase is made. But, at the end of the day, the coupons are batched up by the retailers and sent to the manufacturers with the understanding, *we sold your product so you owe us the money for the total face value of the coupons plus a handling charge.*

Because there are no controls on this, there's widespread fraud. And no one ever proved that point better than Rick Bowdren, today a very senior supervisory agent with the US Postal Inspection Service. In 1977, as a young agent assigned to the New York office, Bowdren was working on a number of different investigations, looking at a lot of different criminal enterprises, when he discovered that some organized crime groups were making a lot of money working discount coupon fraud.

He started contacting people in the coupon business to find out more. They concurred that this was a huge money spinner for organized crime. In normal fraud cases, jurisdiction would go to the local police. Coupon fraud wasn't an obvious area of concern for a postal inspector. But to cash in the coupons the retailer had to mail them, and the moment he put a fraudulent coupon in a letter and stuck a stamp on the envelope and dropped it in a mail box, that was mail fraud.

'The mail fraud statute,' Bowdren explains, 'was created in about 1865 because there were frauds occurring between states and no law enforcement agency had jurisdiction. We were the only people set up to do anything about it. Today, that's changed. But the statute hasn't. Today, if you commit a crime and use the mails, you've got mail fraud. It's a catch-all type statute.'

Armed with that, Bowdren set up a catch-all type sting. The way to prove that a retailer didn't sell the product, he decided, was with coupons offering a discount on a product that didn't exist.

So he invented Breen – 'The detergent that cleans away dirt and grime.'

The coupon he designed offered 25-cents off the next purchase. It contained all the standard warnings: purchase required; non-transferable; any other use constitutes fraud. The address on the back, for retailers looking to reclaim the coupon, was a company he invented called 'CFCP Coupon Redemption', with a PO box in Clinton, Iowa.

After securing the co-operation of three greater New York–New Jersey newspapers – the *Daily News* in New York City, *Newsday* on

Long Island and the *Newark Star Ledger* across the Hudson in New Jersey – a totally legit-looking Breen coupon was an insert on one day, 11 December 1977, and only in those newspapers. The combined circulation of the three papers was 3.38 million.

Bowdren then waited to see what would happen. 'Within four months we got back over 77,000 coupons from over 2,100 stores in 42 different states It was unbelievable. This was a product that did not exist.'

The coupons he got back weren't copied or counterfeited, they were real. In some cases they never found their way into the newspapers. In other cases they were stolen by the newspaper delivery drivers. In some instances the stores themselves got hold of them before any consumers did. In other instances the coupons were stolen by criminals and sold to the retailers.

'We arrested 300 merchants in the New York–New Jersey area', Bowdren explains, 'and charged them with grand theft for fraudulently submitting bogus coupons. It wasn't a lot of arrests, considering how many coupons we got back. But we couldn't take everybody down. We wanted to show how prolific the crime was and that's what we did. Unfortunately, the industry never learned its lesson because coupon fraud is still today as prolific as it was then.'

The industry might not have learned that lesson, but terror groups did. Palestinian terrorists realized that there were thousands of neighbourhood grocery stores – *bodegas* and corner shops – across the United States owned by people from the Middle East who would be sympathetic to their cause. The Florida-based Adnand Bahour controlled a network of 800 grocery stores across the country, solely to defraud the grocery manufacturers with coupons against sales that never happened. His significance became apparent when undercover agents caught him on videotape claiming to be the nephew of Palestinian Liberation Front leader George Habash. Ten postal inspectors went undercover for five months to expose Bahour and his group who, over a two-year period, fraudulently submitted $186 million worth of coupons.

In 1987 the manager of a Brooklyn video store was arrested in connection with a ring that turned over millions of dollars in fraudulent coupons. The man was Mahmud Abouhalima, now serving a 240-year prison sentence for masterminding the 1993 attack on the World Trade Center. There is some evidence that Omar Abdul Rachman, the blind sheikh who is also serving a life sentence for the

1993 attack, was involved in coupon fraud, as well. The suggestion is that the two funded that first attack on the World Trade Center using those monies from those frauds.

Some groups move discount coupons, others move diamonds. Bought in Sierra Leone, Al-Qaeda has been smuggling embargoed 'conflict' diamonds into Europe where they're resold in cities like Antwerp. The money is laundered through legitimate banks in the Middle East. At the same time, the illicit trade in diamonds continues to fuel civil strife, not just in Sierra Leone, but in Liberia and Angola as well.

Throughout the rest of Europe and all over North America, there is a huge trade in knock-off designer goods – Chanel tee-shirts and Nike running shoes, Mont Blanc pens and Rolex watches. One statistic indicates that 5–7 per cent of world trade is counterfeit goods and another suggests that as much as half of that is controlled by terrorist organizations.

It's much the same for cigarettes. Although the movement of cigarettes across borders and state lines by terrorist groups is driven almost entirely by taxes. In Northern Ireland, for example, over the past 30-plus years, the IRA has actively funded mainland activities with cigarette tax fraud.

One recently traceable IRA money trail leads through Malta. There, an alleged IRA business associate – himself purportedly involved with Gerardo Cuomo, a Mafia chieftain named in the EU law suit against the major cigarette companies – has used Liberian shells to launder money. Which is hardly a coincidence given the fact that the man in Malta has tenuous ties to Andrew Warren and Stewart Creggy.

There may also be an IRA arms link through Malta as part of the cigarette smuggling.

In 1999 drug cops working at the airport in St Louis spotted a young Lebanese man acting suspiciously. They recognized the behaviour and, knowing that he was carrying something, intervened. Instead of drugs, they found $700,000 worth of counterfeit cigarette tax stamps. That rang alarm bells because similar counterfeit cigarette tax stamps were found in the apartment of one of the Islamic Jihad cell members who bombed the World Trade Center in 1993.

But even $700,000 worth of counterfeit cigarette tax stamps turned out to be a minor bust, compared with what was going on in Charlotte, North Carolina.

A federal law in the United States says that you cannot transport more than 300 cartons of cigarettes per person across a state line unless state tax has been paid on them. So several young Lebanese men would head for JR Tobacco – a wholesaler in the tiny town of Statesville, about 40 miles from Charlotte who calls himself the world's largest cigarette outlet – and each buy 299 cartons of untaxed cigarettes. They'd load them into their van, then drive 13 hours to Detroit, Michigan – nearly 700 miles away – because neither North Carolina nor Michigan puts tax stamps on cigarettes. North Carolina's taxes are 5 cents a pack and Michigan's are 75 cents. With 20 packs to the carton, multiplied by the 70-cent difference – in business it's called arbitrage – and then multiplied by 299, it works out to $4,186 per person, per trip, before expenses.

Sometimes there would be as many as four guys on a trip, with 299 cartons each. And some weeks they would make five trips.

Needless to say, the trip was not without its perils. They'd get stopped for speeding. Or cops would spot a van load of Arab men and pull them over to find out what they're doing. It's not politically correct to do 'profiling' any more, but that's what they called it pre-9/11 and that's what it still is. The cops would see the cigarettes and start asking questions. Because the answers were never very satisfactory, the cops would confiscate the cigarettes. On one return trip when the cops pulled them over, they found nearly $46,000 in small bills that none of the Lebanese men could account for, so the cops confiscated that.

After a while the cigarette smugglers reckoned they could fool the cops by pretending they were on vacation and strapped mountain bikes to the outside of the van. When that didn't work, one of them married a non-Arab woman and got her to drive the van to make it look less suspicious.

By then, it was probably too late because the security guard at JR Tobacco – who'd seen these guys every few days buying 299 cartons each with shopping bags full of cash – had tipped off the Bureau of Alcohol, Tobacco and Firearms (ATF).

Unbeknown to the ATF, the Canadian Security Intelligence Service (CSIS) had already taken an interest. One of these men, Said Harb, was delivering money in Vancouver to his old childhood friend, Mohamad Dbouk. The CSIS had identified Dbouk as Hezbollah's purchasing agent in Canada. He'd received intelligence training from the Iranians and reported directly to Hezbollah's military procurement chief. He was spending the money on night-vision goggles, mine-detection equipment, laser range finders, software that was otherwise restricted from export, munitions, global positioning systems and even ultrasonic dog repellents.

In the beginning, Harb would either bulk cash to Dbouk or, when he could, he'd wire it. As the amounts of money from the cigarette tax scam mounted, Harb established no fewer than 800 bank accounts and juggled hundreds of credit cards. Almost as if it was *de rigueur*, when Harb was ready to discard a bank account or a credit card, he worked a scam to defraud the bank of whatever he could get away with.

Most of the electronic surveillance that CSIS was getting on these guys was collected by Canada's Communications Security Establishment (CSE). Along with the US National Security Agency and Britain's GCHQ, they form ECHELON, a global electronic surveillance network that shares information. So as CSE narrowed in on Dbouk and Harb. It told the NSC and, in turn, the NSC told the FBI.

The Lebanese cigarette smugglers didn't have a clue how closely they were now being monitored. But they'd been trained to expect some surveillance and so to make their trail more difficult to follow each one used several variant spellings of his name on dozens of bogus IDs. They had phoney passports, licences, social security numbers, credit cards, credit card histories and Immigration and Naturalization Service (INS) papers. For good measure, they befriended Arab students at local universities and when those student left for home, these guys bought their passports and IDs, to use them too.

In five years, the first-ever Hezbollah terrorist cell in Charlotte, North Carolina generated more than $2 million for its cause.

The cell leader was Mohamad Youssef Hammoud. He'd come to New York in 1992 at the age of 27, travelling from Venezuela on a fake visa in his Lebanese passport. When his request for asylum was turned down, he started marrying American women to stay in the country. Apparently, each time the INS ruled his marriage bogus, he got married again.

By the time the Feds were ready to pounce on this crew of 17 men, they knew they had the cell cold on cigarette tax fraud, conspiracy and money laundering. What they didn't have was enough of the Hezbollah connection. But they had the Canadians. After a lot of negotiation, CSIS agreed to give up some wire tap transcripts. The judge accepted three paragraphs as grounds for a search warrant on 18 locations. They found weapons, including an AK-47 automatic rifle, and enough evidence to grab Harb. Once he agreed to talk, the rest of the cell crumbled. Most of them plea bargained. Hammoud was too stubborn and took it to trial.

He was charged with providing material support to a designated terrorist organization. The judge allowed nearly 100 pages of Canadian wire tap transcripts to be heard, a senior CSIS officer testified, the jury said guilty, and the judge sent Hammoud away for 155 years.

When terrorist groups pay for black market products by cheque or wire, if they know how to do it, the money trail can disappear in a nano-second. Where the product is paid for with cash, other problems arise, like how to get that money back to the people who need it.

One of the first financial victims of 9/11 was a company called Al-Barakaat. Within a few weeks of the attack, the White House issued a list of 27 companies whose funds the government was freezing for their suspected links to Al-Qaeda. High on the list was Al-Barakaat, perhaps the largest financial institution in Somalia and certainly the most widely exported.

With a bank in Mogadishu and store-front wire remitters scattered around North America, Al-Barakaat served Somalis wanting to send money home to their families, much the way that American Express has served American tourists in Europe.

The freeze blocked almost $1 million. Arrest warrants saw Al-Barakaat managers handcuffed and taken away. What worried the Americans was that some of the cash coming from North America heading eastward was earmarked for terrorist activities in Afghanistan, and that cash coming out of the Middle East destined for North America was being collected by terrorists to fund their activities.

It's a case that, more than three years later, remains to be proven. But the targeting of Al-Barakaat was an understandable reaction – even if nothing ever gets proven – because Al-Barakaat was really just a *hawallah* banking network with a sign out front. And the first place anyone who understands money laundering and the Middle East would look for bin Laden's money, is at a *hawallah*.

The most direct, most traditional and most invisible way for terrorists to move money is an ancient system of IOUs. Invented by the
Chinese, who named it *fei ch'ien* – literally, 'flying money' – it's known
in other parts of the world as *chop* or *hundi*.

A system born out of political turmoil and a hearty distrust of
banks, it is almost always based on family or tribal connections and
traditionally reinforced with retributive violence.

In its simplest form, chits or tokens are substituted for cash.
Money deposited at a gold shop in Karachi is exchanged for a small,
innocuous piece of paper that has been secretly coded, or a $10 bill
stamped with a special seal. When the object is presented to a money
changer in Dubai, the bearer is given cash. That particular example
is one that matters in the terrorist world because the mammoth
hawallah triangle operating between Pakistan, Dubai and India is
estimated to be worth $4–$5 billion annually. That's four to five
times greater than the sums making the same trip through normal
banking channels.

While cash machines were used by some of the 19 hijackers of the
9/11 atrocity, *hawallah* banking can never be ruled out as a main
funding source for Al-Qaeda's master plans in North America. That's
made abundantly clear by one the bin Laden group's many relationships in the Balkans.

By 1991 the war in Yugoslavia had seriously interrupted the traditional heroin route from Turkey and Afghanistan – where heroin was
the major export – into Europe. Two alternative routes developed, one
through Bulgaria, Romania and Hungary, the other from Bulgaria
through Kosovo and Albania. That became the route of choice.

Albanian gangs moved drugs across the Adriatic into Italy, which
created a new alliance between the Italian Mafia and the Kosovo
Liberation Army (KLA). Together they smuggled people from the
Balkans into Italy, moved counterfeit prescription medicines from
Italy to the Balkans, and traded drugs for arms. They also dealt with
the Russians who paid for heroin with rocket launchers and automatic weapons. Drugs alone were bringing the KLA more than $2
billion a year during those years, turning Albania into the Colombia
of Europe.

As the war intensified, Albanian refugees spread out across the
world. Like the Russian émigrés of the 1970s, these Albanians
extended the KLA's influence into Europe and North America, where
young Albanian gang members do burglaries, armed robberies and

car theft. Some Albanian émigrés also raise money for Albanian and
Kosovo charities. All of which gives them a lot of cash. Bank accounts
related to the KLA and certain Kosovo disaster relief charities have
been located in Canada, Germany, Sweden, Italy, Belgium and the
United States.

Any money the bin Laden group might need in one of those countries can easily be provided. It is known that the Taliban traded heroin
with the Chechens for arms. Moving the arms to Kosovo, means that
cash is available to be picked up at disaster relief charities in the rest
of the world.

That's one of the reasons why, when the world went looking for
bin Laden's money, they didn't find any.

To begin with, he didn't need to spend his own. Anyway, by 9/11,
he might not have had any of his own left to spend. When the world's
attention was focused on him that September, bin Laden's personal
fortune was estimated at slightly more than $300 million. It's
anybody's guess if that's accurate, but it sounded good and so that
was the figure that got repeated. But at the time bin Laden was living
in a cave and that's a terrible place to keep your life savings. These
days there is reason to suspect that by 9/11 he was either broke or
about to be.

There's no doubt that bin Laden once owned several businesses in
Sudan and Yemen. There was an import-export firm, a concrete
factory, a honey business, an Arabic gum business — which manu-
factures an important ingredient for the production of fruit juices —
an investment house that supposedly maintained properties in the
west and, perhaps most significantly, a share of Al-Shamal Bank.
There is also said to be a Sudanese front company with accounts in
Cyprus.

However, the bulk of his assets were in a part of the world where,
if you leave your goat untethered someone helps it walk away. He's
been out of there for quite a while, with very little prospect of showing
up at the next board meeting. Who knows how much, if any, of those
assets are under his control or, for that matter, still intact. The Sudanese
threw him out, which suggests that his assets there have been looted.
In his absence from Yemen many of his assets there, if not all, could
have suffered a similar fate.

With that in mind, and based on the way Al-Qaeda is known to
operate, bin Laden was probably never more than the Chairman of a
holding company that franchised terrorist activities to autonomous

and semi-autonomous subsidiaries. Al-Qaeda maintains cells and alliances throughout the world, most interestingly in Lebanon (secret banking), Malaysia (organized Asian criminal gangs), Uruguay (money laundering), the United Kingdom (off-shore banking) and Canada (easy border access to the US). He didn't fund any of them because he couldn't, because he didn't have to, or both. His backers were wealthy businessmen throughout the Islamic world. Some of them may have included disaffected members of the Saudi royal family. Others might have been encouraged to support him through extortion and blackmail. Anyway, whatever cells are out there, 'sleeping', they almost certainly fund themselves, much the way that the Montreal cell funded itself.

That leaves the possibility of finding offshore shells and bank accounts with bin Laden's name on it very remote. There was the alleged charity connection in Jersey which draw a lot of attention in the aftermath of 9/11. But whatever money goes through charities to support terrorist activities, anywhere in the world, are disguised as just that – charities. Sure, money that funds terrorism may move through an account, but the problem is that none of it gets clearly labelled blood money.

Finding Saddam Hussein's stash is a much more straightforward task, because there are offshore shell companies, somewhere. And Swiss connections, too.

In May 2003 reports out of Baghdad revealed that more than $900 million in cash had been withdrawn from Iraq's Central Bank by Saddam's son Qusay only a matter of days before the allied bombing of the city began. Apparently, Qusay and his associates walked into the bank with some sort of official document signed by his father and ordered that the money – made up of US dollars and around $90 million Euros – be loaded onto three articulated lorries. The press then reported that all three lorries had been spotted heading for the Syrian border.

Undeniably the biggest bank robbery in history – a desperate act of a dictator on the run – it was also a really dumb stunt because it was, simply, too much money.

To begin with, $900 million dollars in its smallest, most portable form – crisp new $100 bills – would have weighed just about 10 tons and stacked 3,300 feet high. That's two and a half Empire State Buildings. Other denominations would have increased the weight and height. So right from the beginning, he had a very serious bulk problem.

As it turned out, bulk proved fatal. He couldn't move it efficiently enough and much of it was quickly found. Around $600 million turned up hidden in one of Saddam's palaces, and another $100 million, plus the 90 million Euros, were found packed into Iraqi armoured vehicles. Later, US soldiers would stop two vans heading for Syria with more than half a billion dollars worth of gold bullion.

But even if they hadn't found a nickel of it, and even if Saddam had worked out how to bulk it out of the country, he never stood a chance of his seeing any of it. The drug traffickers learned this lesson a long time ago. To get money out of a country, you have to trust people whom you can control. And Saddam lost control long before he lost the money.

Even if he had somehow managed to get it into Syria, he would have had to trust someone over whom he had no control – a banker, a member of the ruling party – somebody who would be sleazebag enough to help Saddam and, by definition, be sleazebag enough to steal the money. What could Saddam possibly have done had he got the money out, and then somehow got himself out, should the person looking after it in Syria then announced, regretfully, *but I never saw a penny of it.*

Besides, as soon as news of the theft hit the wires, a lot of people started looking for the money, including the FBI, US Customs and, perhaps most importantly of all, the US Federal Reserve Bank.

One of the jobs of the Fed is to monitor the flow of dollars around the world. It is estimated that as much as 70 per cent of America's currency is in circulation outside the US. Some 60 per cent of that is believed to be inside Russia or otherwise controlled offshore by Russians. While a billion isn't much by Fed standards, were it suddenly to show up in Syria it would still cause a small blip on the Fed's radar screens.

Saddam's attempt to launder a billion is cash is up there with the war against Iran and the Gulf War on the list of 'his mother-of-all stupid mistakes'.

It's not even as if he needed an extra billion. His wealth was probably, at the time, already in the $30–$40 billion range. Much of that having been laundered well. Some of that having been washed through Britain.

It is known that in 1990 when he raped Kuwait, Saddam ordered his soldiers to commandeer whatever automobiles they could drive away. A few of the more expensive cars – Rolls, Mercedes, Lamborghinis, Porches, BMWs and Ferraris – were given to Ba'ath Party officials as a gift. However, 50 of the choicest cars, including an armour-plated Mercedes and an armour-plated BMW, were driven from Baghdad to Amman, then flown to Geneva by Royal Jordanian Airline cargo planes, under the protection accorded diplomatic shipments. Once in Switzerland, they were put on the market and turned into cash.

Not that he needed that money, either. He'd long before taken a lesson straight out of the Calouste Sarkis Gulbenkian textbook of how to run an oil company.

A Turk of Armenian descent, Gulbenkian founded what was then the Iraqi Petroleum Company. For his efforts, he laid claim to a royalty on every drop of oil, giving birth to his nickname, 'Mr Five Per Cent'. When he died in Lisbon in 1955, the oil royalty was passed on to his son Nubar. Some 17 years later, Saddam confiscated Nubar's 5 per cent in the name of the Ba'ath Party, and personally assumed joint custody of the funds, sharing signature authority with Defence Minister Adnan Khairallah and Petroleum Minister Adnan Hamdani. In 1979, Saddam ordered the execution of his old friend and co-signatory, Hamdani. Ten years later, his pal Khairallah died in a mysterious helicopter crash.

According to a document claiming to be a true accounting of those funds, $51 million was deposited in a major Swiss bank in Geneva in 1972. The balance in the account climbed to $92 million the following year and, as the price of oil quadrupled during the Yom Kippur War, to $327 million in 1974. By the time the Iran–Iraq war broke out, with Saddam firmly in control of the country, the account held in excess of $1.69 billion.

In 1995 it was reliably believed that Saddam controlled funds worth far in excess of $32 billion. At the end his reign in 2003, that figure wasn't likely to be less, and could have been twice as high.

As witnessed by his palaces, Saddam wasn't shy when it came to spending money, although his monthly outgoings on reverence, loyalty and, especially, personal security, must have been astonishing. He also frequently spent money on whims and fancies. When the Empress

Faradiba, wife of the late Shah of Iran, sold a few of her jewels, Saddam pulled $352 million out of Switzerland to buy them for his wife. Faradiba denies it, for obvious reasons. But two sources, both reliable and each independent of the other, confirm the story.

Some sources say, and there is good reason to believe they're right, that Saddam spread gigantic amounts of money throughout the offshore world as a giant safety net for himself, his family and his closest Ba'ath Party associates. Clearly, he moved money through Geneva and a network of companies. One of them, Montana Management, is registered in Panama and controlled by Midco Financial, a Geneva shell. In 1981, Midco, through Montana, began buying into the French broadcasting and publishing conglomerate, Hachette SA. At one point, Saddam is said to have owned as much as 8.4 per cent of Hachette's shares.

Another Saddam company is Al-Arabi Trading, headquartered in Baghdad, which purchased a large stake in the British-based Technology and Development Group (TDG). In 1987 TDG bought a precision engineering firm called Matrix-Churchill. A few years later HM Customs and Excise became aware of the connection, took a closer look at Matrix-Churchill, moved in on the firm, and confiscated parts of an alleged super-gun that was destined for Iraq.

The Americans have been searching for Saddam's money since he came to power. In April 1991 the US Treasury's Office of Foreign Asset Control identified 52 businesses and 37 individuals with direct financial links to him and/or his Ba'ath Party. Of those 52 companies, 24 were in the UK, a number of them using the same address – 3 Mandeville Place, London W1. Of the 37 named individuals, a dozen also had addresses in Britain.

For the most part, 'Saddam International Inc' was run by his half-brother Barazan al-Takriti, who was living in Switzerland as Iraq's special ambassador-at-large. Barazan was captured right after the fall of Baghdad in April 2003. He knows the intimate details about currency, gold and jewels that arrived by diplomatic pouch from his half-brother, because he was the one who dumped them into Swiss banks. He also knows about an estimated 500 shell companies that are believed to have been formed, how they fit into each other, and which direction money has flowed through them. After all, Barazan was there for nearly 20 years, bedding down money for safe keeping.

However, here too, Saddam has a serious problem.

In setting up the network of shells, Barazan built up a cadre of

Iraqis outside the country, plus some Jordanians and Palestinians to help him. Saddam's money is said to be in their names – so that there could never be any links back to Saddam or his family – thoroughly washed through double-back loans, investments and trusts, then fed into legitimate businesses that are said to be in Spain, France, Brazil, Indonesia, Hong Kong, Britain and the US.

As long as Saddam was in power, as long as he could shove a gun in someone's mother's ear, his front-men wouldn't dare steal a penny. The price for bad accounting would be death.

But that threat no longer exists.

The downside of dealing this way in the offshore world is that you have to do business with untrustworthy sons-of-bitches.

Just as that statue of Saddam in central Baghdad was yanked down, his money was getting washed yet again, through more shells and secret bank accounts and tropical island trusts, this time by those untrustworthy sons-of-bitches who knew they could get away with stealing it.

CHAPTER SEVENTEEN

Future Crime

I have seen the enemy and he is us.
— Walt Kelly's 'Pogo'

A few years ago, at a major money laundering conference in Montreal sponsored by the RCMP, one of the keynote speakers had just finished when a young man raised his hand to ask a question.

'Please tell me, what we are supposed to do?' He explained, 'I come from the eastern Caribbean. Europe and the United States have taken away our bananas. We have no manufacturing. After September 11th, there are no more tourists. Now you are saying that we should not be licensing offshore banks and we should not be selling shell companies. But we are already starving today. How will we feed ourselves tomorrow?' He stared, then asked again, 'Please tell me, what we are supposed to do?'

The speaker looked at the young man for a long time, then told him the truth. 'I don't know.' He said, 'I can only tell you what we, what all of us, should not be doing.'

That speaker still wishes he'd had a better answer.

After the government of Antigua granted an offshore licence to Hanover Bank, and after a bunch of Russians moved $4.2 billion through the Channel Islands and the Bank of New York, and after the Al-Shamal Bank in Khartoum turned out to have a connection with Osama bin Laden, the preachers who were leading the congregation in the anti-money laundering Sunday mass wanted the world to believe that KYC – know your customer – was the Messiah who would lead us all out of evil.

And the choir sang, *if every financial institution in every country practiced KYC, then dirty money couldn't get into the system and that would be the end of that.*

But in the real world, KYC is money laundering's answer to snake oil. Where it is voluntary, it is too often ignored. Where it is legislated, it is too often fudged.

So along came 'gatekeepers'.

This was the group to target because they could disrupt the movement of dirty money simply by withholding their co-operation. They are bankers, lawyers, accountants, investment brokers, middlemen, fund managers, real estate brokers, auctioneers and so forth. People who, by virtue of their professional experience, know money laundering when they see it. Or, at least, should know the right questions to ask to properly identify it. And who, by virtue of their professional status, are in a position either to facilitate it or to stop it.

To guide the 'gatekeepers', the key term became 'beneficial owner'.

Everyone needed to establish who beneficially owned the money that they were being asked to handle. And they were reminded that, should they not be able to establish the beneficial owner, they should not be doing the business.

Gatekeepers fired back, 'impractical' and 'a violation of our established right to privacy with our customers', and 'a Big Brother-like violation of human rights'.

While certain aspects of the USA Patriots Act might have brought Big Brother a few steps closer, at least where money laundering is concerned, there's no doubt that it changed the lexicon. KYC and gatekeepers were still in, but now the two Acts – USA Pats-I and the amendments that followed, called USA Pats-II – combined to put a real burden on financial institutions operating in the United States. By proxy, that included foreign financial institutions with subsidiaries and offices in the US as well. With the images of 9/11 still fresh in everyone's mind, Congress was getting serious about money laundering and the financing of terrorist organizations.

The Acts prohibit financial institutions from establishing, maintaining, or managing correspondent accounts on behalf of foreign banks that do not have a physical presence in the country of registration. In other words, if an offshore shell doesn't have a roof, you can't do business with it. Every financial institution operating in the US is also subject to stiff penalties for not determining the sources of large overseas private banking accounts. Sanctions under the Acts can be imposed on nations, as well, if they refuse to provide information about depositors to US law enforcement.

Because USA Pats I and II apply to everyone who deals with money

– including *hawallahs,* which must now be licensed and online payment systems, which must satisfy stricter KYC requirements – renewed emphasis has been placed on gatekeepers and beneficial owners. It goes back to the basic concept that the people who allow money to come into the system are the ones who can best keep it out. Which, like the concepts of KYC and gatekeepers, is fine on paper. But unless you start throwing gatekeepers in jail because they didn't adequately KYC, even the tough talking USA Pats acts won't work. If you don't disincentivise those people who could to stop it – those same people who are otherwise incentivized to make it happen – why would they bother?

'Implementation is the word', notes Ted Greenberg, former special counsel for international money laundering at the US Department of Justice and now head of money-laundering investigations at the World Bank. Greenberg is also the man generally acknowledged as the father of the gatekeeper concept. 'You can have all the legislation in the world, but if you don't implement it, what good is it?'

His point is driven home soundly in a quirky little survey. To determine how seriously the nations of the world were about their own money laundering regulations, codes, treaties and laws, the survey looked at 103 countries with stock exchanges to see how well they were regulated. Insider trading laws existed in 87 of those countries, which at first glance is not bad. But prosecutions for insider trading had only occurred in 38.

This is not to say that change hasn't begun to happen. The Proceeds of Crime Act in the UK is forcing people to file more suspicious transaction reports. There was a period during the 1990s when the National Criminal Intelligence Service received 20,000 of them a year, but didn't have the money or the personnel to handle them all. In 2001 they received 31,000. In 2002, anticipating the Proceeds of Crime Act, the number nearly doubled. But staff and budget have not.

In Canada, reporting of cash transactions greater than $10,000 is now mandatory. But FinTRAC – the Canadians' money laundering reporting unit – can't work in tandem with it's US counterpart, FinCen, because Parliament legislated ultra-strict privacy safeguards that severely limit the sharing of information. Even Canadian law enforcement has trouble getting intelligence out of FinTRAC.

In Liechtenstein, where banking and related services account for 40 per cent of the tiny nation's economy, legislators made it a crime for bankers and financial institutions to fail to report suspicious financial activity. Bankers fought it for years, stalling as long as they could, insisting that it wasn't necessary because all was fine in Lilliput. That is, until those bankers got caught hiding a slush fund for former German Chancellor Helmut Kohl; got caught hiding the profits of an illegal arms deal by Jean-Christophe Mitterand, son of the late French President; got caught hiding money stolen by a whole slew of African despots; and got caught hiding drug money for Latin American traffickers. The burghers of Vaduz had to come up with something, so rather than knock down the house, they opted for wallpaper. There is legislation. But bankers and financial institutions aren't getting prosecuted for failure to report. Nor are they necessarily reporting everything that is suspicious. Oh well, at last Liechtenstein can say that its complying.

In Nauru, parliament passed legislation abolishing the country's controversial offshore banks. But that only happened when the United States declared economic war on the island, which was near bankrupt anyway. Which is why Nauru continued selling citizenship and passports, until the US agreed to pay them to stop.

In Niue, the government announced that they won't sell any more banks. But they refused to stop selling phoney shell companies. After all, they argued, why should we?

In Delaware and Nevada and Montana, life goes on as normal. If they were islands somewhere, FATF would jump on their case. But they happen to be in the United States and Washington carries a bigger stick than any of the islands. That's why, when certain offshore jurisdictions found themselves getting slapped across the wrists for doing the same things that were happening in Delaware and Nevada and Montana, they objected. FATF raised its eyebrows in the direction of Washington, and Washington told the FATF to take a hike. There's no way that US trust law was going to get changed just because FATF didn't like it. In the United States, trusts are the business of attorneys and Washington is one place where attorneys wield real power.

In mid-2000, when FATF bared its teeth and published its 'Report on Non-Co-operative Countries and Territories', placing 15 jurisdictions on its blacklist – Russia, Liechtenstein, Israel, Lebanon, the Bahamas, the Cayman Islands, Cook Islands, Dominica, the Marshall Islands, Nauru, Niue, Panama, the Philippines, St Kitts and Nevis, and Saint Vincent and the Grenadines – all 15 feigned shock and horror. Especially Panama, where the head of the country's financial analysis unit told the press, 'Panama cannot afford to have a bad reputation.'

For bad, substitute the word, worse.

But then, considering how easy it is to fool the FATF most of the time, the fact that Panama was included on the list can only be down to that nation's naked venality. Instead of change, when FATF said Panama was 'unco-operative', the Panamanians did what they had to do to pretend to be co-operative. Sure enough, FATF fell for it. So did some US officials, who should have known better, and praised Panama for becoming co-operative.

Except Panama still has secret banking and still has phoney shell companies and still has the Colon Free Trade Zone which is regulated by people who don't believe in regulation because it would cost them too much money. Panama simply passed a few new codes that no one ever intended to enforce, and publicly proclaimed that terrorist money would not be welcome there.

Declaring war on terrorist money is like being in favour of apple pie and motherhood. So Panama got removed from the FATF blacklist and it's business as usual, as long as bin Laden's money never turns up.

'When the 11th happened,' announced a senior representative of Panama's Banking Association, 'we immediately got in touch with all the banks and said terrorist activities are now on the front page. We always said we were committed to helping in this fight.'

But the war on drugs has been on the front page for 35 years, and so has the growing menace of transnational organized crime, and so has fraud and so has tax evasion, and for that matter, so has the Free Zone, where all these financial viruses breed the same way mosquitoes did in the swamps where they built their canal.

The Caymans got off the black list, too. So did the Bahamas.

That Nigeria didn't even make that black list – nor did the Ukraine – tells you a lot about the FATF blacklist. The problem is that when the FATF bares its teeth, its dentures fall out.

This is not to say that the FATF hasn't bitten a few people. Just that it chooses its biting too carefully and stops biting too easily. It would be different if, instead of embarrassing a few jurisdictions, there was a way to ostracize them instead.

This is not just about reputational risk, it's about 'terminal' reputational risk. It's about drawing a line in the sand and saying, you're either on-side or off-side, and if you're off-side it's going to cost you dearly, and if you're on-side, you're going to have to work hard to stay there.

It's all well and good that the FATF embarrasses the Caymans by sticking the island onto its blacklist for a few months. But the FATF, albeit well meaning, needs a cattle prod. It's too gullible. It's also too political. And, in the end, it bottles out when the big kids show up.

If you're going to be a bully, you'd better be able to take out the biggest kid on the block. If reputational risk is really going matter, then entry to the good guy's club must be so strict that membership means something. If Cyprus is going to register a shell to some Russian looking to sell fissile materials on the black market, that should jeopardize all of the other 47,000 shells in Cyprus. If Dominica is going to charter a bank that doesn't have a roof or tellers or real clients, that should put at risk every other company and every other bank chartered on the island. If the Caymans is going to have a Euro Bank; or if the Bahamas is going to sell shells to anyone who wants one over the phone; or if Belize is going to sell a passport to anyone with enough money to pay for it; then the future of those jurisdictions should be put in jeopardy. If you're willing to sell your soul to anyone with $100 and a maildrop address, you need to be put on notice that there is no halfway point between on-side and off-side.

If reputational risk is going to matter, then off-side must be terminal. Or, at least, draconian enough to require life support. It comes down to this: why should the world recognize any offshore entity if the jurisdiction in question will allow even one sleazebag to run one shell or own one sham bank?

The price of admission must be a clear cut distinction between acceptable privacy and unacceptable secrecy.

Is it Bermuda's problem that some re-insurance company registered there has fooled around with reserves in so many other jurisdictions that, when disaster strikes in Europe or Africa or the Far East, there is no money to make things right? Is it the Bahama's problem that a bank there has issued a credit card to someone in Canada or Britain or Australia or the United States, allowing that person to spend money at home without the paying tax on it? Right now, Bermuda and the Bahamas say no, it's not their problem. But the day that Canada, Britain, Australia and the United States – and everyone else – make it their problem, that's the day that the offshore world will take a very different attitude towards responsible citizenship.

Any system that operates outside of legitimate regulatory control – and it doesn't necessarily matter where that regulatory control is, as long as it's legitimate – jeopardizes every other system that feeds into and off of that one. Think of the offshore world like a series of tributaries flowing into the river that is the global financial system. If one of those tributaries is dangerously polluted, what happens to the river? Does someone downstream have the right to say, hey you up there, stop dumping mercury into the water and killing my fish?

It may take time, it may be clumsy, it may cost a lot of money, but it can be done. Why should the world tolerate abuse of its financial system by a bunch of crooked politicians who have hood-winked their own people into believing that this has something to do with sovereignty?

This is not about sovereignty, any more than it's an assault on freewheeling free market capitalism. It's about gross abuse, corruption, tax evasion, crime, terror, and dirty money. It's about providing safe harbour to people who have paid whatever it costs to avoid responsibility somewhere else.

What's right with the present system, that each jurisdiction knows whether or not it is complying, is also what's wrong with the present system, that each jurisdiction must decide whether or not to let the rest of the world in on the secret.

The concept of 'consolidated supervision' means that each jurisdiction employs a local regulator who is responsible for oversight of the financial sector. And when the watchdog comes to visit, it is the local regulator who becomes the tour guide.

Over here, ladies and gentlemen, you will see all the wonderful anti-money laundering regulations we have put in place, and if you look now to your left, you will see the beautifully bound volumes of anti-money laundering codes that every bank must have on its shelves.

The problems with that are obvious, magnified a hundred-fold by the smoke and mirrors nature of the offshore world, where financial institutions in some places aren't necessarily there, and financial institutions in other places are there, but you can't see them.

The first question is, who polices this? The answer is, it's supposed to be the legitimate financial institution in the legitimate financial centre.

The next question is, how well can they do it? The answer is, only as well as some minor employee in some forgotten outpost is willing to let them.

Recognizing that even the most sincere and best-regulated offshore centres are incapable of controlling anything financial beyond the three mile limit, certain banks have taken it upon themselves to fill that void. Arguably, the most interesting initiative has been the Wolfsberg Principles.

In October 2000, 11 of the world's major private banking groups got together in Wolfsberg, Switzerland, to draw up a set of anti-money laundering procedures which, they hoped, would create a level playing field for international private banking. The original 11 were: ABN Amro, Barclays, Banco Santander Central Hispano, Chase Manhattan, Citibank, Credit Suisse, Deutsche Bank, HSBC, J.P. Morgan, Société Générale and UBS. Since then, Chase and Morgan became J. P. Morgan Chase and Goldman Sachs joined.

Collectively, the banks moved beyond standard KYC practices, putting in place a much stricter, more precise level of client disclosure. They agreed: to collect as much information as possible about the people whose money they were handling, and about the source of that money; to put curbs on accepting business from politically exposed persons; to define and monitor high risk category clients, such as senior corporate executives; and to heighten vigilance of money coming from certain jurisdictions where laundering controls were inadequate. Although, if inadequate really means inadequate, they should be eliminating their businesses in Africa, South and Central America, Eastern Europe, a good chunk of Asia, and more than a few of countries in Europe.

Still, they went as far as they did, which is much further than anyone had gone before.

Hand in hand with the watchdog group Transparency International, the Wolfsberg Principles set out to prevent the use for criminal purposes of any subscribing bank's world-wide operations. It's strictly voluntary, so there is no oversight and there are no obligations besides a commitment to try to do better than they have in the past. But the concept is sound. And the next step might be to make the Wolfsberg Principles 'seal of approval' the most exclusive club in banking. The day that other banks are banging down the doors to get in, the day when any bank not in the club is automatically suspect, the day when the 11 toss out one of their own for not trying hard enough – that's the day Wolfsberg will really mean something.

Jonathan Winer, now in private law practice, has spoken about this very road since leaving his post at the State Department. He's observed that too many international financial institutions have weathered scandals that would otherwise have brought down a government. In some cases, where corruption and money laundering scandals have brought down a head of state – witness Marcos, Mobuto and even Richard Nixon – the banks at the heart of them go merrily along. The reason is, because the world runs on profit. If a financial institution is profitable enough, shareholders will remain tame enough to save the neck of the man at the top. How else can anyone explain, for example, shareholders not screaming for blood when someone at the Bank of New York gets a bonus while the ink is still wet on the worst scandal in the bank's history?

In Winer's view of the world, a compliance officer is a bottom line debit – the cost of doing business – and a trader is a bottom line credit because that's where the profits are generated. 'Under the circumstances, it is easy to understand why, at any given bank on any given day, those creating a profit-making scheme involving an offshore trust in Belize, that in turn owns a Turks and Caicos company, tend to win battles with those asking questions about the venture.'

To change that might be to change a lot. His suggestion is the creation of, not another blacklist, but a white list of financial institutions with real incentives to stay on it. And there is plenty of anecdotal evidence to suggest that a totally transparent, totally open, totally dirty-money-free-zone that bears a real seal of approval can be more profitable than the alternative.

Consider the concept of reputation by association and the case of Guernsey. When that island made its deliberate decision to help foreign law enforcement find dirty money on the island, much of the dirty money that was there went elsewhere. Guernsey now believes that people doing business on the island can boast, we're clean otherwise we wouldn't be here. Any hiccup could, and should, prove to be a very expensive stumble. So a white list, which would promote reputation by association, has enormous merit.

The framework for it might lie in a permanent Wolfsberg secretariat with the power to decide who's on-side. The stricter the admission policy, the more valuable the membership. Staying on-side should be a ticket to make money. That way, getting thrown out becomes a solar-plexus blow to the bottom line. If the Wolfsberg Group can bottle real incentives to do the right thing, if reputational risk can be tied directly to profits, then the 11 banks that came up with Wolfsberg will have done the world a greater service than they ever envisioned.

Winer even suggests a way to jump start a white list. He says that a select group of organizations – start with the United Nations, the World Bank, the International Monetary Fund and add a few hundred big time NGOs – could pledge to keep their money only in white list financial institutions. If those white list financial institutions then had to pass an independently administered 'Wolfsberg' test every year – at the risk of losing their status and therefore losing the business of these organizations – at that point, he says, things would change very quickly.

'Financial transparency,' Winer continues, 'is not a criterion for the selection of one financial institution over another. An international bank involved in money-laundering scandals or terrorist finance has about the same chance of obtaining a lucrative source of government resources as does an international bank that has imposed the highest standards of transparency and anti-money laundering policies. No wonder the compliance officer is seen as a profit drain.'

Change that, and it doesn't matter what kind of window dressing some offshore jurisdiction puts up because now you've changed the shape of the world. If the threat of losing white list status comes down to a business in some two-bit laundromat, those folks on the white list will be on the first flight out of town.

Change is inevitable.

At the beginning of 1999, a quiet, almost unnoticed but nevertheless watershed moment happened in England. A man named Ussama El-Kurd was sent to prison for 14 years.

The story made the papers, but only just, and then it was about how this man who'd treated his staff so abominably had laundered £70 million through his Notting Hill bureau de change and, at least for a moment or two, was labelled Europe's biggest money launderer.

Whether or not he was Europe's biggest money launderer is immaterial. Nor is there anything particularly remarkable about the way this 50-year-old man laundered money over a relatively short period of time, from April 1994 to November 1996. What makes him notable is that he was the first person in Britain ever to be sent down for 'outsourced money laundering'.

Until El-Kurd, the only people who got done for money laundering

were somehow involved with a drug or terrorist offence. El-Kurd was
a guy who simply washed dirty money. He had nothing to do with
the underlying offence that made the proceeds dirty.

'That case helped to reshape the way that the current money laundering laws are interpreted,' explains Detective Superintendent Terry
Burke of the National Crime Squad's money laundering unit. 'Before
El-Kurd, through the mid-1980s and into the 1990s, if we knew you
were a money launderer with no source of legitimate income, we
couldn't do anything unless we could prove that this money came
from that pile of drugs. After El-Kurd, if the money is dirty, that's
enough, we don't have to prove the crime behind it.'

Which, he notes, was a sea change in the way the British police
can now deal with the financial aspects of crime. 'In more than 20
years of working money laundering cases, this is the first time when
we have what we need to really be effective.'

Burke, one of the most knowledgeable and experienced police officers in Europe on the subject of money laundering, has been in the
field since long before it became chic.

'Back in the early 1980s we couldn't go after the money because
there were no money laundering laws. The courts wouldn't let us do
it. In the mid-1980s we got a law that required us to tie the money
to drugs or terror. That was better than nothing and a bunch of us got
stuck into some good investigations. But the bar and judiciary didn't
understand the new laws. We got some bad decisions and money laundering never became as effective here as it should have been.'

By the mid-1990s some of those prosecutors were on the bench,
younger prosecutors were being better trained and better decisions
started coming down. In 2003, the UK finally had a workable Proceeds
of Crime Act, which means the police can go after dirty money, prosecute money laundering offences effectively and seize dirty money to
deprive villains of the fruits of their crimes. But to get to this point,
a lot of work needed to be done behind the scenes. It began with a
handful of people who understood money laundering. Three in particular stand out. Peter Vallance at the Home Office, Paul Evans at HM
Customs and Burke. He modestly insists that it would have happened
anyway, because its time had come, but modesty aside, it wouldn't
have happened as quickly or as well had those three not been in a
position to help it happen.

In that sense, the tall, powerful Burke has been in the right place
at the right time for much of his career. He was one of the first offi-

cers to jump on the money laundering bandwagon, having worked on the UK's first major money laundering case. Dubbed 'Operation Cougar', it was the hunt for the money from the Brink's Mat robbery in 1983. His job was to deal with the principal laundrymen in the case – possibly one of the best money launderers of his era – Shaun Murphy.

An Irish-born accountant, Murphy sat in a shack on a beach in the Caribbean, forming companies for his clients in the BVI, using those companies to open accounts at banks on the Isle of Man, forming more companies in Antigua to open more accounts at Swiss banks in Panama. He then wired the money out of Man, through Panama and into an account at a UK bank in the BVI which he opened in the name of a Bahamian shell.

It was as good a method as any, except that after a while he got bored with it and hung a huge map of the world in his office so that he could make money trails even more difficult to follow by discovering all sorts of strange places. Part of the Murphy legend has it that for one client he registered 40 shells and opened 90 different bank accounts in 40 different places around the world. That client later dropped a Samsonite suitcase to him from a passing airplane, with $2.3 million stuffed inside.

'Some of the same systems that Shaun employed are still being done today,' Burke confirms. 'Like back-to-back loans. It's funny, but young officers look at something today and say, this is a new method, and I tell them, Shaun Murphy was doing that. Unfortunately, it makes me realize that we haven't passed along our knowledge as well as we should have.'

When he and a few of the other pioneers in the field – cops like Graham Saltmarsh, Charlie Hill, Tim Wren and Rowan Bosworth-Davies – tried to impart the knowledge they were gaining about money laundering, senior managers in law enforcement didn't believe this was a way forward in fighting crime. They didn't realize that if you want to dismantle an organized crime group, you can pick it apart at the seams by getting at the money and taking it away.

'In the old days,' Burke goes on, 'the only way you got evidence out of banks was if you knew someone there. Today, the financial aspect becomes a key element of every operational strategy. Whatever else we do, it's also about the money and now, how we take that money away.'

After a stint on the money laundering desk at the National Criminal

Intelligence Service, Burke was seconded for a few years to Miami. There, along with his partner, Met detective Dick Marston, they joined forces with FBI special agent Ross Gaffney to form the WCCIT – the white-collar Criminal Investigation Team – a group specifically aimed at offshore money laundering.

This was 1993, the heyday of Medellin and Cali. Drug money was raging through the islands and some people there were serious about trying to clean it up. Burke put a business plan and budget together and got the Foreign Office to help fund it. But WCCIT ran headfirst into the bureaucracy that is the FBI.

Burke shrugs. 'They were interested in doing FBI cases that affected the islands. We wanted to put a British contingent in to work with the islands to get the information out and help the prosecution.'

It wasn't exactly oil and water because they managed to get a lot done, and there are still people in the islands who are totally supportive of WCCIT. But on more than one occasion, the Bureau dug in its corporate heels and good cases that might have come out of WCCIT, didn't. The Caymans, for example, got very frustrated. They were happy to have British officers help them in an investigation, but they insisted that any evidence uncovered had to remain in the Caymans until the proper requests came through proper channels to share it. Burke and Marston were free to follow any leads off the island but the Caymanians didn't want FBI agents dictating what should happen with evidence.

Those years running around the islands gave him a wealth of experience with offshore money laundering. Experience, he feels, that is paying off handsomely now. 'Law enforcement must be allowed to act on information when there are legitimate reasons to do so. As long as these places have the legislation to allow that, then they should be supported. However, if they don't put the legislation in place, or they don't enforce the legislation, or they put hurdles in the way, then the world community needs to isolate them. You can do that in a lot of ways. You can isolate them by saying no dollar deals, no sterling deals. But they have to understand that they have to co-operate and, I believe, that's how strong you need to be.'

At the same time, he openly acknowledges that London is an offshore centre for other countries. 'Yes. And there is loads of criminal money sitting in the City of London. What makes the country workable, though, is that once you know the criminal money is here, a process exists to go after it.'

At the National Crime Squad, Burke set up a unit specifically designed to deal with money laundering on a national basis. It's the first of it's kind in the country. The team is 200 strong, around 70 per cent of the members being non-police. There are people from the financial industry, accountants, analysts and former financial investigators who add a huge amount of experience and energy to the process. He's also put into place joint working groups with Customs and Immigration, so that the unit can provide financial investigative support for them.

Hopefully, he says, the unit can become the model for all financial investigations in the future and, eventually, might just be one of the foundations for the British version of the FBI. 'I am convinced that we will eventually see a national investigating agency in Britain to deal with the majority of major crime. Perhaps it will be formed by uniting the investigative arms of Customs and the National Crime Squad. That's one way of going about it. Maybe it will take five years, maybe it will take 10 years, but it will happen. It's got to come.'

Any effective international strategy to defeat organized crime – and also to limit terrorist activities – must include money.

Willie Sutton robbed banks because, as he often said, 'that's where the money is.' It's the same reason why the Colombian cartels deal drugs, Nigerian criminal enterprises run 419s, Triad societies loan-shark, the LCN does gas tax scams and the Russian Maffiya extorts. Product doesn't matter. Cocaine, fissile materials, tobacco, people smuggling – bad guys go where the money is.

So, too, must the good guys.

One estimate has it that 1.5 million Ecstasy tablets are dropped in Britain every weekend. Adults can reason with teenagers until they're blue in the face, and the Ecstasy death of a teenager every six to eight weeks – a horrifyingly regular event – are still not enough to make kids understand that club drugs are a gamble with a lethal downside. At the same time, the country can patrol its borders and turn itself into a fortress, but drugs will get in.

It's when you factor money into the problem that the picture changes. Even at a cut-rate £10 a pill, that's £15 million a weekend, £60 million a month, £720 million a year. That Ecstasy is generating a mountain of cash and it has to go somewhere. At some point, while being funnelled into the banking system, spun around the world, moved through shells and secret bank accounts, and brought out the other end, it's under the control of a lawyer, a banker, an accountant, a company formation agent, a broker, someone. If you can locate that someone, then interrupt the cash flow and reinvestment that this money represents, the business will go bust.

Bankrupt the business and there is no product being made or sold.

It really isn't any more complicated than that.

The illicit drug business is a business. Global terrorism is a business. The product may be different, but they both depend on cash flow and reinvestment. Like all multinational enterprises, transnational organized crime and global terrorism need the legitimate financial world. In this respect, criminals operate exactly like multinational corporations. They use the same global financial infrastructure to handle their corporate affairs.

At the height of its power, the Cali cartel had annual profits of close to $7 billion – more than three times those of General Motors – and was organized exactly along the same lines. As a business, it could not possibly have survived without the direct help of lawyers, bankers, accountants, company formation agents, brokers, foreign governments and others who, for a fee, echoed the philosophy of the Hong Kong banker when he proclaimed, 'It's not our business to inquire into our client's morals.'

Because criminals shifting drugs hire professionals to handle money, and because professionals handling money never have to touch drugs, those professionals – the laundrymen – live comfortably in a world of 'plausible deniability'. Lawyers, bankers, accountants, company formation agents and brokers may or may not know the origins of the money they're handling, but most of them know they don't want to know. The excuse goes, 'My client is an attorney and I don't need to risk losing my fee by probing too deeply about his client.'

That is precisely what must change.

If politicians are serious about going after the bad guys, then lawmakers need to look no further than the laundrymen. Criminals may deliberately put themselves beyond jurisdiction but their money is local and the laundrymen are local, too. Without cashflow and investment, no business can survive. So the aim must be to cut into the cash flow and reinvestment to bankrupt these criminal businesses.

Again, no business, no product.

It is a fact of life that there will always be someone willing to do the wash. Much like sticking your finger into a balloon, the air doesn't come out of it, you simply displace it. Unfortunately for Europe, as America cracked down on money laundering, the criminals turned to softer jurisdictions. And the European Union is one of the softest. A collection of 15 borderless countries – with more countries to come – not one of them has a truly effective money laundering law. All of them depend on suspicious cash reporting at a time when cash is not the problem, leaving the laundrymen themselves to decide what suspicious means.

The new Proceeds of Crime Act in the UK doesn't prevent money laundering, it's a tool designed to prosecute money laundering. Yet none of the other countries in Europe have anything even half as good. Instead, Europe combines inefficient laws with a lack of commitment in many countries to enforce the law. The double-edged sword of intra-European free trade means that if it's great for business, it's great for illicit business, too.

Now add into the mix a single currency that comes in very large denominations.

Before the EU invented the euro, it was impossible to stash $1 million in an attaché case. Today, with 500-euro notes, it is possible. Equally unfortunate, the euro furnishes for free a service that drug traffickers used to pay for. The euro automatically separates the money from the crime, which is one of the most necessary stages in any money laundering cycle.

Pre-euro, if you smuggled coke into Spain and sold it on the streets of Madrid, you wound up with a pile of pesetas. You needed to reduce the bulk – high volume sales with small value pesetas created too much paper – and to get out of pesetas because Spanish cash was a sure indication that you'd sold drugs in Spain. So you pre-washed, turning pesetas into deutchsmarks and then washed, turning deutchsmarks into dollars. At every step you had to pay a commission. But at least you wound up with dollars going into your offshore accounts.

Along came the euro and while dollars are still easy, euros are almost as easy. Now you sell your coke in Madrid and your stash of euros gives no indication of where you committed your crime. That means there's no reason to pre-wash. In fact, you might not even need to wash, at all. If your laundering strategy includes businesses or real estate within the euro-zone, you're home free. Euros are also welcome in every jurisdiction doing business in Europe, many of which are happy to take cash. Try Eastern Europe. Try the Baltic states. Try the Middle East and the Gulf states.

If Walt Disney had designed 'Moneylaundryland', it would look exactly like Europe.

But tell that to Europe's politicians and the first thing they'll tell you is how wonderful the money laundering legislation is throughout Europe.

What they don't want to understand is that legislation which pretends to make specific kinds of financial transactions more transparent, doesn't work.

If tomorrow, magic wand in hand, total and absolute transparency was imposed in, say, Switzerland and Liechtenstein, the only tangible result would be unemployment in Switzerland and Liechtenstein, because the money would instantly re-locate to a more user-friendly jurisdiction.

Somewhere, there will always be an aspiring Antigua.

EPILOGUE

Worse is yet to come.

Cuba is one heart attack away from throwing the offshore world into total Pandemonium.

While the 40-plus years of the American embargo have prevented American businesses from developing interests in Cuba, both the Brits and the Canadians have been busy establishing a foothold there. Before Fidel's body is even slightly cold, British and Canadian open-market-capitalists will flood the island with holiday resorts and casinos.

America's whore house will rise gleamingly from the ashes.

At the same time, Cuba's long-time trading partners – the Russians – are poised to claim their rights to do business there. Russian organized crime has had a presence in Cuba since the demise of the Soviet Union. Their interests include gambling, drugs and prostitution. With vast amounts of dirty money to invest, the Russians are preparing to solidify their base, from which they can safely operate throughout the Caribbean.

Once that happens, Cuban exiles and Russian organized criminals living in Miami – who are firmly tied into Florida's Colombian and traditional Italian organized criminal groups – will build a crime-bridge linking Havana with south Florida.

Eager to respond to demand, casinos, offshore banking, shell companies and money laundering will flourish, marking Cuba's successful return to it's crime capital roots. But this replay – in digital colour and Dolby Surround Sound – of the 'wild west' that Meyer Lansky and Lucky Luciano built before Castro, will be at the expense of the other islands.

Cuban prosperity will sound a death knoll to casinos, offshore banking, shell companies and money laundering throughout much of the rest of the Caribbean. That is, unless those other islands are willing to compete.

With survival is at stake, they will compete.

They will offer better facilities to criminals looking to launder money; create new markets with designer drugs; put out the welcome mat for tomorrow's Enrons and Halliburtons and Carlyle Groups;

establish better, more efficient transhipment routes for cocaine and heroin; become the world's major transhipment point for the global trade in illegal aliens; offer safe haven to anyone's money, while all the time 'plausibly denying' that it has come from, or is destined for, a terrorist cell.

Ironically, those banks and financial institutions that are lining up impatiently to march into Cuba, will flourish off the back of all this criminality.

But then, the United States, Great Britain and Canada have – either deliberately, short-sightedly or simply through greed – spent years putting all the pieces in place for exactly this to happen.

JR/ London

GLOSSARY

back-to-back loans	loans that are guaranteed with money hidden, usually offshore
BCCI	Bank of Commerce and
bearer share	an anonymous company owned by whoever happens to have physical possession of the share certificate
BMPE	Black Market Peso Exchange
BoE	Bank of England
BoNY	Bank of New York
BSA	Bank Secrecy Act
CD	Certificate of Deposit
CFATF	Caribbean Financial Action Task Force
CI	Confidential Informant
CSE	Communications Security Establishment
CSIS	Canadian Security Intelligence Service
CTR	Cash Transaction Report
DEA	Drug Enforcement Administration (US)
EC	European Community
ECHELON	US organized spy system operated by the National Security Agency in conjunction with Canada, the UK, Australia and New Zealand
FATF	Financial Action Task Force
FinCen	Financial Crimes Enforcement Network (US)
FinTRAC	Financial Transactions and Reports Analysis Centre (Can.)
FISAC	Financial Investigation and Special Access Centre (GB)
FIU	Financial Intelligence Unit
FRU	Financial Reporting Unit
FSA	Fnancial Services Authority
FSF	Financial Stability Forum
FTC	Federal Trade Commission
G8	The eight industrial nations grouped together under the auspices of the OECD
GCHQ	Government Communications Head Quarters (UK)
Hawallah	Traditional Third World underground paperless banking system

IBC	International Business Corporation (shell company)
IFO	Independent Foreign Owner
IPB	International Private Banking
IRS	Internal Revenue Service
KLA	Kosovo Liberation Army
KYC	Know Your Customer
LCN	La Cosa Nostra
MCCA	Money Laundering Control Act
MROS	Money Laundering Reporting Office (Switz.)
NASD	National Association of Securities Dealers
NCIS	National Criminal Intelligence Service (GB)
NORAID	IRA-backed charity
NSC	National Security Council (US)
NTFIU	National Terrorist Financial Investigation Unit (GB)
OCC	Office of the Comptroller of the Currency
OECD	Organization for Economic Cooperation and Development
PTA	Pass-Through Account
Public Citizen	Washington based government watchdog
PWC	PriceWaterhouseCooper
SAR	Suspicious Activity Report
SBA	Swiss Bankers Association
SEC	Securities Exchange Commission
SHARE	Shareholders Association of Canada
shell bank	A company licensed to operate as a bank without having a physical presence anywhere
Smurf	Named for the cartoon characters, these are armies of workers who deposit small amounts of cash in banks, as part of the money laundering process
SO-12	Special Operations – Intelligence (UK)

ACKNOWLEDGEMENTS

There are many people to whom I owe a sincere debt of gratitude for their time, insights, inspiration, help and encouragement.

In the United States, I wish to thank: Judy Fitzgerald and Dave De Young at the National Insurance Crime Bureau; plus Betty Cordial, and James Gordon of Maryland First; Jim Vaules and Don Wadsworth of the National Fraud Center; Les Joseph, Ted Greenberg and Stephen Flamer at the Department of Justice in Washington DC; special agents Bill Waldie, Tom Fuentes, Ross Gaffney and Drick Crawford at the Federal Bureau of Investigation; special agents Joe Webber, John College and Mickey Pledger at US Customs; Wayne Carlin, Stephen Cutler and Alex Vasilescu at the Securities and Exchange Commission; attorney Jonathan Winer; from various US Attorney's Offices, Donna Gallucio, John Carney, Marvin Smilon, Herbert Hadad, Steve Cole, Thom Mrozek and Marjorie Selige; Rick Bowdren of the United States Postal Inspection Service; special agent Joe Kilmer of the Drug Enforcement Administration; former law officers Philip Deming, Joe Occhipinti and Lenny Lemer; professors Holger Henke, Howard M. Wachtel and Mike McIntyre; Dan Glazer at the US Department of the Treasury; Steve Kroll at the US Senate; Jody Myers at the National Security Council; Elise Bean and Robert Roach at the United States Senate's Committee on Governmental Affairs, Permanent Sub-committee on Investigations; David Marchant at Offshore Alert; Joan Wright in Chicago; Howard Arvey in California; Warren Tyron and Gerry Cashin in the office of Representative Spencer Bachus, United States House of Representatives; the Chicago Crime Commission; historical societies and museum resources in Miami, Chicago, Las Vegas and Cuba; plus various friends and acquaintances.

In Europe, may I thank: Metropolitan Police detectives James Perry and Steve Ratcliffe; former Met detectives Gordon Hutchins, Martin Wood and Neil Jeans; Henk van Zwam of the Dutch police; Stan Morris at Interpol; Denis Maxwell, on the Isle of Man; Doug Reeman at the City of London Police; Dave Monk at the Bank of New York; Mark Steels at the National Criminal Intelligence Service; Geoffrey Rowland, Steve Butterworth and Peter Neville in Guernsey;

Dave Minty and David Hall in Jersey; Gerhard Muller of the German National Police; plus various friends and acquaintances.

In Canada, a very sincerely thank you to the following law enforcement officers, current and retired: John Unger, Brad Demarais and Tom Hansen in British Columbia; Doug Coates, Brian Guinard, Bill Henderson, Don Panchuk, Kevin Burk, Dave Truax, Mark Sheffer, Dave Taylor, Tony Warr, Garry Clement and Garry Nichols in Ontario; John Mair and Pierre Camire in Quebec; plus various friends and acquaintances.

And in the Caribbean, my many thanks to: David Thursfield, Commissioner of the Royal Cayman Islands Police; Brian Gibbs, Marshall Langer, Marcus A. Wide, Sir Ronald Sanders, Michael Alberga, Lauriston Wilson, Michael Creft, plus various friends and acquaintances.

Several people contributed information, helped make contacts and provided leads, but did not wish their names to be known or the extent of their participation to be mentioned. I trust they know that I am grateful.

May I also say a very special thank you, for all sorts of reasons, to a bunch of people I am very proud to call my pals: John Moscow and Gilda Mariani at the New York District Attorney's Office; the best press officer on the planet, Dean Boyd at US Customs; Ron Rose; John Forbes; Bob Levinson; Joe Petro; Jack Blum; Tim Baldwin; Terry Burke; Rod Carscallen and the inimitable Ben Soave.

Of course, my enormous gratitude also goes to Carol O'Brien and Dan Hind at Constable & Robinson Ltd; Jonathan Webb at McClelland and Stewart; my Canadian agent Linda McKnight; my London agents Eddie and June Bell, Pat Lomax and Paul Moreton; and, *comme d'habitude*, La Benayoun.

SELECTED BIBLIOGRAPHY

BOOKS

ADAMS J: *The Financing of Terror*; New English Library, London, 1986

ADAMS, JAMES RING AND FRANTZ, DOUGLAS: *A Full Service Bank – How BCCI Stole Billions Around the World*; Pocket Books, New York, 1992

ALEXANDER, SHANA: *The Pizza Connection*; Weidenfeld, New York, 1988

ALLSOP, KENNETH: *The Bootleggers*; Hutchinson, London, 1961

ANDERSON, ANNELISE GRAEBNER: *The Business of Organized Crime*; Hoover Institution Press, Stanford, 1979

ABADINSKY, HOWARD: *Organized Crime*; Nelson Hall Chicago, 1990

ABADINSKY, HOWARD: *The Mafia in America – An Oral History*; Praegar, New York, 1987

ALBANESE, JAY: *Organized Crime in America*; Anderson Publishing, Cincinnati, 1996

ANASTASIA, GEORGE: *The Goodfella Tapes*; Avon Books, New York, 1998

APPLETON, PETER and CLARK, DOUG: *Billion $$$ High – The Drug Invasion of Canada*; McGraw-Hill Ryerson, Montreal, 1990

BALBONI, ALAN: *Beyond the Mafia – Italian Americans and the Development of Las Vegas*; University of Nevada Press, Reno, 1996

BALSAMO, WILLIAM and CARPOZI, GEORGE: *Crime Incorporated, or Under the Clock – The Inside Story of the Mafia's First Hundred Years*; New Horizon Press, New Jersey, 1991

BAUM, DAN: *Smoke and Mirrors – The War on Drugs and the Politics of Failure*; Little Brown, Boston, 1996

BEARE, MARGARET E.: *Criminal Conspiracies – Organized Crime in Canada*; Nelson, Scarborough, 1996

BESCHLOSS, MICHAEL: *Kennedy Versus Khrushchev – The Crisis Years 1960–1963*; HarperCollins, New York, 1991

BLOCK, ALAN: *Masters of Paradise;* Transaction Publishers, New Jersey, 1991

BLUM, HOWARD: *Gangland – How the FBI Broke the Mob*; Simon and Schuster, New York, 1993

BLUMENTHAL, RALPH: *Last Days of the Sicilians – At War With the Mafia,The FBI Assault on the Pizza Connection*; Times Books, New York, 1988

BONANNO, JOSEPH and LALLI, SERGIO: *A Man of Honor*; Simon and Schuster, New York, 1983

BONAVOLONTA, JULES and DUFFY, BRIAN: *The Good Guys*; Pocket Books, New York, 1996

BRASHLER, WILLIAM: *The Don – The Life and Death of Sam Giancana*; Harper and Row, New York, 1977

CAMPBELL, DUNCAN: *That was Business, This is Personal*; Secker and Warburg, London, 1990

CARRIGAN, D. OWEN: *Crime and Punishment in Canada – A History*; McLelland and Stewart, Toronto, 1991

CHARBONNEAU, JEAN-PIERRE: *The Canadian Connection*; Optimum, Ottawa, 1976

CLARK, T. and TIGUE, J. J.: *Dirty Money*; Millington Books, London, 1975

CLIFFORD, CLARK: *Counsel to the President*; Random House, New York, 1991

CLUTTERBUCK, R.: *Terrorism, Drugs and Crime in Europe after 1992*; Routledge and Kegan Paul, London, 1990

COLODNY, LEN and GETTLIN, ROBERT: *Silent Coup – The Removal of Richard Nixon*; Gollancz, London, 1991

CUMMINGS, JOHN, and VOLKMAN, ERNEST: *Goombata*; Little Brown, Boston, 1990

DAVIS, JOHN H.: *Mafia Dynasty – The Rise and Fall of the Gambino Crime Family*; HarperCollins, New York, 1993

DEAN, JOHN: *Blind Ambition*; Simon and Schuster, New York, 1976.

DE GRAZIA, JESSICA: *DEA – The War Against Drugs*; BBC Books, London, 1991

DENTON, SALLY and MORRIS, ROGER: *The Money and the Power – The Making of Las Vegas and its Hold on America*; Vintage Books, New York, 2002

DINGES, JOHN: *Our Man in Panama*; Random House, New York, 1990

EDDY, PAUL: *The Cocaine Wars*; Century Hutchinson, London, 1988

EISENBERG DENNIS, DAN URI and LANDAU ELI: *Meyer Lansky – Mogul of the Mob*; Paddington Press, New York, 1979

FERER, TOM, ed: *Transnational Crime in the Americas*; Routledge, New York, 1999

FIORENTINI, G. and PELTZMAN S.: *The Economics of Organized Crime*; Cambridge University Press, Cambridge, 1995

FOGEL, JEAN-FRANÇOIS: *Le Testament De Pablo Escobar*; Grasset, Paris, 1994

FOX, STEPHEN R: *Blood and Power – Organized Crime in Twentieth Century America*; Morrow, New York, 1989

FRIMAN, H. RICHARD: *Narco Diplomacy – Exporting the US War on Drugs*; Cornell University Press, Ithaca, 1996

FAITH, NICHOLAS: *Safety in Numbers – The Mysterious World of Swiss Banking*; Hamish Hamilton, London, 1984

FRANCES, DIANE: *Contrepreneurs*; Macmillan, Toronto, 1988

FRANKLIN, R.: *Profits of Deceit*; Heinemann, London, 1990

FREEMANTLE, BRIAN: *The Fix*; Michael Joseph, London, 1985

GAGE, NICHOLAS: *Mafia, USA*; Playboy Press, Chicago, 1972

GAMBETTA, DIEGO: *The Sicilian Mafia – The Business of Private Protection*; Harvard University Press, Cambridge, 1993

GARDNER, PAUL: *The Drug Smugglers*; Robert Hale, London, 1989

GARRISON, JIM: *A Heritage of Stone*; Putnam's Sons, New York, 1970

GARRISON, JIM: *On the Trail of the Assassins*; Penguin, London, 1992

GATELY, WILLIAM and FERNANDEZ, YVETTE: *Dead Ringer – An Insider's Account of the Mob's Colombian Connection*; DI Fine, New York, 1994

GENTRY, CURT: *J. Edgar Hoover – The Man and The Secrets*; New American Library, New York, 1992

GIANCANA, SAM and GIANCANA, CHUCK: *Double Cross*; Warner Books, New York, 1992

GOLDFARB, RONALD L.: *Perfect Villains, Imperfect Heroes – Robert F. Kennedy's War Against Organized Crime*; Random House, New York, 1995

GOODE, JAMES: *Wiretap – Listening in on America's Mafia*; Simon and Schuster, New York, 1988

GOSCH, M.A.: *Last Testament of Lucky Luciano*; Little Brown, Boston, 1975

GUGLIOTTA, GUY and LEEN, JEFF: *Kings of Cocaine*; Simon and Schuster, New York, 1989

GUNST, LAURIE: *Born Fi' Dead – A Journey Through the Jamaican Posse Underworld*; H. Holt, New York 1995

HESS, HENNER: *Mafia and Mafiosi*; Saxon Hall, New York, 1973

HOGG, ANDREW; MCDOUGAL, JIM and MORGAN, ROBIN: *Bullion*; Penguin Books, London, 1988

IANNI, FRANCIS and REUSS-IANNI, ELIZABETH: *The Crime Society*; New American Library, New York, 1976

JENNINGS, ANDREW; LASHMAR, PAUL and SIMSON, VYV: *Scotland Yard's Cocaine Connection*; Cape, London, 1990.

JACOBS, JAMES B: *Busting the Mob*; New York University Press, New York, 1994

JOHNSON, VASSEL: *As I See It*; The Book Guild, Sussex, England, 2001

KARCHMER, CLIFF: *Illegal Money Laundering – A Strategy and Resource Guide for Law Enforcement Agencies*; Police Executive Resources, Washington DC, 1988

KATCHER, LEO: *The Big Bankroll*; Harper and Row, New York, 1959

KEFAUVER, ESTES and UNITED STATES SENATE: *Crime in America – Special Committee to Investigate Organized Crime in Interstate Commerce*; Doubleday and Co, Garden City, 1951

KELLY, ROBERT J.: *Handbook of Organized Crime in the United States*; Greenwood Press, Westport, 1994

KEMPE, FREDERICK: *Divorcing the Dictator – America's Bungled Affair with Noriega*; Putnam, New York, 1990

KENNEY, DENNIS JAY and FINCKENAUER, JAMES: *Organized Crime in America*; Wadsworth Publishing, California, 1995

KERRY, JOHN: *A New Kind of War – National Security and the Globalization of Crime*; Simon and Schuster, New York, 1997

KESSLER, RONALD: *The FBI*; Pocket Books, New York, 1993

KESSLER, RONALD: *The Richest Man In The World – The Story of Adnan Khashoggi*; Warner Books, New York, 1986

KLEINKNECHT, WILLIAM: *The New Ethnic Mobs – The Changing Face of Organized Crime in America*; Free Press, New York, 1996

KOBLER, JOHN: *Capone*; Michael Joseph, London, 1972

KOCHAN, NICK WITH WHITTINGTON, BOB and POTTS, MARK: *Dirty Money – The Inside Story of the World's Sleaziest Bank*; National Press Books, Washington DC, 1992

KOSTER, R.M. AND BORBON, G.S.: *In the Time of the Tyrants*; Secker and Warburg, London, 1990

KWITNEY, JONATHAN: *The Crimes of Patriots*; Touchstone, New York, 1987

KWITNEY, JONATHAN: *The Fountain Pen Conspiracy*; Knopf, New York, 1973

LACEY, ROBERT: *Little Man – Meyer Lansky and the Gangster Life*; Little Brown, Boston, 1991

LALLEMAND, ALAIN: *L'Organizatsiya – La Mafia Russe à L'Assaut Du Monde*; Calmann-Lévy, Paris, 1996

LAMOTHE, LEE and NICASO, ANTONIO: *Global Mafia – The New World Order of Organized Crime*; MacMillan, Toronto, 1994

LANCE, BURT: *The Truth of the Matter*; Summit, New York, 1991

LANE, MARK: *Plausible Denial*; Plexus, London, 1992

LAVIGNE, YVES: *Good Guy, Bad Guy – Drugs and the Changing Face of Organized Crime*; Random House, Toronto, 1991

LERNOUX, PENNY: *In Banks We Trust*; Anchor Press, New York, 1984

LOFTUS, JOHN and MCINTYRE, EMILY: *Valhallas Wake*; Atlantic Monthly Press, New York, 1989

LYMAN, MICHAEL D. and POTTER, GARY W.: *Organized Crime*; Prentice Hall, New Jersey, 1997

LYMAN, MICHAEL: *Gangland – Drug Trafficking by Organized Criminals*; Charles Thomas, Illinois, 1989

MAAS, PETER: *The Valachi Papers*; Putnam, New York, 1968

MACDONALD, SCOTT: *Dancing on a Volcano – The Latin American Drug Trade*; Praeger, New York, 1988

MCALARY, MARK: *Crack War*; Robinson Publishing, London, 1990.

MCCARL, HENRY N.: *Economic Impact of the Underground Economy – A Bibliography on Money Laundering and Other Aspects of Off-the-Record Economic Transactions*; Vance Bibliographies, Monticello, Illinois, 1989

MARCHETTI, VICTOR and MARKS, JOHN D.: *The CIA and the Cult of Intelligence*; Dell, New York, 1980

MARTIN, JOHN M. and ROMANO, ANNE T.: *Multinational Crime – Terrorism, Espionage, Drug and Arms Trafficking*; Sage, California, 1992

MILGATE, BRIAN: *The Cochin Connection*; Chatto and Windus, London, 1987

MILLS, JAMES: *The Underground Empire*; Doubleday, Garden City, NY, 1986

MOKHIBER, RUSSELL AND WEISSMAN, ROBERT: *Corporate Preditors*; Common Courage Press, Maine, 1999

MUSTAIN, GENE and CAPECI, JERRY: *Mob Star – The Story of John Gotti, the Most Powerful Man in America*; Penguin, New York, 1989

NADELMANN, ETHAN: *Cops Across Borders – The Internationalization of US*

Criminal Law Enforcement; Pennsylvania State University Press, University Park, 1993

NASH, JAY ROBERT: *World Encyclopedia of Organized Crime*; De Capo Press, New York, 1993

NASH, JAY ROBERT: *Hustlers and Con Men*; Evans, New York, 1976

NAYLOR, R.T.: *Bankers, Bagmen and Bandits*; Black Rose, New York, 1990

NAYLOR, TOM: *Hot Money and the Politics of Debt*; Unwin, London, 1987

NICASO, ANTONIO and LAMOTHE, LEE: *Global Mafia – The New World Order of Organized Crime*; Macmillan Canada, Toronto, 1995

O'BRIEN, JOSEPH and KURINS, ANDRIS: *Boss of Bosses*; Simon and Schuster, New York, 1991

O'KANE, JAMES M.: *The Crooked Ladder – Gangsters, Ethnicity, and the American Dream*; Transaction Books, New Jersey, 1992

O'NEILL, GERARD and LEHR, DICK: *The Underboss – The Rise and Fall of a Mafia Family*; St Martin's Press, New York 1989

PADILLA, FELIX M.: *The Gang As an American Enterprise*; Rutgers University Press, New Jersey, 1992

PETERSON, VIRGIL W.: *The Mob*; Green Hill Publishers, Illinois, 1983

PETRAKIS, GREGORY J.: *The New Face of Organized Crime*; Kendall/Hunt Publishing, Iowa, 1992

PILEGGI, NICHOLAS: *Wise Guy – Life in a Mafia Family*, Pocket Books, New York, 1985

POSSAMAI, MARIO: *Money on the Run*; Viking, Toronto, 1992

PERISCO, JOSEPH: *Casey*; Penguin, New York, 1990

POWERS, THOMAS: *The Man Who Kept the Secrets – Richard Helms and the CIA*; Pocket Books, New York, 1981

RAUFER, XAVIER: *Les Superpuissances Du Crime*; Plon, Paris, 1993

ROBINSON, JEFFREY: *Minus Millionaires*; Grafton, London, 1988

ROBINSON, JEFFREY: *The Laundrymen*; Simon and Schuster, London, 1998

ROBINSON, JEFFREY: *The Merger – How Organized Crime is Taking Over The World*; Simon and Schuster, London, 1999

ROEMER, WILLIAM F. JR: *Accardo – The Genuine Godfather*; Ballantine Books, New York, 1994

ROEMER, WILLIAM F. JR: *The Enforcer*; Ballantine Books; New York, 1994

ROEMER, WILLIAM F. JR: *War of the Godfathers*; Ballantine Books, New York, 1990

RUSSO, GUS: *Live by the Sword – The Secret War Against Castro and the Death of JFK*; Bancroft Press, Baltimore, 1998

RUSSO, GUS: *The Outfit – The Role of Chicago's Underworld in the Shaping of America*, Bloomsbury, New York 2001

RYAN, PATRICK J. and RUSH, GEORGE E.: *Understanding Organized Crime*; Sage, California, 1997

SCHEIM, DAVID: *The Mafia Killed President Kennedy*; WH Allen, London, 1988

SCOTT, PETER DALE: *Deep Politics and the Death of JFK*; University of California Press, Los Angeles, 1993

SHANA, ALEXANDER: *The Pizza Connection – Lawyers, Money, Drugs and the Mafia*; Weidenfeld, New York, 1988

SHORT, MARTIN: *Crime Inc*; Thames Mandarin, London, 1991

STERLING, CLAIRE: *Thieves' World – The Threat of the New Global Network of Organized Crime*; Simon and Schuster, New York, 1994

STERLING, CLAIRE: *Octopus – The Long Reach of the International Sicilian Mafia*; Norton, New York, 1990

STRONG, SIMON: *Whitewash – Pablo Escobar and the Cocaine Wars*; Macmillan, London, 1995

STEWART, JAMES B.: *Den of Thieves*; Simon and Schuster, London, 1992

TANZI, VITO, ed: *The Underground Economy in the United States and Abroad*; collected articles for the International Money Fund, Lexington Books, Lexington, Mass. 1982

THEOHARIS, ATHAN and COX, JOHN STEWART: *The Boss*; Temple University Press, Philadelphia, 1988

TRUELL, PETER and GURWIN, LARRY: BCCI; Bloomsbury, London, 1992.

TYLER, GUS: *Organized Crime in America*; University of Michigan Press, Ann Arbor, 1962

VAKSBERG, ARKADY: *The Soviet Mafia*; Weidenfeld, London, 1991

VILLA, JOHN K: *Banking Crimes: Fraud, Money Laundering and Embezzlement*; Clark Boardman, New York, 1987

WALTER, INGO: *Secret Money*; Unwin, London, 1989

WILLIAMS, B. FREDERIC and WHITNEY FRANK D.: *Federal Money Laundering – Crimes and Forfeitures*; Lexis Law Publishing, Virginia, 1999

WOODS, BRETT F.: *The Art And Science Of Money Laundering – Inside The Commerce Of The International Narcotics Traffickers*; Paladin Press, Colorado, 1998

WOODWARD, BOB: *Veil – The Secret Wars of the CIA*; Simon and Schuster, New York, 1987

WOODWARD, BOB and BERNSTEIN, CARL: *All the President's Men*; Secker and Warburg, London, 1974

WOODWARD, BOB and BERNSTEIN, CARL: *The Final Days*; Avon Books, New York, 1976

NEWSPAPERS AND WIRE SERVICES

AGENCE FRANCE PRESSE

7 December 2002: *Tax Haven Sails With Winds Of Change*
3 June 1999: *London Court Freezes Accounts Of Late Nigerian Ruler*

ASSOCIATED PRESS

5 February 2003: *Two Convicted, One Cleared In Miami Securities Fraud Sting*
14 January 2003: Fowler, Jonathan – *Abacha's Shady Dealings Come Home To Roost*

6 December 2002: Wilson, Catherine – *Insurance Helps Launder Drug Money*

9 December 2002: Wilson, Catherine – *Judge In Miami Orders Man Charged With Tax Fraud Held Without Bond*

5 December 2002: Anderson, Curt – *Man Sought In Multinational Tax Evasion Case Extradited From Costa Rica*

5 November 2002: *Worldcom Fraud May Top $7.68b*

16 August 2002: Veiga, Alex – *Dozens Indicted on Fraud Charges*

14 May 2002: *Former NY Broker Charged With Fraud*

17 May 2001: LaHay, Patricia – *Strip Club Tied To Mob In Testimony*

6 March 2001: *IRS Raids Suspected Tax Evaders*

6 March 2001: Gordon, Marcy – *Money-Laundering Proposals Denounced*

7 March 2000: *13 Charged With $130 Million Metals Fraud Scheme*

22 December 1999: *Fake Stock Brokers Bust Coke Ring*

8 November 1999: Gordon, Marcy – *Citibank Didn't Question Deposits*

8 July 1999: Maull, Samuel – *Former Broker Sentenced To Prison*

17 June 1999: King, Jeanne – *British Lawyer Indicted In $17 Million Stock Fraud*

23 February 1999: Nurse, E – *Caribbean Drugs*

22 February 1999: *Cayman Islands Economy – Tax Regimes Under Scrutiny*

16 November 1998: *Three Sentenced In Insurance Scam Will Testify In Other Cases*

10 November 1998: *Abacha Family Returns More Dollars*

2 November 1998: *President Of Gabon's Appeal Against Account Block Rejected*

19 July 1996: Gold, Jeffrey – *Industry Believes Undercover Probe Saved Operators More Than $100 Million*

26 June 1998: *UK Police Quiz, Release Pair Over Alleged Fraud*

ATLANTA BUSINESS CHRONICLE

7 February 2000: Rankin, Bill – *Nebraska Outfits Accused Of Pirating Scientific-Atlanta Cable TV Boxes*

3 January 1997: Murray, Brendan – *Wyoming Court Convicts Atlantan in Investor Scam*

ATLANTA JOURNAL AND CONSTITUTION

2 August 2001: Rankin, Bill and Visser, Steve – *Plea Deal Could Give Gold Club To Feds $5 Million Fine, Prison Time Likely For Kaplan*

22 July 2001: Rankin Bill – *Witness Silence Imperils The Case*

20 July 2001: Visser, Steve – *Video Kiss Tells Plenty, Prosecution Contends*

19 July 2001: Rankin, Bill and Visser, Steve – *Defense Grills Key Witness*

14 July 2001: Visser, Steve – *Defense Lawyer Says Witness Just Trying To Buy Less Jail Time*

13 July 2001: Rankin, Bill – *This Time, Tapes Testify For Defense Of Kaplan*

12 July 2001: Visser, Steve – *Witness Details Mob-Style Justice*

11 July 2001: Rankin, Bill and Visser, Steve – *Fraud Blamed On Renegade*

28 June 2001: Visser, Steve – *Witness-Prosecution Relying On Serial Liars*

27 June 2001: Visser, Steve – *Lawyer Has A Beef With Prosecutors After Testifying, Says Other Witnesses In Gold Club Trial Are Liars*
26 June 2001: Visser, Steve – *Witness Links Kaplan To Mob*
26 June 2001: Visser, Steve – *Witness Admits Contradicting Testimony*

BARRON'S

19 April 1996: *Easy Money*

BERGEN (NEW JERSEY) RECORD

4 February 2000: Voreacos, David – *Con Man's Plea Can't Assuage Victims*
9 November 1999: Lavelle, Louis – *2 In Brokerage Fraud Have To Repay $6.6m*
19 June 1997: Demarco, Jerry – *FBI Asks For Assets Of Cable TV Thieves*
28 June 1996: Demarco, Jerry – *In FBI Sting, 14 Accused Of Cable Television Piracy*

BLOOMBERG NEWS

27 December 2002: *Morgan Defends Enron Trades*
21 November 2002: Mumma, Christopher – *Lawyers Convicted Of Helping Orchestrate Offshore Stock Swindle*
4 May 2001: *Finders, Keepers: Lawmen Get Meyers Pollock's Ill-Gotten Gains*
27 July 1995: *AR Baron, Officers To Pay $1.5 Million For Markups*

CANADIAN PRESS

18 January 2003: Young, Gerard – *Bogus BC Cleric Ordered To Pay $37 Million US For Bilking Polish Farmers*
8 January 2003: Erwin, Steve – *Valentine Breached Order: Osc Disgraced Broker Denies Violating Ban On Trading Complaint Says He Improperly Traded Futures Contracts*
7 January 2003: Erwin, Steve – *OSC Alleges Former Thomson Kernaghan Chair Broke Trading Ban Order*
16 August 2002: *High-Flying Canadian Stock Broker Mark Valentine Has Been Arrested In Germany On Charges Related To A Two-Year FBI Sting Operation Into Stock Fraud And Money Laundering*

CHICAGO TRIBUNE

21 May 2000: Franklin, Stephen – *Cayman Thriving As Tax-Dodgers' Shangri-La, Is Under Scrutiny*

CHRISTIAN SCIENCE MONITOR

12 February 2002: Kuzio, Taras – *Ukraine-Look Into Arms Export*
3 November 1999: Tidwell, M. – *Fanning The Flame Of Colombia's War*
7 August 1999: Richey, W. – *If Drug Smugglers Can, What About Terrorists?*
27 July 1999: La Franchi, H. – *Drugs Pulling US Into Columbia's War*

9 July 1999: Abel, D. – *Holes Open In US Drug-fighting Net*

27 August 1998: Baldauf, Scott – *Why It's So Hard for US to Pick Terrorists' Pockets*

DALLAS MORNING NEWS

21 October 2001: Robberson Tod – *Investigators Hope Money Trail Is Path To Stopping Drug Flow Unlikely Helpers Aid Effort Against Complex Global Transactions*

10 April 1997: Lodge, Bill – *18 Months Added To Man's Sentence*

21 September 1996: *Houston Man Reportedly Says He Led Phony Nation*

27 July 1996: *Authorities Are Tracking Scam Artist*

10 April 1996: Lodge, Bill – *Insurance Salesman Confesses In Fraud Case*

EDMONTON JOURNAL (CANADA)

18 January 2003: *Judge Orders Man To Pay $37m US For Flour Fraud-Man Said He Was A Minister Sending Aid Overseas*

EUROPEAN

3 March 1995: Parry, John and Patey, Tony – *King Of Europe's Cash Bernie Cornfeld Dies*

EXPRESS (UK)

11 April 2000: Connett, David and Gillard, Michael – *UK Lawyer Faces Extradition*

FINANCIAL POST

13 November 2002: Fitzpatrick, Peter – *Dirty Funds Haunt Small Exchanges Osc Comments About Money Laundering, Criminal Elements Earn Rebuke*

27 September 2002: Brieger, Peter – *Brokerage Regulator Can't Be Sued By Investor Ruling On Suit Against IDA*

FINANCIAL TIMES

September 24 2002: Parker, Andrew; Burns, Jimmy and Peel, Michael – *Banks Set To Avoid Charges In Abacha Funds Case*

23 September 2002: Parker, Andrew; Burns, Jimmy and Peel, Michael – *Sorry Tale Of Efforts To Recover Abacha Loot To Repatriate Funds Stolen From The Country's Central Bank Now In Tatters, The Government Is Turning To The International Courts*

23 September 2002: Parker, Andrew; Burns, Jimmy and Peel, Michael – *Nigeria Seeks To Recover Stolen Abacha $1bn*

23 March 2002: Winer, Jonathan – *How To Clean Up Dirty Money*

13 February 2002: *Caribbean Tax Haven Offers Assistance*

29 November 2001: Willman, John – *Trail of Terrorist Dollars that Spans the World*

26 January 2001: Mason, John and Parker, Andrew – *Government Drive to Seize Criminal's Assets*

30 October 2000: *Banks Clean Up*

20 October 2000: Willman, John – *Laundering Probe Targets London*

21 August 2000: *Cyprus Tries to Shake Off Tax Haven Image*

12 May 2000: *Islands Ask For Help On Offshore Rules*

23 July 1999: *Nigeria Seeks Help in Tracing Billions 'Taken' by Former Military Leaders*

25 March 1998: Cartel Laundered Millions Through Bank

23 March 1998: *Time To Take A Stand On Assets*

24 January 1998: Graham, George and Wright, Robert – *Winds Of Change On Treasure Islands*

17 February 1998: *Panama To Capitalize On Clean Bank Image*

26 November 1997: *Moves To Tame The Tiger*

31 October 1997: *Secrecy Laws – Screen Has Been Drawn Back Briefly*

8 August 1995: *Action Taken on Pyramid Scheme*

GAINSVILLE SUN (FLORIDA)

30 December 1998: Fisher, Lise – *Drug Smuggler Sentenced to Life, Convict to Forfeit Millions*

GANNETT NEWS SERVICE

2 March 2002: Scott, Katherine Hutt – *Antigua Bank Owner Was Largest Soft-Money Contributor To Daschle*

GLOBE AND MAIL (CANADA)

26 March 2003: Marron, Kevin – *Banks Investing In Systems To Bring Terrorists To Account*

4 February 2003: Belford, Terrence – *Brokers Affected By Money-Laundering Legislation*

31 January 2003: Stewart, Sinclair And Howlett, Karen – *Court Halts Tracking Of Valentine*

10 December 2002: McNish, Jacquie – *Trustee Slaps Former TK Staff With Suit Space*

23 October 2002: McNish, Jacquie – *Valentine Sells Assets To Cover Defaulted Loan*

24 September 2002: Alphonso Caroline – *Valentine Proclaims His Innocence. Trader Freed On Bail, But Can't Leave US*

23 September 2002: Alphonso, Caroline – *Valentine Spends Weekend Behind Bars In Miami*

21 September 2002: Alphonso Caroline and McNish, Jacquie – *Valentine Plans To Plead Not Guilty*

20 September 2002: McNish, Jacquie and Dixon, Guy – *Lawyer In Sting Seeks Debt Relief, Man Charged By FBI Has Posh Lifestyle*

18 September 2002: McNish, Jacquie and Freeman, Alan – *Valentine Sought German Brokerage Venture, Indicted Canadian Caught In FBI Sting Eyed Troubled Firm*

26 August 2002: Saunders, John – *Greed Was The Bait For FBI Stock Sting*

18 August 2002: *RCMP Expect Further Arrests From Bermuda Short Sting*

16 August 2002: McFarland, Janet; Mckenna, Barrie and Kennedy, Peter – *FBI Arrests Star Canadian Trader*

8 July 2002: McNish, Jacquie and Saunders, John – *The Rise And Fall Of Broker Mark Valentine*

15 June 2002: Oberman, Mira – *Pot Farms Conceal Deadly Risks*

GUARDIAN

7 March 2003: Teather, David – *Enron Scams Fill 2,000 Pages, Second Report From Investigator Tells Of Increasingly Desperate Efforts To Conceal Financial Disaster*

14 December 2002: Levene, Tony – *An Elite Police Unit Is Using The Internet To Fight Back Against International Electronic Fraudsters*

18 May 2000: Osborn, Andrew – *Nigerian Ex-dictator's Stolen Millions in British Banks*

12 May 1997: Plommer, L – *Islands Link Drug Cartels To Economy*

HOUSTON BUSINESS JOURNAL

October 22, 1999: Perin, Monica – *From Mexico To Antigua, R. Allen Stanford And Family Have Created A Financial Firm Catering To The Affluent*

INDEPENDENT (UK)

28 June 1998: Ricks, Michael – *International Fraud Squad Arrests London Lawyers*

INDEPENDENT ON SUNDAY (UK)

28 January 2001: Lashmar, Paul – *Banking Fugitive Woos Uganda*

INTERNATIONAL HERALD TRIBUNE

15 March 2003: Sullivan, Aline – *World Watchdogs Make Life Unpleasant Offshore*

12 May 2001: Milbank, Dana – *US Quits OECD's Drive To Rein In Tax Havens*

4 December 2000: Ignatius, David – *Getting Serious about Money Laundering.*

25 October 2000: Buerkle, Tom – *Havens See Benefits In Tough New Rules*

12 May 2000: *Luxembourg Freezes Loot Abacha Took From Nigeria*

27 November 1997: Walsh, Sharon – *Mob Bust On Wall Street*

IRISH TIMES

6 July 2002: *Business and Political Figures Names in Ansbacher Report*

5 July 2002: *Walking Bank Who Financed Haughey's Secret Lifestyle*

28 September 2001: Cusack, Jim – *CAB To Lead Anti-terrorism Efforts*

JERUSALEM POST

8 October 1995: Rodan, Steve – *Home-Grown Terrorists May Return To Haunt The US*

KNIGHT-RIDER

16 July 2000: Ivanovich, David – *Houston Banker Tries To Create Caribbean Empire, Runs Into Problems With Feds*

LOS ANGELES TIMES

22 December 2002: Kristof, Kathy M. – *Author, Attorney Indicted In Offshore Account Case*
5 November 2002: Hiltzik, Michael and Weinstein, Henry – *Cigarettes Portrayed As Currency Of Crime EU Suit Against R.J. Reynolds Describes A Worldwide System Of Money Laundering*
31 October 2002: Weinstein, Henry and Levin, Myron – *Eu Alleges Mob Ties To Tobacco*
7 April 2002: Meyer, Josh and Lichtblau, Eric – *Crackdown On Terror Funding Is Questioned*
25 August 1999: Leeds, Jeff – *Cayman Islands Lifts Veil of Bank Secrecy*
17 May 1994: *The Troubled Reign of Bhutto II*
8 September 1989: *Witness Tells Of Mob Influence In Penny Stocks*

MAIL (UK)

13 October 2002: Beaton, Graeme – *Duo Face Jail In US Over £11 Million International Share Scam*

MAIL ON SUNDAY (UK)

16 September 2001: Robinson, Jeffrey – *Following The Money*
1 December 2002: Beaton, Graeme – *Ex-Magistrate Guilty In Huge Shares Sting Graeme Beaton*

MIAMI HERALD

16 August 2002: Fields, Gregg – *Traders Charged In Fund Scheme Money Laundering And Kickbacks Alleged*
15 April, 2001: Fields, Gregg and Whitefield, Mimi – *Prosecutions Helping Lift the Veil of Secrecy from Offshore Banks*
21 February 2001: Fields, Gregg and Whitefield, Mimi – *Offshore Governments Close Three Banks – Money Laundering Report Spurs Move*
27 October 2000: Lebowitz, Larry – *19 From Crime Family Indicted*

MOBILE REGISTER (ALABAMA)

14 January 1997, Wilson, Michael – *The Hollywood Guy*

13 January 1997, Wilson, Michael – *The Informants*
12 January 1997, Wilson, Michael – *Operation Skymaster – Undercover in Mobile*

MONTREAL GAZETTE

14 February 2003: Macdonald, Don – *Montreal Lawyer Sentenced For His Role In Stock Scheme – Harry Bloomfield Gets Five Years Probation Plus Fine And 500 Hours Community Service*
26 November 2002 – *Bloomfield Guily Of Conspiracy To Bilk Investors*
16 October 2002: Hutchinson, Brian – *Disgraced Broker Had Bags Of Loot –*
. *Witness At Montreal Philanthropist's New York Trial Says His Name Never Came Up*

MOSCOW NEWS

1 May 1997: *Caribbean Havens For Money Launderers*

NAPLES DAILY NEWS (FLORIDA)

9 November 2001: Zollo, Cathy and Edwards, Gina – *Marchiano Gets 10–30 Years In Prison, Ordered To Pay $8m Restitution*
6 November 2001: *Marchiano Negotiating Restitution Amount With Prosecutors*
4 June 2001: Edwards, Gina – *Brother Testifies In AS Goldmen Case*
20 April 2000: Edwards, Gina – *AS Goldmen – Broker Linked To Naples Firm Pleads Guilty To Corruption*
10 July 1999: Edwards, Gina – *Marchiano Freed On $1 Million Bail*
24 October 1998: Edwards, Gina – *Troubled Naples Brokerage Firm Trims Operations*

NASSAU GUARDIAN (BAHAMAS)

19 March 2003: Thompson, Lindsay – *Clients' Job To Provide Credit Card Data To US IRS*

NATIONAL POST (CANADA)

26 November 2002: *Montreal Philanthropist Bloomfield Guilty Of Conspiracy To Bilk Investors Businessman And Partner Conspired In Criminal 'Pump-And-Dump' Stock Scheme*
19 October 2002: Hutchinson, Brian – *Lawyer Used Envoy's ID, Court Told Liberian Diplomat Says He Helped Harry Bloomfield Send Money To Switzerland*
12 October 2002: Hutchinson, Brian – *Bloomfield Drawn Into Devious Scheme*
10 October 2002: Hutchinson, Brian – *Letters Show Bloomfield Part Of Sophisticated Fraud, Judge Told – Private Faxes And Correspondence Seized In UK Raid*
9 October 2002: *Leading Montreal Lawyer Facing Fraud Charges Harry Bloomfield: Accused Of Aiding In US $17m 'Pump And Dump' Scheme*
28 November 1997: Tomkins, Richard – *Mob Linked To Pump And Dump Scheme*

NEWSDAY (NEW YORK)

28 November 2002: *Bank Admits Laundering $123M*

2 August 2001: Harrigan, Susan – *Stratton Player Pleads Guilty/Ex-fashion Exec Was Last To Face Prosecution*

1 August 2001: Harrigan, Susan – *Businessman Convicted in LI Brokerage Scheme*

10 July 2001: Harrisgan, Susan – *Views of Shuster's Role Are At Odds*

25 March 2001: Harrigan, Susan – (Part Two) *Boom To Bust – How Authorities Turned 2 Crooked Brokers From High Rollers To Witnesses Against One Of America's Top Shoe Designers*

24 March 2001: Harrigan, Susan – (Part One) *Castles Made of Sand – Brokers Who Rode Fraud to Riches Now Federal Witnesses*

15 July 1999: *S. Mazzeo, 41, Involved In Stock Fraud*

14 May 1997: *13 Indicted In $75M Theft – Accused of Bilking Investors.*

3 April 1997: Hurtado, Patricia – *Stock Swindle/US Alleges Millions Lost In Securities Scam, 18 Indicted*

NEW YORK DAILY NEWS

15 October 2001: Ross, Barbara – *Banks Back off Anti-Terror, Laundering Laws in Slow Spin Cycle*

10 September 2000: Smith, Greg – *Mob Muscles In On Market*

3 May 1997: Peterson, Helen – *Mafioso Held In Stock Fraud*

9 January 1997: Ross, Barbara and Feiden, Douglas – *Sting Nets Bad Stock*

NEW YORK TIMES

12 December 2002: Johnston, David Cay – *10 Are Charged In Tax Evasion Case Said To Involve 2,000*

6 December 2002: Lichtblau, Eric – *New Hiding Place For Drug Profits: Insurance Policies*

28 November 2002: Worth, Robert F. – *Bank Failed To Question Huge Deposits*

16 November 2002: Johnston, David Cay – *Two Plotters Are Sentenced In Big Tax Evasion Scheme*

12 November 2002: Berkeley, Bill – *A Glimpse Into A Recess Of International Finance*

16 October 2002: Gerth, Jeff and Miller, Judith – *Report Says Saudis Fail to Crack Down on Charities That Finance Terrorists*

8 October 2002: *Plan to Stop Tax Evaders Hits Snag*

19 September 2002: Andrews, Edmund L. – *US Proposes Hedge Fund Rules To Prevent Terrorist Financing*

19 September 2002: Frantz, Douglas – *Front Companies Said to Keep Financing Terrorists*

10 September 2002: *Germany Probes Import-Export Firm*

28 June 2002: Weiser, Benjamin – *Ex-Broker Helped to Launder Drug Money, Prosecutors Say*

26 June 2002: Eichenwald, Kurt and Barboza, David – *Enron Criminal Investigation Is Said to Expand to Bankers*

15 June 2002: Lambert, Bruce – *Four Admit Using Bank To Launder Money*

13 June 2002: Weiser, Banjamin – *Officials Say Heroin Arrests Show New Supply Routes*

23 May 2002: Sengupta, Somini – *UN report Says Al Qaeda May Be Diversifying Its Finances*

15 May 2002: Johnston, David Cay – *Nine Are Indicted In Investment Fraud Case*

24 April 2002: Stevenson Richard and Wayne, Leslie – *More Regulations To Thwart Money Laundering Are Imposed*

26 March 2002: Johnston, David Cay – *IRS Says Offshore Tax Evasion Is Widespread*

25 February 2002: Atlas Riva – *Insurers Say JP Morgan Disguised Loans To Enron*

18 February 2002: Eichenwald, Kurt – *Records Raise Questions Over Some Enron Gas Trades*

17 February 2002: Holstein, William J. – *Hounds and Foxes Match Wits in Pursuit of Hidden Assets*

11 December 2001: Wayne, Leslie – *Fight Against Money Laundering Widens*

11 December 2001: Wayne, Leslie – *Wall St Faces Rules on Money Laundering*

10 December 2001: Eichenwald, Kurt – *Terror Money Hard to Block, Officials Find*

8 November 2001: Sanger, David and Eichenwald, Kurt – *US Moves to Cut 2 Financial Links for Terror Group*

14 October 2001: Frantz, Douglas – *Pakistani Trader Denies He Ever Helped Bin Laden*

14 October 2001: MacFarquhar, Neil – *Saudis Reject US Accusation They Balked on Terror Money*

19 August 2001: Schoenberger, Karl – *Regulators Check The New Economy's Books*

6 April 2001: Morgenson, Gretchen – *2 Accused of Fraud Using Shell Companies*

6 March 2001: Johnston, David Cay – *IRS Steps Up Tax-Evasion Raids*

11 February 2001: Morgenson, Gretchen – *Striking A Blow For The Little Guy*

7 November 2000: Daley, Suzanne – *Europeans Suing Big Tobacco In US*

20 October 2000: Johnston, David Cay – *Taking Aim at Tax Havens, IRS Seeks Credit Card Slips*

10 October 2000: Bergman, Lowell – *US Companies Tangled In Web Of Drug Dollars*

27 July 2000: Brick, Michael – *DH Blair & Co Indicted for Racketeering*

21 April 2000: *Former Bear Sterns Executive Barred From Securities Industry*

8 March 2000: Finklestein, Katherine E – *Banker Indicted In Metal Export Fraud Case*

19 November 1999: Eaton, Leslie – *Penny-Stock Fraud Is Billion-Dollar Game*

2 November 1999: Henriques, Diana – *A Brutal Turn In Stock Frauds*

6 August 1999: Morgenson, Gretchen – *SEC Says Bear Stearns Subsidiary Had Central Role in Fraud*

3 August 1999: Smothers, Ronald – *Banker Outlines Money Laundering in Caymans*

4 April 1999: Navarro, M. – *An Outpost In The Banana And Marijuana Wars*

31 May 1998: Navarro, M. – *Upgraded Drug Traffic Flourishes On Old Route*

April 23, 1997: Henriques, Diana and Truell, Peter – *Should a Clearinghouse Be Its Broker's Keeper?*

30 January 1997: Rohter, L. – *Impact Of NAFTA Pounds Economies Of The Caribbean*
3 July 1995: Anderson, J.R. – *Red Dogs' Battle Drugs In The Caribbean*
8 June 1995: Cooper, Michael – *US Indicts A Fugitive Over Drugs*
10 February 1997: Raab, Selwyn – *Officials Say Mob Is Shifting Crimes To New Industries*

OBSERVER (UK)

22 November 1998: *How The Grand Lootocracy Beggared Nigeria's People*

ONTARIO SECURITIES COMMISSION

31 July 2002: *OSC Issues Reasons For Order Against Mark Valentine*

OTTAWA BUSINESS JOURNAL

17 February 2003: *Valentine Trading Ban Extended*
7 January 2003: *Mark Valentine On The Hotseat Again*

OTTAWA CITIZEN (CANADA)

25 March 2003: Tibbetts, Janice – *Government Exempts Lawyers From Money Laundering Law*

PHILADELPHIA INQUIRIER:

1 December, 2000: Webb, Robert – *Offshore Bank Accounts Are Not Secret To IRS*

PITTSBURGH POST GAZETTE

28 January 2001: *Offshore Tax Scam Unveiled by FBI*

REUTERS

6 November 2002: *Worldcom Sees $9 Billion Restatement*
18 September 2002: *US To Propose Tougher Hedge-Fund Scrutiny*
9 September 2002: *Hong Kong Charges Eight in Massive Money Laundering Case*
16 August 2002: Clarke, Toni – *Sting Operation Could Be Tip of Iceberg*
17 July 2002: *US Seeks Rule To Verify Bank Customer Identities*
13 July 2002: Wulfhorst, Ellen – *New York Jury Convicts Algerian In Millennium Plot*
9 July 2002: *US Drops Three from Money Laundering List*
17 April 2002: *Nigeria To Get $1 Billion In Out-Of-Court Deal*
29 January 2002: *Senate Sees Money Laundering Risk for US Brokers*
17 January 2002: Loney, Jim – *Enron Benefited From Caribbean Tax Havens, Lax Law*
8 January 2002: *Atlanta Strip Club Owner Sentenced To 16 Months*
10 July 2001: *Schneider v IRS*
14 May 2000: *More Arrests Seen In Liechtenstein Laundering Probe*
30 March, 2000: Loney, Jim – *Cayman Islands – Human Slave Traders Join Money-Laundering Flood*

14 October 1999: *Swiss Freeze Accounts Of Nigeria's Abacha*

23 September 1999: Zengerle, Patricia – *Russian Report Unwanted Blow To Cayman Islands*

26 June 1998: *UK Police Quiz, Release Pair Over Alleged Fraud*

SAN FRANCISCO CHRONICLE

22 March 1969: *British Plan Anguilla Troop Cut*

22 March 1969: Valencia, F. Scott – *The Anguilla Saga*

21 March 1969: *Anguilla May Face A Long Occupation*

21 March 1969: Valencia, F. Scott – *The Inside Story of the Anguilla Caper*

20 March 1969: *The British Quest Of Anguilla*

SCOTSMAN

28 November 2002: Cox, David – *Briton on $2.7M Fraud Charge*

SOUTH CHINA MORNING POST

8 December 1998: *Melchizedek Case Lawyer Seeks Deportation*

28 November 1998: *15 Banned In Passport Scam*

SOUTH FLORIDA BUSINESS JOURNAL

26 August 2002: Fakler, John T. – *Securities Crackdown Hits Region*

ST. PETERSBURG TIMES

4 February 2002: Freedberg, Sydney P. – *Enron – The Offshore Ventures*

SUNDAY EXPRESS (UK)

23 April 2000: Connett, David and Gillard, Michael – *Solicitor Refuses To Hand Over £20M In Laundered Drugs Money*

TIMES (UK)

11 October 2001: Bremner, Charles and Doran, James – *Britain Denounced as Dirty Money Haven*

11 October 2001: Binyon, Michael – *Island Regimes Make it Easy for Smugglers to Clean Up*

14 October 1999: Lister, David – *Case Of Brainy Don, The Bank And Money-Laundering Briefs*

25 September 1999: Lister, David and Bone, James – *British Lawyers In Bank Inquiry*

8 August 1993: *Plot Thickens in Phony Bank Scheme*

TIMES COLONIST (CANADA)

18 January 2003: *Ripoff Artist Must Pay Millions To Polish Farmers*

TORONTO STAR

20 August 2002: Wells, Jennifer – *Stock Sting Has Quite A Cast Of Characters*
11 July 2002: *Canadian Court Decides Against IRS In Tax Case*
27 February 2002: *Survey Of Brokerages Reveals 13,000 Accounts In Tax Havens*

TORONTO SUN

16 October 2002: Lamberti, Rob – *Twist In Church-Fire Case-Ownership Linked To NYC Trial Figure*
27 February 2002: Lewyckyj, Maryanna – *Investors Head Offshore-Accounts in Money Laundering Havens Worrisome*

UNITED PRESS INTERNATIONAL

5 September 2001: *Funny Business – Honor amongst fraudsters?*

UNITED STATES DEPARTMENT OF JUSTICE

2 August 2001: Press Release – *Harry Schuster, Beverly Hills Businessman, Real Estate Investor and Film Producer Convicted of Money Laundering and Securities Fraud*

OFFICE OF THE UNITED STATES ATTORNEY, SOUTHERN DISTRICT OF NEW YORK:

14 August 14 2000: Press Release – *With sealed complaint against Oleg Zezov and sealed complaint Igor Yarimaka in the matter of the extortion of Bloomberg L.P.*

OFFICE OF THE UNITED STATES ATTORNEY, DISTRICT OF NEW JERSEY

7 March 2000: Press Release – *US Bank Officials and Refining Firm Executives Indicted in Scheme to Defraud Argentinean Government of Export Incentives*

OFFICE OF THE UNITED STATES ATTORNEY, DISTRICT OF NEW JERSEY

2 August 1999: Press Release – *John M. Mathewson, former chairman of Cayman Island bank sentenced for nationwide, multi-million dollar off-shore banking scheme*

OFFICE OF THE UNITED STATES ATTORNEY, DISTRICT OF NEW JERSEY

20 April 1999: Press Release – *William S. 'Trey' Prevost III, Former Fugitive Sentenced To Prison In Connection With Biggest Cable TV Piracy In US History*

USA TODAY

12 September 2002: *Officials Accused Of Using Tyco As Piggy Bank*
16 December 1996: Fairley, Juliette – *Foreign Bank Accounts Offer Profit, Privacy, Protection*

VANCOUVER SUN

18 January 2003: Young, Gerard – *Victoria Man Fined $37m US For Fraud Case: Plot Hurt Thousands Of Polish Farmers*

11 July 2001: Baines, David – *Regulator Cites Broker For Mob Link*

VOA NEWS

28 June 2002: *Former US Banker Indicted In Money Laundering Case*

WALL STREET JOURNAL

8 February 2003: Weinberg Stuart – *Rogue Broker Suspended 10 Years*

23 July 2002: Sapsford, Jathon and Beckett, Paul – *Called To Account-Citigroup, JP Morgan Marketed Enron-Type Deals To Other Firms*

28 February 2001: Beckett, Paul – *JP Morgan Chase, Others Are Criticized Over Correspondent-Banking Standards*

29 February 2000: Allen, Michael – *Grenada Banking Is Great, But Mr Brink Is Off To Uganda Now, Ex-Head Of Firm That Claims Staggering Profits Is Busy Fixing Congo's Currency*

6 April 2000: *Secret Offshore Bank Accounts Not So Secret*

22 February 2000: Beckett, Paul and Allen, Michael – *Bank Of New York Investigation Widens To Include Swiss Financier Rappaport*

17 June 1999: Schroeder, Michael – *Eighty-Five Brokers Are Charged With Allegedly Bilking Investors*

4 February 1999: Gasparino, Charles – *SEC Staff Weighing Civil Fraud Charges Against Bear Stearns In AR Baron Case*

1 July 1998: Jones, Roland – *British Lawyers Tied To AR Baron Investigation*

25 August 1997: Alpert, Bill – *Buyer, Beware! Dizzying Deals Raise Questions About California's Fast-Growing Osicom Technologies*

12 May 1997: Robichaux, Mark – *Cable Pirates Sought Plunder But Blundered Into A Major FBI Sting*

16 March 1990: *Gorbachev's Empire on the Cheap*

WASHINGTON POST

3 October 2002: *Fastow Charged With Fraud, Conspiracy In Enron Case*

15 August 2002: Barbaro, Michael – *Rockville CEO Among Dozens Accused in Stock-Fraud Sting*

3 June 2002: O'Harrow, Robert Jr – *In Terror War, Privacy vs Security – Search for Illicit Activities Taps Confidential Data*

3 April 2002: Samuelson, Robert J – *Tax Haven, Anyone?*

17 February 2002: Farah, Douglas – *Al-Qaeda's Road Paved with Gold*

29 August 2000: DeYoung, Karen – *US, Colombia to Confront Lucrative Peso Exchange*

28 October 1999: Hilzenrath, David – *Russians Use Tiny Island to Hide Billions*

3 February 1999: *Banking With Big Brother*

7 October 1996: Farah, Douglas – *Russian Crime Finds Haven In Caribbean*

5 November 1995 – *The Ruse That Roared*
18 June, 1995: McGee, Jim – *From Respected Attorney To Suspected Racketeer – A Lawyer's Journey*
4 January 1995: *Bagging A Bumbling Band Of Alleged Money Launderers*
22 June 1986: *Moscow's Shell Game – Soviet Bankers Use Our Money Against Us*

WASHINGTON TIMES

6 December 2002: Seper, Jerry – *Money-Laundering Scheme Squashed*
6 September 2002: Rahn, Richard – *Nightmare on FATF Street*
9 August 2002: *Worldcom Reveals Additional Fraud Worth $3.3 Billion*

MAGAZINES, JOURNALS AND OTHER AND PERIODICALS

AMERICAN BANKER

Anti-Laundering Proposal Draws Flood of Complaints; 29 December 1998

ART, ANTIQUES AND LAW

Snaith, Ian: *Art, Antiques and the Fruits of Crime – Laundering, Investigation and Confiscation, Part I* December 1998, *Part II* March 1999

BULLETIN OF ATOMIC SCIENTISTS

Woodard, Colin: *Offshore Banking – Clean Beaches, Dirty Money*; May/June 2000

BUSINESS CRIMES BULLETIN

Mariani, Gilda: *Ungagging The Gatekeepers-Accountants' Sensitive Role In Probes*; August 2002

BUSINESS WEEK

Looks Like Every Day Is Money-Laundry Day; February 2001
Paula Dwyer, Paula and Solomon Steven: *The Citi That Slept?*; 2 November 1998
Weiss, Gary: *Investors Beware – Chop Stocks Are On The Rise*; 15 December 1997
Tax-Haven Whiz Or Rogue Banker? Marc Harris' Doings In Panama Are Raising Eyebrows; 1 June 1998

CARIBBEAN AFFAIRS

Sanders, R: *Narcotics, Corruption And Development – The Problems In The Smaller Islands*; January 1990
Pantin, D: *The Colombian Nightmare – Drugs And Structural Adjustment*; October 1989

CARIBBEAN JOURNAL OF CRIMINOLOGY AND SOCIAL PSYCHOLOGY

de Albuquerque, K. and McElroy J.: *A Longitudinal Study Of Serious Crime In The Caribbean*; 1999

DOLLARS AND SENSE

Petras, James: *US Banks And The Dirty Money Empire*; September–October 2001

ECONOMIC PERSPECTIVES

Joseph, Lester: *Money Laundering Enforcement – Following The Money*, May 2000

ECONOMIST

Small States, Big Money Economist; 23 September 2000
Dirty Linen – Mexico; 17 May 1997

FAR EASTERN ECONOMIC REVIEW

Lintner, Bertil: *Fantasy Island – Melchizedek Passport Scam Reveals How The Internet Can Take Fraud To New Frontiers*; 10 December 1998

FBI LAW ENFORCEMENT BULLETIN

Schroeder, William: *Money Laundering – A Global Threat And The International Community's Response*; May 2001

FEDERAL RESERVE BULLETIN

Houpt, James V: *International Activities of US Banks and in US Banking Markets* September 1999

FOREIGN POLICY

Morris-Cotterill, Nigel: *Think Again – Money Laundering*; May–June 2001

HARPER'S MAGAZINE

Schapiro, Mark – *Doing The Wash – Inside A Colombian Cartel's Money-Laundering Machine*; February 1997

JANE'S INTELLIGENCE REVIEW

Galeotti, Dr Mark: *Crimes Of The New Millennium*; 24 Aug 2000

THE LAWYERS WEEKLY

Harloff, Glen: *Phony Financial Instruments Can Put Lawyers At Risk*; 25 January 2002

MACLEAN'S

Geddes, John: *The Money Trail – Ottawa's Fight Against Laundering is Going Slowly*; 13 May 2002

MOTHER JONES

Silverstein, Ken: *Trillion-Dollar Hideaway*, November-December 2000

THE NATION

Bubble Capitalism, 19 August 2002

NEWSWEEK

The Lost Billions; 13 March 2000

Powell, Bill and Albats, Yevgenia: *Follow The Money – The Latest Kremlin Scandal Involves Billions Of Dollars Moving Offshore Plus Sex And Videotape*; 29 March 1999

NEW YORK TIMES SUNDAY MAGAZINE

Hitt, Jack – *The Billion-Dollar Shack*; 10 December 2000

NEW YORK UNIVERSITY LAW REVIEW

Bellwoar, John M.: *Bar Baron At The Gate – An Argument For Expanding The Liability Of Securities Clearing Brokers For The Fraud Of Introducing Brokers*; October 1999

PLAYBOY

Robinson, Jeffrey: *Terror Dollars*; January 2002

SECURITY AND DEFENCE STUDIES REVIEW

Griffith Ivelaw L.: *Security, Sovereignty and Public Order in the Caribbean*; Summer 2002

SECURITIES REFORM ACT LITIGATION REPORTER

Zweifach, Lawrence J.: *Current Developments and Issues in the Criminal Prosecution of Federal Securities Law Violations*; January 2002

SECURITIES WEEK

9 April 2001: *New York DA Indicts Two In Wide Ranging Securities Fraud Case*

TAX NOTES INTERNATIONAL

Langer, Marshall J.: *The Outrageous History of Caribbean Tax Treaties with OECD Member States*; 1 July 2002

TIME MAGAZINE

Israely, Jeff: *Meet The Mob*; 10 June 2002

Cohen, Adam: *Banking On Secrecy – Terrorists Oppose Scrutiny Of Offshore Accounts – And So Do Many US Bankers And Lawmakers*; 22 October 2001

Wallace Charles P: *Funds In The Sun – Tax Havens Are Coming Under Increasing Pressure To Clean Up Money Laundering*; 10 July 2000

Handelman, Stephen: *Confronting Cross-Border Crime Law Enforcers Must Learn To Move Faster To Snare Global Lawbreakers*; 24 April 2000

Walsh, James: *A World War On Bribery*; 22 June 1998

Booth, Cathy: *Caribbean Blizzard – With Blissful Vacationers Unaware, Tons Of Cocaine Flow Through The Idyllic Islands, Thanks To Sharkish Drug Cartels*; 26 February 1996

US NEWS AND WORLD REPORT

Chesnoff, Richard Z – *Liechtenstein – A Mouse That Roars* 22 June 1987

Zanker, Alfred and Scherschel, Patricia M – *Why Its Getting Tougher To Hide Money*; 2 June 1986

WASHINGTON MONTHLY

Dorgan, Byron: *Global Shell Games – How The Corporations Operate Tax Free*; July 2000

WORLD POLICY JOURNAL

Malkin, Lawrence and Elizur, Yuval: *The Dilemma Of Dirty Money*; Spring 2001

SIGNIFICANT TESTIMONY AND SPEECHES

BAIN JOHN S: *Money Laundering – A Practical Analysis With Particular Reference To Bahamian And Caribbean Offshore Institutions;* submitted to the University of Wales and the Manchester Business School, Wales and England, 1998

BENN, HILARY: *Money Laundering As A Threat To International Development*; Money Laundering Conference, London, 26 February 2002

GURULE, JAMES: *International Cooperation In The War On Terrorism*; delivered before the Commission on Security and Co-operation in Europe, Washington DC, 8 May 2002

LANGER, MARSHALL J: *Harmful Tax Competition – Who Are The Real Tax Havens?*; presented at a meeting of the International Tax Planning Association, New Orleans, 20 November 2000

RICHARDS, LORI A, Director, Office of Compliance Inspections And Examinations US Securities & Exchange Commission: *Money Laundering: It's On The Sec's Radar Screen*; delivered at the Conference on Anti-Money Laundering Compliance for Broker-Dealers Securities Industry Association, Washington DC, 8 May 2001

ROTH, JEAN-PIERRE, Chairman of the Governing Board Swiss National Bank: *The Challenges Of An International Financial Centre – The Swiss Case*; delivered before the British-Swiss Chamber of Commerce, London, 26 February 2002

STATE OF NEW JERSEY, State Crime Commission, *Hearings on Money Laundering*; Trenton, 9 and 14 December 1993

SUMMERS, LAWRENCE H: Secretary of the Treasury – *Combatting International Money Laundering*; remarks to the American Bar Association, Washington DC, 2 March 2000

UNITED NATIONS: *Attacking The Profits Of Crime – Drugs, Money And Laundering*; A panel discussion, including: Ian Hamilton Fazey: *Setting The Context – Ten Years On From The 1988 Convention*; Pino Arlacchi: *The Need For A Global Attack On Money Laundering*; Jack Blum: *Financial Havens And Banking Secrecy*; Vito Tanzi: *Macro-Economic Aspects Of Offshore Centres And The Importance Of Money Laundering In Offshore Financial Flows*; Carla Del Ponte: *Practical And Legal Obstacles To International Judicial Cooperation In Financial Investigations*; N.K. Singh: *New Money Laundering Threats For Emerging Economies*; Timothy Donaldson: *Offshore Financial Business And Banking Regulation*; New York, 10 June 1998

UNITED STATES HOUSE OF REPRESENTATIVES:

Committee on Banking And Financial Services:

Dismantling The Financial Infrastructure Of Global Terrorism; Washington DC 2001

Hearing On Money Laundering; *testimony of former money launderer* Kenneth Rijock, 9 March 2000

Russian Money Laundering; Washington DC, 1999

Money Laundering Deterrence Act Of 1998 And H.R. 1756 – Money Laundering And Financial Crime Strategy Act Of 1997; Washington DC, 1998

Money Laundering And Financial Crimes Strategy Act Of 1998, Report To Accompany H.R. 1756; Washington DC, 1998

Efforts To Combat Money Laundering; Jack Blum, 11 June 1998

Committee on Commerce, Subcommittee on Finance and Hazardous Materials:

Organized Crime On Wall Street; Prepared Statement of Richard H. Walker Director, Division of Enforcement Securities and Exchange Commission, 13 September 2000

Committee on Commerce, Subcommittee on Finance and Hazardous Materials:

On Organized Crime; statement and testimony by special agent Tom Fuentes, FBI, Washington DC, 13 September 2000

Committee on Financial Services:

Cutting Off The Financial Life Blood Of The Terrorists; Dennis M. Lormel, Chief, Financial Crimes Section, Federal Bureau of Investigation, 3 October 2001

Committee on Financial Services, Subcommittee on Financial Institutions and Consumer Credit:

Recovering Assets Stolen by Corrupt Foreign Leaders – Opening Statement, Chairman Spencer Bachus; *Recovering Dictator's Plunder*, Jack Blum; *Social and Political Costs of Theft of Public Funds by African Dictators*, Michael Chege; *Recovering Dictator's Plunder*, John Conyngham; 9 May 2002

Committee on Financial Services, Subcommittee on Oversight and Investigations:
Patriot Act Oversight – Investigating Patterns Of Terrorist Financing; Washington DC, 12 February 2002
Preventing Identity Theft by Terrorists and Criminals; joint hearing before the Subcommittee on Oversight and Investigations of the Committee on Financial Services and the Subcommittee on Social Security of the Committee on Ways and Means; 8 November 2001
Committee on Government Reform, Subcommittee on Criminal Justice:
Drug Policy, And Human Resources – Combating Money Laundering; Washington DC, 2000
Committee on International Relations
    International Organized Crime – The Larger Issues; Jack Blum, 1 October 1997
    Committee On The Judiciary, Subcommittee On Crime: *2000 Money Laundering Crisis*; 10 February 2000

UNITED STATES SENATE:
Committee on Banking, Housing, and Urban Affairs:
Prime Bank Schemes; Herbert Biern, deputy associate director, Division of Banking Supervision and Regulation, 17 July 1996
Committee on Banking, Housing, and Urban Affairs, Subcommittee on International Trade and Finance:
The Role Of Charities And Nongovernmental Organizations In Financing Terrorist Activities; 1 August 2002
Committee On Governmental Affairs:
Crime And Secrecy – The Use Of Offshore Banks And Companies; a report to the Senate, August 1985
Committee on the Judiciary, Subcommittee on Technology, Terrorism and Government Information:
Narco-Terror – The Worldwide Connection Between Drugs And Terror; Rand Beers, Assistant Secretary for International Narcotics and Law Enforcement Affairs; and Francis X. Taylor, Ambassador-At-Large For Counterterrorism, 13 March 2002
Committee on Governmental Affairs, Permanent Subcommittee On Investigations:
Offshore Tax Havens; Robert M. Morgenthau, District Attorney for the County of Manhattan, City of New York, 18 July 2001
National Money Laundering Strategy; Joseph M. Myers, Acting Deputy Assistant Secretary (Enforcement Policy), United States Department of the Treasury, 6 March 2001
Law Enforcement Activities Related To Our Anti-Money Laundering Efforts And Correspondent Bank Relationships; Mary Lee Warren, Deputy Assistant Attorney General, Criminal Division, United States Department of Justice, 6 March 2001
Money Laundering And Correspondent Banking; testimony of Jack Blum, 2 March 2001; Robert Evans, 2 March 2001; statement of John M. Mathewson; 1 March 2001

Hearing On Private Banking And Money Laundering: Abacha Sons – A Case Study Of Opportunities And Vulnerabilities; 9 November 1999

Hearing On Micro-Cap Stock Fraud; testimony of Arthur Levitt, chairman US Commission; testimony of Barry R. Goldsmith, Executive Vice President NASD Regulation; testimony of Joseph P. Borg Director, Alabama Securities Commission; Washington DC, 22 September 1997

Committee on Finance:

Tax Schemes, Scams And Cons; Jack Blum, 11 April 2002

MAJOR REPORTS, COURT DOCUMENTS
AND DISSERTATIONS

ASSEMBLÉE NATIONALE FRANÇAISE: *La Lutte Contre Le Blanchiment Des Capitaux En Suisse–Un Combat De Façade*, Paris 2001

AUSTRALIAN INSTITUTE FOR GAMBLING RESEARCH: McMillen, Jan and Woolley, Richard – *Money Laundering In Australian Casinos*, Canberra, 2001

BEARE, MARGARET E.: *Critique Of A Compliance-Driven Enforcement Strategy – Money Laundering And The Financial Sector*; draft working paper, Toronto, 2002

Facts From Fiction–Tactics And Strategies Of Addressing Organized Crime And Organized Criminals; Perspectives on Organized Crime in Canada for the Canadian Police College, Ottawa, 2000

BEARE, MARGARET E. AND NAYLOR R.T.: *Organized Crime within the Context of Economic Relationships*; Nathanson Centre For The Study Of Organized Crime And Corruption, Toronto, 1999

BELL, DR R.E.: *Discretion And Decision-Making In Money Laundering Prosecutions*; from the office of the director of public prosecutions for Northern Ireland, writing in a personal capacity, undated

BIRD, GRAHAM and RAJAN, RAMKISHEN: *Economic Globalization – How Far and How Much Further?*; Centre For International Economic Studies, Adelaide, Australia, April 2001

BROOKINGS INSTITUTE FOR PUBLIC POLICY EDUCATION: Caux Roundtable – *Dirty Money – Nourishing Poverty And Terrorism*; Remarks by Richard Newcomb, Director, Office of Foreign Assets Control, US Treasury Department, and Robert Morgenthau, District Attorney, County of New York, Washington DC, 2002

CANADIAN SECURITY INTELLIGENCE SERVICE: *Counter-Terrorism*; Ottawa, 2002

COUNCIL ON FOREIGN RELATIONS: *Report of an Independent Task Force – Terrorist Financing*; New York, 2002

EXECTUIVE OFFICE OF THE PRESIDENT OF THE UNITED STATES: The President's Commission On Organized Crime: *The Impact-Organized Crime Today*; Washington DC, 1986

A Report To The President And The Attorney General Of The United States – America's

Habit-Drug Abuse, Drug Trafficking And Organized Crime; Washington DC, 1986

Cash Connection – The Interim Report On Organized Crime, Financial Institutions And Money Laundering; Washington DC, 1984

FINANCIAL ACTION TASK FORCE: *Report On Money Laundering Typologies,* Paris, 2003

Review Of The FATF Forty Recommendations, Paris, 30 May 2002

FRASER, A. GABRIELLA: *Can The Sir Stafford Sands Model Of The Bahamian Economy, Survive Today's Global Economy?,* 33rd Conference of the Caribbean Centre for Monetary Studies, Belize, November 2001

GENERAL ACCOUNTING OFFICE: *Anti-Money Laundering – Efforts In The Securities Industry;* Washington DC, 2001

Money Laundering – Oversight Of Suspicious Activity Reporting At Bank-Affiliated Broker-Dealers; Washington DC, 2001

Money Launderingraul Salinas, Citibank, And Alleged Money Laundering; Washington DC, 2001

Money Laundering – Regulatory Oversight Of Offshore Private Banking Activities; Washington DC, 2001

Suspicious Bank Activities – Possible Money Laundering By US Corporations For Russian Entities; Washington DC, 2000

Money Laundering – Observations On Private Banking And Related Oversight Of Selected Offshore Jurisdictions; Washington DC, 1999

Money Laundering – Fincen's Law Enforcement Support Role Is Evolving; Washington DC, 1998

Money Laundering – Fincen Needs To Better Communicate Regulatory Priorities And Timeliness; Washington DC, 1998

Report To The Chairman, Subcommittee On General Oversight And Investigations, Committee On Banking And Financial Services, House Of Representatives: Money Laundering – Regulatory Oversight Of Offshore Private Banking Activities; Washington DC, 1998

GILLESPIE, KATE: *Smuggling and the Global Firm;* Third Annual International Business Forum, Temple University, Philadelphia, 2002

GOREUX, LOUIS: *Conflict Diamonds;* World Bank, Africa Region Working Paper Series No. 13, Washington DC, March 2001

GOVERNMENT ACCOUNTING OFFICE: *Extent Of Money Laundering Through Credit Cards Is Unknown;* Washington DC, 2002

GOVERNMENT OF CANADA: *Canada-US Cross Border Crime and Security Cooperation;* Ottawa, September 2002

GOVERNMENT OF GREAT BRITAIN: *Report Of Mr Rodney Gallagher Of Coopers And Lybrand On The Survey Of Offshore Financial Sectors In The Caribbean Dependent Territories;* London, 1990

GRAND COURT OF THE CAYMAN ISLANDS: *Indictment – The Queen V Donald Stewart, Brian Cunha, Ivan Burges, Judith Donegan;* Georgetown, Cayman Islands, 2002

INTERNATIONAL MONETARY FUND: *Governance, Corruption & Economic*

Performance; Corruption Around The World – Causes, Consequences, Scope And Cures; Institutionalized Corruption And The Kleptocratic State; Corruption, Extortion And Evasion; Corruption, Structural Reforms And Economic Performance In The Transition Economies; Improving Governance And Fighting Corruption In The Baltic And Cis Countries – The Role Of The IMF; Washington DC, September 2002

Caribbean Offshore Financial Centers – Past, Present And Possibilities For The Future; a working paper prepared by Esther C. Suss, Oral H. Williams and Chandima Mendis, Washington DC, May 2002

Enhancing Contributions To Combating Money Laundering; Washington DC, 2001

Financial System Abuse, Financial Crime And Money Laundering; Washington DC, 2001

Offshore Financial Centers; Background Paper, Washington DC, June 2000

Offshore Banking – An Analysis Of Micro- And Macro-Prudential Issues; Errico, Luca and Musalem, Alberto, Washington DC, January 1999

Money Laundering And The International Financial System; Tanzi, Vito, Washington DC, 1996.

The Structure and Operation of the World Gold Market; Washington DC, September 1993

LAIDLOW, PHILIP: *Shams*; Association Of Corporate Trustees, July 2000

LIBRARY OF CONGRESS, CONGRESSIONAL RESEARCH SERVICE: *The USA Patriot Act – A Legal Analysis*; Doyle, Charles, Washington DC, 2002

The USA Patriot Act – A Sketch; Doyle, Charles, Washington DC, 2002

NAYLOR, R.T.: *Follow-The-Money Methods In Crime Control Policy*; A study prepared for the Nathanson Centre For The Study Of Organized Crime And Corruption, Toronto, 1999

OXFAM: *Tax Havens, Releasing The Hidden Billions For Poverty Eradication*; London, June 2000

PETRAS, JAMES: *Dirty Money Foundation Of US Growth And Empire Size And Scope Of Money Laundering By US Banks*; report to the Centre for Research on Globalization, Mexico, 19 May 2001

PHILLIPS, DION E.: *Another Look At The Royal Bahamas Defence Force*; Center For Hemispheric Defense Studies, University of the Virgin Islands, St Thomas, August 2002

PUBLIC CITIZEN: *Congress Watch – Congressional Leaders' Soft Money Accounts Show Need for Campaign Finance Reform Bills*; Washington DC, February 2002

ROBB EVANS AND ASSOCIATES LLC: *Various Reports Of Receiver's Activities In The Matter Of JK Publications, MJD Service Corp, et al*; California, 2002

SANTINO, UMBERTO: *The Financial Mafia – The Illegal Accumulation Of Wealth And The Financial-Industrial Complex*; private paper, 1986

SECURITIES AND EXCHANGE COMMISSION: *A.S. Goldmen And Co, Inc, And Employees Charged With Variety Of Microcap Related Violations*; Washington, DC, 1999

SIRIUS, FRANCIS J: *Cubans In Miami – An Historic Perspective*; Division of Humanities, St Thomas University, Miami, Florida. Prepared for delivery at the annual meeting of the Florida Historical Society, Miami, Florida, 13 May, 1988

SUPREME COURT OF THE STATE OF NEW YORK, COUNTY OF NEW YORK: *The People Of The State Of New York Against Harry Bloomfield And Stuart Creggy*; New York, 2002

SWISS BANKERS ASSOCIATION: *Switzerland And The Fight Against Money Laundering*; Basle, 2001

UNITED NATIONS: *Report Of The Policy Working Group On The United Nations And Terrorism*; New York, 2002

UNITED NATIONS, OFFICE FOR DRUG CONTROL AND CRIME PREVENTION, GLOBAL PROGRAMME AGAINST MONEY-LAUNDERING: *Financial Havens, Banking Secrecy and Money Laundering*; authored by Blum, Jack; Levi, Michael; Naylor, R. Thomas; Williams, Phil; New York, 1998

UNITED NATIONS, SECURITY COUNCIL: *Report Of The Monitoring Group Established Pursuant To Security Council Resolution 1363 (2001) And Extended By Resolution 1390 (2002)*; New York, 13 May 2002

UNITED STATES OF AMERICA: *An Act To Deter And Punish Terrorist Acts In The United States And Around The World, To Enhance Law Enforcement, Ionvestigatory Tools, And For Other Purposes (United And Strengthening America By Providing Apprppriate Tools Required To Intercept And Obstruct Terrorism – USA Patriot Act)*; Washington DC, 2001

UNITED STATES COURT OF APPEALS FOR THE DISTRICT OF COLUMBIA CIRCUIT: *Final Report Of The Independent Counsel For Iran/Contra Matters*; Washington DC, 1993

UNITED STATES DEPARTMENT OF JUSTICE, UNITED STATES ATTORNEY CENTRAL DISTRICT OF CALIFORNIA:
Malibu Man Pleads Guilty To $37 Million Internet Credit Card Fraud Scheme; 22 January, 2001

UNITED STATES DEPARTMENT OF JUSTICE, UNITED STATES ATTORNEY, DISTRICT OF NEW JERSEY: *Letter to Hon. Alfred J. Lechner, Jr re: United States v John Mathewson*; 29 July 1999

Plea Agreement With John Mathewson, 3 March 1997

Letter To Mr. William T. Walsh, US District Court Clerk, re: Johnson And Dinan V United States Of America: Brief Of The United States In Opposition To The Petitioners' Motion For Return Of Property; Affidavit Of Special Agent Sean W. Mccarthy; Declaration Of James P. Springer; Proposed Order; 27 November 1996

UNITED STATES DEPARTMENT OF STATE: BUREAU FOR INTERNATIONAL NARCOTICS AND LAW ENFORCEMENT AFFAIRS – *International Narcotics Control Strategy Report*; Washington DC, 2003, 2002, 2001, 2000

UNITED STATES DEPARTMENT OF THE TREASURY: *National Money Laundering Strategy Report*; Washington DC, 2002

International Counter-Money Laundering Act Of 2000, A Section By Section Analysis; March 2000

An Introduction To Electronic Money Issues; Staff paper for the conference 'Toward Electronic Money and Banking,' Washington DC, 1996

UNITED STATES DISTRICT COURT, DISTRICT OF NEW JERSEY: *Amended*

Judgement In A Criminal Case, United States Of America V John Mathewson, Attempt To Commit Tax Evasion; Newark, 1999

Amended Judgement In A Criminal Case, United States Of America V John Mathewson, Conspiracy To Commit International Money Laundering; Newark, 1999

Indictment, United States Of America V. Francis Joseph Russo, Joann Russo, Joseph Russo, Frank Russo Jr, Joseph Olkowski, Daniel Zielinski, William S. PREVOST III, Anthony Lee Marinacco, John Mathewson; 1996

UNITED STATES DISTRICT COURT, EASTERN DISTRICT OF NEW YORK: *The European Community v RJR Nabisco, Inc, and others.*

UNITED STATES DISTRICT COURT, SOUTHERN DISTRICT OF NEW YORK: *Security And Exchange Commission V Invest Better 2001, Cole A Bartiromo And John/Jane Does 1–10, Declaration Of Craig S. Warkol In Support Of Plaintiff's Motion For Summary Judgement And An Order Of Preclusion; Exhibits To Declaration Of Craig S. Warkol, Volumes 1–4*; 2002

UNITED STATES GENERAL ACCOUNTING OFFICE: *Report To The Chairman, Permanent Subcommittee On Investigations, Committee On Government Affairs, United States Senate – Anti-Money Laundering Efforts In The Securities Industry*; Washington DC, 2001

UNITED STATES SENATE: *Report To The Committee On Foreign Relations – The BCCI Affair*; Kerry, John and Brown, Hank, December 1992

UNITED STATES SENATE: PERMANENT SUBCOMMITTEE ON INVESTIGATIONS:

Report On Correspondent Banking: A Gateway To Money Laundering; Minority Staff, Washington DC, February 2001

WACHTEL, HOWARD M: *Corporate Governance And Tax Distortion In The Global Economy*; Inter-Disciplinary Council on the Global Economy, Washington DC, 2000

The Mosaic Of Global Taxes; Global Futures – Institute for Social Studies Washington DC, 2000

WHITE HOUSE TASK FORCE: *International Crime Threat Assessment*; Washington DC, 2000.

WINER, JONATHAN M: *Illicit Finance and Global Conflict – Economies of Conflict: Private Sector Activity in Armed Conflict*; Fafo Institute for Applied Social Science, Programme for International Co-operation and Conflict Resolution, Oslo, 2002

WRISTON, WALTER B: *Dumb Networks And Smart Capital*; Cato Institute, Annual Monetary Conference, New York, 1997

INDEX